The Production of Personal Life

Class, Gender, and the Psychological in Hawthorne's Fiction

The Production of Personal Life

Class, Gender, and the Psychological
in Hawthorne's Fiction

Joel Pfister

Stanford University Press, Stanford, California

Stanford University Press, Stanford, California
© 1991 by the Board of Trustees of the Leland Stanford Junior University
Printed in the United States of America

CIP data appear at the end of the book

Silhouette design by Kristine Pfister.

For Elizabeth, my mother
and in memory of Joseph, my father

Acknowledgments

The Production of Personal Life was written while I was a lecturer in American Studies at Yale University and then an assistant professor of English and American Studies at Wesleyan University. My thinking has been stimulated by the presence of rigorous and supportive colleagues at both universities. A fellowship at the Center for the Humanities at Wesleyan University and a fellowship from the American Council of Learned Societies permitted me to devote the necessary time to revising my manuscript; I gratefully acknowledge their support. I also wish to thank the Wesleyan administration for financially supplementing my ACLS fellowship and for funding the compilation of the index.

Going back in time, I owe more than I can possibly say to the encouragement, generosity, and critical acumen of my teachers, such as Daniel Javitch, Robert Egan, and Sacvan Bercovitch at Columbia University, Peter Stallybrass and Alan Sinfield at the University of Sussex, Eric Mottram at the University of London, and Alan Trachtenberg, Bryan Wolf, Richard Brodhead, and Fredric Jameson at Yale University. Dick Brodhead, whose understanding of the complexities of Hawthorne's writing and historical situation never ceases to astonish me, was especially generous in making time to offer valuable comments on the penultimate draft of several chapters. Bryan Wolf's expansive theorizing and startlingly brilliant close readings of American paintings and literature have inspired me throughout all phases of my own project. Alan Trachtenberg and Fred Jameson have been models for me of politically committed, antidisciplinary risk takers.

I remain indebted to Raoul Ibarguen, not only for his adept criticisms of the earliest drafts of would-be chapters, but for helping to clarify my theorizing of the historical relationship between mid-nineteenth-century American "psychological" fiction and psychoanalysis. Wendy Owen, in New Haven, and Elizabeth Allen, in London, taught me to grasp the "feminization" of women as a cultural and ideological process. My first forays into the history of family life commenced with raids on the bookshelves of Sally Pindar. I thank her also for demanding that I let her teach me how to use the computer and for many years of happiness. Clive Bush, of the University of London, convinced me—through his scholarship and his poetry—that "only the range must be taken."

Nancy Schnog, Richard Lowry, and John Evans were very kind to comment on the entire first draft of my book. I am particularly grateful to Nancy Schnog, who pushed me to keep expanding my history-of-personal-life approach. Her own work on sentimental fiction and our wide-ranging conversations have shaped my thinking at key junctures. Clare Carroll and Marina Leslie, two sharp Renaissance scholars, helped knock the rust off my own Renaissance skills in their reading of two chapters. My *Marble Faun* chapter has profited from the art history expertise of Elizabeth Milroy, John Paoletti, and Sally Gross. The Yale librarians and libraries also contributed to making the writing of this book a pleasure.

Laura Wexler's smart comments and enthusiasm were instrumental in the revision of my introduction. In *The Politics and Poetics of Transgression*, Peter Stallybrass and the late Allon White acknowledge that Nancy Armstrong and Leonard Tennenhouse "have been constantly supportive in ways too numerous to mention." I feel the same. Like many others, I talk, write, and teach a little differently because of their influence and example. Most recently, my work has benefited from the editorial sagacity of my two wonderful editors at Stanford University Press, Helen Tartar and Ellen F. Smith.

I have discussed the arguments developed in this book more substantively with my students than with anyone. It was in the seminar rooms of Yale and Wesleyan that some of my most crucial learning and unlearning took place. I am indebted to too many students—more like younger colleagues—to list all their names, but I hope that Jennifer Nold, Steven Ecker, and Ann Hess will stand for my Yale students and Sarah Ellenzweig, Sasha Meyerowitz, Erika Lindholm, Kathleen Storms, and Rebecca Rossen will stand for my Wesleyan students.

My most profound and long-lasting debt is to my family: to my mother, Elizabeth, to my sister, Kristi, and to my brother, Jordan.

Contents

A Note to the Reader

Unless otherwise indicated, quotations from Hawthorne's works are from the volumes of *The Centenary Edition of the Works of Nathaniel Hawthorne* (Columbus: Ohio University Press, 1962-   ). References are cited by volume number and page number.

The Production of Personal Life

Class, Gender, and the Psychological in Hawthorne's Fiction

Introduction

Hawthorne and the
History of Personal Life

My intent in this book is both to demystify and to reconstitute "Hawthorne" as an object of literary, cultural, historical, and political study by rereading Hawthorne's fictions, mainly those from the early 1840's to 1860, in the context of the history of personal life. Studies of the emergence in the mid-nineteenth century of a personal life characterized by intense emotional bonds have suggested to me that Hawthorne's much celebrated preoccupation with the "psychological" in his fiction should not be thought of solely in a conventional way, as an expression of authorial insight into a transhistorical "human nature" or timeless personal relations. Rather, his persistent thematic focus on subjectivity and personal life can be read as a literary expression of historically specific cultural and ideological concerns.

Of course, the dominant theory that those of us in the late-twentieth-century academic middle class have at hand to think about subjectivity and personal life is still psychoanalysis, a distinctly individualistic and often ahistorical vision. Indeed, Frederick Crews, in his classic psychoanalytic study of Hawthorne, *The Sins of the Fathers* (1966), suggests that Hawthorne anticipates Freud's genius as an explorer of the psyche, quoting, for example, the preface to *Snow-Image* (1851), in which Hawthorne imagines himself as one "who has been burrowing to his utmost ability into the depths of our common nature, for the purposes of psychological romance." By implication, Hawthorne and Freud were "burrowing" into the *same* "depths of our common nature."

My work on Hawthorne departed from such assumptions as I began to focus on the question of *why* Hawthorne's writing is so psychological. When I considered the large number of mid-nineteenth-century authors who chose psychological, affective, and sentimental relations—personal life—as their subject, I found it increasingly problematic to "apply" psychoanalysis to Hawthorne's fictions. Early on I came to realize that my question is fundamentally a *historical* one. That Hawthorne, like Freud, would engage in the production of a psychological common sense about "the depths of our common nature" was an impulse Crews took as a given rather than as a culturally grounded "burrowing" that invites historical explanation. Although Crews later recanted some of his psychoanalytic presuppositions, principally because he judged them to be empirically unverifiable, he has also acknowledged recently that his book's persuasive construction of a "proto-psychoanalytic Hawthorne" succeeded in steering "the premises of subsequent Hawthorne criticism" away from "cultural history."[1] Drawn as I was to many of Crews's shrewd psychological readings, I also began to rethink the premises of such readings (and the origins of these premises) in the light of new historical scholarship—particularly on women and family life—that expands the conventional notion of history to include the private sphere, gender roles, and emotional life. This historical work convinced me that one must be attentive to the cultural pressures generating the representation of psychologized relations both in Hawthorne's fiction and that of his contemporaries.

Gradually, I began to recognize that the cultural context for what Henry James called "the deeper psychology" in Hawthorne's writing is the history of a distinctively *middle-class* personal life that encompasses the family, gender, emotional relations, the body, and sexuality. Recent histories of family life, privatization, the body, and gender have established that a middle-class personal life as it consolidated in the mid-nineteenth century made certain assumptions about "family," "private," "public," "masculine," "feminine," and psychological "depth" (which modern critics have coded as "natural") seem commonsensical. As we shall see, they were historical constructions integral to both the formation and the reproduction of the middle class.[2] The formation of class identity through the production of such "personal" categories was, historically, something new.

Stuart Blumin, in chronicling the prehistory of the American middle class, observes that the eighteenth-century "middling rank" was largely made up of artisans whose manual labor placed them in a social category subordinate to the dominant mercantile and professional elite, closer in status and wealth to the bottom than the top of society. The term "middle class" is a nineteenth-century category whose emergence Blumin ties to a "stretching" of the category of the "business class" and to the growing perception of a sharper "boundary between manual and nonmanual worlds of work." The burgeoning marketplace, geared toward specialization, brought along with it changing conditions of work and new, socially elevated, nonmanual, "white-collar" occupations. "White-collar" workers, such as retailers, wholesalers, clerks, salesmen, accountants, and supervisors, were neither associated with "the poor and 'inferior' inhabitants of the city, as were the mainly artisanal 'middle sorts' of the eighteenth century," nor "were they members of the mercantile elite." Nevertheless, their places of work and the location, construction, and furnishings of their homes distinguished them by mid-century as members of an enlarged, literate "business class" that typically dissociated itself ideologically from "the social stigma of manual labor."[3] Hawthorne, who moaned about having to tally the productivity of coal shovelers on a barge during the winter of 1840, when he worked as a weigher and gauger of coal and salt at the Boston Custom House, was clearly an alienated member of this emerging nonmanual, "white-collar" middle class.[4] Brook Farm, where Hawthorne lived from April until November in 1841, was a middle-class, transcendentalist-Fourierist experiment that, in the words of George Ripley, its founder, was established "to insure a more natural union between intellectual and manual labor than now exists; to combine the thinker and the worker, as far as possible, in the same individual."[5]

This manual-vs.-nonmanual boundary, Blumin notes, became even more hardened as a result of the changing ideological significance of personal life. "White-collar" families began to perceive "their homes and their domestic strategies to be distinct from those of manual workers, as well as from those fashionables who did not . . . aspire to the domestic ideal." Hence Blumin, following the lead of Mary Ryan, claims not simply that "middle-class formation" was linked to woman's work but that it *was* woman's work. By mid-century, increasingly privatized and "feminized" emotional relations within family life distinguished families as middle-class. Judging from Blumin's account, neither femininity nor intense sentimental relations within the household had played key ideological roles in defining social status in the eighteenth century's "culture of rank." Ryan's studies of the mid-nineteenth-century "woman's

sphere" explore how the middle-class family established boundaries between itself and other classes not only through gender construction but
through the cultural production of specific kinds of psychological bonds,
dependencies, expectations, and norms.[6]

Men and women in the colonial household often labored together
and performed overlapping tasks in a family business that was located
in the house. Colonial child rearing, as John Demos notes, had a com-
munal dimension, as it "was shared among a variety of people and
institutions." Neither the bond between parents and children nor that
between spouses was defined as an "exclusive" emotional relationship.
"Love was not the main axis of family relations," observes Stephanie
Coontz: "Family, church, and government all taught roughly the same
things and demanded roughly the same commitments, though perhaps
in different degrees; relationships in each area did not require qualitatively different ways of behaving and feeling." Social reproduction was
conducted through community institutions and the household (not yet
sentimentalized as the "home"). Privacy was not considered a domestic
value; rather, the household itself was imagined as a "little commonwealth."

In the mid-nineteenth century, "white-collar" men typically worked
outside the home, often in the employ of others, and left behind a
"woman's sphere" in which affective ties had become less communally
based and more concentrated around the individual hearth. Middle-
class women, who less frequently produced (with their husbands) their
own goods and instead purchased them as commodities, specialized in a
domestic management now gendered as "women's work." This management featured the psychological labor of building "character" in children (now conceptualized as a more private, domestic process) and of
ministering to the emotional needs of men returning from the marketplace. By the mid-century, boundaries between "woman's sphere" and
"world," husband and wife, and adults and children came to seem natural. Different social roles for men and women were now legitimized—
particularly by medical texts—as the logical outcome of biological differences. Comparing seventeenth-century and mid-nineteenth-century
constructions of femininity, Coontz writes: "Being female in colonial
America involved 'Restraints' rather than incapacities." Bonding within
the home, as experienced through these role divisions and categories,
had become more symbolic, sentimentalized, and psychologized.

By the mid-nineteenth century, marriage was categorized as what
Coontz terms a "private compact," a concept that superseded the colo-

nial notion of marriage as a social institution "with roles and duties fixed by the place of the family in a hierarchical social order." Thus the emotional soil was rich for what Demos calls "the flowering of a . . . 'hot-house family.' "[7] The "expansion of inner life" and personal life in the nineteenth-century middle class, writes Eli Zaretsky, is a sociological development that must be seen in dialectical relation "to capitalist expansion."[8] Hawthorne's writings, as well as those of other mid-century "psychological" and sentimental authors, grew out of, helped produce, and *profited* from the "expansion of inner life" in middle-class families.

"The middle class" is not unproblematic as a term. Neither Ryan nor Blumin nor I wish to represent this class-in-formation as a fixed or uniform group. The frighteningly unpredictable rise and fall of fortunes, the migration from East to West, the influx of immigrants, the effect of the 1848 Seneca Falls women's rights convention on gender roles, and the impact of the campaign for the emancipation of slaves on domestic ideologies are just a few of the factors that make the historical study of the not particularly stable "middle class" a complex enterprise. More work needs to be done in this field. Yet it is striking that the letters, diaries, advice books, and fictions written by diverse members of this class testify to the ideological significance of the personal for them, even as its meaning evolved from the 1830's to 1860's.

To refer to the cultural formation of a *middle-class* personal life is a redundancy, for no other class set out to produce such domestic arrangements as a means of reproducing itself. Hawthorne's "psychological themes" are of great historical and ideological importance because, when reread in the context of the cultural production of personal life, they tell us much about what Peter Stallybrass and Allon White call the "subject-formation of the middle classes."[9] By rooting the ideological construction of the *category* of the "psychological" within the middle-class reshaping of emotional relations, I endeavor to develop some historically specific implications of historian Richard Johnson's argument that "subjectivities are produced, not given, and are therefore the objects of inquiry, not the premises or starting points."[10] My work on Hawthorne's texts and the history of personal life has oriented me toward asking not how Hawthorne and other authors in his class explored a Freudian psychological "self" but how their writing helped produce as commonsensical what Chris Weedon has termed "an already existing subjectivity which awaits expression."[11]

If the original question that I brought to this project asked *why* much of Hawthorne's fiction was so psychological, it was not long before I also began to question why it was that *women* in this fiction were psychological targets of male monomaniacs in the home. Mid-century fiction, especially that written by men, represents female characters who get drained of blood, buried alive, or drowned out of the plot when they reach outside of feminine roles (or even look as if they might do so). When Chillingworth confesses to Hester that he had drawn her "into my heart, into its inmost chamber, and sought to warm thee by the warmth which thy presence made there!" (1: 74) in *The Scarlet Letter* (1850), his obsession was not of seventeenth-century vintage. Rather, his privatized expectations compulsively fed upon a nineteenth-century middle-class sentimental discourse that represented womanhood as a human hearth whose domestic function was to keep a beleaguered masculinity, chilled in the marketplace, emotionally warm and psychologically secure. Characterizing seventeenth-century attitudes about adultery, Coontz notes, "Rebellion by a female evoked especially harsh responses because it threatened the household authority in which larger political hierarchies rested."[12] Hawthorne, writing in 1850, stresses Chillingworth's *psychological* response to Hester's adultery. I came to understand that it was impossible to make historical sense of the production of the category of the "psychological" within the middle class without considering its relationship to the symbolic and ideological significance of the category of the "feminine."

Hawthorne did not have to be a feminist practitioner of "social constructionism" to grasp that femininity and masculinity are culturally produced categories. In *The Blithedale Romance* (1852), Zenobia, an advocate of women's rights, classifies her pale, emaciated, feminine half-sister as "the type of womanhood such as man has spent centuries in making it" (3: 122). Before one engages wide-ranging arguments such as those developed in Barbara Welter's "The Feminization of American Religion" (1973) and Ann Douglas's *The Feminization of American Culture* (1977), it is crucial for reasons of theoretical clarity to recognize that the *feminization of women* within middle-class culture was a precondition for the processes they have studied. I will argue that Hawthorne, who together with other mid-century authors understood this process quite well, alternatively participated in and blew the whistle on feminization (I expand on what I mean by feminization in Chapters 3 and 4). The "payoff" question, it seems to me, is why this feminization of women took place in the way that it did and what relation it bears to the discourse of the "psychological" that we see emerging in middle-class literary and nonliterary writings.

This is not a question posed by Jane Tompkins in *Sensational Designs* (1985), a book to which my thinking is indebted in a number of ways. Tompkins argues that the cultural work of the "Other" American Renaissance, that of women writers, should be included in the literary canon molded by English departments. She has an understandable political interest in underscoring the "sentimental," rather than the "Freudian" psychological, aspects of Hawthorne's fiction (aspects that are often interwoven), because her revisionary concern is to establish the value of works written by female sentimental writers who fictionalize emotional life within "women's sphere."[13] Thus she quotes reviews, mostly from the 1830's, that praise Hawthorne's stories with sentimental language identical to that used by female authors. But in basing her critique on the value of the "Other" Feminine American Renaissance, Tompkins is on problematic ground because she does not address the political implications of the fact that the feminine qualities she wishes to see valued were socially constructed within and for a class. Mary Ryan, Stuart Blumin, and Stephanie Coontz, unlike Tompkins, have focused on ideological connections between gender construction and the establishment of middle-class identity. The literature of *both* Renaissances should be understood as having contributed to the stereotyping of a femininity that was essential to the ideological and psychological formation of the middle class.

The middle class that Hawthorne and sentimental female authors represented in and through their fiction was constituted by antagonistic class and race relations as well as unequal gender relations. As Laura Wexler has argued, the debate over the literary value of sentimental fiction "has tended to elide . . . [the] imperial project of sentimentalism." The "sentimental power" of this white middle-class fiction was designed "as a tool for the control of others," writes Wexler: "it aimed at the subjection of different classes and even races who were compelled to play not the leading roles but the human scenery before which the melodrama of middle-class redemption could be enacted."[14] The political question to engage here is what roles the literatures of both Renaissances played in producing subjectivities that enabled the middle class to dominate "others" with a clean conscience.

The psychological imagining of the "self" that Hawthorne both produces and contests is difficult to evaluate politically. On the one hand, it promotes a more privatized sense of self integral to the middle-class ideology of individualism. On the other hand, it problematizes sentimental assumptions about the middle-class home as the source of emotional warmth and well-being. By representing overheated relations between the sexes in a psychological rather than a sentimental discourse (a domestic discourse that he valued), Hawthorne suggests that the emerging category of the "psychological" is symptomatic in part of ideologically rooted emotional needs to construct, enforce, and sometimes resist categories of sexual difference. Thus by connecting the enforcement of "feminine" roles and the appearance of psychological tension between the sexes, Hawthorne's fiction intermittently launches a critique of the sentimental construction of "masculine" and "feminine" roles upon which the economic and cultural ascendancy of his class relied.

At various phases in the research and composition of this project I have asked myself or been asked by others: Why write on Hawthorne, who has for well over a century been enshrined within the American literary canon? The book itself provides my response, but the very fact that Hawthorne has been so thoroughly canonized raises political questions—several of which Tompkins addresses—about what resultant ideological appropriations of "Hawthorne" have supported in specific historical moments (e.g., the construction of the twentieth-century middle-class psychological self and the equation of the fictional "exploration" of this middle-class psychological self with literary value).[15] The contributions of Ann Douglas, Nina Baym, Bell Gale Chevigny, Jane Tompkins, Judith Fetterley, and others, however, have now established a more comprehensive canon. As Tompkins notes, mid-nineteenth-century women's fictions don't always mesh easily with either the Freudian psychological model or conventional assumptions about literary value. Hawthorne's literary, historical, and ideological place in this new canon remains to be worked out. I move toward this reevaluation in my efforts to situate Hawthorne's works in relation to writings by Margaret Fuller, Sarah Grimké, Fanny Fern, Lydia Maria Child, Harriet Beecher Stowe, Elizabeth Stuart Phelps [Ward], Lizzie Linn, Catherine Sedgwick, and Sarah Hale.

Still, I chose to write primarily on Hawthorne, not on one of these authors, and I did so, in part, for what may seem to be a traditional reason—a critical interest in the self-reflexive dimension of Hawthorne's writing. Yet Hawthorne's highly praised self-reflexivity—to thematize the processes of his art—has functioned for me more as an invaluable source of *historical* insights than as the conventional sign of his work's canonical "greatness." Because Hawthorne uses his self-reflexive fiction to make visible and to criticize *ideological* processes in which his writing is also complicit, I find his work rich both as a critique and as an ideological symptom of what Stallybrass and White term "the formation of the cultural Imaginary of the middle class."[16]

My scope in each chapter has been expanded by the theoretical, historical, and cultural themes I have outlined. Throughout the book I draw on contributions of historians of family life, Marxist and feminist theorists, sociologists of privatization, cultural anthropologists of the body, and historians of subjectivity. I read Hawthorne's texts in the context of medical representations of women's bodies, phrenological courtship guides that stereotype women's cranial "organs," masturbation "manuals" that teach readers to detect signs of the "solitary vice," women's rights journals that challenge the representation of women as "angels" and "dolls," "lady's" books that inscribe and sometimes contest femininity, and conduct books that teach little girls middle-class, republican fantasies. Yet I should emphasize that the "cultural studies" dimension of my project has gained both clarity and historical complexity because of its focus on Hawthorne's texts. The literary historical readings that follow are indebted to exemplary "close readings" of Hawthorne, such as Charles Feidelson's "The Scarlet Letter" (1964), Nina Baym's *The Shape of Hawthorne's Career* (1976), and Richard Brodhead's *Hawthorne, Melville, and the Novel* (1977).

I begin in Chapter 1 with a discussion of the relationship between "The Birth-mark" (1843), an allegory that serves as a leitmotiv throughout the book, and the mid-century cultural production of a middle-class psychological self. Rather than suggesting that it is Freud who explains the psychological tension between the sexes depicted by Hawthorne, Poe, and others, I propose that a historical study of this fiction and its ideological origins helps to account for the production of a bourgeois "Freudian" discourse that surfaces predictably later in the century. Chapter 2, which focuses on "Rappaccini's Daughter" (1844), builds on my efforts in Chapter 1 to discern *why* women's bodies in Hawthorne's fiction and his culture were stereotyped as unstable or disordered. Here I suggest that fears of women's bodies as biologically "monstrous" should be reconsidered as displaced anxieties about women as social actors and authors. An understanding of Margaret Fuller's unusual upbringing provides the basis for my reassessment of Beatrice Rappacini's so-called empowerment through being made "poisonous." Chapter 3, on *The Blithedale Romance*, establishes that Hawthorne and other mid-century writers clearly understood that gender is socially constructed and that they thought about the role their writing played in that ideological process. I reinterpret the narrative account of Zenobia's drowning as well as stories discussed previously in the context of the feminization of women. Chapter 4 reads two stories by Herman Melville as revisions of Hawthorne's "The Birth-mark"—but far-ranging theoretical re-visions that place the cultural feminization of women in a broader industrial and class context. Melville prompts us to consider how the cultural production of femininity relates to the plastering over and even the legitimation of social contradictions at the base of early industrial capitalism.

Moving to *The Scarlet Letter* in Chapter 5, I argue that Hawthorne's anxiety about the cultural revolution that might result from the emancipation of women from middle-class angelhood underlies his revealingly awkward narrative endeavors to feminize Pearl and her scarlet mother. Chapter 6 reads *The House of the Seven Gables* (1851) as Hawthorne's attempt, having just published *The Scarlet Letter*, to move away from a gothic-psychological discourse of subjectivity into a sentimental one, premised on the political hope that the middle-class feminine woman, though acknowledged and even parodied as a discursive construct, is powerful enough to "humanize" (resocialize) both America's aristocracy and its working class. I close, in Chapter 7, with an analysis of one aspect of *The Marble Faun* (1860): Hawthorne's paradoxical tendency to call the reader's attention to (and thus to compromise) his narrator's efforts to feminize our reading of Miriam's feminist artwork.

In his prefaces Hawthorne profiles the sympathetic reader for whom his work has been written. My own ideal readers would recognize the importance of making ourselves as much the subject of inquiry as the author's text and culture. If we wish to interrogate successfully the ideological categories of Hawthorne and his class, we must be willing to challenge our own. Antonio Gramsci writes, "The starting point of critical elaboration is the consciousness of what one really is, and is 'Knowing thyself' as a product of the historical process to date which has deposited in you an infinity of traces, without leaving an inventory." [17] *The Production of Personal Life* seeks to provide a partial inventory of some of these traces, our own historical birthmarks.

Historical Birthmarks

Hawthorne and the Cultural Production of the Psychological Self

I felt a little sleepy & lay down upon the couch till it should be time to call Mary to get my bath. At half past six, it was still quite dusky, but I summoned her. In the tub I read a part of Count Louis's article on Mr. Brownson in the Demo: & my dear husband came in before I was out.[1]

Nathaniel Hawthorne and Sophia Peabody were married on July 9, 1842, and from all indications blissfully so. This candid journal entry of December 7, 1843, inscribed by the pregnant Sophia, expresses the generally relaxed nature of her early married experience with her "dear husband" at the Old Manse in Concord. Nathaniel's notebooks and other writings reveal a newlywed intoxicated not only with his bride but with the exhilarating influence of domesticity itself. She was his "Dove" and he her "Lord." Sophia's journal portrays a notably cultural household in which he wrote, she painted (when not too nervous), they both read widely, and he read aloud to her *The Tempest*, *Hamlet*, and many other plays by Shakespeare, in addition to his own works-in-progress.

This idyllic chapter of domestic life was a fertile one for Hawthorne. He published 21 short stories, many of which were later collected in *Mosses from an Old Manse* (1846). His introductory piece for this volume, titled appropriately "The Old Manse," greets his readers with the homey epigraph: "The Author makes the Reader acquainted with his Abode." In a notebook entry of August 5, 1842, he queries himself: "And what is there to write about at all? Happiness has no succession of events, because it is a part of eternity; and we have been living in eternity ever since we came to this old manse" (8: 315). But write he did, and I have long thought it curious that some of Hawthorne's "mosses" from

1843 and 1844 seem dramatically at odds with the idyllic domesticity described in his introduction and their notebooks.

This devotee of domesticity, a mere nine months after his wedding, began publishing allegories about male monomaniacs obsessed with re-coding the bodies of their beloveds within allegories, sometimes to the death.[2] In "The Birth-mark" (1843), "Egotism; Or, the Bosom Serpent" (1843), and "Rappacini's Daughter" (1844), courtship or wedlock is anything but salubrious. Although "The Old Manse" celebrates domes-ticity with sentimental zeal, many of the images of domesticity evoked in this 1846 introduction first appeared with less auspicious associations two or three years earlier in these tales.

Hawthorne may have alluded to this anomaly in "The Old Manse," if only symbolically, when he sketched his apple "orchard."[3] In profiling its attributes, Hawthorne distilled the essence of domesticity from the con-ventions of popular sentimental literature: "The trees possess a domestic character; they have lost the wild nature of their forest-kindred, and have grown humanized by receiving the care of man, as well as by con-tributing to his wants" (10: 12). This is the contemporary middle-class ideology of domesticity as a humanizing institution. Domesticity *human-izes* husband, wife, orchards, and, presumably, the fruits of one's literary labors. Yet, when we peruse some of Hawthorne's literary "mosses," it is evident that they, like these apple trees, also assumed a "variety of grotesque shapes" that "take such hold of the imagination" (10: 12), rather than appearing to be unambiguously "humanized." Hawthorne offers us two very different genres of domesticity in his collection: a sen-timental, "humanizing" domesticity expressed in the preface, and one that grips our imagination in some of the stories as it branches into the "grotesque."

Before seeing where some of these "grotesque" branches lead, it is crucial first to appreciate how much Hawthorne reveled in the middle-class ideology that domesticity humanizes. "The glimmering shadows, that lay half-asleep between the door of the house and public highway, were a kind of spiritual medium," he writes in "The Old Manse," "seen through which the edifice had not quite the aspect of belonging to the material world" (10: 3). Ideally this soft-focus domesticity eludes the hardened marketplace surrounding it and is, like the nearby preindus-trial Concord River, "happily incapable of becoming the slave of human ingenuity" (10: 6). Public life is illusory, while privacy harbors reality: the Old Manse "had grown sacred in connection with the artificial life against which we inveighed. . . . it seemed to me that all the artifice and conventionalism of life was but an impalpable thinness upon its surface" (10: 25). *Privacy* is a magical prerequisite for a humanizing domesticity.[4] The shared psychological codes constructed within this sentimental space keep "tumult" (10: 28), "trouble" (10: 29), and "turmoil" (10: 33) where they belong—in the world. It is "you that give me reality," Nathaniel wrote to Sophia in 1841, "and make all things real for me."[5] Home, that "so powerful opiate" (10: 29), enables them to believe that they can live and love apart from "the world."

Such sentiments reflect a specific phase in the emergence of middle-class ideology and its "history of feelings." In broad strokes the historian Philippe Ariès has traced when and in what ways the family came to be imagined not just as a social, economic, and moral unit but as a "sentimental reality." He has argued that the industrial revolution and the urbanization that accompanied it in France and England in the late eighteenth and early nineteenth centuries precipitated an "emotional revolution" as a response. The "emotional revolution," so evident in "The Old Manse," not only transformed the family into a value, a theme of expression, and an occasion of emotion, its ideological intensity also germinated what Ariès terms an "obsessive love" within the domestic sphere.[6] Mary Ryan has examined this "privatizing tendency" in the domestic ideology of the nineteenth-century American middle-class family. The "utilitarian and practical view of the family," still common in the 1820's, was by mid-century "displaced" by "a vague, rhapsodic, and emotion-packed treatment of home virtues."[7] By 1864 John Ruskin, in a classic evocation of the domestic ideal, could represent the middle-class "home" as a construct of psychic order within a world of social disorder: "It is the place of Peace; the shelter, not only from injury, but from all terror, doubt and division." Significantly this psychic space is predicated on the presence of a specific kind of womanhood: home, Ruskin adds, "is yet wherever she is."[8]

Hawthorne's manse also is figured as a "magic circle" of therapeutic enchantment: "What better could be done for anybody who came within our magic circle than to throw the spell of a tranquil spirit over him?" (10: 29). This "magic circle" originates from occult lore. As one scholar has observed, it demarcates for the magician a "sacred precinct within which the demon or spirit could not intrude." Hawthorne imbues this occult "circle" with domestic sentiment. Domestic alchemy exorcises the demons that arise from intercourse with the outside world.[9] In his notebook entry of August 13, 1842, Hawthorne rhapsodized: "The fight with the world,—the struggle of man among men,—the agony of the universal effort to wrench the means of life from a host of greedy competitors,—all this seems like a dream to me." [10] Hawthorne's "circle" became "Eden." In his notebooks and letters Nathaniel fantasizes that he and his newlywed are a nineteenth-century Adam and Eve.

Yet this Edenic soil, so rich for the domestic imagination, also yielded those "grotesque shapes," in the form of several allegories included in *Mosses*. When situated in the context of these tales, the self-conscious sentimentalism of "The Old Manse" seems like Hawthorne's belated attempt to paper over a stockpile of psychological explosives that he has deposited or discovered in the center of the "magic circle." In such tales the "magic circle" marks off a precinct filled not with sentiment but with what one critic has called "buried psychological conflicts." [11] It is tempting to wonder whether the early phase of Hawthorne's marriage, exalted in his notebooks, letters, and "The Old Manse," made him conscious that certain kinds of psychological tensions were peculiar to this middle-class sentimentalized encirclement and that such tensions took on a "variety of grotesque shapes."

My interest, however, is not biographical speculation. In this chapter I am concerned with how Hawthorne viewed the role his own writing played in the construction of a cultural discourse that helped *produce* the tensions he writes about. In no story is Hawthorne's awareness of the ideological forces influencing his aesthetic more explosive than "The Birth-mark," which, interestingly, directly follows his sentimental introduction to *Mosses*, "The Old Manse." This is a tale of two newlyweds, published (curiously enough for a story with this title) nine months after Hawthorne's wedding, in March 1843.

Toward Historicizing Constructions of Psychological Codes

In "The Birth-mark" the home is no sanctuary of psychic order, as Hawthorne and Ruskin would have it; rather, it appears to be a space of psychological coercion and sexual tension. In place of a manse "sheltered from the turmoil of life's ocean," we find a home perched over a maelstrom. Before we look into this vortex, however, it is important to note that recently critics have begun to challenge the more traditional "buried psychological conflicts" approach to Hawthorne's tales. [12]

Michael J. Colacurcio, for example, has argued powerfully that the

"inherent arrogance of the psychoanalytic" approach is that it evapo-
rates the history in Hawthorne. Proposing that Hawthorne's talent as an
"intellectual historian" "may well surpass his Freudian acumen," Colacurcio prescribes "a full-scale historical analysis" to boot "Hawthorne's
characters off the couch."[13] These monitions, however, to my mind beg
theoretical questions about what should be regarded as "history" in the
eyes of the literary and cultural historian.

Hawthorne's puritans in "The Maypole of Merrymount" (1836),
who chop down "maypoles" and put a stop to merrymounters, constitute a historical subject, as Colacurcio demonstrates so thoroughly,
although the history informing Hawthorne's 1836 version is certainly
as much that of the 1830's as of the seventeenth century.[14] Historical
subjects like Leo Marx's industrial "machine in the garden" of course
offer concrete literary evidence of mid-nineteenth-century social concerns.[15] And when Hawthorne was not writing about monomaniacs
in the early 1840's, he was in fact publishing allegories and sketches
whose "historical" dimension is manifest: Hawthorne wrote critically
and sometimes satirically about "the demon of machinery," the ideology
of technology-as-progress, "destructive modes of labor," the exploitation
of seamstresses in urban sweatshops, growing class divisions in cities,
and money-mad millionaires.[16] But if Hawthorne's outlook is indeed
social and historical, as Colacurcio and others, including myself, maintain, we might wonder how Hawthorne's "grotesque" stories about male
monomaniacs and psychological tension between the sexes fit into this
history.

At stake here is a recognition of Hawthorne's "psychological" preoccupations as historical evidence of his contemporary *social* concerns.
There does seem to be what one might term a proto-psychoanalytic
dimension of the postnuptial stories I am about to discuss, but I will
suggest that one can reassess this dimension historically without con-
signing Hawthorne's characters to the couch and trading history for
psychobabble. As will become clear, the very resemblance between
Hawthorne's psychological allegories and what we are now familiar with
as psychoanalytic thinking and categories is one that must be theorized
as a historical connection.

A psychological reading of "The Birth-mark" is one we will have
to rethink historically in the framework of the social construction of
psychological codes and the emergence of the "psychological" as a category produced within the middle class; nevertheless, it will be useful

to commence our rethinking by reading one level of tension between Hawthorne's newlyweds as sexuality and the tale itself as an allegory of failed "sublimation." Less than a decade after he published "The Birth-mark," Hawthorne would present himself as a writer of "psychological romance" preoccupied with imagining the "motives and modes of passion" (1: 33). Hawthorne's "The Birth-mark," like Freud's case studies, does seem to train readers to translate behavior allegorically in search of latent and repressed motives. From the outset of the allegory, Hawthorne hints that we should sift much of what we read for underlying sexual meaning.

Even as we are introduced to an alchemist who has put aside his "love of science" for matrimony, "a spiritual affinity, more attractive than any chemical one" (10: 36), we are led to doubt the "spiritual" meaning of Aylmer's latest "affinity." His chemical affinity seems rather a dirty business, for we first see Aylmer washing up, and soon learn that face and hands, though not his own, acquire for him compulsive significance. Through his choice of verbs, Hawthorne insinuates that our spotless scientist may still have dirty work in mind: he "cleared his fine countenance from the furnace-smoke, washed the stain of acids from his fingers, and *persuaded* a beautiful woman to become his wife" (10: 36; emphasis mine). As the narrative unfolds, we find that where there's smoke, there's fire. This first cleansing is key: we see his effort to "clear" himself of signs of his "chemical" affinity, furnace-smoke, and the stain of acid.

Aylmer's arts of persuasion succeed in the age of the "comparatively recent discovery of electricity" (10: 36)—a curious way of dating the tale. By then alchemy was already "antique." Hawthorne's reference to the age of the "discovery of electricity" carries another meaning besides: Aylmer seems to have discovered his own "electricity" comparatively recently. "Chemical" affinity, furnace-smoke, the stain of acid, and the discovery of "electricity" are just some of the double entendres that bedevil this well-scrubbed scientist before we get much beyond the opening sentences.

So it is of particular interest that by the second paragraph the "beautiful woman" whom he has persuaded soon "shocks" him. Not long after their marriage Aylmer notices and directs Georgiana's attention to a birthmark on her left cheek, which he hesitates "to term a defect or a beauty." Undaunted by such ambiguity, he admits that it "shocks" him "as being the visible mark of earthly imperfection." Her response is electric: "Shocks you, my husband! . . . You cannot love what shocks you!" (10: 37). In contemporary dictionaries "electricity" transmits an instinctual charge: dangerous "bodies" that "when rubbed . . . draw substances, and emit fire." [17]

The newlywed's birthmark stands out like "a crimson stain upon the snow" and "bore not a little similarity to the human hand, though of the smallest pygmy size" (10: 38). Her "hand" is no tabula rasa, how-ever, for the public eye has already distinguished it with a history of interpretation. Rather a busy hand, it signals "every pulse of emotion" to the world, thus making it a (perhaps too) well-read hand. It is read "according to the difference of temperament in the beholders" (10: 38), who fall into three groups.

Georgiana's "lovers," passionate readers all, mythologize its sexual allure and testify to its "magic endowments," which "give her such sway over all hearts." Many a "desperate swain" would risk his life "for the privilege of pressing his lips to the mysterious hand" (10: 38).

Another group, "fastidious women," also read the mark as a sign of sexuality, or perhaps reproductivity, a "bloody hand" (10: 38) that, once exposed to the public, renders her expression hideous. The "en-dowments" that make a woman charming, magical, desirable, and full of life in the eyes of some are recoded as shameful and hideous by the gaze of others. Here Hawthorne seems to be suggesting that these "fas-tidious" women *project* something shameful or "bloody" in their own temperaments, perhaps shame of blood, onto Georgiana.

A third group of "masculine observers" also adopt the aesthetic analogy, but for contrary purposes. Georgiana is an objet d'art and would be "ideal" if not for this one "semblance of a flaw" (10: 38). Aylmer "discovered" (10: 38) that he too felt this way, and after his betrothal he begins to interpret the mark as a flaw. Like women who project some-thing "bloody" in themselves, these "observers" may be projecting fear of their own imperfection. If we credit the readings of the first two groups and encode the birthmark as a sign of sexual power, this third group is neither openly drawn to nor overtly ashamed of this power; instead, it transfigures female sexuality by aestheticizing it as a "flaw."

The alchemist allegorizes his wife's hand as signifying everything foul. Yet his reading skirts the issue of sexuality. Georgiana's birthmark becomes "the fatal flaw of humanity, which Nature . . . stamps inefface-ably on all her productions" (10: 38–39). Her "Crimson Hand" is figured as expressing the "ineludible gripe in which mortality clutches the highest and purest of earthly mould, degrading them into kindred with the lowest." It signaled her "liability to sin, sorrow, decay, and death." Her mark is the "spectral Hand that wrote mortality" (10: 39). Georgiana is penned into a myth of the fall. In his love letters Hawthorne named Sophia his "sinless Eve!" [18] and his redeemer: "God gave you to be the salvation of my soul." [19] But in "The Birth-mark" Hawthorne shows how this Edenic role playing can turn insidious as Georgiana is emplotted not as Eve the redeemer but as Eve the original sinner. No longer a threatening sexual charm, this woman's "Hand" has been recontextualized and universalized as that which makes the human condition a shameful and forlorn predicament.

The red hand is rewritten as a *dead* hand. Shaken by her husband's allegorical rewriting, Georgiana revises her reading of herself and grows to loathe what she terms her "horrible stigma" (10: 52). Fearing "madness" (10: 41), she begs to become the subject of an alchemical experiment to edit it out.

Several clues point to sexuality or jealousy as Aylmer's motives for editing her. In the opening paragraph we learn that his "scientific" aspiration is to "lay his hand on the secret of creative force" (10: 36). Perhaps the censorship of his wife's "shocking" red hand is really a repression of his own "electricity," his own lust to lay his hands on her "creative force." Even his aversion is ambivalent. Near the conclusion of his experiments, as Georgiana is sleeping and her birthmark is fading, Aylmer kisses it though his "spirit recoiled . . . in the very act" (10: 54).

Several passages lead us to consider what exactly this ambivalent "spirit" is repressing. Hawthorne does this in one instance by resurfacing the image of the hand and allowing us to catch Aylmer rather than his wife red-handed. At one point Georgiana intrudes upon the alchemist's labors in his laboratory where she spies her husband, "pale as death" (10: 50), and Aminadab, earlier described as his "under-worker" (10: 43), engaged in dirty work over their furnace. The images associated with this "under-worker" are physical, sexual, and industrial: "a man of low stature, but bulky frame, with shaggy hair hanging about his visage, which was grimed with the vapors of the furnace" (10: 43). Hawthorne's narrator mentions "his great mechanical readiness" (10: 43), while Aylmer hails his assistant as "thou human machine" (10: 51). Yet he is also called "man of clay" (10: 51), "clod," "earthly mass," and "thing of senses" (10: 55). Allegorically, "he seemed to represent man's physical nature; while Aylmer's slender figure, and pale, intellectual face, were no less apt a type of the spiritual element" (10: 43). Aminadab is a recognizable character in Western literature: the "wild man." Bearing in mind Shakespeare's *Tempest*, here he plays a seemingly servile Caliban ("thou earth") to Aylmer's intractable Prospero.[20] Both "wild men" can be read along psychoanalytic lines as representing the wildness their masters seek to manage in themselves through alchemy.

What Georgiana spies has industrial as well as sexual resonances: "The first thing that struck her eye was the furnace, that hot and fever-ish worker, with the intense flow of its fire, which, by the quantities of soot clustered above it, seemed to have been burning for ages" (10: 50). Shocked, or perhaps embarrassed, by his wife's intrusion upon the "intense flow" of his "fire," Aylmer's erubescent face and hand tell all: "Aylmer raised his eyes hastily, and at first reddened, then grew paler than ever, on beholding Georgiana. He rushed towards her, and seized her arm with a gripe that left the print of his fingers upon it." Leaving his own handprint on Georgiana, Aylmer encodes her as a contaminat-ing force: "Would you throw the blight of that fatal birth-mark over my labors?" (10: 51).

Nowhere is this fusion of sexuality and aggression so stark as in Aylmer's dream of ruthlessly penetrating Geogiana to abort the "hand." Aylmer had "fancied himself, with his servant Aminadab, attempting an operation for the removal of the birth-mark. But the deeper went the knife, the deeper sank the Hand, until at length its tiny grasp ap-peared to have caught hold of Georgiana's heart; whence, however, her husband was inexorably resolved to cut or wrench it away" (10: 40). His dream of penetration is simultaneously an amputation and a brutal concidence with historical fact.

The first "sexual surgery" of women was performed by J. Marion Sims in 1843, the year "The Birth-mark" was published. Since he required "endurance, passivity, and utter helplessness" in his patients (and since he could not marry them all), Sims conscripted female slaves from co-operative slaveholders and even purchased his own for his experiments. That Georgiana has become Aylmer's experimental slave is suggested when the mark burns her like the brand of a "red-hot iron" (10: 46). By the 1860's and 1870's clitoridectomies, ovariotomies (female castra-tion), and new techniques of sexual surgery were developed to obtain "scientific" mastery over the "flaws" of female sexuality and procre-ativity. The uncanny resemblance, including metaphors of alchemy, that the rhetoric of "pioneering" mid-century gynecologists bears to

Aylmer underscores how astute Hawthorne was in perceiving the forms that tension between the sexes was taking in his culture.[21]

The alchemist's dream also bears striking resemblances to the rhetoric of the notorious "moral" reformer of the 1830's, the Rev. John R. McDowall. His *Magdalen Report* (1831) set out to expose the "gangrenous canker" of prostitution and alleged that 10,000 painted women lurked in the dark forest of New York City. McDowall figured this "moral impurity" as a gorgon: "Slay this gorgon monster, and the evils that infest society will disappear." His reform mania, like Aylmer's, led him to prescribe surgical amputation:

Reformers must approach their duties like surgeons, with prepared assistants and instruments to dissect putrescent sores, a task, from which nature shrinks, but to the performance of which a sense of duty urges. Even ulcers the most foul must be laid open before they can be healed; and reformers, surgeon-like, must nerve their hearts and helpers to work before them. . . . [They must] exert themselves to the utmost to strip from its every aspect a seducing charm.[22]

The fallen women he sought to reform were responsible, in his rhetoric, for more than selling sexual favors; they embodied the forces of social chaos. "These women now scatter fire-brands, arrows, and death through the land."[23] By 1834 the impulse driving this "moral reform" became so questionably obsessive that Rev. McDowall was himself accused of "polluting the purity of American youth" by printing lurid tales in *McDowall's Journal* and thus lost both his journal (taken over by women reformers) and his presbytery. In his next campaign, directed against pornography, he toted around a valise full of books such as *Fanny Hill* as evidence for all who would peruse them.[24]

As in the surgical dream, the alchemical "reform" of his wife brings Aylmer curious gratifications. "Believe me, Georgiana, I even rejoice in this single imperfection, since it will be such a rapture to remove it" (10: 44). "There was a rapture in his work," wrote *Harper's Weekly* in praise of the founder of sexual surgery, "like that of a lover's pursuit or a great artist's creation."[25] And when the final experiment begins to show its effect, Aylmer is overtaken by an "almost irrepressible ecstasy" (10: 55). Even Georgiana participates in this displacement of sexuality onto alchemical editing and seeks to "satisfy" her husband's "highest and deepest conception" (10: 52).

I am moving in the direction of arguing that the psychoanalytic "explanation" for such behavior is itself in need of historical explanation.

But for the moment, if we wish to "explain" these actions in reference to psychoanalytic discourse, then the psychological process at work in Aylmer's relationship to Georgiana should be termed "sublimation." Freud defines sublimation as a "transmutation": a diversion of the sexual drive to "higher, asexual aims," which in turn "provide the energy for a great number of our cultural achievements."[26] As Norman O. Brown explains it, in language descriptive of the hubristic alchemist, "sublimation is the essential activity of soul divorced from body"; *homo sublimans* "attempt[s] to be more than man" and "aims at immortality." Sublimation, however, like the sanitized Georgiana, is merely a "pale imitation" of the impulse repressed.[27] Despite this "sublimation," the latent sexuality fueling the whitewashing irrepressibly shows its hand.

Aylmer's pattern of sublimated satisfactions resembles what Freud would recognize as an "obsessive ritual." Obsessive ceremonials function as "defensive and protective measures" that enable one to disguise one's penchant for switching on one's sexual "electricity." But over time something paradoxical happens: obsessive practices reproduce "something of the identical pleasure they were designed to prevent."[28] "When you think it fled," Melville writes on madness, "it may have but become transfigured into some subtler form."[29] Aylmer's *defensive* alchemical practice stands in place of the prohibited act and delivers a substitute gratification, though it is what Brown calls a "pale imitation." Alchemy, as may have been the case with McDowall's "moral reform," functions as an ostensibly innocent alibi to commit the offending act in "subtler" form.

Aylmer's prenuptial scrubbing invites comparison to psychoanalytic studies of obsessive ceremonials, for the private rituals analyzed often take the form of a purification devised to disguise "dirty thoughts," usually the desire to masturbate. Otto Fenichel observes that washing can become a symbolic means of undoing, a "baptismal" compensation for an act of touching or thinking about something "dirty."[30] Without meaning to "diagnose" Aylmer's compulsion to "wash" or "undo" his wife's hand as anxiety over his own desire to touch himself, it is, nonetheless, important to note that paranoia over masturbation reached an intensity in the 1830's and 1840's that it never had before in American history, and that in the immensely popular literature on the subject the "hand" was singled out as the offending organ.[31]

"Hand—stay thy lasciviousness!" the Rev. John Todd enjoined his young readers in Latin: "More than perpetrating an enormity in young boys—it SINS." Marriage was frequently prescribed as a cure for masturbation; although, as the sex reformer Sylvester Graham warned, this haptic "shamefacedness" can persist in wedlock.[32] One physician admonishes his readers that the fear of encountering the "trials of matrimony" can bring on a "resort to unnatural excitements as a substitute."[33] Many of these sex manuals, as guides for the detection of masturbators, fostered paranoia. Onanists, Graham advises, "cannot meet the look of others, and especially of the female sex, with the modest boldness of conscious innocence and purity." The blush is decoded (encoded) as a tell-tale sign of "mingled shame and confusion." Bites, running sores, suppurating blisters, pimples, and paleness constituted damning symptoms of polluted practices.[34] With the aid and encouragement of such guides, social intercourse became textualized as a lived sexual allegory. Thus Aylmer's effort to "clear" *himself* of the "stain of acid" resonates with the way in which sexuality was becoming, to use Michel Foucault's term, peculiarly "problematized" (focused on *as* a problem) in Hawthorne's middle-class culture. These texts, by constructing a "hermeneutics of desire," functioned ideologically to implant "sex" in the middle-class self as the essence of subjectivity.[35]

Aylmer's hairy "under-worker," curiously, shares something in common with Georgiana. When he first sees Georgiana, who has fainted in response to her husband's disgust, the "man of clay" mutters: "If she were my wife, I'd never part with the birth-mark" (10: 43). Aminadab values the "hand." One pun that links them, a pun not made explicit, is that Aminadab may be considered, as an "under-worker," Aylmer's "hand." Georgiana, then, may be cast as the wild woman Aylmer strives to restrain and sublimate.[36] Aylmer never attains the stage of self-knowledge and acceptance where, like Prospero, he can say: "this thing of [redness] / I acknowledge mine." Nor does he conclude, "this rough magic / I here abjure." Instead, like Melville's Captain Ahab, the alchemist's "special lunacy stormed his general sanity, and carried it, and turned all its concentrated cannon upon its own mad mark."[37]

When Georgiana's redness is whitewashed, she reassures her alchemical editor "with a more than human tenderness": "you have done nobly! Do not repent that, with so high and pure a feeling, you have rejected the best the earth could offer. . . . I am dying!" (10: 55). Anna Freud might observe that this response resembles "altruistic projection," a powerful identification with someone else upon whom one projects or displaces one's "instinctual impulses." Altruistic surrender can preclude even fear of death.[38] "Danger is nothing to me," Georgiana assures Aylmer: "I shall quaff whatever draft you bring to me" (10: 41, 51). This too, like Aylmer's dream of sexual surgery and his own fastidious handwashing, has historical resonances. Altruistic projection may be the process that best illuminates the psychological positioning of middle-class women in mid-century domesticity.

Georgiana's perception that her husband has "rejected the best the earth could offer" is significant on a number of levels. As Hawthorne undoubtedly knew from the first book of Spenser's *Faerie Queene*, the name George signifies the earth, or husbandry. Thus even Georgiana's telluric name allies her with Aminadab, that "earthly mass." Her dying words, "you have done nobly," refer to the etymological root of Aylmer's name, which signifies nobility.[39] The story, however, casts doubt on a cocksure nobility that allegorically debases the physicality of an earth-woman in order to manufacture something "more than human." The last laugh, a "gross hoarse, chuckle" (10: 55), belongs to the underclass representative of Nature and the body, Aminadab, whom we finally recognize as having been in an unstated contest with his sublimating master (Caliban's revenge).

In an early case study, Sigmund Freud contended "that sexuality is the key to the problem of the psychoneuroses and of the neuroses in general." "No one who disdains the key," he added slyly with double entendre, "will ever be able to unlock the door."[40] Sexuality *seems* to be one "key" into "The Birth-mark." Here Hawthorne is representing not only the "motives" but especially the "modes of passion." Aylmer's science transmits the same electrical charge as McDowall's cathected "moral reform": husband and wife seem to spiritualize but, in fact, eroticize their relation to one another.

But if "the motive force" underlying the alchemist's "fiendish passion for knowledge . . . is the thwarting of [his own] sexual feeling," as Frederick Crews suggested in 1966,[41] and we neatly classify the allegory as a case study of failed sublimation, questions remain about the historical and ideological status of "sexuality" and sublimation in the story. To begin to see this we need only turn from Freud to Foucault. Aylmer, Freud, and Crews read within what Foucault identified as a middle-class "deployment of sexuality," which Hawthorne saw come into being.[42] The sexualized reading practices that one finds in Aylmer, McDowall, and the masturbation manuals are all manifestations of what

Foucault would recognize as a discursive sexualizing of middle-class subjectivity. The gynecological rhetoric of Sims and the "moral" reform symbolism of McDowall also suggest that the figuring of female bodies as sexual, biological, and social disorder is, within this historical moment, integral to the "deployment" of the discourse of "sexuality." Sublimation must likewise be historicized. What people are made to believe should be "sublimated" is inscribed through historically specific discourses of power. Sublimation, write Peter Stallybrass and Allon White with the nineteenth-century bourgeoisie in mind, is "the main mechanism whereby a group or class or individual bids for symbolic superiority over others: sublimation is inseparable from strategies of sexual domination."[43] Georgiana is susceptible to reading her body as fallen, "bloody," or too sexual—a body whose essence must be "sublimated"—because historical conditions give rise to ideological discourses that encode female sexuality as a flaw and that discipline the way we read it. Sublimation is a semiotic rather than a "natural" practice: the ideological encoding of something "inner" or "biological" that demands "sublimation." The ideological alchemy at work in the very concept of sublimation is that it renders unquestionable the presupposition that something threatening inside ("thwarting of sexual feeling") *needs* to be sublimated.

To ignore the historicity of "sexuality" and a specific notion of sublimation that supports this discourse of "sexuality" is to reproduce a universalizing ideology that helped shape the identity of Hawthorne's middle class. Diverse modern critics of Hawthorne and his "classic" contemporaries have reproduced these inherited ideological assumptions, thereby dehistoricizing the literary construction of the "psychological." Even Henry Nash Smith, whose American Studies emphasis is resolutely historical, applauded the courage it took for mid-century (male) authors to "explore the dark underside of the psyche."[44] Judith Fetterley, a feminist literary critic committed to recovering the historical dimension of mid-century women's writing, has similarly argued that "classic" works by mid-century male authors "frequently serve as the means for projecting, encountering, and exploring their own psychic territory."[45] But in reviewing such assumptions, we must not relegate this literary preoccupation with "psychic territory" to a position somehow outside the "historical" mainstream. Jane Tompkins maintains that this literary fascination with the "dark underside" is indeed historical, but that it is a mid-twentieth-century preoccupation. She has proposed that literary critics pinned behind Freud's mid- and late-twentieth-century cultural grid transform Hawthorne's fictions "into vehicles of 'psychological insight'" because they have projected their own culturally conditioned psychoanalytic concerns onto his texts.[46] There is much truth in this contention. Yet long before Freud held sway over critics, nineteenth-century reviewers promoted Hawthorne's fiction as a kind of pop psychology for the middle class.

Reviewers of Hawthorne's writings in the 1840's and 1850's described his psychological concerns by employing metaphors of surface and depth—what we would now term manifest and latent. In 1842 one reviewer characterized Hawthorne's "favorite study" in fiction as "unveiling . . . the affections and inward impulses of man."[47] *The Scarlet Letter*, wrote another reviewer in 1850, shows "genius" in its exploration of "the region of great passions and elusive emotions."[48] Also in 1850, *The Literary World* characterized it not as a "novel" but as "a tale of remorse, a study of character, in which the human heart is anatomized." Hawthorne exhibits "character in its secret springs and outer manifestations."[49] In 1852 Charles Hale read it as "an awful probing into the most forbidden regions of consciousness."[50] A few years later Anne C. Lynch Botta lauded Hawthorne for his ability to delineate "the darker passages of life."[51]

As one reads these reviews, Hawthorne begins to sound like a mid-century Freud who possessed the courage and "genius" to traverse the darkest interiors of the tabooed self. In his 1851 review of Hawthorne, Henry T. Tuckerman wrote: "What the scientific use of lenses—the telescope and the microscope—does for us in relation to the external universe, the psychological writer achieves in regard to our own nature."[52] And, of course, Henry James praised Hawthorne's "anatomizing" as "the deeper psychology."[53]

However, this "anatomizing" of the latent "regions of consciousness" in Hawthorne's works, reviews of his writings, and the antimasturbation manuals should all be interpreted as historical evidence, not of individual genius, but of the emergence of psychological codes still expressed in sentimental language that are beginning to *construct* middle-class readers' assumptions about interiority. Therefore, our theoretical focus over the course of this chapter must shift from chronicling Hawthorne's "psychological insight" to examining the role that his fiction played in the production of the "psychological" and to specifying the cultural conditions for its emergence. What we must reconsider are, in the words of Fredric Jameson, the underlying historical "conditions of possibility"[54] that account for correspondences between the symbolic systems and psychological themes used by Hawthorne and Freud to inscribe bourgeois interiority.

These psychological codes frequently form a pattern in Hawthorne's fiction, one that also can be identified as symptomatic of historical change. As "The Birth-mark" and other texts by Hawthorne that I shall discuss make clear, Hawthorne often represents the interiority that intrigues him as peculiarly prone to obsession. The historicity of Hawthorne's interest in obsession merits rethinking in the context of research by historians which suggests that patterns of psychological disorders can be contextualized as caricatures of historically specific, class-specific, and gender-specific social and ideological stress. Christopher Lasch, for instance, has proposed that we read what the psychoanalytic community calls narcissism as a sociological sign of our own times. Today, he notes, cases of obsessional neurosis are infrequent, but "in Freud's time, hysteria and obsessional neurosis carried to extremes the personality traits associated with the capitalist order at an earlier stage in its development—acquisitiveness, fanatical devotion to work, and a fierce repression of sexuality."[55] G. J. Barker-Benfield, writing on the mid-nineteenth-century American middle class, arrived at much the same conclusion about monomania as a caricature of the bourgeois ethos: "Monomania was the appropriate form of derangement for a society preoccupied with self-making and individualism."[56]

As critics we would do well to heed the warnings of Colacurcio and Tompkins and not get all absorbed in simply making psychological sense out of psychological tales. But if we wish to launch a "full-scale historical analysis" of Hawthorne's works, we must also begin making sociological and historical sense of fiction that *was* recognized as psychological in its own time. We find in both literary and nonliterary texts of the period the discursive production of what Chris Weedon calls "an already existing subjectivity which awaits expression."[57] Notwithstanding the theoretical differences among them, Smith, Fetterley, Tompkins, and Colacurcio all tend to extract this construction of the "psychological" from its mid-nineteenth-century social context. But as we shall learn, "classic" and popular mid-century fiction produces the "psychological" for sociological and historical reasons.

Gender and the Biological Expression
of Anxieties About Social Change

There is no "machine in the garden" in "The Birth-mark" as in Hawthorne's "The Celestial Railroad" (1843) to signify history, but Hawthorne's tale does represent a male pseudoscientist obsessed with persuading a woman to participate in his rewriting of her body. This compulsion to remake the female body is not a natural manifestation of a universal male psyche; rather, it says much about historically produced gender roles. "The Birth-mark" must not be understood simply as an allegory of sexual repression; more specifically it is problematizing why *female* bodies were subjected to ideological reinscription. As Stallybrass and White observe, "the body is actively produced by the junction and disjunction of symbolic domains and can never be legitimately evaluated 'in itself.'" I will argue that once the female sexuality represented by the "crimson stain" is situated in a broader social and discursive frame, it should be read as symbolic of women's creative powers.[58] Masculine control over the female body *and* its creative powers is a theme that appears in Hawthorne's other writings as well as in writings by his contemporaries.

One episode recounted in Hawthorne's *English Notebooks* shows that Hawthorne, like Aylmer, sometimes thought the man-made woman a better design than the original. In September 1854 Hawthorne recorded his visit to a British scientific association, where the sight of some society matrons aroused him to unsheathe his surgical pen. He portrays "the English lady of forty or fifty" as "the most hideous animal that ever pretended to human shape" and expresses sympathy for "the respectable elderly gentlemen whom I saw walking about with such atrocities hanging on their arms—the grim, red-faced monsters!" Ideal types ("womanhood," "mother," "wife") determine the content of these women. These "greasy animal[s]" are perhaps "unconscious of the wrong they are doing to one's *idea* of womanhood" (emphasis mine). "Who," Hawthorne inquires, *shocked* as Aylmer, "would not shrink from such a mother! Who would not abhor such a wife?"

Hawthorne's repugnance puts into play a Pygmalion-like urge to mutilate these "monsters" so that they can be squeezed into his stereotypes of femininity: "Surely, a man would be justified in murdering them—in taking a sharp knife and cutting away their mountainous flesh, until he had brought them into reasonable shape, as a sculptor seeks for the beautiful form of woman in a shapeless block of marble." In their "gross, gross, gross" form these ("flawed") women do not meet Hawthorne's allegorical requirements ("delicacy of soul existing within") and therefore "ought to be killed, in order to release the spirit so vilely imprisoned."[59]

No doubt Hawthorne was thinking of the sculptor Pygmalion and his fictile Galatea in the above passage from his notebooks as well as in "The Birth-mark." "Even Pygmalion," Aylmer boasts, anticipating the climax of his experiment, ". . . felt not greater ecstasy than mine will be" (10: 41). Let us not forget, as Ovid tells us, that Pygmalion, until making and mating with his "snowy ivory statue," had "long lived a bachelor existence" having been "revolted by the many faults which nature has implanted in the female sex." Presumably the ostensibly girlish, yet sexually available, "ivory maid" Pygmalion has "fashioned" with such a "yielding surface" so easily "worked by men's fingers" will display no such "faults."[60]

But Susan Gubar puts a different construction on this male creation and the editorial squeezing that accompanies it. "Not only has he created life," she argues, Pygmalion "has created female life as he would like it to be—pliable, responsive, purely physical. Most important, he has evaded the humiliation, shared by many men, of acknowledging that it is *he* who is really created out of and from the *female* body!" Pygmalion's "ingenuity seeks to usurp the generative powers of the womb" and "tries to re-create the female in the male's image."[61] In "The Birth-mark" not only does Aylmer exhibit the aesthetic compulsion to recreate a woman, but Hawthorne suggests that this scabrous "hand" scrubber, like his Ovidian prototype, gets a distinctly sexual charge out of his effort to appropriate female reproductive power for himself.

There is much in the story that guides us to reflect on the encoding of female reproductive power as a source of domestic tension. Georgiana exhibits on her face not God's hand, or Nature's hand, but "Mother" (10: 42) Nature's hand.[62] Hawthorne's decision to call this sign a "birthmark" was probably unusual; his other option, as we shall see, links Georgiana's hand even more intimately to "Mother." The word "birthmark," a difficult one to trace, does not appear in some of the more well-known dictionaries or encyclopedias that Hawthorne's generation would have consulted. In "The Rape of Lucrece" (1594) Shakespeare refers to an infant's "birth-hour's blot" ("nature's fault, not their own infamy").[63] Many early-nineteenth-century observers would have called this "birth-hour's blot" a mother's mark, or *naevus maternus*. Robert Hooper's *Lexicon Medicum* (1841) defines this as "A mark on the skin of children, which is born with them, and which is said to be produced by the longing of the mother for particular things, or her aversion to them; hence these marks resemble mulberries, strawberries, grapes, pines, bacon & c."[64] Aylmer's battle against Mother Nature, then, is focused on what Hawthorne's contemporary readers would have recognized as the mark of the mother. Thus far Mother has retained the upper hand.

Hawthorne's Pygmalion pits his signifying prowess against Mother's reproductive monopoly to demonstrate that, by effacing her trademark, he can remodel "her masterpiece" (10: 42) as *his own* "sculptured woman" (10: 41). Aylmer's desire to appropriate the secrets of "our great creative Mother," a "jealous patentee" (10: 42), has led him to probe some suggestive areas. His past experiments have "investigated" aspects of nature that sound curiously anatomical: the "fires of the volcano," and the "mystery of fountains . . . how . . . they gush forth . . . from the dark bosom of the earth" (10: 42). Georgiana calls this his "deep science!" (10: 41). But the narrator tells us that Aylmer's most far-reaching experiments were "invariably failures" (10: 49). When perusing her husband's journal, Georgiana learns that his most *creative* labors have miscarried.[65]

"Had she been less beautiful—if Envy's self could have found aught else to sneer at—he might have felt his affection heightened by the prettiness of this mimic hand" (10: 38). "Envy" is a possible motive, but it may well be that Mother's *creative* potency has been what Aylmer has envied in the "hand" all along. Another of Hawthorne's postnuptial allegories sheds light on this.

Hawthorne's "Egotism; Or, the Bosom Serpent" (1843), published the same month as "The Birth-mark," elaborates on the peculiar contours of this masculine obsession and confirms that "Envy's self" is indeed a motive worth pondering. Roderick Elliston, another mad allegorist, is a man who has been mysteriously possessed by an "egotism" that fixates on a "serpent" in his bosom.[66] Aylmer's allegorical obsession here assumes a public dimension. Elliston (like Aylmer) resembles the Rev. John McDowall. Both are keen to see "gorgon monsters" hidden in the hearts of even their well-appointed neighbors.[67] Allegorized bosoms suffer the fate of allegorized red hands elsewhere: he made "his own actual serpent—if serpent there actually was in his bosom—the type of each man's fatal error, or hoarded sin, or unquiet conscience"

(10: 277). In a significant shift of dominant conventions, he instructs his neighbors to hear psychological snakes hiss rather than sentimental hearts throb.

Hawthorne's allegory is of special interest when we speculate on *why* Roderick undertakes his venomous yet self-mocking crusade. Roderick's perplexed friends originally wondered if he had been stricken by an "insanity" or a "moral" "canker of the mind" (10: 271). Some, possibly nearer the mark, "looked for the root of this trouble in his shattered schemes of domestic bliss—wilfully shattered by himself." His "singular gloom" began, after all, four years before, not long "after Elliston's separation from his wife." His friends, nonetheless, "could not be satisfied of its existence there" (10: 270–71). Yet the hypothesis of shattered "domestic bliss" invites further consideration when we reflect on Herkimer's passing observation that his friend Roderick resembles the bust he has sculpted of "Envy." "Envy," like Medusa, has "snaky locks" (10: 269). Roderick also has "glittering eyes and long black hair" (10: 268). We never learn the prehistory of Roderick's "domestic bliss," but could "Envy," his envy, have been the snake in his garden?[68] Could Roderick's features have metamorphosed into a distorted image of *her* whom he envies?

Several passages that represent Roderick with imagery and language conventionally used to portray pregnant women point to this interpretation. Elliston, for instance, becomes convinced that he carries inside himself "the hidden monster" (10: 278) and "the living mischief" (10: 270). He cannot "hide the secret" (10: 273). Like a woman queasy from the kicking of her baby, "he felt the sickening motion of a thing alive," and even worse "the gnawing of that restless fang which seemed to gratify at once a physical appetite and a fiendish spite" (10: 272). The mad allegorist may be experiencing the labor pains accompanying Hawthorne's growing consciousness of a nascent force in his own writing, an interiorized Muse represented as resembling a gorgon. Perhaps this is what his allegory announces, disguises, and aborts. Aylmer's allegorical experimentation on Georgiana's "hand" performs a similar function: to recognize, recode, and finally erase this "creative force."

Such clues point to the possibility that the "bosom fiend" (though occasionally referred to as "he") should be reread as a fiend with a bosom, and the "bosom serpent" as a serpent with a bosom. In the third paragraph, after Roderick has been identified as a man with "a snake in his bosom," Herkimer, thinking of Roderick's estranged Rosina, muses that, "No second man on earth has such a bosom-friend!" (10: 268). She too, in other words, is associated with "bosom." This is not surprising when one bears in mind that the cult of domesticity prescribed that the wife act as a therapeutic mother for her husband—a symbolic bosom.[69] In *Elsie Venner* (1861), which reworks themes and symbolism from "The Birth-mark," "Rappacini's Daughter," and "Egotism; Or, the Bosom Serpent," Oliver Wendell Holmes portrays a "monstrous" young woman with an "ominous birthmark" in the shape of a snake coiled round her neck. Holmes's symbolism suggests, unconsciously no doubt, that once the angel in the house is assigned a halo by her culture, it can drop too easily upon the neck as a serpent-like noose.[70] I suspect that Roderick has recast his domestic "bosom friend" as Medusa or "Envy" with her "snaky locks" and then interiorized her as his "bosom fiend."[71]

Roderick does not merely encode Rosina as a "bosom fiend"; he gets pregnant with one. She impregnates him. Roderick's imagination and figurative power as an allegorist, pathological as they are, rely on his ambivalent attachment to his "bosom fiend"—"the foulest of all created things!" (10: 279). Likewise, Aylmer's "creative force" as an alchemist is beholden to Georgiana's availability as a woman he can encode as a "flaw." Hawthorne the allegorist, at his self-referential best, is telling us that the gestation of a bosom fiend is what gives Roderick the allegorist his creative sting. He loves, hates, fears, and, most revealingly, *identifies* with his "hidden monster" (10: 278). Roderick, with "glittering eyes and long black hair," seems to become a caricature of a woman men might fear as a (snake) "charmer." Hawthorne is suggesting that this allegorist of bosoms is envious of women's reproductive creativity and that his figurative potency as a psychological allegorist feeds on stereotyping woman as "the foulest of all created things." This envy is concomitantly a tormented identification with woman with a sting—woman with a bite.

What we are seeing in "The Birth-mark" and "Egotism; Or, the Bosom Serpent," I believe, is the tendency to express social anxieties or ambivalence about women's behavior in biological terms. This was a pattern of displacement within the larger middle-class effort to control and reform bodies. The body received a great deal of cultural attention as a biological or sexual force in need of control and reform in the mid-century. Popular "reforms," such as temperance, vegetarianism, phrenology, and, as we have seen, taboos against masturbation, stressed not only control over the body but what entered and left it. Mary Douglas, a cultural anthropologist who has studied taboos, suggests that we interpret the female body subjected to pollution rituals "as an image of society," thus reading the control of the female body as a symbolic effort to exert "social control."[72] Carroll Smith-Rosenberg, who draws on the work of Douglas, has argued that the taboos propagated by health reformers such as Sylvester Graham and William Alcott, when situated in the context of mid-century social stress, have an "emotional if not cognitive logic." In an effort to account for the anxieties that filter through advice books on health and courtship, Smith-Rosenberg suggests that sweeping changes in social experience produced anxiety about change itself.[73] Fears regarding bodily pollution are linked to underlying anxieties about socioeconomic uncertainty. She argues that mid-century middle-class Americans responded to an overload of social stress, change, and contradiction by condensing "their sociosexual anxieties into a symbolic system," so that "change and chaos assumed a sexual form."

When reconsidering the historicity of psychological stories like "The Birth-mark" and "Egotism," we would do well to heed evidence that the change and chaos which required ordering came to assume a specifically female form. G. J. Barker-Benfield, in his study of the emergence of nineteenth-century gynecology, argues that the management of women's health, sexuality, and procreativity represented for "pioneer" American gynecologists ("obsessed with female power") a symbolic restoration of "social order."[74] By extending the logic of this thesis, we can suggest that not only were cultural anxieties about women recast as biological flaws, but more to the point women's biological processes were *pathologized* as "change and chaos" so that their reordering would be tantamount to a symbolic reassertion of patriarchal middle-class notions of cultural stability.[75]

It is no coincidence that the language used to characterize Georgiana's "horrible stigma" resonates with mid-century representations of women's bodies as biologically flawed, disordered, and dangerous. Hawthorne's story about a wife made to feel ashamed of and obsessed with a "mark" of birth the size of a pygmy's hand (as Philip Young notes, a "baby's hand") fits into a cultural logic within which women were sometimes embarrassed to disclose signs of procreativity.[76] In *The Abuse of Maternity* (1875), for instance, Elizabeth Edson Evans tells of a pregnant woman much like Roderick Elliston at the outset of his snake gestation: she "is often so ashamed of her altered form and countenance as to shun the sight of acquaintances, and even to refrain from taking necessary exercise, receiving the punishment of her disregard of the laws of health in the agonies of protracted labor, including, not infrequently, the loss of her child." [77] As a public sign of sexual activity, pregnancy could indeed be experienced by middle-class women as a monstrosity to be hidden. Thomas C. Grattan's journal of his American travels records his impression that pregnant women seem to have been banished to isolation chambers: "The newspapers . . . abstain, on a point of delicacy from ever announcing the birth of a child. . . . No lady allows herself to be seen publicly while she is visibly enceinte." [78] Cultural attitudes toward women in labor were surely on Hawthorne's mind, for "The Birth-mark" and "Egotism" were published just one month after Sophia's first pregnancy had tragically miscarried. [79]

The fear of an excessive and unstable, perhaps angry, female imagination usurped by the womb partly accounted for this confinement. Michael Paul Rogin cites "the story in two popular medical books . . . of a pregnant wife who killed her husband and ate him." Dictionaries from the eighteenth and nineteenth centuries commonly include "hysterical passion" as one of several definitions for "mother." [80] Hence it is not surprising that, as both Ann Douglas and Nina Baym have pointed out, most mid-century sentimental novels written by and for women eschewed reference to the female body and sexuality, as if to bypass their cultural bondage to "anatomy is destiny." [81]

The other "horrible stigma" was, of course, women's "issue." Here too cultural anxieties over women's social behavior assumed biological form. Some medical authorities thought that menstruation, like pregnancy, had a dangerous destabilizing effect on women. Dr. Charles Knowlton's best-selling *Fruits of Philosophy* (1832) defined women with the "turns" as "out of order" and in need of isolation from the world. In 1844 Dr. George Rowe identified the function of menstruation as "controlling violent sexual passions" and preventing "promiscuous intercourse which would prove so destructive to the purest and holiest aspects of civil life." Here we see the fear that the menstruous woman's chemical affinities can get out of hand and thus precipitate "change and chaos." [82]

This mid-nineteenth-century anxiety corresponds to fears shaped by tribal pollution rituals in which women are confined to huts during the menarche, menstruation, or childbirth, and, becuase of the "threat" their bodies pose, are "tabooed" from touching certain people or ob-

jects. Georgiana's curtained decontamination chamber ("the secluded
abode") bears more resemblance to a respectable middle-class "hut";
yet it serves a purifying function similar to what Roger Williams, in
the seventeenth century, called the "little house" and James Adair,
in the eighteenth century, termed the "lunar retreat" in their writings
about Native American practices. Hawthorne could have learned about
"taboos" from a variety of sources including contemporary narratives of
Western "exploration" and accounts of Polynesian customs.[83] The scene
in which Georgiana bursts into the laboratory, when Aylmer accuses
her of throwing a "blight" over his "labors," resonates with the taboo
that isolates menstruating women whose presence was said to endanger
the hunt. Pollution rituals provide perhaps the clearest model of how
a culture can symbolically displace its fear of what Smith-Rosenberg
calls "change and chaos" onto women's bodies. "Purity," writes Mary
Douglas, "is the enemy of change, of ambiguity, and compromise."[84]

Change and chaos assumed a more specific literary nature in "The
Birth-mark." The "fastidious women" who read Georgiana's birthmark
as a "bloody hand" linked it by association with women's reproductive powers.[85] Fear of these reproductive powers, following the cultural
pattern we have traced, could be taken as a displaced expression of ambivalence about a female creativity that, once unleashed, could inspire
"disorder." Along these lines, it is significant that Georgiana's facial
hand publically exhibits *writerly* characteristics. Perhaps herein lies its
threat.

Aylmer figures his wife's "imperfection" as "the spectral Hand that
wrote mortality" (10: 39). Authors *write* "mortality." Her "mark" possesses a "disastrous brilliancy" that scared "away all their happiness" (10:
55). Hawthorne stresses that the synecdochic "Hand" that signals emotions has been well read. As noted earlier, her "mimic hand," like that
of a sentimental writer, could be read "glimmering to-and-fro with every
pulse of emotion that throbbed within her heart." Female sentimental
authors of the mid-century, like Georgiana, exercised a "sway over all
hearts"—though not quite all. Hawthorne himself, seemingly stung by
the book sales of women writers, wrote to his publisher in 1852 that he
wished women "were forbidden to write, on pain of having their faces
deeply scarified with an oyster shell."[86] Thus the "Envy" underlying the
experiment may be envy of a female author's "creative force." Within
this literary context the alchemist's symbolic decree, HANDS OFF MY
WIFE, assumes new and nefarious meaning.

Therefore it is worth noting briefly some parallels as well as differences between Hawthorne's tale and Charlotte Perkins Gilman's "The Yellow Wallpaper" (1892). Here the doctored wife is married, not to an alchemist, but to a cocksure physician, and is encoded as flawed, not within a vaguely biblical discourse ("sin, sorrow, decay, and death"), but within a late-nineteenth-century medical discourse ("temporary nervous depression—a slight hysterical tendency"). This discourse reflects professionalization of gynecology just beginning to gear up in the 1840's. Both stories suggest that domestic experiments designed to "normalize" a wife are more like gothic experiments that can destroy her.

Hawthorne merely hints that Georgiana's too "brilliant" hand is the object of envy, whereas Gilman's narrator knows and resents the fact that her "power," her creative writing, has been wrongfully encoded as a flaw, as that which causes her to be "nervous" and "hysterical." The stakes are clear: a woman's creative power is pathologized as a *psychological* problem. The narrator, as a female author, is under house arrest for being too imaginative to conform to her middle-class sex role. If this is the less explicit tension motivating Aylmer's HANDS OFF policy, then we can see Hawthorne himself reproducing features of a cultural process of mystification that he finds deadly in the alchemist's obsessive behavior. Hawthorne may have *biologized* and thus disguised his professional anxieties about literary women who, by virtue of their publishing success, were threatening to gain (in his mind) the upper hand. This possibility complicates our approach to our recurring question—why the editing?—because Hawthorne himself may, as a member of middle-class culture, have displaced (biologized) the motive.

Allegory and the Discursive Context for Psychological Tension

But along with the possibility that Hawthorne is himself operating within a discourse that biologizes cultural anxieties about creative women, we must also acknowledge his acute perception of the power of discourse to produce oppressive forms of subjectivity. In "The Birthmark" we see Hawthorne's self-critical awareness of an ideological process of representation that was working itself out in his aesthetic, an ideological process that helped *produce* the discursive conditions for both heated-up psychological tension between the sexes and the control of women's bodies. Hawthorne makes it evident that Georgiana is caught in the grip of discursive practices more cultural and far more powerful than the well-scrubbed hands of an isolated monomaniac. When she is carried across the threshold, she enters a literary laboratory. We are invited to ponder the implications of Aylmer's fatal cosmetic operation as an experiment in representation.

Our narrator represents the responses of the three groups to Georgiana's "hand"—magical endowment, "bloody" hand, and aesthetic flaw—as attributable to the distinct "temperaments" of the beholders. Yet upon a review of these responses, it becomes clear that Hawthorne is taking us on a tour of the ways in which female sexuality has been discursively produced by his culture. He does this in "Egotism" as well, by hinting that Rosina has been typed as a serpent with a bosom.

Our consideration of this stereotyping raises questions that the text of "The Birth-mark" leaves open. Does Aylmer react to Georgiana's "hand" per se, whatever the "hand" means, or does he respond to the way her "hand" has been responded to, that is, to the way it has already been allegorized by her culture? Does he respond to her sexuality or, in more mediated fashion, respond to stereotyped readings of female sexuality? Georgiana's tragic "flaw" is not how she looks but how she is looked at. The tale should be read not only as a historically specific "psychological" allegory but as an allegory about the way in which Hawthorne's own writing is complicit with and critical of a cultural process that discursively produces the female body as pathological. From this perspective the point of tension is not sexuality or biology conceptualized apart from culture, but systems of representation, including the literary, that color our readings of female sexuality through stereotypes.

Hawthorne would likely have been aware that women in the 1830's and 1840's, even women who wrote for conventional "lady's" magazines, sometimes saw themselves as having been abused by literary stereotypes. In 1832, for example, an anonymous female critic writing for *Godey's Lady's Book* took male authors to task for editing female bodies in their fiction. She accused male authors of misrepresenting heroines by shrinking their hands:

But why should small hands be accounted a characteristic of beauty? If we rightly understand the matter, a hand, or foot, or nose, in order to look well, should be in due proportion to the rest of the body. It is not the smallness of the hand that makes it beautiful—but the just relation it bears to the parts. A small hand, therefore, unless it be upon a small person, is an absolute deformity; and the novelists, while they think themselves beautifying their heroines by giving them tiny hands, are making them absolute frights.

"Do, gentlemen authors, get something original;" she concludes, "your stock of small hands must be exhausted by this time."[87] The *Godey's* critic intervenes in a discursive practice that teaches men how to read women and women how to read themselves. Miles Coverdale, the narrator of *The Blithedale Romance*, offers a splendid example of the aesthetic maltreatment parodied in *Godey's*: Zenobia's "hand, though very soft, was larger than most women would like to have—or than they could afford to have—though not a whit too large in proportion with the spacious plan of Zenobia's entire development" (10: 15). Literary aesthetics functions ideologically as a policing of the female body; women recognize that they cannot "afford to have" unconventional hands. The shrunken hand is an *infantalized* hand, a "pygmy" hand, a more vulnerable hand that vanishes in the grip of a larger male hand. The *Godey's* critic goes on to speculate that male authors edit the hands of their heroines to protect "their husband's ears." She suggests, by implication, that anxieties other than those relating to beauty underlie this aesthetic disciplining of bodies: female *resistance* is contained (shrunken) through male representation.

In January 1843, two months before "The Birth-mark" was published, *Godey's* criticized its own cultural power to produce distorted representations of women in their "fashion plates." An indignant artist complains that there has not been one woman illustrated in the magazine "whose waist is not so small as to be absolutely deformed. Nature never makes such, except when she perpetuates her malformations." Harriet Beecher Stowe, in a letter to the editor, recommended that *Godey's* artists portray women who "have *room to breathe*." A few months later the editor, Sarah Hale, testified that it is "absurd" to standardize "female forms": "As well prescribe the length of noses as the breadth of waists."[88] In this shift of policy, *Godey's* acknowledged not only its power of representation but more specifically its capacity to use these aesthetic judgments to put the squeeze on women.

These too are Hawthorne's concerns in "The Birth-mark." He suggests that representation is the name of the alchemist's game and that Aylmer's representations put the squeeze on his wife behind closed doors. Aylmer would have Georgiana believe that "he could draw a magic circle round her, within which no evil might intrude." Protected within this "magic circle," he endeavors to "release" Georgiana's "mind from the burden of actual things" (10: 44). In domestic "seclusion" Georgiana's view of the world is replaced by a "procession of external existence" that flits "across a screen." Like Shakespeare's Prospero, Aylmer's "alchemy" creates "optical illusion[s]" (10: 45): "Airy figures, absolutely bodiless ideas, and forms of unsubstantial beauty" (10: 44). At the climax of his experimentation Georgiana herself will become abstracted as a "bodiless idea," a "beauty" without substance, an "illusion." Aylmer's projections are designed "to warrant the belief" that he "possessed sway over the spiritual world" (10: 45). His representations are deployed to encode himself with allegorical authority in his newlywed's eyes.

This domestic experiment in the patriarchal production of womanhood has a singularly *literary* quality. Georgiana discovers that the volumes of her husband's "scientific library" contain "chapters full of romance and poetry" (10: 48). That Hawthorne, like others before him, is experimenting with alchemy as a figure for writing is likely.[89]

The "deformed" Georgiana awaits her alchemizing and is entertained by her husband's "bodiless" representations in a "secluded abode," a decontamination chamber that Hawthorne compares to "a pavilion in the clouds" (10: 44). This "pavilion," like the "alchemy" that perfects and beautifies, is literary in character. "Cloud-land" is a literary space that Hawthorne referred to often. In *The House of the Seven Gables* (1851) Hawthorne calls romance his "atmospherical medium" (2: 1) and assures his literal-minded reader that he infringes on nobody's "private rights" by "building a house, of materials long in use for constructing castles in the air" (2: 3). By the same token he reminds readers of *The Scarlet Letter* that his Salem is really "an overgrown village in cloud-land" (1: 44). Michael Davitt Bell has aptly described this characteristic of Hawthorne's "romance" as a "sacrifice of relation."[90] Georgiana has been transported to a private zone of romance or allegory for a *literary* operation.

Hawthorne also depicted "cloud-land" as a space in which allegorical operations could go awry, especially when they involved the representation of women. For instance, in the preface to "Rappaccini's Daughter" Hawthorne's narrator playfully but revealingly criticizes M. de l'Aubepine, the fictive allegorist of the tale that follows. Aubepine happens to have written stories with the same titles as Hawthorne's, though in French. His tales "might have won him greater reputation but for an inveterate love of allegory, which is apt to invest his plots and characters with the aspect of scenery and people in the clouds and to steal the human warmth out of his conceptions" (10: 91–92). Although the tone is light, "cloud-land" is represented as a privatized vampire space within which allegory almost automatically drains the life out of an author's "conceptions." We also find Hawthorne musing on the blood-letting effect of his allegory in his 1851 preface to *Twice-Told Tales*. He acknowledges that "even in what purport to be pictures of actual life [in his tales], we have allegory, not always so warmly dressed in its habiliments of flesh and blood, as to be taken into the reader's mind without a shiver" (9: 5). The character whose "human warmth" is chilled by allegory in "Rappacini's Daughter" is a young woman. Not surprisingly, the obsessive allegorist who ices her is a young man.

In "A Select Party" (1844), published one year after "The Birthmark," Hawthorne also expressed literary concern over the frigid fate of his isolated women-in-the-clouds. The narrator invites us to an "entertainment" in a "castle in the air" whose foundations "were quarried out of a ledge of heavy and sombre clouds" (10: 57). This castle is occupied by an author, a "Man of Fancy." Our host is unexpectedly "thronged" by a crowd of characters he had inscribed in his "visionary youth," among which is a "beautiful dream-woman" (10: 63). His characters appear mechanical rather than human, especially his "peerless dream-lady": "there advanced up the saloon, with a movement like a jointed-doll, a sort of wax-figure of an angel—a creature as cold as moonshine—an artifice in petticoats, with an intellect of pretty phrases, and only the semblance of a heart—yet, in all these particulars, the true type of a young man's imaginary mistress" (10: 63). This "unreality" graces him with a "sentimental glance" as a reminder of their "former love-passages" (10: 64). But the more mature Man of Fancy now fancies "what Nature makes, better than my own creations in the guise of womanhood." "Ah, false one," the dream lady shrieks, when banished to her plot, "your inconstancy has annihilated me!" To this charge the "cruel" Man of Fancy retorts: "good riddance too" (10: 64). Hawthorne mocks the male author, perhaps himself in the 1830's, who is capable of fabricating only dolls or angels, parodies of womanhood. In "The Birth-mark" and "Rappacini's Daughter" Hawthorne sketches women who are subjected to the "inveterate love of allegory" of male author figures; but in "A Select Party" the problem is that of a frustrated author who is able to sketch women only as mechanical stereotypes.

Hawthorne's diffidence about his ability to "make" lifelike female characters in his postnuptial narratives, and his apprehension that his "love of allegory" could "steal away the warmth out of his conceptions," especially conceptions of females, are twin concerns critical to rereading and rethinking the "sublimation" of Georgiana in "The Birth-mark." Hawthorne is exploring not simply what a literary alchemist does to a woman in marriage but what a male author figure does, *in spite of* himself, through plot and forms of representation to a woman in his text. He is questioning how the very form of his art, allegory, sets off deadly stereotypes.

Walter Benjamin has written that the allegorized object is rendered "incapable of projecting any meaning of its own; it can only take on that meaning which the allegorist wishes to lend it. . . . In his hands the thing in question becomes something else, speaks of something else, becomes for him the key to some realm of hidden knowledge, as whose emblem he honors it."[91] Georgiana gradually learns to recite her husband's allegory of her. At the climax of his experiments, Aylmer is left with what the more mature Man of Fancy rejects as failed art: "a sort of wax-figure of an angel . . . cold as moonshine"—a dead wife.

If Hawthorne does see himself locked in the grip of a discourse that produces wax angels with bloodless bodies, he also reflects on how this discourse helps to create the conditions that make this production possible and perhaps even predictable. Hawthorne's tale of two newlyweds and their "pavilion in the clouds" problematizes the privatized "magic circle" romanticized in "The Old Manse." Domestic "seclusion" such as Georgiana's should not be taken as a direct reflection of daily life in the 1840's; nevertheless, a variety of mid-century writers did think that the middle-class wife had undergone a "sacrifice of relation" that was too great a sacrifice.

For example, in 1840 Tocqueville noted that the unmarried American girl "makes her father's house an abode of freedom and of pleasure"; but if she weds, she is sequestered "in the home of her husband as if it were a cloister." After her betrothal she is expected to surrender her freedoms "without a struggle and without a murmur."[92] In her poem entitled "Home" (1857), Lydia Hunt Sigourney (no radical) did more than murmur: "Man's *home is everywhere!* . . . *It is not thus with* Woman!"[93] Marx Lazarus, a Fourierist critic of middle-class domesticity, decried the tyranny of domestic privacy as well as the jealousy that he saw as a product of its confines. "As soon as a girl marries," he protested, "she is placed under a sort of ban in most parts of this country, neglected by her former companions, and excluded from their festivities."[94] Anxieties about the privatization of married women sometimes surfaced in the correspondence and diaries of young people. Upon learning of his childhood friend's engagement in 1843, one young man confided to his diary, perhaps with Edgar Allan Poe in mind, that the "idea of her being married seems to me much the same as being buried."[95] And Elizabeth Cady Stanton, herself married and not having heard from Susan B. Anthony for quite a while, wrote to her friend in 1856, "Are you dead or married?"[96] The "magic circle" that casts "the spell of a tranquil spirit" around visitors to the domestic Eden becomes in Hawthorne's story a magic snare that drops on unsuspecting women. The connotations of Aylmer's "magic circle" are not only troubling, they are antidomestic.

Such comments attest to the "privatizing tendency" that historian Mary Ryan has studied in mid-century family life. Tocqueville's remarks about the 1830's, however, precede the period, the 1850's, in which Ryan finds this trend to be dominant. In the 1820's and 1830's, Ryan argues, the middle-class family was envisioned as a "corporate household" that was "benevolently ruled by a patriarch" (what Tocqueville calls "her father's home"), whereas in the late 1840's and 1850's there is a recognizable shift to the "privatized home" and a "feminine domesticity" in which the wife enacted the role of the preeminent socializing agent. Women also left the home in the 1830's and 1840's as active participants in benevolent and reform associations that encouraged them to "override meek, retiring, and feminine qualities." Tales like "The Birth-mark," which represent men and women in private spaces seemingly divorced from the public sphere, were written on the cusp of the transformation in domestic ideology that Ryan has charted.[97] Stories such as "The Birth-mark" suggest that even before nineteenth-century privatization became recognized as a cultural trend, it showed signs of becoming a psychologically airtight experience.

This *historical* process is thematized in tales by Poe. Like Hawthorne, Poe reflected critically upon how his own aesthetic participated in both the privatization and the cultural "editing" of women. Wedded life behind closed doors provides both a breeding ground for masculine obsession and a challenge to the signifying powers of one of Poe's artist figures in a story that Poe published shortly before Hawthorne's appeared, "The Oval Portrait" (1842). Poe's tale probably influenced Hawthorne's reflections on his own representational routines.[98]

Poe's story within a story is about a newlywed painted to death by her husband. The narrator is a wounded aristocrat who takes refuge in a vacant gothic chateau. While reclining on a bed in what seems to be an art gallery, his curiosity is aroused by an oval portrait of a "young girl ripening into womanhood." The "absolute *life-likeness* of expression . . . confounded, subdued, and appalled" him. He learns its eerie history in a journal. There once was an artist who, like Aylmer, had already "a bride in his Art" but who married nevertheless. His "Art" was his new wife's sole "rival." Like Georgiana, the newlywed consents to become the subject of her husband's art to vie for his gaze. In the seclusion of the art studio the gothic artist "*would* not see" that his "humble and obedient" wife suffered and "withered" as she posed. Her "sacrifice of relation" within this artistic privatization is total. The artist "turned his eyes from the canvas rarely, even to regard the countenance of his wife. And he *would* not see that the tints which he spread upon the canvas were drawn from the cheeks of her who sat beside him." A soft kiss after lovemaking is substituted by "one brush upon the mouth" to complete his image. "This is *Life* itself!" the painter exults, as his wife dies to live only in his canvas. His privatizing realism becomes her new home.[99]

Poe comments more explicitly on the role that the literary aesthetic itself plays in *constructing* male obsessions about women in "Berenice" (1835), which also bears important similarities to "The Birth-mark." Like the vampire artist of "The Oval Portrait," Egaeus, the narrator, seems empowered by privacy. Egaeus was born in a library, a textual space that appears to be the origin of his representational obsessions. Berenice, his conventionally pastoral cousin, seems like a parody of the uncloistered unmarried girl depicted by Tocqueville. She had been "agile, graceful, and overflowing with energy" and rambling through the hills until "struck" by a "fatal disease." One suspects that Egaeus and his library may be the *gothic* sources of her "disease," very like starvation.

As the new target of her narrator's representational obsession, Berenice is perceived only as what he has signified her to be: "not . . . the living and breathing Berenice, but . . . the Berenice of a dream." When Berenice's teeth ("excessively white"), her distinguishing feature, signs of her identity, are disclosed "in a smile of peculiar meaning," the narrator encodes them as his central fixation. Like hands, an adult woman's teeth give her a certain autonomy. The meaning he inscribes upon her teeth is "*Des idées!*—ah *therefore* it was that I coveted them so madly!" A female character or wife with "idées" and smiles of "peculiar meaning" cannot be. Thus she, like other Poe heroines, is buried alive (penned in), though disinterred briefly to undergo censorship with some "instruments of dental surgery": her distinctive "idées" are yanked with

Berenice (who won't roll over and play dead) screaming toothless in the grave.[100] "Then as now," observes Mary Ryan, in reference to the court records of mid-century Oneida County, New York, "wife beating was the most common violent crime."[101]

Both Poe and Hawthorne suggest connections linking a privatizing literary aesthetic, hyperpsychological relations between the sexes, and a cultural signification of women that can prove fatal. "The Birth-mark," however, problematizes a cultural process not addressed by Poe's tales. Aylmer gains psychological power over his wife through a sociological sleight of hand: he trains her to read herself as an aesthetic problem. As we have seen, even writers in *Godey's* recognized this kind of representational bamboozling as mass-produced stereotyping. A major ideological tension between "The Old Manse" and "The Birth-mark" is that in "Manse" Hawthorne represents home as exempt from the "artifice and conventionalisms of life"; in his allegory he depicts domestic Eden as a space in which stereotyping germinates like weeds in a hothouse.

"The Birth-mark," like the preface to "Rappacini's Daughter," raises the possibility that Hawthorne sees himself penned up in an allegorizing mode that *produces* the masculine obsession to stereotype how women read themselves.[102] He sees his allegorical form producing his content. Hawthorne, of course, liked to read Spenser, Bunyan, and Milton, and no doubt reflected at length on allegory as a literary form.[103] But I shall argue that Hawthorne's keen interest in Spenser and other allegorists also betokens more historically specific cultural concerns.[104]

It makes sense that Hawthorne problematized the *allegorizing* of women at a historical moment when an emphasis on the reading of character and bodies in middle-class culture—a nervous response to sweeping social changes—was transforming into a practice that was peculiarly allegorical. The mid-century antimasturbation guides that taught middle-class readers to detect (that is, to produce) evidence of onanism in blushes, blisters, pimples, and paleness suggest that mid-century men and women were learning to read one another as texts and that sexual desire was becoming the allegorical key to such texts. We must also take into account the growing popularity of that curious allegorical system of reading character called phrenology.[105] This pseudoscience achieved notoriety in America by the 1820's and became even more publicized in the 1830's with the American tours of Johann Gaspar Spurzheim and George Combe. As early as 1830 Sophia Peabody, after reading

Combe's best-selling *Constitution of Man* (1829), recorded in her diary her inclination "to believe in phrenology."[106]

Keeping in mind the prompt allegorizing of Georgiana, it is noteworthy that one particular genre of phrenology guides promised its readers control over personal relations, especially sexual relations. By the 1830's many phrenological publications warn young lovers to beware courtship and offer a "science" by means of which they can decode one another's character. In 1839 one lecturer counseled prospective lovers to think of all 35 "mental instincts" when sizing up one another in order to avert a "harvest of affliction."[107] Orson Fowler's *Fowler on Matrimony* (1841) described courtship as a "school of deception" in which "artificial smiles" are plastered over "hidden faults": "Every thing [is] white-washed for the occasion." The first edition of this phrenology manual sold out its 5,000 copies in three months; a second edition went in four.[108] "We can tell the rake, and designate the wanton," Fowler wrote in 1846, "and say truly who hath known the other sex and how; as well as who seeks solitary gratification, and who is pure. The *signs* of all these things *come to the surface*, and cannot be disguised."[109]

Although these popular books and pamphlets were written for readers of both sexes, the advice given most frequently seems to have been directed to the male reader who must screen his prey. Occasionally these pieces sway in the direction of droll self-parody, though without muting their phrenological zeal.[110] Sometimes the most prominent bulge in these pieces is the tongue in the cheek, as in the poem "Phrenology Applied" (1840). This remarkable lyric promotes phrenological courtship by recounting an array of bump-ridden women who suffer detection: Emma's big bump of "Destructiveness," Fanny's overdeveloped "Organ of Speech," and Hannah's undomestic organ of "Locality" ("a passion to roam . . . she will ne'er be home"). Not only does the authority of phrenological discourse allow the "poet" to project his culturally conditioned fears onto *autonomous* women, it gives him permission to allegorize them with an arsenal of stereotypes. This, too, is the fate of Georgiana.

It is likely that Hawthorne was conversant with some of this phrenological literature, including the parodies. While editing *The American Magazine of Useful and Entertaining Knowledge* in 1836, Hawthorne wrote parodies of both the "sciences" of phrenology and physiognomy and ranked phrenology (like alchemy) among "the doubtful sciences." In "Phrenology" Hawthorne reproduced illustrations that map the front and rear of the head, and he listed the 35 cerebral functions, albeit only to underscore the silliness of classifications more useful for encoding than decoding character. His "Science of Noses" parodically introduced the nose as an organ that betrays the self, and he suggested that the man who fears speaking unconsciously through his nose might attach "his handkerchief" over it. This undercover arrangement, however, would stir speculation about his "atrocious nose" as well as advertise his urge to conceal. In 1836, perhaps with this nasal fig leaf in mind, Hawthorne also published "The Minister's Black Veil," another piece that suggests that it doesn't pay to advertise.

John Neal's "The Young Phrenologist" (1836) appeared in the same issue of *The Token* as "The Minister's Black Veil." Neal's story clearly grows out of the genre of phrenological courtship manuals and also shows signs of having influenced "The Birth-mark." Nelly, like Georgiana, is an unsuspecting newlywed. From Ned's talk in his sleep Nelly learns that she has married not an alchemist but a *"Phrenologist!* Ay, a Phrenologist!"* Rummaging through her husband's drawers she discovers "a miniature of herself, with her hair wiped off, and her bare ivory skull, written all over with unutterably strange characters. . . . The beautiful hair she had been so proud of, and so celebrated for!" Ned awakens to explain that he charted her character during their courtship and that she is "indebted to Phrenology for a husband." Her organs include positive traits but also "Destructiveness—very large." At which point Nelly usurps his allegorical authority by seizing his chart and rewriting Ned: "Audacity—unparalleled! . . . Obstinacy—unspeakable!" Nelly, unlike Georgiana, is a resisting reader who refuses to speak her husband's allegory of her.[111]

In "The Young Phrenologist" the issues at stake revolve around power rather than sexuality: the power to resist a phrenological discourse that helps to construct, legitimize, and activate gender stereotypes, and the power to interpret oneself. "The Birth-mark" also is not just about sexuality but about power and the construction of stereotypes that produce female sexuality as a flaw.

Hawthorne's decision to write allegories about male allegorists is culturally meaningful because it demonstrates how Georgiana's conjugal socialization as a female flaw is an internalization of patriarchal stereotypes. Gender roles, Hawthorne implies, can be like lived allegories. Women, the story suggests, can be produced to read their distinctiveness not simply as an aesthetic problem but even more destructively as an allegorical problem. "The Birth-mark" has its origins in a culture in which women were sometimes trained to read talents or attributes that distinguished them from the crowd as "sin, sorrow, decay, and death."

In its self-reflexive operations Hawthorne's "anti-allegorical allegory"[112] is progressive: it becomes a hermeneutic for examining the ideological role that literature plays in the social construction of unambiguous roles for women. Hawthorne is subtle (more so than Neal) because he gets us to think about how and why the form of his own allegory, *had it* taken the form of Aylmer's, would have contributed to the discursive field in which phrenology had become a fad. Hawthorne reflects upon how his own aesthetic was capable of participating in the discursive reproduction of allegorical reading habits that *promote* psychological tension between the sexes—a tension that both he and Neal criticize through parody.

Hawthorne's parody not only encompasses literature written by men but also conventions and values gradually becoming popular in sentimental fiction written by women who contributed to what Jane Tompkins calls the "Other" American Renaissance. Using Susan Warner's *The Wide Wide World* (1851) as her model, Tompkins profiles the mid-nineteenth-century "ethic of submission," which she "values" as the expression of an alternative female culture: "This fiction presents an image of people [females] dominated by external authorities [fathers, parents, guardians, or husbands] and forced to curb their own desires; but as they learn to transmute rebellious passion into humble conformity to others' wishes, their powerlessness becomes a source of strength." This "religion" of submission (similar to Anna Freud's altruistic projection) yields "sensual pleasures, spiritual aspirations, and satisfaction in work accomplished." Such satisfactions, which help transmute submission into an "ethic," are only made possible by socializing women to allegorize their victimization as a test of their virtue. Social historians tend, unlike Tompkins, "to take a dim view of the domestic ideology" promoted by this fiction of submission; Hawthorne seems to have done so as well.[113]

"The Birth-mark" is anything but a middle-class fairy tale espousing the romance of married life. It is, rather, an unsentimental domestic parody of a newlywed who demonstrates her "true womanhood" and obedience to her husband by killing off a part, perhaps the creative part, of herself (and thus killing herself). Georgiana's "mark" is read as expressing her inner self, and this expression seems to be something that her ambivalent husband cannot look at or let the public see or allow his wife to view for herself.

Hawthorne Explains Freud (Historically)

By way of conclusion let us review some key considerations that will contribute to a more complex awareness of history in "The Birth-mark." I have argued that Hawthorne's postnuptial allegory is about a woman who has been socialized to read part of herself as an aesthetic, biological, and even psychological flaw; she has been subjected to a *cultural* rewriting. Questions remain about how to read the significance of Hawthorne's decision to represent this cultural censorship as one imposed by a monomaniacal male alchemist on his new wife.

If these overheated psychological relations between the sexes are read, in lieu of "machines in the garden," as signposts of history, as I have argued, there are several theoretical approaches we can take to interpret this history. For instance, we might begin by classifying "The Birth-mark" as an example of mid-century psychological fiction that probes the darkest corridors of the psyche. By paying attention to cultural and family history as well as literary history, we might follow this up by suggesting that the story *is* a historical text in the sense that it explored the transhistorical self at a particular historical moment when family life was undergoing an "emotional revolution" that produced "obsessive love." In his study of the "bourgeois experience" in America and Europe, Peter Gay concludes: "Intimate love, intimate hatred, are timeless. . . . But the nineteenth-century middle-class family, more intimate, more *concentrated* than ever, gave these universal human entanglements exceptional scope and complex configurations. Potent ambivalent feelings between married couples, and between parents and children, the tug between love and hate deeply felt but rarely acknowledged, became more subject to censorship than before, to the kind of repression that makes for neurosis." [114] And Mary Ryan, in describing the shift in family bonds from the 1820's to the 1850's, concludes: "The ties between the generations were knit of more intangible materials of affection, self-sacrifice, guilt, and all the mysterious machinations of conscience." [115]

This historical approach to the transformation of middle-class emotional life speaks to Colacurcio's apprehensiveness that a critical emphasis on the (apparent) psychological content of Hawthorne's fiction means putting his characters on the "couch" and vaporizing history in the bargain. By establishing that middle-class domestic relations were in fact undergoing an emotional intensification, one would make sense of why reviewers in the nineteenth century as well as critics in the twentieth century have privileged the psychological content of Hawthorne's writings in their readings. This historical approach might modify Tompkins's contention that twentieth-century critics have simply imposed their psychoanalytic preoccupations onto their reading of Hawthorne.[116]

But I now wish to push this historical approach further. The historicizing of Hawthorne's writing challenges the very notion of a transhistorical psychological self. Rather than reading Hawthorne as a proto-Freudian mid-century genius who anticipates Freud's insights into a transhistorical human nature,[117] I propose that we read his work another way: Hawthorne is telling us, through his "psychological" fiction, about the cultural production of a more psychologically privatized and domesticated middle-class subjectivity that, from our twentieth-century perspective, makes Freud's invention of psychoanalysis later in the century historically *predictable*. Mid-century psychological fiction such as "The Birth-mark" is exhibiting more than "insight" into obsessive rituals, projection, repression, ambivalence, and displacement; it is revealing, through what is present and absent from it, the conditions requisite for the production of a psychological hermeneutic that helped construct middle-class forms of subjectivity.

Fredric Jameson has argued that the "symbolic possibilities" of psychoanalysis historically rely on "the preliminary isolation of sexual experience" and "the autonomization of the family as a private space within the nascent sphere of bourgeois society."[118] Hawthorne explored some of these "symbolic possibilities" sixty years before Freud, not because he was a "genius," but because he was enmeshed in an earlier phase of the same transformation of middle-class domesticity and identity—the split between the public and private spheres and between masculine and feminine roles that resulted in what Philippe Ariès has termed the "emotional revolution." The absence of a conventionally historical context, like the industrial revolution, in stories like "The Birth-mark" and "The Oval Portrait" *is* their context. When Hawthorne observes in "The Old Manse" that his sketches have "so little of external life about them" (10: 34), this "sacrifice of relation," what Ryan calls a "privatizing tendency," makes historical sense.

We must move beyond conventional concepts of causality as well as of context if we wish to clarify the historical connection between Hawthorne's and Freud's writings. Nineteenth-century literature was a major discursive source for the symbolic and narrative possibilities of psychoanalysis. Middle-class psychological, sentimental, and romantic fictions, such as Hawthorne's, were historically antecedent to specialized "scientific" theories of subjectivity. These fictions in Europe and America actively transformed not only what was written and read but what was felt, desired, dreamed, daydreamed, and imagined. The representation of the "emotional revolution" in literature was an important force in the success of that revolution, whose political effects we are just beginning to fathom.

To recognize all of this is, of course, neither to embrace psychoanalysis as a theoretical solution to Hawthorne and his characters, as Frederick Crews did in 1966, nor simply to brush aside "Freudianism" as empirically unscientific, as Crews later did in his most recent "recantation" in 1989.[119] Instead, the theoretical and historical contributions of Jameson, Foucault, Ariès, Ryan, John Demos, Stephanie Coontz, Richard Brodhead, and others suggest that we situate the thematic concerns and symbolic preoccupations of Hawthorne and Freud in a more encompassing history of privatization, intimacy, gender roles, sexuality, the body, literature, and not least of all class, so that we can see how their writings addressed needs and discursively produced needs in an emerging middle class in New England and in the bourgeoisie in Vienna. Crews now acknowledges that his earlier literary perception "that Freud and Hawthorne were both Romantic thinkers" gave him an opening he did not take to situate their writings in "cultural history." But even his current conception of "cultural history" does not seem cognizant of contributions to a history of personal life published over the past two decades that have begun to illuminate the conditions within which the nineteenth-century middle class in both Europe and America was producing the "psychological" as a category.

To suggest that one should reread the writings of Hawthorne and Freud within this historical frame is not to propose any oversimplified equivalence between the two periods. In trying to explain why psychoanalysis was accorded a more enthusiastic reception in America than in Europe in the early twentieth century, Demos has argued that we must turn to the nineteenth-century history of family life for some answers. He traces this American "cultural readiness" for psychoanalysis to the nineteenth-century emergence of the "hothouse family" and a "domestic bonding [that] had become a matter of life-and-death." Psychoanalysis made psychological sense to middle-class Americans because of their "historically specific patterns of domestic relationship"—intense affective bonding with the mother and, in the case of the male, ambivalent rivalry with the father. The nineteenth-century "white-collar" male who felt the early psychological tug of mother grew to maturity in an ideological climate feeling the capitalist pull of the "success creed" and the myth of the "self-made" man ("a covert inducement," says Demos, "to competition in the relation of fathers and sons"). The cultural production of the cults of domesticity, motherhood, and success established conditions "in which oedipal issues [had] become highly charged for many people." [120]

Nineteenth-century Europe experienced some similar "trends": "the bounded quality of nineteenth-century family life; the sharpened definition of sex roles; the 'Victorian' culture of sexual repressiveness; and the 'discovery' of childhood." On the other hand, there was no significant "cult of success" in Europe, Demos adds; nor was the "intensity" of other factors equivalent ("the cult of motherhood; the shift to a child-rearing regime based on guilt more than shame; the declining birth rate; the sense of exclusive responsibility among the family members for one another"). Demos concludes that psychoanalysis (although Freud would have denied it) was in some respects more American than European.[121] Hence the history of nineteenth-century family life suggests that the age of Hawthorne (the "hothouse family") helps to explain Freud.

Even Gloria Erlich's account of Hawthorne's relationships to members of his family stays at the theoretical level of conventional family *biography* and does not recognize that Hawthorne's family was, like other middle-class families, deeply affected by social transformations that were bringing into being radically different assumptions about gender, sexuality, intimacy, motherhood, fatherhood, and individualism.[122] Just as Erlich would have benefited from situating her study of Hawthorne's family in the larger context of the history of middle-class family life, Crews, in both his Freudian and anti-Freudian modes, could have profited from placing Hawthorne's psychological themes in the context of an emerging middle-class pop psychology that is manifest in other mid-century literary and nonliterary texts.

For example, pioneering works of psychological realism by Richard Henry Dana, Sr., and William Gilmore Simms, published before "The Birth-mark," confirm a correlation between extreme middle-class pri-

vacy (Jameson's "autonomization") and supercharged psychological relations between the sexes.[123] In "Domestic Life," an essay published in
the same volume as *Paul Felton* in 1833, Dana commended domesticity
as "the safest way of coming into communion with mankind."[124] Yet
domesticity in Dana's *Paul Felton* is by no means safe. After the death of
his mother, whom he loved excessively, Paul Felton's domestic isolation
led him to "speculate on his feelings." As he grew up, "the pent up and
secret action" of his "character" got worse. Into the web of such expectations walks Esther, who evinces the unfortunate tendency to interact
with human beings in addition to her new husband. "The creatures are
beautiful and fair," Paul reasoned, "and would be innocent as flowers,
did none but heaven's winds visit them; but the world's breath blows
on them, and taints them." As Paul himself admits to Esther, "the very
intenseness of love calls up misgivings." Paul's misgivings take the form
of his proclivity to "speculate" on Esther's feelings, which are indistin-
guishable from his doubts about himself. As Freud would interpret it, the
jealous husband becomes obsessed with reading his wife's unconscious
("shall I kill her for her thoughts?") while actually projecting his own
insecurities upon the content of that reading.[125] This unstable project
climaxes when Paul stabs Esther with a rusty knife while she is sleeping
in bed.

In Simms's *Confession or The Blind Heart: A Domestic Story* (1841),
Edward Clifford, who suffered from lack of love while growing up in the
house of his uncle, cautions his reader that children reared in isolation
develop extravagant psychological expectations and "ask too much from
their neighbors." This results in his adult propensity to psychologize his
relations with others. Julia, his wife, is merely a text to be projected
upon. For Edward, Julia's sigh is not a sigh; it is taken as a psychological
code that she loves his best friend. Like Dana, Simms suggests a connection between the couple's domestic privacy and the psychologized
system of meaning that is taking hold in the home. On one occasion
Julia remonstrates to Edward that she has "few female friends—few
friends of any sort—how small is my social circle." Edward associates
the uncertainty of the mid-century marketplace with the unstable intensity of privatized romantic love when he compares himself to one of
those "petty traders" who "invested" his "whole capital of the affections
in one precious jewel" and lost the venture.[126] Poisoned by Edward, Julia
loses her life.

Both novels, like several of Poe's tales, depicted isolated domestic spaces well before the 1850's, from which Mary Ryan dates the decisive emergence of the ideology of the privatized home. Relations between men and women in these novels are *psychologically* airtight before privatization became a conspicuous mass-mediated reality for the middle class.[127] The gestures, assurances, and sociability of Esther and Julia are susceptible to being allegorized psychologically as signs of illicit sexual desires. Historians have observed that mid-century authors of conduct books offered their advice on the basis of their belief in "character," which signified "the marks or impressions made upon the mind."[128] But Dana, Simms, Poe, and Hawthorne are equally if not more preoccupied with representing what psychoanalysis calls "instinctual drives" and tracing how these "drives" are shaped within the domestic sphere. The novels of Dana and Simms are making a sociological point: the home that becomes too isolated from the community can produce psychologized relations between men and women. By suggesting this, these novels, like "The Birth-mark," "Berenice," and "The Oval Portrait," are destabilizing sentimental assumptions about the "humanizing" atmosphere of the middle-class home.

It can be argued that such hyperpsychological novels *reflect* changes in emotional relations between men and women in the middle-class home, but also that they are *ushering in* to cultural prominence a new psychological way of reading and imagining the middle-class self. Like the antimasturbation manuals of the 1830's and 1840's, what these novels may be doing is socializing middle-class readers to encode sexuality as the true essence that is locked up and thus awaits discovery in the self. Returning to "The Birth-mark," we might conclude that Hawthorne trains his reader to recognize when the unnamed sexuality shows its hand and that the detection of this in its myriad displacements, in Foucault's words, is presented as the "discovery" of "the truth of their being." But we might also take Hawthorne's postnuptial tale as an allegorical *warning* to middle-class culture that readings based on this discursively produced psychological common sense can be deadly, particularly for women.

I shall plead for the latter reading. Here the difference between Hawthorne and Poe, on the one hand, and Dana and Simms, on the other, is crucial to establish. One can make a case that the psychological novels of Dana and Simms are literary contributions to the exploration of a transhistorical self. If one situates them within the "bourgeois experience" described by Peter Gay, for instance, one might view their novels as fictional studies of a transhistorical self whose psychological relations have grown more intense in specific historical conditions. But "The Birth-mark," by virtue of its self-reflexivity, points us in theoretical directions charted by Jameson and Foucault: Hawthorne's story reflects upon the origins of its own "symbolic possibilities." "The Birth-mark" should be understood historically as a socially symbolic allegory about a psychological *discourse* (as opposed to a set of universal psychological truths) that was emerging, a psychologized system of meanings and displacements—a psychological realism—that characterized the way the middle class was beginning to produce its concept of "self." [129]

The same can be argued for "Egotism; Or, the Bosom Serpent." Roderick Elliston's compulsive snake-charming grows intriguingly ridiculous until it becomes obvious that Hawthorne wishes us to read it not as a psychological allegory or a case study of obsession which posits a snake-infested self, but more dialectically as a self-critical *parody* of a psychological allegorist run amok. Hawthorne is rethinking his bag of figures and hinting that the self can become obsessively psychologized by the cultural allegories ("dark fantasies") made available to represent it. His parody thus problematizes the author's cultural complicity in both figuring an interiority that cannot be known and installing ideologies of subjectivity. What "The Birth-mark" and "Egotism" are telling us, by implication, is that the socioeconomic pressures that made women susceptible to cultural censorship were now experienced and expressed by middle-class men and women in a peculiarly psychological register.

This development in the "psychological" imagining of middle-class subjectivity encountered resistance from another mass-produced discourse. In reviews of Hawthorne's writings of the 1850's we find an entrenched sentimental view of the self conventionally expressed through the language of the "heart" clashing with what was read (or misread) as Hawthorne's participation in an emerging psychological discourse. Some reviewers recoiled from Hawthorne's psychological "insights" as the townspeople did from Roderick's and wrote off his characterizations as "morbid." They read the "anatomized" heart as a spurious representation of the "human heart."

The most articulate and feisty critic of Hawthorne's "psychological romance" was Margaret Oliphant, the English novelist, who wrote as "Mrs. Oliphant." Hawthorne's puritans, she wrote, "are exhibited to us rather as a surgeon might exhibit his pet 'cases,' than as a poet shows his men and women, brothers and sisters to the universal heart." Her most provocative criticism is sociological; she identifies Hawthorne's psychological emphasis as just one cultural expression of an emerging psychological discourse in America: "it is not wonderful . . . that the new science which is called 'anatomy of character,' should be in great request among them. For ourselves, we have small admiration of the spiritual dissecting-knife, however skillfully handled, and very little tolerance for the 'study of character,' which has been quite a fashionable pursuit for sometime past." Mrs. Oliphant seems on the verge of suggesting that Hawthorne's psychological case studies should be assessed sociologically as signs of cultural malaise rather than as insights into an essential human nature: "How thoroughly worn out and blasé that young world must be." She concludes by suggesting that the dark regions probed by Hawthorne are really his own mystifying constructions of self, custom-made for members of the "intellectual" class.[130]

Mrs. Oliphant's critique is of Hawthorne's novels of the 1850's rather than his stories of the 1840's. But what she overlooks is that Hawthorne himself was at times problematizing the cultural production of a psychological discourse (a "study of character") that she pulls back from as a weird cultural phenomenon. Hawthorne's "mosses" that branch into a "variety of grotesque shapes" tend in their self-reflexivity to touch upon the discursive roots of their historical emergence. In these allegories home is the site of rather than the refuge from "artifice and conventionalisms." An increasingly privatized middle-class family life that was sentimentalized through Oliphant's domestic discourse of the "universal heart" should be understood as one precondition for the emergence of a literary pop psychology that portrayed middle-class sentiment as becoming obsessively overheated. Both discourses, which overlapped, were part of the same history. Hawthorne writes about a discursive sentimentalization of personal life and women that backfires and contributes to the production of psychological tension.

Of course, other social processes worked in tandem with the discursive sentimentalization of the middle-class family to set the conditions for the psychological tension between the sexes that Hawthorne fictionalized. Smith-Rosenberg's contributions, mentioned earlier, are valuable because they clarify causal connections between a history that focuses on the rise of industrialization and railroads (once again, Leo Marx's "machines in the garden") and a history of emotional tensions surrounding the control of the body. Her work on the mid-nineteenth century proposes what is in effect an inversion of psychoanalytic premises: rather than assuming that social activity is symbolic of deeper wishes or desires, sexuality is seen as both shaped by and symbolic of surrounding social contradictions, transformations, and pressures.

Smith-Rosenberg's explanatory narrative begins with socioeconomic transformations that recast personal life and its symbolic significance. The rise of commercial and early industrial capitalism, along with the burgeoning transportation network, expanded a marketplace that contributed to wide-ranging stress in the middle decades of the nineteenth century: many fathers lost the power to help determine the economic choices of their sons; artisans became hired laborers and, in factories, mere "hands"; city dwellers feared mobs of the poor; and farm girls who left for the city shocked moral reformers such as McDowall by becoming prostitutes. If the best-selling advice books are any gauge of actual behavior, by the 1830's we can see a widespread sexual repression more extreme than ever before in American history. Smith-Rosenberg, as I have noted, argues that mid-century reform movements to manage the body (including phrenology) should be read as cultural symptoms of emotional rather than cognitive efforts to compensate for lack of control over a socioeconomic world that was perceived as "disordered": "When the social fabric is rent in fundamental ways, bodily and familial imagery will assume ascendency. . . . The last intuitive resource of any individual is his or her own body, and especially its sexual impulses."[131] This symbolic compensation (controlling the body in place of society) was also achieved by controlling the definition of sex roles.

"The Birth-mark" is about a domestic experiment, not simply to re-order a body, but to require a body to conform to a *symbolic role*, a compensatory role, that middle-class women, in these times of cultural stress, were directed to play. Hawthorne's allegory (as a parody) can be read as an articulation of middle-class gender roles that were being produced within this rent "social fabric," as can "The Old Manse" and Hawthorne's notebooks from the mid 1840's. "The Old Manse" and the notebooks not only exhibit the emotional and symbolic significance of domesticity (Smith-Rosenberg's "familial imagery") in this context of "change and chaos"; they are indirectly about the need to use domesticity (with its clearly delineated gender roles) to form a *class* identity.[132] Therefore "The Birth-mark" and "The Old Manse" are not merely symptomatic literary responses to the experience of social change and contradiction; they reveal aspects of the formation of the subjectivity of a middle class that rose to economic and cultural hegemony within the whirlpool of rapid social transformations.

Yet these two ideological representations of middle-class subjectivity are at odds, for if "The Old Manse" is taken as an idealized construction of a class-specific sentimental interiority, then "The Birth-mark" must be read as an effort to disrupt this conventional class discourse by complicating the psychological codes attached to it, the sentimental psychological codes that are the signatures of the middle-class "humanizing" ideology. But in the process of criticizing this interiority, Hawthorne's allegory displaces middle-class domestic discourse from the story; his critique does not confront this discourse directly. Had it been otherwise, "The Birth-mark" might have hit too close to "home" both for its author and for its contemporary readers.

"The Birth-mark," then, is about the urge to control, not just a female body, but a female role, and this discursive management of the way women envisioned their womanhood was crucial to the ideological production of middle-class identity in uncertain times. Bearing this causal link in mind, we must in the coming chapters strive to think about the middle-class *uses* of definitions of gender, bodies, and domesticity, and the role that Hawthorne saw literature play in constructing, disseminating, and contesting such definitions.

2

Monsters in the Hothouse

Monstrous Expectations
in "Rappacini's Daughter"

I have suggested that "Egotism; Or, the Bosom Serpent" is an allegory about a "hidden monster"—perhaps a "serpent" with a "bosom"—that is gestating as a critical force in Hawthorne's fiction. The implications of this "monster" birth are more historically multivalent when we consider that the key word which connects mid-century male anxieties about female fertility and women authors is *monster*. Monstrosity is alluded to in "The Birth-mark." The narrator dismisses the idea that the "bloody hand" renders Georgiana's countenance "hideous" by noting that such an absurdity would be like calling the statue of "Eve Tempted" by Hiram Powers a "monster" simply because of a blue stain in the marble (10: 38).

This wordplay was literal: Hawthorne's culture, if not Hawthorne himself, would have considered Georgiana a "monster." Infants with a naevus maternus were classified as monster births. The *Encyclopaedia Britannica* of 1797 defined monstrosity as "too many members, or too few; or some of them are extravagantly out of proportion, either on the side of defect or excess." Abraham Rees's *Cyclopaedia* (1819) observed that monstrosity "deviates remarkably from the accustomed formation." The etymology of "monster" reminds one of the birthmark's disclosure of emotions, its tendency to show its hand: it is derived "from the Latin *monstrum*, or *monstrando*, 'showing.' "[1]

The presupposition underlying the concept of monstrosity-as-deviancy is that one is able to classify what is original, normal, or natural. Webster's 1829 dictionary described monstrosity as "any unnatural production; something greatly deformed" and "a person so wicked as to appear horrible." Shakespeare's "mis-shapen" Caliban, for example, is repeatedly called "monster." Dr. Johnson defined monstrosity as "deviating from the stated order of nature" and, most interesting of all, "shocking." But the 1797 *Encyclopaedia Britannica*, less confident than Dr. Johnson that we really know the "stated order" of Nature, regarded monstrosity as a sign of an excessively capricious and unfathomable Mother Nature whose "order" is frequently unstated: "we seem as yet to be very little acquainted with Nature in her sports and errors."

By associating Georgiana with the word "monster," even while dissociating her from it, and by making the sign of contention what would have been recognized as a "mother's mark," Hawthorne is connecting Aylmer's alchemy with a medical tradition of turning women into scapegoats for a Mother Nature that masculine science could neither pin down nor explain. Although Shakespeare wrote that birth-hour blots are "nature's fault," not the child's "own infamy," this infamy was eventually laid in the lap and on the conscience of the mother. Monstrosity was blamed on female conceptions that had gotten out of hand.

Eighteenth-century encyclopedias even contain discussions of mother's marks under the entry for "Imagination."[2] The *Britannica* quotes Malebranche's notion that when pregnant women who are "startled" by something or "agitated with any extraordinary passion" rub "some hidden part of the body," this impression is transmitted to a "hidden part" of the child. Rees's *Cyclopaedia* mentions another belief that when a pregnant woman's imagination is stimulated by "violent desire," the impression results in the too fertile birth of a monster. As Rees points out, the word for mother's mark in French is "envie," also meaning longing. As "the very image of his mother's desire," notes one critic, "the monster publicly signals all aberrant desire, reproves all excessive passion and all illegitimate fantasy."[3]

Thus it is noteworthy that in "Rappacini's Daughter" (1844) Hawthorne represents a female "monster" who is not a living symbol of her mother's unregulated desire and imagination but, the narrator concludes, "the poor victim of man's ingenuity and of thwarted nature" (10: 128). The patriarchal scientific imagination and its overreaching ambitions take the place of maternal "longing" as that which produces a monster. The "monster" is Beatrice Rappacini, a hybrid in sexual transition, "half childish and half woman-like" (10: 104), therefore ambiguous, and thus dangerous. Yielding to the narrative recoding devised by her suitor, Beatrice herself beseeches him to "forget that there ever crawled on earth such a monster as poor Beatrice" (10: 125). Dr. Rappacini, a medical botanist, has made the flowers in his garden and his daughter—his experiments both—literally dangerous to anyone from the outer world who touches them: their chemistry is poison. It is the social and ideological significance of this "monstrous" male experimentation that we shall explore in this chapter.

Beatrice's colorful features, like the "disastrous brilliancy" of Georgiana's "crimson stain," run to excess: she exhibited "a bloom so deep and vivid that one shade more would have been too much" (10: 97). In this respect her "bloom" resembles the excess of Rappacini's monstrous plants, which have curious characteristics. Some, for instance, have "flowers gorgeously magnificent" with "gigantic leaves" (10: 95). Others seem to have an unnatural, sexual quality and "would have shocked a delicate instinct by an appearance of artificialness indicating that there had been such commixture, and, as it were adultery, of various vegetable species, that the production was no longer of God's making, but the monstrous offspring of man's depraved fancy, glowing with only an evil mockery of beauty" (10: 110). What is fascinating about these "monstrous" flowers made by man is their tendency to be excessive.

One can easily get the impression that Hawthorne, in these curious descriptions, has in mind more than "monstrous" flowers. Rappacini's "vegetable existences" (10: 96) produce "gigantic leaves." And he, like a wary editor, prunes their contaminating leaves armed with "a thick pair of gloves" and a "mask": "he avoided their actual touch, or the direct inhaling of their odors, with a caution. . . . the man's demeanor was that of one walking among malignant influences, such as savage beasts, or deadly snakes, or evil spirits, which, should he allow them one moment of license, would wreak upon him some terrible fatality" (10: 96).

These seemingly sentient beings whom one should not "allow . . . one moment of license" are Beatrice's "sister" plants. She often communes with them in what seems erotic, not to say incestuous fashion: "Give me thy breath, my sister, . . . for I am faint with common air! And give me this flower of thine, which I separate with gentlest fingers from the stem and place it close beside my heart" (10: 102). But even Beatrice withdraws from some of her "sisters" who are endowed with a disastrous brilliancy too excessive. "There are many flowers here," she confesses with maidenly propriety, "and those not the least brilliant, that shock and offend me, when they meet my eye" (10: 111). Yet her mysterious father seems obsessed with inventing "brilliant" plants that, in the words of Giovanni, Beatrice's suitor, "seemed fierce, passionate, and even unnatural" (10: 110).

The story illustrates the disastrous things that can happen when characters like Beatrice get too intimate with such excessive "sisters." Dr. Rappacini had "succeeded in mingling plants individually lovely into a compound possessing . . . [a] questionable and ominous character" (10: 110). Colored by this context, at least in the eyes of Giovanni, Beatrice, the sexually alluring "compound," half child and half woman, takes on their "questionable and ominous character." From this point of view, her "fierce, passionate, and unnatural" sisters, perhaps too "brilliant" for their own good, are no sanguine influence.

Of course, blame is never so easy to place in a Hawthorne story. The narrator makes it obvious that Rappacini is not the only maker of female "monsters" in the picture. If his monster making is botanical and biological, that of Giovanni and Baglioni, his pompous advisor, is insidiously literary. Their injection of narrative poison into Beatrice's bloodstream is more toxic than Rappacini's accomplishment. Like Georgiana, Beatrice is rewritten as monstrous by their *narrative* experiments.

When drinking with Baglioni, Rappacini's envious rival, Giovanni first swallows narrative poison. After recounting Rappacini's experiments in "vegetable poisons" (10: 100), Baglioni turns the subject to Beatrice, whom he has never met: "Rappacini is said to have instructed her deeply in his science, and that, young and beautiful as fame reports her, she is already qualified to fill a professor's chair. Perchance her father destines her for mine!" (10: 101). With wine and the association of Beatrice with "vegetable poisons" coursing through his veins, Giovanni returns to his room overlooking Rappacini's garden.[4] There he thinks he sees a "small orange-colored reptile" destroyed by moisture from the "broken stem of the flower" (10: 102-3). The narrator, who is less clear about what happens, is definite about how taken Giovanni is by Beatrice. The scene is sexual: "he was compelled to thrust his head quite out of its concealment in order to gratify the intense and painful curiosity which she excited." Thrusting his head into her garden, he also "fancied that while Beatrice was gazing at [an] insect with childish delight, it grew faint and fell at her feet" (10: 103). Here, too, the narrator's choice of verbs makes what really occurs indeterminate. Giovanni's perception is filtered through Baglioni's narrative of poison experiments. His narrative helps render Beatrice "questionable and ominous." The more desirable and womanly she is to Giovanni, the more ambiguous she becomes. Like Georgiana, Beatrice is stereotyped as either "angel or demon" (10: 109).[5]

Stereotypes inform an ambivalence that in turn activates stereotypes. "Blessed are all simple emotions, be they dark or bright!" our narrator warns us: "It is the lurid intermixture of the two that produces the illuminating blaze of the infernal regions" (10: 105). Giovanni, as one "who was not unstudied in the great poem of his country" (10: 93), may measure his own garden-variety Beatrice by the standard of Dante's. Clearly, Dante's Beatrice was always more allegorical than human. But Hawthorne may have had another literary Beatrice of more recent vintage in mind when naming his character. In Mary Shelley's *Valperga* (1823), which is also set in medieval Italy, there is a thoroughly ambiguous Beatrice who fraternizes with witches when on the verge of taking the veil. In a half-crazed oration this mercurial "prophetess" philosophizes that "all beauty wraps deformity as the fruit the kernel; Time opens the shell, the seed is poison."[6] This is Giovanni's obsessive dread. Beatrice's predicament, like Georgiana's, is that her *humanity*, her signs of life, put into play the stereotype that "beauty wraps deformity" and that angel masks demon.

At the prodding of Baglioni, Giovanni seeks to transform Beatrice's "questionable" nature into something more sharply defined by inserting her into the classical fable of Alexander the Great and the poisonous lady sent to seduce and kill him. Like Giovanni, Alexander is warned by an advisor, and he conquers as usual. Giovanni uses this narrative as "gloves" to handle, or reclassify, the ambiguous Beatrice. Once pressed within the pages of this narrative, Beatrice is allegorized or *stereotyped* to death. The Alexander fable affords Giovanni a pretext to administer her Baglioni's "antidote" (10: 119), which, like Aylmer's "solution," is fatal. Thus Hawthorne's anxieties about the lethal effects of his own "inveterate love of allegory," as revealed in his preface, are reenacted specifically in the detoxification of a colorful female character. Like the Man of Fancy's dream-lady, Beatrice could easily have charged: "false one . . . your inconstancy has annihilated me." And so she does. Less a product of the "ethic of submission" mold than Georgiana, the dying Beatrice probes Giovanni's motives: "Oh, was there not, from the first, more poison in thy nature than in mine?" (10: 127).

The contradiction is that Hawthorne makes Beatrice poisonous and dangerous literally but not morally. Hawthorne has inverted the sentimental ideology that "romantic love" within home and garden constitutes an Edenic antidote to the "poisonous" world outside. In this garden, male love is not an antidote but the poison.[7] It is Giovanni who is monstrous: he "was startled," though undeterred, by the "horrible suspicions that rose, monster-like, out of the caverns of his heart, and stared him in the face" (10: 116). In contrast to the encyclopedia entries, male rather than female passion is responsible for the conception of "monsters." Like Aylmer's project to sanitize his wife, the detoxification of Beatrice has underhanded sexual meaning: she is fatally deflowered.[8]

"Rappaccini's Daughter" suggests that Hawthorne did his homework on monstrosity and thought through its literal and figurative meanings. He probably knew that "monster" was a botanical term: "plants producing any part different from the same part, when growing wild"; or "irregularities in plants . . . such as double flowers . . . [or] a superfluity or scarcity of juices."[9] He may also have known that botanical science was in crisis. Its confidence in scientific naming had been shaken. New discoveries of unclassifiable plants, as one botanist observed in 1834, required "more enlarged views": "Nature has instituted neither classes, orders, nor genera." Between 1825 and 1845 at least twenty "natural" systems were introduced by scientists. One source of danger to "order" was the discovery of "monstrous" plants, the apparent result of commingling.[10] These discoveries raised doubts for botanists as to whether some monsters were deviant or the true original from which plants previously classified as natural had deviated.[11]

In "The Birth-mark" and "Rappaccini's Daughter," Hawthorne reproduces this scientific anxiety about signifying and classifying female nature. Monstrosity is a metaphor for female ambiguity, desire, and *power* in the eyes of males. Conversely, monstrosity serves as a trope for male ambivalence about desirable and therefore questionable women. Most important, the metaphor of woman-as-monster reveals the rigidity of sex-role classification for women: any deviation from the stereotype (the stated order of feminine nature) produces the appearance of dangerousness, deformity, and monstrosity. Hawthorne's story therefore is not simply a psychological allegory about the tragic effects of male ambivalence toward female sexuality but a social allegory about the scientific and literary *administration* of classifiable sex roles.

In asking why this narrative experiment is initiated, we must entertain several related possibilities. Hawthorne's interest in "flowers," for instance, has multiple layers of cultural and literary meaning. When

Georgiana heeds Aylmer's request to stroke his magic flower, "the whole plant suffered a blight . . . as if by the agency of fire" (10: 45). We see the same "blighting" in "Rappacini's Daughter." Giovanni's gift of flowers to the "poisonous" Beatrice, a bouquet from outside her father's garden, may also be blighted by her touch (so Giovanni believes). This "blight" was a popular folk myth handed down from Pliny's *Natural History*, which held that "crops touched by it [menstrual blood] become barren, grafts die, seeds in gardens are dried up, the fruit of trees falls off." [12] Hawthorne's poisonous flower imagery is a significant metonymy when we recall the prohibitions from Leviticus 15:24 that figure menstruation as "flowers": "if any man lie with her at all, and her flowers be upon him, he shall be unclean seven days." "Flowers" was also used as a euphemism for menstruation in nineteenth-century medical texts. The possibility that Hawthorne is associating monstrous with menstruous in "Rappacini's Daughter" is not far-fetched, although the botanical term "menstruous" plant, an excessive flowering "lasting for a month," may not have entered the lexicon until the 1860's. [13] Both Beatrice and Georgiana are isolated, "tabooed," and condemned within pollution narratives that destroy them. Hawthorne is suggesting that a male dread of women's biological "issue"—as it is constructed *within* discourse—conflicts with pure stereotypes of the feminine woman.

The blighting of flowers, however, refers to more than this "issue"; in the mid-nineteenth century flowers served as metaphors of well-socialized femininity. In John Ruskin's classic apologia of the ideology of women's separate sphere, "Of Queen's Gardens," the garden is a metaphor of domestic "order." The middle-class woman both tends flowers and is herself a sympathetic "flower": "the harebells should bloom, not stoop, as she passes." Within her garden, woman assumes a symbolic burden as "the centre of order, the balm of distress, and the mirror of beauty." As a symbol of order and sweet submission, she must appear as safe and disinfected as her home, with no room for ambiguity. If disorder contaminates her hermetic garden, blame is clear: "within his house, as ruled by her, unless she herself has sought it, need enter no danger, no temptation, no cause of error or offence." [14] Describing taboos imposed upon English middle-class privatized "flowers," historians Leonore Davidoff and Catherine Hall observe, "Woman's virtuosity lay in her confinement, like the plant in the pot, limited and domesticated, sexually controlled, not spilling out into the spheres in which she did not belong nor being overpowered by the weeds of social disorder." [15]

Flower imagery sprouted everywhere in the well-ordered feminine culture industry. Bonnets illustrated in *Godey's*, for example, framed women's faces as the petals of a flower.[16] In *The Blithedale Romance* Priscilla and Zenobia are consistently represented and judged through metaphors of flowers. Priscilla is either a "poor, pallid flower" (3: 193) or "budding and blossoming" (3: 72). As a fertile advocate of women's rights Zenobia is more like one of Rappacini's renegade flowers, overgrown with a mind "full of weeds" (3: 44). And "ranker vegetation," says Coverdale, "grew out" (3: 244) of her heart. Pseudonyms of sentimental female authors (Fern, Greenwood, Forrester, Myrtle) and titles of their books (*Fern Leaves from Fanny's Portfolio*, Julia Ward Howe's *Passion Flowers*) also associated feminine writing with "flowers."[17] Read within this context, the blighting of flowers suggests that Georgiana's well-read hand and Beatrice's purple poison blight femininity itself. Neither Georgiana nor Beatrice is quite "another flower."

The association of authors, writing, and flowers would have been obvious to Hawthorne. His own name, which he changed from Hathorne, was a bush: "*Class* 12. *Order* 2. Principally a N. American genus, but found in Europe, the Levant, and India. Flowers scarlet."[18] Scarlet "flowers," since the Renaissance, could also be read metaphorically as "scarlet" rhetoric or "scarlet" writing. But the mid-nineteenth-century association between "flowers" and authorship usually pertained to flowery writing by women. Thus Sarah Hale, editor of *Godey's*, published *Flora's Interpreter* (1832), an anthology of poetry about flowers accompanied by their botanical descriptions, which followed "the classification of Linnaeus partly because I think twenty-four seems most gracefully to round the number of classes." Linnaeus's "order" is, says Hale, "the most poetical." Hale's "philology of flowers" is, in effect, stereotypes of uncontaminated, well-socialized feminine sentiments; nothing but "pure, tender and devoted thoughts and feelings."[19] No real poisonous or overly passionate flowers, and certainly no unclassifiable "monsters" who produce "gigantic leaves" are permitted to take root in *Flora's Interpreter*.

Hale's *Godey's Lady's Book* self-consciously served as cultural proof that women could write and maintain their femininity by religiously inscribing femininity. An English "authoress" wrote *Godey's* in praise of American female poets who express "tender sentiment with flowers of the minute beauties of nature." She complimented Hale on the magazine's biographical sketches of "poetical ladies" because they show "that so many of them are married and have families, whom they educate and manage so well." *Godey's* published a well-tended garden.[20]

But Hawthorne is fascinated by "vegetable existences" that are "commixtures": "flowers gorgeously magnificent" with "gigantic leaves," and "brilliant" characteristics that "shock" a "delicate instinct." He is drawn to contaminating flowers so exceptional that they "no longer" seem to be of "God's making." The flowers he cultivates in Rappacini's garden are far from ordinary—and "ordinary" is a key word in Hawthorne's tale. Baglioni's "antidote" is concocted to bring "this miserable child [Beatrice] within the limits of ordinary nature" (10: 119). To restore a woman to the "ordinary" is to make her classifiable, like the suitably feminine flowers in *Flora's Interpreter*. Not only is Beatrice's "bloom" almost "too much," but like Georgiana she is associated with the word "brilliant," another sign of the extraordinary. Yet this "brilliance," like Georgiana's, is aestheticized so that it refers not to how well she thinks but to the way she looks or is looked at.

One other revealing image is associated with this "brilliance." "There came thoughts, too, from a deep source, and fantasies of a gem-like brilliancy, as if diamonds and rubies sparkled upward among the bubbles of the fountain" (10: 113). Beatrice's "fantasies of gemlike brilliancy" sound like they would be the *envy* of any author and remind us of the manifold literary characteristics of Georgiana's "creative force." Perhaps here, as in "The Birth-mark," we see traces of an underlying anxiety that the female literary imagination has gotten out of hand. Baglioni's fear is that Rappacini's teaching and Beatrice's brilliancy have qualified her to fill a professor's chair, namely his own! For a young woman to be "brilliant" and perhaps to be daring as an author is to be irregular, a commixture, a monster outside of the limits of "ordinary"— meaning recognizably feminine—nature.

This too may be Hawthorne's fear: being displaced by poisonous women who cultivate "flowers" not "ordinary." The model of an eccentric and solitary scholar who empowers (and thus endangers) his daughter with "poison" and removes her from the sphere of the "ordinary" is one with which Hawthorne was acquainted in his own circle. Just one month after his marriage to Sophia in 1842, Hawthorne enjoyed an idyllic afternoon in the woods of Sleepy Hollow cemetery near Concord with the editor of *The Dial*, Margaret Fuller, "lying on the ground, and me sitting by her side." [21] The ever reticent Hawthorne was so touched by their intimacy that a few days later he wrote her: "There is nobody to whom I would more willingly speak my mind, because I am certain of being thoroughly understood." [22] They talked about the season, about "getting lost in the woods," and, of particular interest here, "about the experiences of early childhood, whose influence remains upon the character after the recollection of them has passed away."[23] Fuller's upbringing, as we shall see, keeping in mind "Rappacini's Daughter," was nothing like "ordinary."

She described her mother as one would a sentimental poem from *Godey's*: "one of those fair and flower-like natures . . . bound by one law with the blue sky, the dew, and the frolic birds." On her mother's tombstone was engraved the epithet "true woman." Her father, Timothy, a solitary and iconoclastic lawyer who had excelled at Harvard, was her intellectual Pygmalion. Fuller had wanted a boy and gave Margaret an education that would have distinguished her at his alma mater. By age six his daughter was studying Latin as well as English grammar.[24] Trained in the classics, she soon acquired a "gladitorial disposition." Her sharp intellect and erudite learning made interaction difficult, especially with males. Emerson once commented that "men thought she carried too many guns."[25] In what was probably an allusion to Fuller in "The Old Manse," Hawthorne viewed her well-honed intellect as a weighty imposition rather than a charm: "her, on whose feminine nature had been imposed the heavy gift of intellectual power, such as a strong man might have staggered under, and with it the necessity to act upon the world" (10: 29).

Of her relationship to her eccentric and autocratic father, Bell Chevigny concludes, "The duty Timothy had shunned was showing his daughter what to do with what he made her." In a culture suspicious of women whose intellect situated them beyond the "limits of ordinary nature," Fuller "could only be useless and freakish." She saw herself, to use Hawthorne's botanical word, as an ambiguous commixture: "The Woman in me kneels and weeps in tender rapture; the Man in me rushes forth, but only to be baffled."[26] If Beatrice spends her time in homoerotic communion with a community of female flowers, her "sisters," Fuller likewise invested time, energy, and passion in "conversations" with up to forty women every week for five winters from 1839 to 1844, the year "Rappacini's Daughter" was published. Sophia Peabody, before marrying Hawthorne, participated in this group. Hawthorne may have his perception of Sophia's perception of some of these women in mind when Beatrice tells of the "many flowers here, and those not the least brilliant, that shock and offend me when they meet my eye."

Fuller was certainly on Hawthorne's mind not long before he published his tale of a poisonous woman in December 1844. In July 1843 Fuller published her first feminist tract in *The Dial*: "The Great Lawsuit —Man *versus* Men; Woman *versus* Women." The piece caused Sophia some upset, as is apparent in a missive to her mother: "What do you think of the speech which Queen Margaret Fuller has made from the throne? It seems to me that if she were married truly, she would no longer be puzzled about the rights of women."[27] Yet Fuller visited Concord for about a month in July 1844 and stayed at turns with her sister and with the Hawthornes at the Old Manse. Like that idyllic August afternoon in 1842, the time spent with Nathaniel, in this instance a moonlit evening of rowing on the Concord, seems to have been special: "He talked a great deal this time. I love him much, and love to be with him in this sweet tender homely scene. But I should like too, to be with him on the bold ocean shore."[28]

Beatrice can be distinguished from Fuller on several counts. Unlike Fuller, Beatrice is beautiful and has almost "too much" bloom. Fuller's caustic wit and plain physical presence, on the other hand, tended to make her stunning in a different way. Recalling Fuller's schoolgirl days, William Henry Channing wrote, "Words flashed from her of such scathing satire, that prudence counselled the keeping at safe distance from a body so surcharged with electricity."[29] Unlike the egotistical Fuller, Beatrice is self-effacing in the "ordinary" feminine manner and keen to refute "disastrous brilliancy": "Do people say that I am skilled in my father's science of plants? What a jest is there!" (10: 111).

In fact, Beatrice is actively resentful of the empowerment to which she has been subjected by her father. Her dying words, perhaps words that occurred to Fuller, question why he had imposed "this miserable doom" upon her: "I would fain have been loved, not feared." Her paternal Pygmalion sees her transformation differently: "Misery, to be as terrible as thou art beautiful? Wouldst thou, then, have preferred the condition of a weak woman, exposed to all evil and capable of none?" (10: 127). "Terrible," of course, has two meanings: to be made formidable, but also to be made dreadful. In Hawthorne's tale and his culture, men respond to the formidable woman, like Fuller, as dreadful. This disturbs Beatrice.

Margaret Fuller is dangerous and perceived as "monstrous" because of her petrifying intelligence. Her excessive flowering was culturally shocking. Timothy Fuller, like Dr. Rappacini, ruined a good "flower" by injecting her with poison; that is, by arming his daughter with an education that would have prepared a boy for a distinguished career at Harvard. Then Margaret used this "poison" to inject other "flowers" in her weekly "conversations." Beatrice's "brilliancy," unlike Fuller's, seems to be wholly physical: too much "bloom" and a blighting power associated in popular folklore with menstruating women. If Hawthorne did have Fuller in the back of his mind while sketching Beatrice and converted Fuller's intellect, her "frightful peculiarity," into Beatrice's biological "poison," her transmutation into a toxic nymphet is worth questioning.

We must interrogate why Hawthorne chose to figure a woman's intellectual power as bodily poison and to portray a man who seeks to empower a woman as a poisoner. While it is Beatrice's desirability and touch of death that distinguish her as a threat, it is Fuller's capacity to think and to persuade that makes her *culturally* extraordinary and "monstrous." When Giovanni classifies Beatrice "a world's wonder of hideous monstrosity," the word "monster" communicated a range of cultural significance that extended beyond medical or botanical definitions. An awareness of this cultural range of meaning suggests that the correspondence between Fuller's intellectual and literary upbringing and Beatrice's "poisonous" one is not mere coincidence and that the latter's "poison" is distilled from a compound of more encompassing cultural anxieties.

In contextualizing the uses of the concept of "monstrosity," I suggest that in "Rappacini's Daughter," as in "The Birth-mark," we are seeing signs of the cultural tendency to *biologize* masculine social or literary anxieties about women. "Monstrosity" had acquired significance as a term connoting female deviance as far back as the sixteenth century, and since this particular meaning of "monster" becomes important in Hawthorne's novels of the 1850's, we should also consider his use of the word in the 1840's. In 1558 the fanatical founder of Scottish Presbyterianism, John Knox—with Queen Mary in mind—denounced the "monstriferouse empire of women." This association of monstrosity with both heresy and female rule was made prominent again in an event that Hawthorne knew much about: the Puritans' trial of Anne Hutchinson in 1637.

John Winthrop's famous account of the antinomian controversy was published anonymously in 1644 and then reissued twice with a new title and a preface by Theodore Weld in the same year. Weld did what Winthrop refrained from doing: he attributed allegorical significance to two "monster" births that became a symbolic controversy within the larger controversy. He related the monster birth of Mary Dyer, a follower of Hutchinson, to the coincidence that "that very day Mistris *Hutchinson* was cast out of the church for her monstrous errors." Weld allegorized the fetus as the embodiment of antinomian opinions not in His image:

God . . . [testified] his displeasure against their opinions and practices, as clearly as if he had pointed with his finger, in causing the two fomenting women in the time of the height of the Opinions to produce out of their wombs, as before they had out of their braines . . . monstrous births. . . . Mistris Dier brought forth her birth of a woman child, a fish, a beast, and a fowle, all woven together in one, and without an head. . . . Mistris Hutchinson . . . brought forth . . . 30 monstrous births . . . few of any perfect shape, not all of them . . . of humane shape.

The doctrine of the transmission of impressions is invoked and responsibility is laid in the lap of Hutchinson, whom Weld describes as a "woman very helpfull in times of child-birth, and other occasions of bodily infirmities . . . shee easily insinuated her selfe into the affections of many." In both cases what emerges from womb and brain, which are conflated, is excessive, unrecognizable, and unclassifiable. Weld also charges Hutchinson as the "breeder and nourisher of all these distempers."[30]

In another classic account published in 1653, with which Hawthorne was also probably acquainted, Edward Johnson followed Weld's lead and allegorized these monster births as signs of God's censure of a specifically female rebellion. His narrative is of special interest for, even more explicitly than Weld, Johnson ascribes to Hutchinson the wish to displace the father and to impregnate her female followers ("the breeder") with her influence. His account brings to mind Beatrice inhaling the uncommon breath of her poisonous sisters, as well as Fuller's "conversations" with her "flowers": "This Woman was wonted to give drinks to other Women to cause them to conceive, how they wrought I know not, but sure were Monsters borne not long after."[31]

A short piece on "Mrs. Hutchinson," which appeared in December 1830, was one of the first to be published by the 26-year-old Hawthorne, and the near hysteria about women's unregulated and heretical "creative force" disclosed by Weld and Johnson is present here. In a lengthy opening paragraph Hawthorne makes comments, not about the puritans, but on the evolving feelings and occupations of the "gentle sex" in his own century. It becomes evident that Hawthorne's interest in "Mrs." Hutchinson, never referred to by her Christian name, is deeply rooted in his more immediate anxiety about contemporary women who profit so successfully from their "feminine ambition" in the literary marketplace. The "public women," of which Hutchinson was a type in her own times, are on the loose, in the "press," and perhaps worst of all, will soon become "fair orators." Indeed, young Hawthorne complains, the "tottering infancy of our literature" suffers from "a girlish feebleness."

Hawthorne puts these "numerous" women authors in a double bind. If they write sentimental works, the literary equivalent of a "light and fanciful embroidery," they debase the possibilities of a serious national literature; but if they write something different, we may assume, they are blamed for having trespassed the bounds of their domestic sphere and for fomenting a literary revolution: "when a continuance of ill-judged incitements shall have turned their hearts away from the fireside . . . the ink-stained Amazons will expel their rivals by actual pressure, and petticoats wave triumphantly over all the field." At this stage of his career Hawthorne had barely placed his toe on the field. Hutchinson and her banishment from Massachusetts naturally bring up the question of the role of cocky women writers and their heresies in his own day. Public, creative, and artistic women, therefore, with Hutchinson and the puritan fathers in mind, should be examined with a "stricter, instead of a more indulgent eye" for their "irregularity" (monstrosity).[32]

Which women, as early as December of 1830, had gotten under his skin? Hawthorne specifically refers to "cisatlantic" or American women authors. Nina Baym, in her survey of women's fiction of the 1820's, discusses novels by Catherine Sedgwick and Sarah Hale, both of whom seem unlikely candidates for provoking social unrest akin to Hutchinson's antinomianism.[33]

Of course, Fanny Wright delivered a number of much publicized and criticized lectures in 1828 and 1829 that were published just before Hawthorne wrote his sketch. She spoke unabashedly on behalf of women's rights, especially for education, and denounced America's "priestcraft" and its stranglehold on women. One New York reviewer hailed her as "unrivalled by any of the public speakers, of any description, in this city," but other reviewers in the 1830's reviled her as a monstrous hybrid, "a great awkward *bungle* of womanhood, somewhere about six feet in longitude, with a face like a Fury, and her hair cropped like a convict." Catherine Beecher, defender of domesticity, scolded

Wright as "offensive and disgusting."[34] Rev. John R. McDowall envisioned her "path" as "crimsoned with the blood and rendered doleful by the moans of her captives."[35] It is possible that this notorious orator, who refused to see her "sisters" dwarfed by "mental imbecility," was the antinomian "monster" of the 1820's who agitated young Hawthorne to judge women with a "stricter, instead of more indulgent eye."[36]

"Monstrosity" continued to become a sign of the times. The "monstrous regiment," "fomenting women," and "breeders" of "distempers" of the mid-century were often political women. Matilda Joslyn Gage notes that one women's rights convention in 1853 was disrupted by protestors who accused the delegates of being "unsexed," "a hybrid species . . . belonging to neither sex," and "Amazons."[37] In 1871 Dr. Alfred Stille, president of the American Medical Association, pronounced "strong-minded" women who "seek to rival men in manly sports and occupations" "monstrous productions." As such, as Hawthorne might have agreed, these wild women "may command a sort of admiration . . . especially when they tend toward a higher type than their own."[38]

Beatrice Rappacini deviates from her role and is classified as "monster," not because of what she thinks, but because of her "poison," the desire she sparks, and the way she looks. "Monstrosity" in *The Blithedale Romance*, however, refers to women, like Hutchinson, Wright, and Fuller, who deviate from their sex role because of how they act and what they say. Hollingsworth's salvos are aimed at the defender of women's rights, Zenobia: "Man is a wretch without woman; but woman is a monster—and, thank Heaven, an almost impossible and hitherto imaginary monster—without man, as her acknowledged principle!" The "petticoated monstrosities" who engage in feminist and political activities are "poor miserable, abortive creatures, who only dream of such things because they have missed woman's peculiar happiness, or because Nature made them really neither man nor woman!" If necessary, this former blacksmith turned prison reformer would call on his "own sex to use its physical force, that unmistakable evidence of sovereignty, to scourge them back within their bounds!" (3: 122–23). Here women's political and cultural expression, not just facial expression, constitutes evidence of monstrosity.

"Imaginary monsters," or monsters with imaginations, also wrote literature. We see this classification take hold in a review of E. D. E. N. Southworth's sensational novel *The Curse of Clifton* (1853). Although Southworth "possesses many unquestionable powers," she needs "to tame her disposition to exaggerate monstrously the features which she attempts to delineate." Not only is her expression monstrous, she "is content to do few things naturally" and thus gives birth to the "most un-mitigated social monsters" in her characters. If Southworth aspires "to secure a permanent reputation," she must "subdue her paces," "reform her imagination," "mitigate her rages," and "put passion into straight jackets for a season."[39] Like the menstruous woman or the mother who gives birth to a monster, her too-creative imagination can get out of hand. Southworth's passionate and monstrous literary *excesses* are un-feminine, perforce unnatural. Her "flowers" grow wild and her "bloom" is too much. No doubt the critic would agree with Baglioni that South-worth, like the monstrous Beatrice, must be brought "rigidly and sys-tematically within the limits of ordinary nature."

Edgar Allan Poe shared this cultural concern. His *Autography* (1836) measures the "hands" of prominent poetical ladies in terms of their conformity to or deviation from what he takes to be ordinary feminine handwriting. "Mrs. Hale," he concludes, "writes a larger and bolder hand than her sex generally. . . . The whole MS. is indicative of a mas-culine understanding." Catherine Sedgwick's display of "hand," more recognizably conventional, discloses "perfect freedom of manner" while remaining "sufficiently feminine." When the literary commodity was not "sufficiently feminine," doubts about its origins could be raised.[40] The female author who does not submit (or submit to) what Hawthorne called "girlish feebleness" often had, as Fanny Fern (the pseudonym of Sara Parton) observed, a difficult time negotiating with publishing houses ruled by cigar-smoking male editors. "Why," Fern asks indig-nantly, "on the first appearance of 'Uncle Tom's Cabin' did some of the gallant editors of the American world pronounce it 'too powerful to have been written by a woman' and, when driven from this 'chival-ric' opinion, why did they still sneakingly cling to the belief that her *husband* must have assisted her in writing it?"[41]

Bearing in mind the focus on sexual tension in "The Birth-mark," "Egotism; Or, the Bosom Serpent," and "Rappaccini's Daughter," it is important to note that Hawthorne's own nervousness about the "ink-stained" hands of women seems to have found expression often in distinctly sexual terms. The sentimental author Grace Greenwood (pseudonym of Sara Jane Clarke) was no Zenobia or Margaret Fuller; but she was monster enough to arouse Hawthorne's derision in a letter to Sophia in which he praised God that "with a higher and deeper intellect than other women," Sophia never "prostituted" herself "to the public, as that woman has, and a thousand others do." It deprived "women of all delicacy" and produced "much the same effect on them as it would do to walk abroad the streets, physically stark naked."[42] Like Weld and Johnson, Hawthorne represents female discourse as fundamentally carnal. In 1855 Hawthorne wrote his famous letter to his publisher lambasting an America "now wholly given over to a d____d mob of scribbling women." As in "The Birth-mark," the ideal feminine beauty is an unscribbled page. Yet the following month he wrote again, praising the author of the best-selling *Ruth Hall*, Fanny Fern, in the very words he had used to vilify Grace Greenwood and expressed what he admired most about monsters-with-pens in sexually charged language: "The woman writes as if the Devil was in her; and that is the only condition under which a woman writes anything worth reading. Generally women write like immasculated men, and are only to be distinguished from male authors by greater feebleness and folly; but when they throw off the restraints of decency and come before the public stark naked, as it were—then their books are sure to possess character and value."[43] Women's literary achievement is still imagined in carnal terms ("stark naked") but in this case it is considered a laudable transgression ("as if the Devil was in her").

As we saw in his early piece on Hutchinson, Hawthorne had anxieties about powerful (monstrous) women from the start of his career. The way Georgiana's "Hand" was looked at destabilized the male imagination in "The Birth-mark," while in Hawthorne's novels of the 1850's and 1860's, it is when women such as Hester, Zenobia, and Miriam show their political and artistic hands that they are classified as dangerous. Georgiana and Beatrice can be read as sexual prototypes of the women in Hawthorne's later fiction who are intellectually and artistically as well as sexually powerful. In his later works the colorful woman is active as a political and artistic creator, not just a biological creature whose stains or poisons "naturally" excite male ambivalence. Perhaps Hawthorne was ambivalent about women in general,[44] but one can certainly make a case that his fiction registers an ambivalence about women deviating from prescribed sex roles. When we think about the correspondences between an "ink-stained Amazon" like Zenobia and Hawthorne's early monsters-without-voices, we can suggest that, in Hawthorne's early fiction and his culture, social fears about unfeminine women and their toxic potential to transform the political and literary order were biologized and sexualized. Thus male efforts to encode and control the female body must be reinterpreted as culturally symbolic of a more comprehensive middle-class control of roles, ways of seeing, structures of feeling, and modes of expression.

Keeping this pattern of displacement in mind, I propose that the truly threatening tale hidden beneath the surface of Hawthorne's "The Birth-mark" and "Rappaccini's Daughter" is one not unlike that written by Sarah Hale. Hale's *The Lecturess* (1838) tells the story of Marian Gayland, a women's rights advocate. She is of the type of authors and "fair orators" who Hawthorne had feared in "Mrs. Hutchinson" would overrun the field. Hale's novel exemplifies young Hawthorne's judgment in that essay that "woman, when she feels the impulse of genius like a command of Heaven within her, should be aware that she is relinquishing a part of the loveliness of her sex, and obey the inward voice with sorrowing reluctance." [45] Marian's intelligence and talent for oratory are encoded by Hale not as a charm but a curse. Like Hawthorne's characters, her colorfulness is seen not as positive but as a lamentable feature that tempts her to make a spectacle of herself. What Hawthorne means by feminine "loveliness" is not to show one's power, for showing ("monstrando") is tantamount to showing off. Her colorlessly feminine friend Sophia, by contrast, "shrunk," as a proper woman should, "from the publicity to which her friend was exposing herself." [46] Hale may well have been irked by the exposure of Fanny Wright in 1838 as Hawthorne probably was in 1830. Wright had just completed a much publicized tour which fomented a "state of excitement" in more than one state. Marian's lectures, like Wright's, blast slavery as well as patriarchy.

The lecturess weds William Forrester who, sounding like many of Wright's critics, "cannot bear to see a woman so unsex herself." Also like Wright, Marian wins what William calls a "noisy popularity." [47] Thus it behooves him, as it would Henry James's Basil Ransom years later when cloaking Verena Tarrant, to muffle her noise. Hale is critical of William's handling of Marian, but only because her novel seeks to offer better methods for husbands to manage refractory wives who have become overly excited by agitation for women's rights and abolition. The novel itself exacts capital punishment to underscore its moral judgment, with Sophia taking the dying lecturess's confession that she has failed to be a proper wife.

Hale's silencing of the "noisy" lecturess is unequivocal, while Hawthorne's representations of Georgiana and Beatrice remain ambiguous and problematic to interpret. I suspect that Hawthorne does want to sketch a colorful and perhaps "monstrous" woman. But he seems able to do so only in an underhanded and ambivalent fashion.

To see this let us imagine "Rappacini's Daughter" as Hawthorne's monologue with himself about the process of his aesthetic and his relationship to his less conventional "vegetable progeny" (10: 14). Let us suppose that Hawthorne views himself, like Dr. Rappacini, as a "distrustful gardener" (10: 96), and that his ambivalence about his own colorful women is registered in the scientist's attitude toward his untouchable shrubs. That Hawthorne did in fact envision himself as a literary gardener is evident from his two other horticultural ideas for the title of *Mosses*: "Wall Flowers from an Old Abbey" and "Moss and Lichens from an Old Parsonage."[48] Rappacini regards his creations with "a perception of harm in what his own hands caused to grow." Thus he takes measures to protect himself with mask and gloves, and avoids any real "intimacy between himself and these vegetable existences." Yet there is a "deep intelligence on his part" (10: 96) that guides his cultivation. His ego is gratified by making his daughter and her vegetable "sisters" powerful.

We know why Hale's lecturess is powerful: she possesses obvious intelligence, talent, and charm. But Hawthorne's Beatrice, unlike Marian, does not even wish to be powerful. Who can blame her? Hawthorne poisons the way the reader might imagine the possibilities of the powerful woman. Considering that Beatrice's poison prohibits her from circulating in the world outside her garden, who would gainsay her disappointment over being empowered in this manner? "Poison" enforces her privatization. Rappacini's Queen of the Garden is, like Prospero's Miranda, a domestic prisoner on his island. Hale's lecturess threatens the ideology of "true" womanhood and the social order that upholds it, whereas Beatrice is dangerous only as a biological freak. There is no social power in her "poison."

Beatrice's poison however seems vital to Hawthorne not only as her "distrustful gardener" but as her even more distrustful suitor—Giovanni. Aubepine, Hawthorne's pseudonymous author, tells us that Beatrice "had . . . instilled a fierce and subtle poison into [Giovanni's] system." This "subtle poison," once "instilled," gives life to "wild offspring" in his imagination. Giovanni is himself startled by "the wild vagaries which his

imagination ran riot continually producing" (10: 105). Hawthorne's language seems to insinuate that Beatrice *impregnated* Giovanni. Her poison
breathes life into his powers as an allegorist ("continually producing").
Hawthorne, through Giovanni, appears to be designating his poisonous offspring, Beatrice, not only a product but a *source* of his narrative
power, his Muse. Georgiana also functions not just as the object but as
the source of Aylmer's allegorical power. The not too creative alchemist must *persuade* her to enter his allegorical text. He needs a colorful
woman who is willing to *give him a hand*. Roderick Elliston acquires his
creative sting by internalizing the stereotype of woman as serpent with
a bosom. Once Rosina is allegorized as "the hidden monster," she seems
to impregnate him.[49] In "The Birth-mark" and "Rappaccini's Daughter"
the colorful woman whose electricity recharges the male imagination
represents a "creative force" that is courted, allegorized as monstrous,
and detoxified (written off) with ambivalence.

Hawthorne allows Georgiana and Beatrice to exhibit signs of "creative force" but not to exercise it. Although they possess "flaws" that
associate them with authorship, they are neither artistic nor unfeminine. They seem to be colorful in spite of themselves. The monomaniacal males in these tales are the real creators who exercise too much force.
Through his male characters Hawthorne courts a creativity gendered as
female which he deems necessary to the "continually producing" male
imagination but which he curbs as a "force" in its own right. In this
sense Hawthorne's plotting of womanhood is just as conservative and
far more devious than Hale's.

On the other hand, Hawthorne is more progressive than Hale. What
he observes about Rappaccini is true of himself: there is a "deep intelligence on his part." When female creativity is allegorized as a "flaw,"
the interpretive source is a deeply disturbed and ambivalent male consciousness. Hawthorne not only unveils this stereotyping as a patriarchal
invention at times reinforced by "fastidious" women, but self-critically
points to fictions circulated by men as discursive culprits complicit in the
dirty work. On one level Hawthorne seems to recognize that the woman
allegorized by her culture as "unnatural" or "monstrous" is not only "the
poor victim of man's ingenuity" but, in his fiction, the rigged construction of his own "wonder-working fancy" (10: 98): courted, allegorized,
written off with regrets. Hawthorne shows us that male author figures
who trap women within flower metaphors are getting away with murder.
Ruskin's pronouncement about the middle-class Queen of the Garden,

"She grows as a flower does,"[50] takes on insidious connotations in the lurid light of Hawthorne's tale. Let us conclude then that in "Rappacini's Daughter" Hawthorne both represents monstrosity as a nervous patriarchal invention and adopts the very assumptions of the cultural convention (female power equals poison) that he seems to criticize male author figures for acting on so obsessively.

A seventeenth-century puritan couple, whose marriage was based on the discourse of "rational" love and whose home ("the little commonwealth") was not conceptually detachable from the community, would probably marvel at the psychological "hothouses" allegorized in Hawthorne's *Old Manse*.[51] From the vantage point of the history of mid-nineteenth-century gender relations, "The Birth-mark," "Egotism," and "Rappacini's Daughter" exhibit women who suffered from the extraordinary psychological *expectations* thrust upon them within a context in which, as Stephanie Coontz has put it, the middle class "sought a predictability in gender roles that could be set against the changes in their social and work relations."[52] As John D'Emilio and Estelle B. Freedman have observed, the middle-class demand for domestic intimacy became emotionally intense just as men and women were being socialized to occupy increasingly separate gender roles. Privatized middle-class women were forced to be more economically dependent on men, and this too was a social cause of psychological stress.[53] Hawthorne's distinctive contribution to our understanding of the stress produced by these expectations is his own understanding that what Mary Ryan has termed the "psychological services" women were socialized to perform were in fact allegorical or symbolic services.[54] These allegorical or symbolic services required that middle-class women remain identifiably "feminine" in body and mind, a monstrous expectation that, Hawthorne suggests, could prove to be the death of them.

3 Plotting Womanhood

*Feminine Evolution and
Narrative Feminization in 'Blithedale'*

During the past two decades literary critics, historians, and sociologists have begun to theorize gender as a social, historical, and ideological construction. Thus, in her study of the signification of the "feminine" in the works of Henry James, Elizabeth Allen defines the "feminine" as "the whole range of potential meanings for woman which are seen as natural but are in fact socially constructed."[1] The social category of the "feminine," notes historian Mary Ryan, "conspires to dichotomize the human personality according to sex."[2] In the first section of this chapter I will establish that Hawthorne was thinking along these lines and developed a mid-nineteenth-century understanding of the social construction of gender in his works, most elaborately in *The Blithedale Romance* (1852). The second section of this chapter proposes that Hawthorne in *Blithedale* had Zenobia resist her narrator's effort to feminize the way in which we read her death. Zenobia's resistance to Miles Coverdale's narration of her as an Ophelia clarifies the role that Hawthorne saw literature and his own writing playing in the ideological process of feminization.

Hawthorne on the Social Construction of Femininity

Hawthorne's thematic interest in the cultural "making" of women took some seemingly oddball twists and turns, especially in his concept of their evolution. Hence the "not unsubstantial persons" of the women who throng around the scaffold in the opening scene of *The Scarlet Letter* display, in the narrator's mind, specific seventeenth-century characteristics. These substantial women have no compunction about indecorously flaunting their unrefined "persons" in public. "Morally, as well as materially," we are told, "there was a coarser fiber in those wives and maidens of old English birth and breeding, than in their fair descendants, separated from them by a series of six or seven generations; for, throughout that chain of ancestry, every successive mother has transmitted to her child a fainter bloom, a more delicate and briefer beauty, and a slighter physical frame, if not a character of less force and solidity, than her own." These women, still showing evidence of the "beef and ale of their native land," congregated "within less than half a century of the period when the man-like Elizabeth had been the not altogether unsuitable representative of her sex" (1: 50).

Hawthorne then hints at a transformation of puritan women well underway in his own times. These puritan matrons, with "broad shoulders," "well-developed busts," and "round and ruddy cheeks" had "hardly yet grown pale or thinner in the atmosphere of New England" (1: 50–51). This paleness betokens not just a physical alteration, but a different discourse and behavior. The "boldness and rotundity of speech among these matrons" would "startle" the nineteenth-century observer "whether in respect to its purport or its volume of tone" (1: 51). Such public activity is both aesthetically and socially taboo by the nineteenth century. By contemporary standards this "man-like" look and behavior are unfeminine. Hawthorne does believe that femininity existed in the seventeenth century but that it was different from what he knows in the nineteenth. On the scaffold Hester "was lady-like, too, after the manner of the feminine gentility of those days; characterized by a certain state and dignity, rather than by the delicate, evanescent, and indescribable grace, which is now recognized as its indication" (1: 53).

The distinction that Hawthorne makes between rotund English-women and their nineteenth-century New England counterparts is one that he also thinks valid in his own era. This is evident in the passage from Hawthorne's *English Notebooks* in which he eviscerates the "red-faced monsters" who, "unconscious of the wrong they are doing to one's idea of womanhood," accompany their husbands to a meeting of a British scientific association. "American women, of all ranks, when past their prime, generally look thin, worn, care-begone, as if they may have led a life of much trouble and few enjoyments; but English women look as if they had fed upon the fat of meat, and made themselves earthy in all sorts of ways." Hawthorne laments that men are constrained to "choose between a greasy animal and an anxious skeleton"; but, as "a point of taste," he prefers his "own countrywomen."[3] The "delicate, evanescent, and indescribable grace" ascribed to his "countrywomen" in *The Scarlet Letter* is viewed here in a less sanguine light: the American female is "thin, worn, care-begone."

The notion that the American woman has become a cold, passionless skeleton is present even in Hawthorne's final works.[4] In *The Marble Faun* (1860) Hawthorne describes Kenyon's statue of Cleopatra as "the fossil woman of an age that produced statelier, stronger, and more passionate creatures, than our own" (4: 377). Even *Septimius Felton*, the rough fragments of Hawthorne's last effort to write a novel, depicts a Revolutionary War character, Rose Garfield, who tells us that her grandfather has observed the women of present times to have grown "slighter still; so that we are dwindling away" (8: 6).

These representations mystify historically specific shifts in the category of femininity. Comparing gender roles in colonial times and the nineteenth century, Stephanie Coontz notes that seventeenth-century "femininity was often seen as weaker or more prone to evil than masculinity but it was not yet equated with a qualitatively different set of capacities." It was only after the American Revolution that special characteristics were assigned to female nature.[5] Since republican ideology removed many of the limits imposed on character and behavior by the colonial hierarchy, republican wives and mothers were viewed as *naturally* qualified—in the setting of the home—to place moral constraints on males who competed in the marketplace. Rather than rooting changes in the definitions of femininity in the specific contexts of colonial hierarchical relations, republican ideology, and nascent industrial capitalism, the evolutionary description outlined in some of Hawthorne's fictions *biologizes* the historical process.

Hawthorne's idea of feminine evolution (more like a progressive atrophy of women's bodies) is developed most fully in *The Blithedale Romance.* Zenobia's active intelligence, robust sexuality, full body, and "noble earthliness" (3: 101) make her stand out. The "peculiarity" Coverdale refers to in his profile appears to be nothing other than her unemaciated womanhood:

There was another peculiarity about her. We seldom meet with women now-a-days, and in this country, who impress us as being women at all,—their sex fades away and goes for nothing, in ordinary intercourse. Not so with Zenobia. One felt an influence breathing out of her, such as we might suppose to come from Eve, when she was just made, and her Creator brought her to Adam, saying

'Behold! here is a woman!' Not that I would convey the idea of especial gentleness, grace, modesty, and shyness, but of a certain warm and rich characteristic, which seems, for the most part, to have been refined away out of the feminine system. (3: 17)

Coverdale imagines the sexy Zenobia as a female original unmutated by the cultural alchemy of successive "feminine systems."

Zenobia is contrasted to Priscilla, who seems to be the ideal of the nineteenth-century feminine woman. Westervelt, however, views this spurious ideal as a cultural aberration and echoes the sentiments of some mid-century health reformers:

She is one of those delicate, nervous young creatures, not uncommon in New England, and whom I suppose to have become what we find them by the gradual refining away of the physical system, among your women. Some philosophers choose to glorify this habit of body by terming it spiritual; but, in my opinion, it is rather the effect of unwholesome food, bad air, lack of out-door exercise, and neglect of bathing, on the part of these damsels and their female progenitors, all resulting in a kind of hereditary dyspepsia. (3: 95)

Thus he praises Zenobia, in spite of "her uncomfortable surplus of vitality," as "far the better model of womanhood" (3: 95–96). Priscilla's half-starved grace "lay so singularly between disease and beauty" (3: 101).[6]

Hawthorne was not alone in his perception of "anxious skeletons." Sections of mid-nineteenth-century medical texts, even those that stereotype women, criticize the narrowing of woman's sphere and comment upon the appearance of feminine palefaces.[7] Some physicians suggested that women were undergoing a radical transmutation at the hands of the culture: the Georgianas of America were being confined and whitewashed. By 1875 Dr. Edward H. Clarke, who disparaged the idea that women were physiologically capable of pursuing higher education, also despaired that "pale, bloodless female faces" prevailed in American "factories, workshops, and homes." Thus he quipped inanely that men who desired women who had not lost their bloom would soon have to consider importing mothers of the republic from Europe.[8] "Travellers to America during the first half of the nineteenth century usually praised the delicate beauty and high-spirits of the American girl," observes historian Barbara Welter, "but they regretted that she was abnormally pale, collapsed under maternal responsibilities, and was likely to be a faded invalid by thirty."[9]

Zenobia, in what is surely the most provocative statement in Hawthorne's novel, recognizes Priscilla and her kind as cultural *inventions*: "She is the type of womanhood such as man has spent centuries in making it" (3: 122). This awareness appears to have been rare in the mid-nineteenth century, although it can be found in the writings of Sarah Grimké and Margaret Fuller and in the works of female authors who wrote later in the century. In 1838 Grimké held that "intellect is not sexed" and discarded the notion of sexual difference as a pernicious cultural mystification. "We approach each other, and mingle with each other, under the constant pressure of a feeling that we are of different sexes; and, instead of regarding each other only in the light of immortal creatures, the mind is fettered by the idea which is early and industriously infused into it, that we must never forget the distinction between male and female." The "true dignity of woman" is damaged because "she is approached by man in the character of a female" rather than as a social and intellectual equal.[10] Two anonymous contributors to *The Lily* in 1851, who were writing in the tradition of Grimké, published their view of the debate between Sydney Smith, the outspoken English theologian, and T. S. Arthur, a sentimental writer and upholder of "true" womanhood. They quote Smith approvingly: "As long as boys and girls run about in the dirt, and trundle hoops together, they are both precisely alike. If you catch up one-half of these creatures, and train them to a particular set of actions and opinions, and the other half to a perfectly opposite set, of course their understanding will differ."[11]

Like Hawthorne and contemporary physicians, Margaret Fuller worried about whether America's "bodiless ideas," the "ladies," were fit to be "mothers of a mighty race." Unlike Hawthorne and the physicians, the shocking implications she drew were feminist: "There are no American women, only overgrown children." For that reason perhaps Fuller refused to write for *Godey's*, which she dismissed as an "opiate."[12] Elizabeth Stuart Phelps [Ward], in her essay on "The True Woman" (1871), demystifies the "true" woman as patently false, an ideological fiction. Phelps's profile of the "true" woman evokes the image of Pygmalion's silent partner: she is an "empty and powerful figure" who "is patched up by men, and by those women who have no sense of character but such as they reflect from men." In remarks that bring to mind "The Birthmark," she argues that this "sad Sphinx" "has been always experimented upon" and "manufactured . . . to man's convenience."[13]

Hawthorne's occasional mystification of this socializing process as female evolution is intertwined with his understanding of nineteenth-century femininity as a construction. We can describe this evolution, culminating in the wax angels and bloodless "skeletons" of the mid-century, as a process of feminization. Judith Fetterley, in a clever reading of "The Birth-mark," has argued that the story is about "how to murder your wife." I would argue that the tale is about a cultural and discursive process that is more subtle and insidious: the feminization of a colorful and perhaps creative wife. Feminization is the cultural process that contextualizes the psychological disturbance in Aylmer. The story emerges from a culture in which middle-class sex roles, in their stereotyped forms, must remain distinct.[14] Its conflict centers on the removal of a woman's distinguishing mark, a sign of life that might blur that distinction. If the "bloody hand" can be associated with a physiological process that signifies a female's biological maturation from girlhood to womanhood, then its papering over is an infantalization, a feminization that bears out Fuller's remark about American women as "overgrown children."

It is Zenobia who persistently stresses that literature plays a key role in this feminizing "alchemy." She jests that since Priscilla has "hardly any physique," "a poet, like Mr. Miles Coverdale, may be allowed to think her spiritual!" (3: 34). To Coverdale's (mis)representation of Priscilla, "She is as lovely as a flower!" (3: 169), Zenobia retorts: "Well; say so, if you like. . . . You are a poet—at least as poets go now-a-days—and must be allowed to make an opera-glass of your imagination, when you look at women" (3: 170).

Priscilla herself, albeit far less critically aware than Zenobia, calls into question the optic distortions of Coverdale's "opera glass." "You, especially, have always seemed like a figure in a dream—and now more than ever" (3: 168), he confesses. In a rejoinder that would no doubt please the anonymous *Godey's* critic of shrinking hands, Priscilla reminds him that "there is substance in these fingers of mine! . . . Why do you call me a dream?" (3: 169). Priscilla is in truth not quite so "impressible as wax" as "she seemed" (3: 78) to Coverdale and Westervelt. Coverdale, however, sounding like Pygmalion, himself acknowledges that Priscilla excites him not "for her realities—poor little seamstress, as Zenobia rightly called her!—but for the fancywork with which I have idly decked her out!" (3: 100).

Not long after Priscilla's dramatic entrance at Blithedale, Zenobia recognizes that both she and Priscilla are being transformed by Coverdale's "poetical" "light" (3: 33). This "poetical" "light" colors what *we* read. Coverdale, for example, supposes that Priscilla "had read some of Zenobia's stories, (as such literature goes everywhere,) or her tracts in defence of the sex, and had come hither with the one purpose of being her slave" (3: 33). He elects to depict her as a literary "slave" rather than as disciple or student or friend. There is also the fear, as we saw in Chapter 2—stated overtly in Theodore Weld's and Edward Johnson's accounts of Anne Hutchinson's influence and symbolically in the representation of Beatrice's "sisters"—that powerful women infect or even impregnate other women with their heresies (thus making them "slaves"). In response to these speculations Zenobia satirically invites Coverdale to do what she knows he is already in the process of doing: "you had better turn the affair into a ballad. It is a grand subject, and worthy of supernatural machinery" (3: 33). This "supernatural machinery" is a male narrative experiment that reconstructs women.

Feminization is a social process that too easily appears to be invisible; thus, nineteenth-century "female complaints" seem to be the consequence of female "nature" rather than feminine roles. Psychoanalysis often tends to foreclose our consideration of social and historical processes, such as feminization, of which its own mode of thinking is an outgrowth. The use of psychoanalytic labels for psychological processes can provide insight into feminization while simultaneously contributing to its invisibility as a social and historical development. Anna Freud, as I have already noted, helps us see that Georgiana's response to Aylmer's succession of experiments is "altruistic projection," and so it is. Yet there is another way of reading Georgiana's positioning that accounts for this tendency to be obsessively altruistic. The feminizing ideology that Georgiana has internalized is obsession with beauty. John Berger describes this *social* process:

Men survey women before treating them. . . . How a woman appears to a man can determine how she will be treated. To acquire some control over this process, women must contain it and interiorize it. . . . The surveyor of woman in herself is male: the surveyed female. Thus she turns herself into an object—and most particularly an object of vision: a sight.[15]

It is feminization that allegorizes a woman's apparent physical defect as a moral and spiritual blemish and transforms women into allegorical problems for men and for one another.

Conventions of beauty constitute one mode of this historical process of feminization. Feminine beauty acquired obsessive significance for
middle-class women as a substitute for social power and public participation. The *Godey's Lady's Book* line was that beauty should be regarded
as more than ornament: it was "woman's *business.*" Yet no one could
really succeed in this "business." In 1868 Harriet Beecher Stowe complained that the American ideal of beauty had narrowed the concept of
"womanhood" quite literally, disqualifying women with "vigor of outline": "When we see a woman made as a woman ought to be, she strikes
us as a monster." Women consumed arsenic (perhaps Aylmer's "solution," Giovanni's "antidote") to achieve delicate, translucent complex-
ions. By the 1850's women even painted their faces white to look like
the American "angels" that Hawthorne in the 1860's would contrast to
the "beefy" Englishwoman.[16] Aylmer's refusal to accept what he allegorizes as Georgiana's mortality is one important index of how unreal the
"true" woman had become.

Alice James once described herself as "absorbing into the bone that
the better part is to clothe oneself in neutral tints."[17] Wearing no such
"neutral tints," Zenobia had instead "a rich, though varying color" and
"was alive with a passionate intensity" (3: 102). By contrast, Coverdale describes himself as a parasite "suffering my colorless life to take its
hue from other lives" (3: 245). Zenobia can resist his "eye-shot" with
her own powerful vision: her "eyes glowed" (3: 102) on one occasion,
and on another they "were shooting bright arrows, barbed with scorn,
across the intervening space" (3: 158). She is a woman who sees and sees
through others and who refuses, in Berger's words, to be a mere "object
of sight" or a mere face. Georgiana is killed because of the way she is
looked at, whereas Zenobia is done in because of the way she sees. Thus
it is worth challenging how Coverdale represents Zenobia's response to
the fond looks Hollingsworth gives to Priscilla: Zenobia "would have
given her eyes, bright as they were, for such a look" (3: 72). As I shall
make evident below, I harbor doubts that she would have engaged in
this feminine romance of dismemberment.

The Death of Ophelia as the Birth of Medusa

Throughout Coverdale's narrative Hawthorne uses Zenobia to
underscore how she and others are (mis)represented by the "minor"
(3: 246) poet. Near the end of the novel she has *ostensibly* outlived her

narrative usefulness. Zenobia is written off all too blithely by Coverdale, who entombs her in the literary grave of Ophelia, Shakespeare's lovesick maiden who drowns herself when rejected by her Hamlet:

She had seen pictures, I suppose, of drowned persons in lithe and graceful attitudes. And she deemed it well and decorous to die as so many village maidens have, wronged in their first-love, and seeking peace in the bosom of the old familiar stream—so familiar that they could not dread it. . . . But, in Zenobia's case, there was some tint of the Arcadian affectation that had been visible enough in all our lives, for a few months past. (3: 236–37)

Coverdale would have us believe that Zenobia's death represents nothing other than a girlish imitation of Ophelia. But for Coverdale this effort to imitate a "decorous," poetic death has miscarried: "Being the woman that she was, could Zenobia have foreseen all the ugly circumstances of her death, how ill it would become her, the altogether unseemly aspect which she must put on . . . she would no more have committed the dreadful act, than have exhibited herself to a public assembly in a badly-fitting garment!" The brilliant Zenobia, now ugly, has blundered: "Six hours before, how beautiful! At midnight, what a horror!" (3: 236).

Zenobia is, nevertheless, a rather rebellious "horror." The description we get is the opposite of the "quiet, gradual, graceful" and "decorative" death that Ann Douglas identifies as an established convention of women's sentimental fiction.[18] Georgiana's genteel death, which followed the erasure of her "hand," was within the confines of this convention. The most noticeable feature of Zenobia's dead body, by contrast, is her hands. Coverdale is unsure whether her unfeminine hands are "clenched" in "the attitude of prayer," or "in immitigable defiance." Her posture might be termed an anti-pose, a position which offers nothing for the voyeur.[19] It is quite the contrary of what Coverdale, earlier on, would like to see her do: "sit endlessly to painters and sculptors, and preferably the latter; because the cold decorum of the marble would consist with the utmost scantiness of drapery, so that the eye might chastely be gladdened with her material perfection" (3: 44). Positioned thus, Zenobia's role in life would be to serve as raw material for male images of her.

Silas Foster, struck by the rigidity of her arms which "bade him defiance" (3: 236), struggles to straighten her out, but she is eternally bent. During their debate over women's rights at Eliot's pulpit, Hollingsworth invoked man's "physical force" as that "unmistakable evidence of sovereignty" (3: 123) over women. But here Hawthorne makes Zenobia, though dead, refuse to bend to male "force." Zenobia cannot, like the monstrous E. D. E. N. Southworth, be put into "straight jackets for a season." The description of her arms resembles the "crooked and unmanageable boughs" found at Blithedale, which "could never be measured into merchantable cords for the market" (3: 13). And these "cords" resemble the "variety of grotesque shapes" of the trees in Hawthorne's "orchard" at the "Old Manse." By "Why, man, it's not decent!" (3: 236), Foster really means that her posture, rigidly phallic, is unfeminine. Coverdale applies literary mythology, a cultural force, to do what Foster cannot do: straighten out Zenobia. He rechristens her Ophelia.

Coverdale, himself besotted with Hollingsworth, has little problem imagining that Zenobia would kill herself once rejected by the "iron"-willed reformer. But some mid-nineteenth-century critics had difficulty swallowing this ending (this "antidote" or "solution"). "We do not believe in Zenobia drowning herself," Mrs. Oliphant protested in 1855. "It is a piece of sham entirely, and never impresses us with the slightest idea of reality." [20] Of course, *Blithedale* is not "reality"; it is a "romance," a narrative experiment in "cloud-land." Another critic in 1853 charged that Zenobia's suicide was gratuitous, "and positively conflicts with the moral of her portrait as well as of the story." An appropriately conventional ending would have straightened her out in a more didactic manner: "marry her off"—make her a merchantable cord for market. [21]

Perhaps Hawthorne would not have been entirely comfortable emplotting his feminist in this conventional way. He prefers instead to draw our attention to the way, the literary way, that Coverdale tries to stereotype her. In several instances Hawthorne encourages his reader to develop a critical distance from Coverdale in order to problematize the politics and strategies of his narrative prestidigitations.

I shall argue that Hawthorne's Zenobia, as opposed to Coverdale's Zenobia, sends signals that her drowning *should* be read as "a piece of sham entirely." Her botched Ophelia-death is not simply a lovesick suicide but a parody of the way her culture stereotyped women. Some mid-century critics, for example, regarded her narrative submersion as poetic justice: such "unwomanly" women, wrote one, "blaspheme God by stepping beyond the limits he assigned to them through all the ages." Her monstrosity makes this critic "shrink closer every moment from the contact." [22] Zenobia's gestures suggest that her culture, which speaks through Hollingsworth and some of the reviewers of Blithedale, had already tried to drown her out and shut her up when she was alive. "With the last, choking consciousness, her soul, bubbling out through her lips, it may be had given itself up to the Father, reconciled and penitent" (3: 235). Judging from the iconography of her body, Zenobia's "choking consciousness" or consciousness of having *been choked* may well have been her motive for refusing in the end to bend to "the Father."

The message her form of death sends is a distinctively literary one, which should be read in the context of her objections to Coverdale's literary alchemy. When bidding farewell to Coverdale, she alludes indirectly to the image that her narrator will later deploy: "I intend to become a Catholic, for the sake of going to a nunnery" (3: 227). Hamlet taunts Ophelia, "Get thee to a nunnery." [23] Plotting her through the grid of the Ophelia narrative, Coverdale reads Zenobia as a failed copyist; but her message, on the contrary, is original.

Zenobia's commentary on Ophelia is clarified when put in the context of remarks by another female critic of Shakespeare. Mrs. Jameson's *Characteristics of Women* (1833), which Hawthorne had borrowed from the Salem Atheneum on two occasions in 1835,[24] offers profiles of Shakespeare's heroines as plotted on a properly domestic grid. She sketches a sentimental portrait of Ophelia that is antithetical to the proud Zenobia—charmingly helpless and unearthly, "far too soft, too good, too fair, to be cast among the working-day world, and fall and bleed upon the thorns of life!" She is capable of evaporating on contact, "like the snowflake dissolved in air before it has caught the stain of earth." Ophelia's incapacity to resist is the essence of her charm. Her demise is likened to that of a dove who "flitted . . . hither and thither, with its silver pinions shining against the black thundercloud, till, after a few giddy whirls, it fell blinded, affrighted, and bewildered, into the turbid wave beneath, and was swallowed up forever." [25] Mrs. Jameson sentimentalizes Ophelia's death as an aesthetically pleasing event.

From reading Mrs. Jameson it becomes apparent that Coverdale has impressed qualities on Zenobia that he either found in or projected on Priscilla. Mrs. Jameson's Ophelia is closer to a profile of Priscilla than Zenobia: she is "a young girl who, at an early age, is brought from a life of privacy into the circle of a court. . . . She is placed immediately about the person of the queen, and is apparently her favorite attendant." Coverdale, of course, earlier sees Zenobia as the "Queen." Zenobia is far more akin to Mrs. Jameson's portrait of Shakespeare's Beatrice, who displays "high intellectual and animal spirits," "a touch of insolence," and a "satirical humour." [26] Coverdale miscasts Zenobia as Ophelia rather than a Beatrice who fights back. In doing so, Coverdale, like Aylmer, attempts to reconstruct the properly feminine body. But Hawthorne has Zenobia refuse to cooperate.

Thus the intractable Zenobia was not only "fond of giving us readings from Shakespeare" (3: 106) but also of giving us readings *of* Shakespeare. Elaine Showalter, in her provocative historical study of women and madness, has noted the appearance of an Ophelia complex in mid- and late-nineteenth-century English asylums for women. Medical books routinely printed photographs of women decked out as Ophelia. Showalter analyzes the phenomenon as one that can be explained by understanding how "madness expressed conflicts in the feminine role itself." The lovesick Ophelia became a logical stereotype for women who experienced such conflicts to adopt. But the Ophelia photographs also suggest how Victorian physicians, not unlike Coverdale, actively "imposed cultural stereotypes of femininity and female insanity on women who defied their gender roles." Showalter examines the "moral management" of these domesticated asylums as one that institutionalized "the discipline of femininity" ("ladylike values of silence, decorum, taste, service, piety, and gratitude"). Ophelia surfaced as more than a mid-nineteenth-century literary convention; she was a stereotype for how the culture was fashioning femininity and representing women and their "problems" to women. [27]

Zenobia's own narrative of Theodore and the Veiled Lady opens up another reading of her death that conflicts with Coverdale's rendition. The Veiled Lady, a mute theatrical spectacle, pledges herself to young Theodore if he agrees to kiss her no matter what face he discovers beneath her veil. It is her utmost wish to be unveiled and accepted for who she is. Although she most resembles Priscilla, one cannot help but hear the voice of Zenobia in her plea to Theodore: "thou canst lift this mysterious veil, beneath which I am a sad and lonely prisoner, in a bondage which is worse to me than death" (3: 112). She invites both trust and reciprocity, "thou shalt be mine, and I thine, with never more a veil between us" (3: 113). The veil invites multiple readings; but it had specific cultural significance for Elizabeth Stuart Phelps [Ward], who read the nineteenth-century "veil" as the sign of the so-called "true" woman who has been falsified by her culture. When sexual difference is acknowledged as a mystification, she wrote, "only then can we draw the veil from the brows of the true woman." [28]

Priscilla's paper-like veil, Westervelt's "enchantment," seems to have been conjured in the literary laboratory of cloud-land. "It was white . . . like the sunny side of a cloud; and falling over the wearer, from head to foot, was supposed to insulate her from the material world, from time and space, and to endow her with many of the privileges of a disembodied spirit" (3: 6). Her veil bears striking similarities to a domestic ideology that promises to "insulate" woman "from the natural world" and to elevate her as a "disembodied spirit." This paper lady seems very like the feminized woman fetishized by Hollingsworth: she serves as a blank envelope for male messages. The paper veil also may be a symbol for a feminine narrative, a veiled discourse that screens what a woman can explain to a man: "So much may a maiden say behind the veil!" (3: 113) she tells Theodore.

If the veil is a sign of a culturally draped femininity, a paper *shroud*, this discursive femininity also goes hand in hand with myths that figure the female body as dangerous and decayed (as in "The Birth-mark," the body that wrote "mortality"). Thus young Theodore balks at the unveiling: suppose "he should salute the lips of a dead girl, or the jaws of a skeleton, or the grinning cavity of a monster's mouth!" (3: 113). Zenobia herself becomes a "dead girl" who, by Hollingsworth's definition of a feminist, has a "monster's mouth." Earlier in her narrative Theodore and his friends speculate that behind the veil one would find "the face of a corpse . . . the head of a skeleton . . . a monstrous visage, with snaky locks, like Medusa's, and one great red eye in the centre of the forehead" (3: 110).

This Medusa image is crucial. Medusa is the quintessential image of the powerful female stereotyped as horribly corporeal and grotesque. Hawthorne wants us to see that Coverdale misses this connection in his final gaze at Zenobia. Zenobia has made a grievous blunder, he thinks, because she does not resemble poetic images of Ophelia. But the dead Zenobia, when ugly, looks more like Medusa. From another perspective she appears like a petrified victim of some Medusa: "Ah, that rigidity! It is impossible to bear the terror of it" (3: 235). Ophelia is Coverdale's "antidote" for the "terror." Hawthorne wants the rigidified Zenobia to tell us not that she is a lovesick Ophelia but that she has been turned to stone ("cold as moonshine") by an inflexible society and the sentimental literary discourse that ideologically upholds it.

Hawthorne, in fact, retold the Medusa myth in his chapter on "The Gorgon's Head" in *A Wonder-Book for Girls and Boys*, published in 1851, just one year before *Blithedale*. Not unlike the feminists decried by Hollingsworth ("petticoated monstrosities," "neither man nor woman"), the three gorgons "seem to have borne some distant resemblance to women, but were really a very frightful and mischievous species of dragon" (7: 12). These "terrible monsters" (7: 12) have the power, as does Aubepine's allegory ("to steal the warmth out of his conceptions"), to transform those who catch their eye "from warm flesh and blood into cold and lifeless stone!" (7: 13).

Young Perseus is sent on an expedition to behead Medusa by a king who hopes that he will be petrified and fail. His weapons, reminiscent of Rappacini's mask and gloves, have literary associations. The gods give him winged slippers that transport him to the safety of cloud-land: "had he but looked one instant at them [the gorgons], he would have fallen heavily out of the air, an image of senseless stone" (7: 29). His helmet of invisibility enables him to remain unseen as he plots against Medusa. The "bright mirror" of his "shield" (7: 29), most potent of all, allows Perseus to reflect her image without actually looking at her. Her reflection, reminiscent of Rappacini's plants, shows a face "with a strange, fearful, and savage kind of beauty in it" (7: 29). The monsters were "at once ugly and beautiful. . . . there was something partly human about them, too" (7: 28). Once Medusa's image is framed by his shield, the invisible conqueror beheads her. Perseus retreats to cloud-land "soaring up a perpendicular mile or so" (7: 31).

One commentator on the Medusa myth makes explicit what is implicit in Hawthorne's version: Medusa is "transformed into an image"; she is inserted "into a closed system, a relation of identity between seer and seen." After this act of signification is accomplished "she will serve primarily as the support for a long chain of discursive and figurative events, beginning with Perseus's own account of his triumph over Medusa (recounted by Ovid)" and later revised by Hawthorne. Medusa's decapitation is reenacted throughout the ages by male authors. Perseus might be read as a figure for Medusa's original male author. Narrative becomes the cultural shield that enables these conquerors to avoid really looking at their Medusa for the fear, part of the myth, that she will petrify them. The shield, in other words, is what frames Medusa as a stereotype.[29] Ovid's Medusa myth, like Giovanni's fable of Alexander the Great and his poisonous lady, functions as a permission for men to figuratively and culturally decapitate women they deem dangerous, unclassifiable, and impossible to look at.

If Zenobia winds up looking like Medusa rather than the genteel Ophelia, perhaps it is because she herself intends this self-consciously literary suicide to signal her awareness that she has been beheaded by— that is, treated as a gorgon by—her culture and the reifying narratives it deploys. Being subjected to stereotyping is of course a kind of petrifaction, a turning to stone. At the same time this Ophelia-izing can be seen as an ideological veiling. Ophelia is not just a stereotype but a mystifying ideological explanation of Zenobia's actions. Her advocacy of women's rights is shrouded by rewriting her death as "Love has gone against her" (3: 241). Coverdale's designation of love as her sole motive imposes a narrative cover that obscures a frustrated Zenobia who argues that "women possess no rights" (3: 141) and "the whole universe, her own sex and yours, and Providence, or Destiny, to boot, make common cause against the woman who swerves one hair's breadth out of the beaten track" (3: 224). Her death may be an acknowledgment of having been overwhelmed not only by the culture that speaks through Hollingsworth but by the conventional "type of womanhood such as man has spent centuries in making it," as represented by Priscilla.[30]

Coverdale's narrative strategies are downright aggressive. After Zenobia is rejected by Hollingsworth and she leans dejected against a rock, Coverdale muses: "But Destiny itself, methought, in its kindliest mood, could do no better for Zenobia, in the way of quick relief, than to cause the impending rock to impend a little further, and fall upon her head" (3: 223).[31] By replacing an embittered Zenobia with a botched Ophelia, Coverdale can represent her demise as a romantic "tragedy." Hawthorne's Zenobia presents her death not as a tragedy but as a contradiction: rigidity in defiance of rigidity.

Beauty is a cultural construct that Hawthorne has Zenobia break free of through her death. A death that makes Zenobia "ugly" symbolically releases her from myths of beauty that are part of her cultural embodiment. Zenobia's retreat to a river brings Ophelia to mind—but one other literary character as well. Again we turn to Ovid. When Daphne is chased by Apollo, who would rape her, she entreats her father, the river god Peneus, to transform her. Her desperation corresponds to that of Zenobia's, worn out by her culture: " 'Oh father,' she cried, 'help me! If you rivers really have divine powers, work some transformation, and destroy this beauty which makes me please all too well.' "[32] Zenobia may have intended to use the river to destroy a beauty that makes her "please all too well."

Margaret Fuller once teased a young friend who had blossomed into beauty, "Heaven help you."[33] Zenobia understood this. When Coverdale, with syrupy disingenuousness, pleads that he "should love dearly— for the next thousand years, at least—to have all government devolve into the hands of women," Zenobia submits a qualification. " 'Yes, if she were young and beautiful,' said Zenobia, laughing. 'But how if she were sixty, and a fright?' " One sardonic male reviewer of Fanny Wright's "frightening" lectures in 1836 confirmed Zenobia's criticism: "One could very well afford to hear his own opinions of propriety abused by a woman, if the traduction came from between a pretty pair of lips."[34] The drowned Zenobia becomes a "fright" and hence unsuitable as a conventional heroine of romance.

Nineteenth-century critics speculated that Margaret Fuller had undergone cosmetic surgery by Hawthorne's pen, perhaps as she did also as the poisonous and beautiful Beatrice, to make her acceptable as the heroine of *Blithedale*. It was "Fuller's fate to be Zenobia," observed Moncure Conway, "though she was homely and Zenobia beautiful."[35] "It is not difficult to recognize who Zenobia really is," Charles Hale wrote in 1852, "notwithstanding some prominent differences in external condition."[36] It is this Pygmalion process of beautification, under Coverdale's gaze and Hawthorne's pen, that Hawthorne has Zenobia sabotage through her death.

Hawthorne's relationship to Fuller was acutely ambivalent. The only mention of the real Fuller in his text is potent. When the pale and feminized Priscilla delivers a letter sent from Fuller to Coverdale, he thinks he sees a transformation: "it forcibly struck me that her air, though not her figure, and the expression of her face, but not its features, had a resemblance to what I had often seen in a friend of mine, one of the most gifted women of the age" (3: 51). Fuller's power, though obviously intellectual, is represented in sexually charged imagery: emanating from an envelope it seems to take over the "air" and "expression" of feminized women who have only minimal contact with her.

The episode reflects Fuller's influence in literary Boston. Of Fuller's electricity, lovers, and desperate swains, the artist Sarah Freeman Clark wrote: "Encountering her glance, something like an electric shock was felt. . . . No woman ever had more true lovers among those of her own sex, and so many men she also numbered among her friends." Her gaze transmitted "the shock of truth." Holding Fuller's envelope, Priscilla's gaze seems to see into others (3: 51–52).

In the early 1840's Fuller was friend not only to Hawthorne but to Sophia, who was so inspired by Margaret that in appreciation of her "conversations" she composed for her what Bell Chevigny describes as a "rapturous sonnet": "To a Priestess of the Temple Not Made with Hands." After one year of marriage, however, Sophia complained to her mother about Margaret (in language oddly sexual): "It was always a shock to me to have women mount the rostrum."[37] Hawthorne's Sophia censures Margaret just as Hale's Sophia reproaches Marian in *The Lecturess*.

These were probably also the views of her husband, for his relationship to Fuller also underwent a transformation. Fuller felt that the Hawthorne with whom she had had long talks in the early 1840's "might be a brother to me." But her independence gradually caught up to her "brother" who, after her death by drowning in 1850, two years before *Blithedale*, maligned her in a letter in terms that echo Weld's dressing down of Hutchinson: "She set to work on her strange, heavy unpliable, and in many respects, defective and evil nature." Fuller, he scoffed, tried to be "her own Redeemer, if not her own Creator . . . [but] there was something within her that she could not possibly come at, to re-create and refine it." Fuller transgressed by tampering with her own femininity, and perhaps Sophia's. Hawthorne took satisfaction that her marriage to the Marchese Ossoli "proved herself a very woman . . . [who] fell as the weakest of her sisters might" (every Zenobia conceals an Ophelia).[38]

Zenobia, like Fuller, was at times reduced to a stereotype by Hawthorne. In the preface to *Blithedale* she may as well have been placed behind a placard: "high-spirited Woman, bruising herself against the narrow limitations of her sex" (3: 2). A more verbose version of this placard appeared on an earlier women's rights advocate, one of the embittered guests in Hawthorne's "The Christmas Banquet" (1844): "She had . . . driven herself to the verge of madness by dark broodings over the wrongs of her sex, and its exclusion from a proper field of action" (10: 303). This phrasing by Hawthorne's narrator frames her problem not as "the world" but as her own failure to adapt emotionally to "nothing" (10: 303); she drives herself to madness. Had Zenobia been given the opportunity to debate with her maker as well as with Hollingsworth, and had she had access to a later vocabulary, one wonders if she would have emended Hawthorne's classification: "High-spirited woman, bruised by the narrow limitations of her sex role."

Yet Hawthorne's decision to call his stereotype "Zenobia" complicates our understanding of both his attitude toward his "high-spirited Woman" and his intention of how she should be read. The historical Queen Zenobia was profiled in the classical dictionaries of Hawthorne's times. Charles Anthon, whose dictionary Hawthorne consulted when rewriting Greek myths for children in the early 1850's, portrays the fabled Queen of Palmyra as "disdaining the female litter." This "amazon" distinguished herself as a formidable public figure: talented in "jurisprudence and finance," skilled in "the arts and duties of government," and "agile" enough to "direct and share the labours and enterprises of war." Not unlike Margaret Fuller, she was "accomplished in literary endowments."[39]

A variety of mid-century authors paid tribute to Queen Zenobia as a powerful figure. In 1851, the year before *Blithedale* was published, a contributor to one prominent women's rights journal heralded Zenobia as "the celebrated Queen of the East . . . not exceeded by any king on record, for talent, courage, and daring ambition."[40] Lydia Maria Child, in her *Brief History of the Condition of Women* (1835), noted that Zenobia was "said to have been as beautiful as Cleopatra, from whom she claimed descent," and that, in addition to distinguishing herself as a master of languages, hunting, and the arts of war, she ruled "with wonderful steadiness and wisdom."[41] Sarah Grimké quotes from Child in her own salute to Zenobia in her pioneering women's rights tract, *Letters on the Equality of the Sexes and the Condition of Women* (1838). In her *Memoirs of Celebrated Female Sovereigns* (1840) Mrs. Jameson stresses Queen Zenobia's prodigious "passion for study."[42]

But Hawthorne and his reader would probably have been most familiar with the figure of Zenobia through a popular novel published in 1836 by the prominent Boston Unitarian minister William Ware, which a year later he retitled *Zenobia*. Ware offers a historical romance of the reign and fall of Zenobia, Queen of Palmyra, as recorded by the letters of the sympathetic Roman, Lucius Piso. Steel-helmeted and suited for war, Zenobia is viewed as "unequalled for a marvelous union of feminine beauty, queenly dignity, and masculine power." Bent on expanding her empire, even when it meant annexing provinces claimed by Rome, she is represented as supremely confident and ambitious: "I would that the world were mine."[43]

From the outset it is clear that the novel, though set in ancient times, seeks to challenge contemporary assumptions about "true" womanhood. Ware is intrigued by the idea of female androgyny, or in Hawthorne's term, the "man-like" woman. His literary Palmyra has several amazons who revere Zenobia as a role model. Fausta, for example, true to her name, is like Faust: ostensibly an overreacher, but simply developing her abilities in so-called "masculine" as well as "feminine" ways. She is skilled not only at plying the needle but more especially at throwing the lance (replete with glaring phallic associations). To Gracchus's dig, "When will you be a woman?" she replies, "Never, I trust . . . if I may neither laugh, nor cry, nor vex a Roman, nor fight for our queen. These are my vocations, and if I must renounce them, then I will be a man."[44]

Ware's portrait of Zenobia, though certainly romanticized, is that of an *epic* rather than a romantic woman.[45] In fact, Zenobia must be described as anti-romantic.[46] Hollingsworth would not have gotten to first base with Ware's Zenobia, who eschews "that mad and blind passion, which loves only because it will love," and instead prefers "the calm, peaceful lake, which mirrors friendship."[47] Neither a lovesick Ophelia, nor a soggy Edna Pontellier, Ware's Zenobia is far too committed to her role as "head" of state to let her heart be sunk by the emotional tonnage of romantic conventions. In her epic mode Zenobia's haughty dismissal of romantic "love" ("the ocean heaving and tossing from its foundations") distinguishes her as the very antithesis of the Victorian construction of Ophelia.

Rome's Emperor Aurelian who, says Anthon, was "envious of her power," does contrive to sink her and prevails in a symbolic fashion. Once conquered, Zenobia's singular punishment is peculiarly reminiscent of Pygmalion decking out his silent "ivory maid" with jewelry. In Rome Zenobia is publicly transformed from ruler to the ruled, from an epic actor to a romantic mannequin. In the words of Charles Anthon, the woman who disdained the "female litter" was "led along in chains of gold" and "is said to have almost sunk beneath the weight of jewels with which she was adorned on that occasion."[48] Ware's narrator, Lucius Piso, is even more explicit that the "chains of gold . . . passing around her neck and arms" are bonds. His imagery suggests an analogy between her burden and Christ bearing the cross: "My impulse was to break through the crowd and support her almost fainting form."[49] Both Anthon and Ware relate not just an episode in warfare but one in gender imperialism.

Boccaccio underscores this battle in his version. "Having thus overcome feminine softness," he writes of her younger days, Zenobia "was so strong that by her strength she surpassed the young man of her age in wrestling and all other contests." The challenge she faces as a public spectacle is nothing less than a contest of strength: "In spite of her great strength she often stooped, exhausted by the weight."[50] From several accounts, Aurelian, like Hollingsworth, tries to prove that "physical force" constitutes man's (or Rome's) "unmistakable sovereignty over women." Aurelian assumes the feminizing role of Pygmalion. The "high-spirited Woman's" sentence is *feminization*: she is "sunk" by the weight of femininity.

This is also a privatization. Lydia Maria Child observes that "the great Queen of the East sunk into the obscurity of private life."[51] Rome's epic monster was polished off and set in a jewel box on the Tiber. Hawthorne's Zenobia, convention though she be, is the stereotype of a proud and able woman feminized and privatized into silence.

Thus Hawthorne's decision to have his heroine adopt the public name "Zenobia" suggests his own as well as her own keen awareness of the stereotypes and social process she is up against. Zenobia, faithful to her namesake, is used to *parody* the Ophelia suicide just as Hawthorne, in "The Birth-mark," parodies the "ethic of submission." Whether or not this shared tendency to parody indicates Hawthorne's sympathy for her remains ambiguous. Perhaps a word other than "sympathy," a key word for Hawthorne,[52] would be more appropriate.

To clarify this, let us return to Hawthorne's "The Gorgon's Head." Hawthorne's attitude toward Zenobia may in some ways resemble Perseus's use of Medusa. Although Perseus may lock Medusa within his representation of her, his narrative shield, and in so doing behead her, he does not feminize her. In fact, he soon discovers how her unfeminine head can help him survive. Upon his return Perseus is told that the evil King Polydectes and his court demand proof that he has slain the "snaky haired monster." "Show me the Gorgon's head," the king commands, "or I will cut off your own!" Pressed by this corrupt administration, the young conqueror complies. King and court, petrified by the infamous gorgon, become "the mere images of a monarch and his people . . . whitened into marble!" Perseus uses Medusa's gaze and fame to "steal the human warmth" out of his public enemies, thereby reifying them as artwork (statues, wooden images). Medusa's head, by implication, symbolizes the artist's power of representation as a social and political force. In a sentence with a notably sexual resonance, Hawthorne writes that the triumphant Perseus "thrust the head back into his wallet" and went home to "dear mother" (7: 34).

Medusa's head, slipped out of Perseus's "magic wallet," is something that Hawthorne clearly depicts as a kind of currency. At the same time there is a hint of exhibitionism here ("thrust the head back into his wallet"), a fantastic display of his own phallic potency. Of course, the "head" that he exhibits is female. Freud's speculation about Medusa, that her head symbolizes both "the terrifying genitals of the Mother" ("snaky-haired monster") and castration fears, frames this as yet another episode in which female generativity is mythologized as monstrous.[53] Though decapitated, Medusa's head sprouts signs of life (many heads). Her head is almost too creative. But Perseus *needs* this symbol of apparently aberrant generativity and female dangerousness (giving birth to snakes out of one's head) to get ahead. Just as Georgiana must give her husband a "hand" to make him creative, Medusa's dangerously fertile "head" empowers Perseus.

Perhaps we can say of Hawthorne what Hawthorne recognizes about Perseus: once the dangerous woman is in-the-bag, the male author's powers of representation grow more potent. Medusa is a commodity. Both Hawthorne and Perseus profit from the stereotype of Medusa as she whose head petrifies. Since they too subscribe to her power to petrify, their ally, Medusa, cannot be looked at face-to-face. Narrative provides the bag that protects them and contains her. Perseus's narrative "wallet" is another version of the paper shroud that gives Westervelt, the mesmerist, power over Priscilla. In this enchanted state she becomes a paper medium, a conveyor of messages not her own. Like Perseus, Westervelt profits from, in Phelps's words, the "sad Sphinx" behind the veil.

When we bear in mind that Hawthorne's version of the myth was published one year before *Blithedale* and one year after *The Scarlet Letter*, our understanding of Hawthorne's relation to Medusa becomes still more complex. In *The Scarlet Letter* Hawthorne represents his political dismissal from the Salem Customs House and his subsequent manhandling in the press in literary terms: "careering through the public prints, in my decapitated state, like Irving's Headless Horseman; ghastly and grim, and longing to be buried, as a politically dead man ought" (1: 42–43). The reference to Irving may be a red herring to steer us off the track. For Hawthorne's condition is one he may view, if only by implication, as reflecting another literary figure: the "Customs House," he tells us, "may be considered as the POSTHUMOUS PAPERS OF A DECAPITATED SURVEYOR" (1: 43). Perhaps the two most famous decapitated surveyors in Western literature are, curiously enough, Hawthorne and Medusa.

Hawthorne loses his head but finds his art. In his decapitated state Hawthorne, paradoxically, develops the insight to survey his first novel and to represent the first of three artistic and "dangerous" women-of-vision who are at the center of his novels. By whipping Hester out of the bag, Hawthorne is released temporarily from his financial dependency on offensive civil authorities. Once Hawthorne takes up writing novels, he lets more hazardous women out of the bag. Which is to suggest that while Hawthorne turns away from the women whose heads (like currency) stuff his "wallet," he may also *identify* with them and their power to petrify and transform others. If his women-of-vision are stereotypes, the stereotypes both wield power and inspire him to create.

Hawthorne is best understood as an author who identifies with *both* Perseus (he who manipulates an inert and silent representation of a woman's head and profits from the stereotype) and the unfeminine Medusa (the original decapitated surveyor). He may also have partly identified with their peculiar partnership as a revolutionary force.[54] When Perseus flashes the Gorgon's head, he gains control of the political world by changing it. Zenobia, notes the paranoid Coverdale, also possesses such powers: "She made no scruple of oversetting all human institutions, and scattering them as with a breeze from her fan" (3: 464).[55] Perseus is the agent of change; Medusa's reconstituting vision is, once let out of the bag, what enables this change.

A dread of Medusa let out of the bag, like Pandora's box, moves Hawthorne to disqualify his puritan woman of vision, Hester Prynne, as the ideal reformer. Like Hester, the speculative woman who sees through too much discerns "a hopeless [revolutionary] task before her" because in order to liberate women from conventional feminine roles the *entire* culture must be restructured. This calls for literary, cultural, and social upheaval. Medusa stands for cultural revolution as opposed to feminine evolution. As we shall see in our discussion of *The Scarlet Letter*, this petrifies Hawthorne.

In sum, the gender politics of Hawthorne's tales and novels are difficult to describe because Hawthorne (like Aylmer, when he kisses the "hand") seems both drawn to and repulsed by the more petrifying aspects of his art, which he recognizes as critical of the feminization of women within American culture. Hawthorne exposes feminization as a literary and social construction, but sometimes, as in *The Scarlet Letter*, mystifies this process as an evolution caused by "the atmosphere of New England" (1: 50–51).

"The Birth-mark" parodies a process of feminization that has run amok. Yet in "The Birth-mark" and other tales Hawthorne never goes beyond parody to authorize the "real" women that the Man of Fancy aspires to create. We get parodies of femininity addicts making jointed dolls and wax angels, but no sustained effort from Hawthorne to engender something other than that which he criticizes.[56]

Equally troubling, "The Birth-mark" and "Rappacini's Daughter," like Poe's "Oval Portrait" and "Berenice," can be seen as narratives of victimization which, by imagining women *only* as relatively passive victims, reproduce in part the very patterns of stereotyping they would seem to contest. Hawthorne's own narrative decision to drown (out) Zenobia flirts with this pattern even as it unveils Coverdale's ideological (mis)representation. Although Zenobia is allowed to signal that her demise is, in Mrs. Oliphant's words, "a sham entirely," she has nonetheless been made to suffer a dubious heart enlargement and, surprisingly, *loses her head* to Hollingsworth.

I suspect that these contradictory signals betoken Hawthorne's ambivalence about a petrifying yet alluring critical force gathering strength in his writing. In Chapter 1 I suggested that the "monster" gestating in "Egotism; Or, the Bosom Serpent" is a serpent with a bosom and that this bosomy stereotype is not only the creative fount of Roderick's allegorical power but a powerful female force, a *gorgon*, emerging in Hawthorne's writing. Recall that the allegorist has "glittering eyes and long black hair" and is said to have *resembled* Envy (or Medusa) with her "snaky locks." Zenobia and Medusa, both bosomy and both powerful, are full-grown versions of this "restless" force. "Egotism" hints that Hawthorne on one level may have interiorized this decapitated yet vital force. If Hawthorne-as-Perseus seeks to keep his Medusa's restless, snaky head stuffed in his wallet, or supine beneath his pen, he also acknowledges the critical power of Medusa, not only to inspire novels, but to transform (petrify) the world. Medusa may symbolize the revolutionary political work of Hawthorne's fiction, perhaps his *own* "head," that he himself decapitates and shudders to look at.

Melville's Birthmarks

The Feminization Industry

Only one reader of Hawthorne's works has recognized the cultural dimension of texts like "The Birth-mark." He knew Hawthorne personally as well as through his fiction. His daring readings, cast in fictional form, are as complex as Hawthorne's own texts. I refer to Melville. Before we continue with a discussion of Hawthorne's three other novels, let us read Melville rewriting Hawthorne and boldly reimagining his friend's criticism of gender construction and American culture through his own.

What ideological role did the feminized woman play in the workings of mid-nineteenth-century culture? Why and to whom was it important that women be "feminine"? These are the systemic questions that Hawthorne's fictions prompt us to ask and that Melville's readings of Hawthorne help us to address. I shall argue here that Melville, in rethinking the cultural implications of Hawthorne's fictions, suggests how the construct of femininity was connected to and complicit with structural social contradictions at the base of the domestic tensions represented by Hawthorne.

Melville's recognition of this structural relationship was not unique. Some consideration of the connection between widespread material social changes and femininity even surfaces in texts that proselytize on behalf of "true" womanhood. "Of Queen's Gardens," for instance, makes it unambiguous that Ruskin requires women to act as symbols of order precisely because the social world *outside* the garden walls was depicted as disordered. "The literature of domesticity," Nancy Cott concludes, "enlisted women in their domestic roles to absorb, palliate, and even to redeem the strain of social and economic transformation." In the stories we shall discuss, Melville charts the systemic relationship between the ideology of industrial "progress" and the cultural production of feminized women.[1] As we will see, Melville focused on both the themes and the symbolism in "The Birth-mark" and, in his creative rewriting, developed their historical dimension.

Melville probably first read "The Birth-mark" in July of 1850, while writing *Moby-Dick*. His new copy of Hawthorne's *Mosses from an Old Manse* shows that he marked passages of special interest.[2] Symbols and themes in "The Birth-mark" are reworked in Melville's texts from *Moby-Dick* to *Billy Budd* (1890–91),[3] but the most intriguing and fully elaborated correspondences can be found in two of his short stories, "The Bell-Tower" and "The Tartarus of Maids," written in the mid-1850's. These correspondences challenge us to read "The Birth-mark" in a light only hinted at thus far. The social conflict that Melville focuses on in reimagining "The Birth-mark" is industrial capitalism.

Lewis Mumford and others have noted the "Hawthornesque" qualities of Melville's "The Bell-Tower" (1854). Even the sound of its title resonates with "The Birth-mark."[4] But the relation between the tales is more than cosmetic. Melville's fable is about the erection of a "Titanic" bell tower designed by a "great mechanician, the unblest foundling, Bannadonna." The construction takes place during the first flowering of the Renaissance in "the south of Europe, nigh a once frescoed capital, now with dank mould cankering its bloom" (p. 223). Yet Melville's epigraph gives the narrative a relevance to the blight of contemporary slavery on the American Renaissance:

Like negroes, these higher powers own man sullenly; mindful of their higher master; while serving, plot revenge.

The world is apoplectic with high-living of ambition; and apoplexy has its fall.

Seeking to conquer a larger liberty, man but extends the empire of necessity. (p. 223)

The bell towers that stood watch over the factories and armories of New England would have signaled connections in the minds of readers between the emergence of a contemporary "empire of necessity" and the one sketched in the story.[5] So would the conflict that dooms its success.

The battle is between management and labor. During the casting of "the great state-bell," the metals "bayed like hounds" while the workers "shrunk" through "fright" (p. 225). Protective of his bell, the ruthless Bannadonna "smote the chief culprit with his ponderous ladle," thus dashing a splinter "into the seething mass," to become forever part of the mold (p. 225). In a passage that could serve as a bitterly ironic afterword to "The Birth-mark," we learn, "The homicide was overlooked. By the charitable that deed was but imputed to sudden transports of esthetic passion, not any flagitious quality. A kick from an Arabian charger; not a sign of vice but blood" (p. 225). Public awe for the mechanician's individual "triumph" as well as the state's appreciation of the bell as a national symbol account for his "absolution" (p. 225).

The design of the clock tower, a colossal pedestal, signals a symbiotic relationship between the elevation and the oppression of women. "Round and round the bell," the narrator tells us, "twelve figures of gay girls, garlanded, hand-in-hand, danced in a choral ring—the embodied hours" (p. 226). This pastoral band of women, linked hand-in-hand, is battered by a phallic mechanical force: "that stroke shall fall there," Bannadonna boasts with sexual bravado, "where the hand of Una clasps Dua's. The stroke of one shall sever that loved clasp" (p. 228). Rather than uttering cries of anguish or pain, these punctually fractured sisters have been built to warble "strange music" as their hands smash the bell (p. 228). Spectators below will hear a "peculiar resonance" (p. 235) from this "metallic aviary" (p. 223), audible symbols intended to instill national pride. Their shattered clasps provide the culture with an organizing center: "The hour-hands of a thousand watches now verged within a hair's breadth of the figure I" (p. 231); Melville, of course, is writing about the 1850's—"a thousand watches." The "mechanic hand" (p. 233) pressed into Bannadonna's service as a smasher of women's hands is "Talus," his "iron slave" (p. 234), who moves forward "sliding along a grooved way, like a railway; advancing to the clock-bell, with uplifted manacles striking it" (p. 235). As a cultural symbol of either religion or progress (or the nineteenth-century religion of technological progress), it reveals much about the capability of symbols to make discordant relations sound almost harmonious ("strange music," a "peculiar resonance").[6]

Several themes and symbols from "The Birth-mark" resurface, though sometimes in altered form. The subjugation of nature-as-woman is prominent in Melville's version. Winking at Hawthorne's tale, the narrator distinguishes Bannadonna from "the tribe of alchemists" who experiment with "species of incantations"; instead, he is a "practical materialist" who employs "plain vice-bench and hammer": "to solve nature, to steal into her, to intrigue beyond her, to procure some one else to bind her to his hand;—these, one and all, had not been his objects; but, asking no favors from any element or any being, of himself, to rival her, outstrip her, and rule her." Bannadonna invokes no magic but his own "common sense" (p. 234). Underlying the projects of Aylmer and Bannadonna, both driven by "esthetic passion," there is a subtext of envy: Aylmer drains a well-read hand of "creative force"; Bannadonna severs "garlanded" female hands that form a band. Melville hints at something mysteriously erotic in Bannadonna's motivation, thus bringing him closer to Aylmer, when the mechanician himself depicts the entwined hands of Una and Dua as the "loved clasp." Bannadonna's name reveals his aim. "Banna" derivates from the Old Norse, "banna," meaning to prohibit. "Donna" is Italian for woman. This gives us "bannadonna": to prohibit women.

The splinter from the "ponderous ladle" smashed on the "chief culprit" falls into the casting, thereby creating a fatal "defect" (p. 236). This deathmark is lifted from Hawthorne: "All was fair except in one strange spot. But as he suffered no one to attend him in these inspections, he concealed the blemish by some preparation which none knew better to devise" (p. 225). When the bell is tried, "the blemish" proves fatal: tolling a "broken and disastrous sound," it crashes to the earth (p. 236).

The mechanician does not live to see his failure, for another flaw requires the application of his cosmetic skills before the collapse. On a tour of the new bell tower a magistrate spots a peculiarity in Una: an "uncertain smile" (p. 229), perhaps even "a fatal one" (p. 228).[7] In an effort to explain (or explain away) this "strange" and "different" look, Bannadonna observes that the law of art forbids "duplicates" and "evokes fine personalities" (p. 229). Nevertheless, the magistrates compel him to touch up this disturbing irregularity. While altering Una's ambiguous smile (reminiscent of the "suspicious" smile of the prematurely entombed Madeline Usher),[8] Bannadonna falls prey to his own devices. Talus, true to his geological name, slides forward to strike the hands of the women but strikes his master instead. Bannadonna is found dead "at the feet of the hour Una; his head coinciding, in a vertical line, with her left hand, clasped by the hour Dua" (p. 231).

The "peculiar resonance" of "The Bell-Tower" itself is the way in which it both *recognizes* and elaborates upon the less developed social imagery in "The Birth-mark," such as the resemblance between Amina-dab and Talus. Aylmer addresses his "under-worker," Aminadab, as a "human machine" and a "man of low stature." The servant who labors over "furnace-smoke" possesses "great mechanical readiness" (10: 43, 51). Talus, described only briefly, reminds one of both Aminadab and Babo, the crafty insurgent slave in Melville's "Benito Cereno" (1855): "a sort of elephantine Helot, adapted to further . . . the universal conveniences and glories of humanity" (p. 233). He is the prototype for a mechanical laborer who will ever submit to rule.

But more explicitly than Aminadab, whose triumph over Aylmer is only hinted in his laugh, and more like Babo (Melville's "decapitated surveyor"), Talus "plots" revenge on his master. Here we recall the slave revolt prefigured in Melville's epigraph. "The Bell-Tower" revises the end of "The Birth-mark": both slave and woman, though made mechanical, win a retributive triumph over the conqueror who would "rival," "outstrip," and "rule" nature and human beings.

Melville did not develop the pun, but what he narrates more unequivocally than Hawthorne is the revenge of the "hand," the "mechanic hand." In the wake of the worker slain by Bannadonna, Talus takes on the role of "chief culprit." Without literally representing the reincarnation of the one in the other, Melville's tale eerily suggests the revolt of dead labor. This retribution could be interpreted as a prediction for his own times, when workers, not unlike Aminadab or Talus, were finding themselves cuffed in the role of "thou human machine."

Mid-century readers familiar with Spenser's *Faerie Queene* would have recognized the avenging Talus. In Book 5 he is the virtually invincible page of Sir Artegall, knight of Justice: "His name was *Talus*, made of yron mould, / Immouable, resistlesse, without end. / Who in his hand an iron flale did hould, / With which he thresht out falsehood, and did truth unfold."[9] Perhaps Melville was drawn to the industrial associations of this unbending "yron" man. Spenser's Talus, however, is subordinate to authority and seems more like Artegall's henchman than his page. Not only does he rescue Sir Artegall on occasion, he does his dirty work for him. Melville's Talus is just as "resistlesse" with his "iron flale" but has been converted into a rebel.

There is one other pun, unstated in the text, that links "The Bell-Tower" to "The Birth-mark" as Melville's commentary on patriarchal discourse. Melville's tale is about the erection and collapse of a "belle" tower. The "brilliant" belle, illustrated in *Godey's* fashion-plates, was celebrated, not for her intelligence, but for her "brilliant" looks: her success was as an aesthetic construct.[10]

Bannadonna's "esthetic passion" drives him to perform cosmetic surgery not only on a cracked bell but on an imperfect "belle." His mechanization, like Aylmer's alchemy, is an experiment in belle making. Mechanization and molding, like alchemy, were much used metaphors for literary discourse in mid-nineteenth-century texts.[11] Bannadonna's aesthetic precludes the casting of liberty belles who sport "uncertain" or "fatal" smiles, whose "music" is "strange," and whose "resonance" is "peculiar."

Una refuses, with her "uncertain smile," to be stereotyped within his aesthetic as the "belle." Her expression supervenes her role as a false icon of social order and docile femininity, a "gay girl, garlanded." Bannadonna attempts to *feminize* Una. Like Georgiana's distinguishing "charm," Una's contumacious smile is remarkable: she clashes with the other belles. Bannadonna's beautification is meant to standardize her as publicly recognizable and harmonious, that is, invisible, just another belle.

The venerable name "Una" also carried contemporary significance. Spenser's heroine, the other personification of Truth in *Faerie Queene*, was enlisted to lend her name to a publication Melville may have known, which appeared between February 1853 and October 1855: *The Una: A Paper Devoted to the Elevation of Women.* Melville's tale, recall, was published in August 1855. Paulina Wright Davis was the editor of this powerful and provocative women's rights magazine.[12]

Davis explained that Spenser's Una was chosen as their political standard bearer because she symbolized "*Truth* in its reformatory agency on human affairs." "Bigotry" resists "Progress," "Ignorance" flies from the "light," "Poverty" refuses "redemption," and "even Holinesse" deserts the "truth," while Una is "*ever the same.*" Una was radicalized by Davis and her colleagues as the unflinching spokeswoman of women's rights.[13] In *The Una* we hear an expression of the "strange music" and "peculiar resonance" of Bannadonna's belles: "The wail of the winds is not sadder nor more constant, than the groan of anguish from oppressed womanhood."[14] *Una* puts cracks in the ideology of the "belle." Charlotte Brontë, whose works were too "revolting" for many readers, is applauded by *Una* for having written "for no conventional puppets, no dolls of fashion!" "A nobler destiny is hers," writes a second critic, "than to be the doll of the parlor."[15]

In Lizzie Linn's "Marriage the Only Resource," which appeared in the January 1855 *Una*, marriage itself is feared as a belle tower that merely pretends to elevate women. Netta, mortified that her sole career seems to be matrimony, protests to Uncle Ralph: "I am like a man who feels vigor in every muscle, but his hands are chained that he cannot work. . . . how would you feel with nothing to do, nothing to occupy your mind that interested you?" Her uncle is baffled, for his niece no longer chimes like a belle: "What does a woman want to occupy her besides parties and beaux and fashions and novels? . . . why you want to get married, of course. That is what every woman *wants*."[16]

From April of 1853 it was frequently "Dear Una," rather than Davis, to whom letters were addressed from women, often famous, in America and abroad. It is not unlikely that "Dear Una" did much to promote the "uncertain smile." I am suggesting that Melville may have smiled back.[17]

All of these themes—the manufacture of women, the deadening of labor, and even literary gendering—are taken up in Melville's most far-ranging reworking of "The Birth-mark," "The Tartarus of Maids" (1855). Melville's narrative recounts a trip to a paper factory in the Berkshires in which women workers are enslaved by machinery and, as if mesmerized, ritually perform dead labor.[18] That their labor is dead is clear from the title; the factory is a *tartarus* of maids—the first of many specifically literary allusions. In the *Illiad* Homer's Zeus threatens banishment for any god who tries to aid either the Greeks or the Trojans: "into the murk of Tartaros that lies / deep down in underworld . . . the depth from hell / as great as heaven's utmost height from earth."[19] Spenser, who surely was on Melville's mind, also represents Tartarus in *Faerie Queene*. In imagery more anatomical than Homer's, Spenser pictures it as a "dark dreadful hole" of "damned ghosts" who come "Backe to the world, bad liuers to torment."[20] We see this Spenserian sexual imagery in references to the "black notch" through which one must ride on the road to Tartarus. One must also pass through a "Dantean gateway." These literary allusions suggest that Melville writes of dead laborers who are condemned not just to an industrial inferno but to a peculiarly *literary* space in paperland.

Melville moved to the Berkshires in 1850 and was aware of the proliferation of paper factories in the region. In part, the tale is based on an actual trip he made in January of 1851 to a mill to buy paper.[21] Several machines that transformed the character of labor in paper factories are described by Melville. The Wright ruling machine, for example, patented in 1842: "Seated before a long apparatus, strung with long, slender strings, like any harp, another girl was feeding it with foolscap sheets which, so soon as they curiously traveled from her on the cords, were withdrawn at the opposite end of the machine by a second girl. They came to the first girl blank; they went to the second girl ruled."[22] Its more nefarious function is to "rule" labor by leaving the brows of these harp-playing angels "ruled and wrinkled."

Another machine performs an operation with effects similar to those of Aylmer's experiments:

In one corner stood some huge frame of ponderous iron, with a vertical thing like piston periodically rising and falling upon a heavy wooden block. Before it—its tame minister—stood a tall girl, feeding the iron animal with half-quires of rose-hued note-paper which, at every downward dab of the piston-like machine, received in the corner the impress of a wreath of roses. I looked from the rosy paper to the pallid cheek, but said nothing. (p. 215)

The "piston-like machine" to which the girl is attached hints at some deeper sexual or gender oppression that underlies this "metallic necessity." Bleaching powders were incorporated into the papermaking process by the 1830's.[23] Intolerant of origins or nature, bleach whitens all. "At rows of blank-looking counters sat rows of blank-looking girls, with blank, white folders in their blank hands, all blankly folding paper" (p. 215).

The factory, also drained of color and life, is the antithesis of the sentimentalized, rural, whitewashed cottage. The water-wheel of this "frost-painted" "sepulchre" (p. 214), located in "Devil's Dungeon," is propelled by a "turbid brick-colored stream," a "strange-colored torrent Blood River" (p. 211). Once again our narrator suggests that the factory is powered by the blood of its hands:

"You make only blank paper; no printing of any sort, I suppose? All blank paper, don't you?"

"Certainly; what else should a paper-factory make?"

The lad here looked at me as if suspicious of my common-sense.

"Oh, to be sure!" said I, confused and stammering; "it only struck me as so strange that red waters should turn out pale chee—paper, I mean." (pp. 216–17)

This is Melville's point; one must focus, at the risk of having one's "common-sense" doubted, on how the factory manufactures not only products but workers. Twelve years later Marx would take the same risk and use similar imagery: "Capital is dead labour, that vampire-like, only lives by sucking living labour, and lives the more, the more labour it sucks." [24]

Melville's two versions of "The Birth-mark" tell us much about his creative readings of Hawthorne's tale. "The Bell-Tower" and "The Tartarus of Maids" may be regarded as two parts of a continuous "letter" ("a thousand—a million—a billion thoughts") that Melville once promised to send Hawthorne on an "endless riband" of paper. [25] Both of these "letters" are about the management of labor, labor-slaving devices, and the conquest of female nature, and both *recognize* industrial or labor imagery registered but not developed in "The Birth-mark."

The alchemical extraction of a woman's birthmark led Melville to envision not more fables about domestic tension but tales about mechanized women whose hands were regulated and smashed and women paper workers whose hands and faces were drained of blood. The alchemical erasure of a sign of origins, creativity, birth, and desire in a wife reminded him of industrial processes that were erasing the "birthmarks" of workers and contributing to the overall deadening of labor. As Melville wrote in "The Bell-Tower," Bannadonna set out "to devise some metallic agent, which should strike the hour with its mechanic hand, with even greater precision than the vital one" (p. 233).

That Melville would reread Hawthorne's tales within an industrial frame of reference is not surprising, for the body metaphors Melville found in "The Birth-mark" generated associations relating not only to sexuality but to processes shaping the political economy. In mid-century writings we find the "hand" figured as a synecdoche of labor and class, a symbol of contradiction, and a sign pointing to social fragmentation. [26] Theodore Parker's "Thoughts on Labor" (1841) invoked the classical analogy of the body politic, not to suggest the traditional organic harmony, but to allegorize a social body at war with itself. Two classes had developed, made up of consumers and producers: "They glory in being the Mouth that consumes, not the Hand that works. . . . when the Mouth and Hand are on different bodies . . . natural restraint is taken from appetite, and it runs to excess." [27]

Parker, Orestes Brownson, and others saw that the schism between

Head and Hand was not natural but was of social, economic, and often industrial origin.[28] In 1875 Lucy Larcom, a former worker at Lowell, published *An Idyl of Work*, which recounts the experience of mill labor in the 1830's and 1840's. She, too, recognized the social origins of fragmentation and unleashed her invective: "this woman-faculty / tied to machinery, part of the machine." Minta, full of "right aspirings," Esther, "an intellectual equal," and "sweet" Eleanor: "These counted but as 'hands!' named such!" The poet foresaw "The time must come when mind itself would yield / To the machine, or leave work to hands / Which were hands only."[29] And in "The Education of the Laboring Classes" (1843) Parker argues that education must now try to compensate for a system of work that stunts rather than cultivates workers' faculties: "He becomes hands, and hands only; a passive drudge, who can eat, drink, and vote. The popular term for working men, 'hands' is not without meaning; a mournful meaning, too, if a man but thinks of it. He reads little—that of unprofitable matter, and thinks still less than he reads."[30] Thus "The Birth-mark" was not alone in its cultural admonitions against perceiving a person as a "hand" or reducing someone to a "hand" (a "hand only").[31]

There are other reasons why Melville would have recognized this industrial imagery interwoven with psychological symbols. When he made a distinction between the "practical materialist" and "the tribe of alchemists" in "The Bell-Tower," he was not the first to do so. Alchemy was employed in popular and especially political rhetoric both as a metaphor for mid-century industrialization and as an example of a less rational and less practical science that had to be distinguished from modern mechanization.

Edward Everett, for instance, used alchemy as a metaphor for industrialism in numerous speeches. In his address on "American Manufactures" (1831) the manufacturer practices an "alchemy" that transmutes "the inanimate growth of the forest or the field" and "rough and discordant elements" into gold. The industrial Bannadonnas of the mid-nineteenth century, he argues, are more efficient at reconstructing the face of nature: "The mechanician, not the magician, is now the master of life. . . . [He makes] mighty chain-pumps descend, clanking and groaning, to the deepest abysses of the coal mine, and rid them of their deluge of waters; and spindles and looms ply their task, as if instinct with life." Capital personified is the editor of Mother Nature: "a mighty genius, bidding the mountains to bow their heads, and the village to rise, the crooked places to be straight, and the rough places plain."[32] The capitalist-alchemist, "master of life," perfects Nature to his liking and makes it pay.

Industrial capitalism did more than promote the invention of machinery; along with such technological changes it assembled a machinery of discourse designed to enchant its readers. In his emphasis on the besieged "hand" who operated the machinery rather than the "alchemist" who owned it or the pastoral scenery that surrounded it, Melville went against conventional representations of American industry that helped construct the prevailing "common sense." These representations could be found in articles about factories that were printed along with "The Tartarus of Maids" in *Harper's Weekly*. Jacob Abbott's "The Armory at Springfield" (1852) is a typical example of this factory tourism genre: the factory—Leo Marx's "machine in the garden"— "appears simply like a grove with cupolas and spires rising above the masses of forest foliage. . . . It presents everywhere the most enchanting pictures of rural health and beauty." The stream "pressed into its service," so different from Melville's "Blood River," is described as "a rivulet that meanders through a winding and romantic valley." Such enchanting harmony between factory and nature encourages the tourist to read the armory not as an "embodiment of a vast machinery incessantly employed in the production of engines of carnage and death," but rather as a pastoral institution that manufactures "instruments of security and peace."[33]

Melville subverts the ideology of the republican factory-in-nature that had its roots in eighteenth-century American thought.[34] By the mid-1850's Melville saw the notion of an enlightened "moral" factory in nature (crowned by its quaint bell tower) as a deceptive whitewash for the exploitation of labor. Nature had become a public relations sign used to sell the factory as not merely socially acceptable but desirable. This is apparent in some of the workers' literary magazines produced by and for women operatives. In her "Letters from Susan" (1844) column, the editor of *The Lowell Offering*, Harriet Farley, described a well-ordered factory environment inside and out: "the girls so pretty and neatly dressed, and the machinery so brightly polished or nicely painted. The plants in the window, or on the overseer's bench or desk, gave a pleasant aspect to things." In Melville's language, Farley offers her readers only portraits of "gay girls, garlanded." The factories in nature are not, like Spenser's Tartarus, "close and black as—as the Black Hole of Calcutta";

rather they are "high spacious well-built edifices, with neat paths around them, and beautiful plots of greensward." The workers' rooms are kept "whitewashed" with "white curtains in the windows." Signs of nature and domesticity can be seen not only in the plants in the windows but in the "beautiful and uniform" machinery: "green looms . . . the lathes moving back and forth, the harnesses up and down, the white cloth winding over the rollers . . . I have thought it beautiful."[35]

Nature and domestic touches are employed as signs to *naturalize* the factory and its social relations of production. Melville's de-natured maids inside and blasted landscape outside the factory jam this literary machinery of beautification to a halt. As in "The Bell-Tower," Melville's tale disrupts ideological modes of representation. Melville's factory maids are not the "gay girls, garlanded" so often (mis)represented by *The Lowell Offering* and its counterparts. The operatives of Tartarus are not spiritualized or "nicely painted" or "brightly polished"; they are sunk by the weight of the paper. Beneath its snow-white veil the American factory can be more insidiously infernal than its filthy counterparts in Manchester.[36] The blood, not the paper, is its most telling product. If industrial America looks great on paper, the paper used by *Harper's Weekly* and other middle-class literary magazines, Melville suggests that it looks less pure when we look into its origins and restore its labormarks.

Yet, as several critics have understood, "The Tartarus of Maids" cannot be classified only as a critique of mid-century industrialization. Marx's "vampire" imagery is subordinate to his central aim: a critique of industrial capitalism. Looking at "The Birth-mark" and "Tartarus," we find bleached women, a dead white woman and "maids" who experience a living death, a "bloody" hand and bloody "boiling" waters that turn a mill wheel, and the *isolation* of women by men who subject them to an alchemical or technological experiment. Melville, whose familiarity with Polynesian taboos on women is explicit in *Typee* (1846), seems to imagine these women papermakers imprisoned within a mechanical pollution ritual. His imagery of women workers drained of blood suggests multiple levels of meaning and criticism that make a Marxian reading of the oppression in Devil's Dungeon more complex. It is here that the dialogue between "The Birth-mark" and "The Tartarus of Maids" proves crucial.

Spenser's representation of women in thrall in *Faerie Queene* is an important source for both tales, I would argue, and as such clarifies the link between them. In Book 3 we find the lovely Amoret imprisoned in the castle of the enchanter Busyrane, yet another literary alchemist, who has magically entranced her for many months. Amoret is described in terms that reappear in images associated with Georgiana ("the spectral hand that wrote mortality"). Propped up and propelled forward by Cruelty and Despight, Amoret "Had deathes owne image figurd in her face."

> Of her dew honour was despoyled quight,
> And a wide wound therein (O ruefull sight)
> Entrenched deepe with knife accursed keene,
> Yet freshly bleeding forth her fainting spright,
> (The work of cruell hand) was to be seene,
> That dyde in sanguine red her skin all snowy cleene.[37]

The "work of cruell hand" resurfaces in Aylmer's dream of surgical penetration. Amoret walks with "her trembling hart" in a basin bathed with a continuous ("steeming fresh") flow of blood.

What probably intrigued Melville, in addition to the images that Hawthorne reworked and the blood river flowing continuously from Amoret's chest, was the character who next appears and in whose power she is enslaved: Cupid. He rides on a "Lion ravenous" to flaunt his mastery of nature and to survey his female conquest. Following the conventions of the factory tourism genre, Melville's narrator has a guide, also named Cupid: "a dimpled, red-cheeked, spirited-looking, forward little fellow, who was rather impudently, I thought, gliding among the passive-looking girls" (p. 216). This sexually offensive, "usage hardened" (p. 218) Cupid of the industrial age has become blindly mechanical.[38] However, like the magic of Spenser's Cupid, the mechanization that this mid-nineteenth-century Cupid represents also causes his spellbound "maids" to lose heart and much else.

"The Tartarus of Maids" is not only about industrialization and the exploitation of women laborers; it proposes that mechanization in Devil's Dungeon, like Aylmer's alchemy and Busyrane's enchantment, operates to drain the sexuality and, more precisely, the procreativity of these women-in-labor. In Hawthorne's tale a mark of birth and mother's desire is erased; in Melville's story birth itself appears to be *replaced* by the machine. "Labor," in the double sense of productive labor fit for human beings and maternity, has been made sterile.

The symbol Melville uses to condense associations of labor and birth is the papermaking machine. Cupid suggests that the narrator make a "mark" on a slip of paper so that it can be put through the papermaking process. This is a test to back up his boast that the machine can produce paper in only nine minutes. The narrator inscribes the word "Cupid." Nine minutes later "a scissory sound smote my ear, as of some cord being snapped; and down dropped an unfolded sheet of perfect foolscap, with my 'Cupid' half faded out of it, and still moist and warm" (p. 220). The Cupid-mark, like Georgiana's birthmark, has been erased.

Papermaking machines, like alchemical authors, not only manufacture paper women, they erase signs of identity. Melville does not suggest, as does Hawthorne, that the bleached maids possess a "secret of creative force," a "disastrous brilliancy," or a charm that "sways" hearts, all qualities that we might associate with female authorship. But Melville thematizes the same patriarchal effort to expunge signs of female reproductive power. The sheet with the faded Cupid-mark on it becomes identical with other sheets, just as the straightening out of Una's smile would standardize her as just another belle. At last the paper falls into the "waiting hands" of an "elderly" operative who, no longer able (or perhaps permitted) to work as a midwife, now delivers machine-made paper rather than infants.[39]

As Marvin Fisher has pointed out, the papermaking machine is "a grotesque parody" of the nine-month (nine-minute) birth process; it "mocks conception, rationalizes gestation, and industrializes birth."[40] And as Michael Rogin has noted, the story abounds with imagery ("white pulp," "Blood River," "cord being snapped") which suggests that the factory is like one great mechanized womb. Here technological alchemy erases signs of both love (Cupid) and labor: mechanized "productivity" is more like an abortion.[41]

By linking the industrialization of women workers with menstruation imagery (Blood River), Melville is suggesting a perverse motivation fused with the rationalization of labor, just as there is a "peculiar resonance" to Bannadonna's delight in shattering the "loved clasp" of Una and Dua. Like "The Birth-mark," Melville's "Tartarus" can be read on one level as an allegory of sexual repression or oppression; but more fundamentally "Tartarus," again like "The Birth-mark," can be reinterpreted as an allegory of feminization. In *The Scarlet Letter* Hawthorne suggests that the "atmosphere" in New England makes women grow "pale or thinner." Melville's story shows specific social conditions for this. Devil's Dungeon, like Aylmer's pavilion in literary cloud-land, is an institution set up to alter angels who bleed; their procreativity is sanitized and *made* safe. "Why is it sir," the narrator asks the factory owner, Old Bach, "that in most factories, female operatives, of whatever age, are indiscriminately called girls, never women?" (p. 222).

It is this discursive angel making, this denial of womanhood, represented in "Tartarus" and "The Birth-mark," that adult critics writing for *The Una* protested: "Angels, there are none." "We love our human nature," wrote another contributor in 1853. "If angels, then we are fallen angels. . . . We always grow suspicious when the term is applied, and shrink from the use of it, for we have little faith in its honesty, and much fear of its design and influence."[42] The angels in Devil's Dungeon tied to that "long apparatus, strung with long slender strings, like any harp," may well have agreed through their whispers—had they been asked.

By situating the process of feminization in a factory, Melville can suggest that this infernal angel making is carried out because of profit. Motives of Old Bachelors are not purely psychological. There are at least two economic motives for angel making. Greenswards, flowers in the window, and "nicely painted" green looms all function as signs that naturalize the factory as the "machine in the garden." Feminization serves as a similar ideological alchemy. The "gay girls" are "garlanded," perhaps manacled, not only with signs of nature but with signs of femininity. As icons of purity and order, flawlessly feminine operatives are employed to whitewash the ideological presence of the factory in America.

Bloodless "angels," moreover, are malleable and manageable: blank sheets are more easily scribbled on. The "mill girls make excellent wives," boasted Harriet Farley, editor of *The Lowell Offering*, as if advertising wind-up dolls: "They are good managers, orderly in their households, and 'neat as waxwork.'"[43] Many of the factory magazines edited and written by female operatives set in motion a discursive machinery of feminization. *The New England Offering*, Farley's successor to *The Lowell Offering*, as Bertha Stearns put it, inculcated "calm demeanor in factory girls, pointing out to them the 'bad taste' involved in abusing 'those from whom one is voluntarily receiving the means of subsistence,' and offering them stories, poems, essays, advice, and book notices as irreproachable as those presided by Mrs. Sarah J. Hale in the *Lady's Book*." When Sarah Bagley took over the editorship of the radical *Voice of Industry* in 1846, a pro-worker alternative to the *Offering*, she orchestrated what Stearns calls a "feminization of the *Voice*": "There was less of insistent agitation for a ten-hour day . . . and more emphasis upon the social and personal concerns of women."[44] The original title of the celebrated *Lowell Offering*, interestingly, was *The Garland of the Mills*. Another operatives magazine that promoted management and femininity was the *Factory Girl's Garland* (1844). The "gay girls, garlanded" were cuffed to green looms as well as a machinery of signification, both "nicely painted."

Melville's story offers more than a criticism of the ideological discourse in factory magazines and politicians' speeches, for he seems to be quoting from or drawing on some of the key works we have previously discussed that thematize the patriarchal literary representation of women. In Devil's Dungeon we find a factory owned by an "Old Bach" who, like an industrial Pygmalion (who also had "long lived as a bachelor"), is in the business of producing "snowy ivory maid[s]" easily manipulated and "neat as waxwork." "Tartarus" is set up to mold the kinds of female characters that Hawthorne's Man of Fancy, much to his mature embarrassment, created in his youthful fictions: wax angels, jointed dolls, all left "cold as moonshine." Like Aubepine's allegory in "Rappaccini's Daughter," Old Bach's factory "steal[s] the human warmth out of his [female] conceptions." "The human voice," the narrator observes of the "whispering" maids, "was banished from the spot" (p. 215).

When the narrator acknowledges that he "looked from the rosy paper to the pallid cheek, but said nothing," Melville is reworking imagery from Poe's "The Oval Portrait": the egotistical artist "*would* not see that the tints which he spread from the canvas were drawn from the cheeks of her who sat beside him." Here, too, both Poe and Melville may have been thinking of Spenser's "Enchaunter," Busyrane, who figures "straunge characters of his art" with the "living bloud" of Amoret's "dying hart."[45] Spenser, Poe, and Hawthorne all see the male aesthetic as thriving on women's lifeblood. Poe, like Melville, represented the woman as complicit in this aesthetic emplotment. To rewrite a phrase from Melville's narrator, the artist's wife wet the very brush that slew her. Melville is also suggesting that feminization involves a self-defeating component: that the "girls" or "belles" authorized by bachelor-authors wet/whet the pens ("swords") that slay them (p. 218).

One historian of technology has criticized Melville for downplaying the advantages women enjoyed by working in the Berkshire paper factories rather than Lowell's cotton mills. Yet these women worked long hours, suffered industrial "accidents" (snapped tendons, severed fingers, deep paper cuts), and were usually paid only one-third the salary of men. It may be that Melville perceived the women workers he witnessed as drained not only by a particular paper factory but by a capitalist culture industry (a paper machinery) with which he was even more familiar. Melville, I would argue, understood the factory both as a material reality and as an appropriate *metaphor* for the cultural production of femininity.[46]

The same year that Melville published "Tartarus," Harpers (which published *Moby-Dick* in 1851 and *Pierre* in 1852) "manufactured books on an efficient assembly line, putting forth no less than thirty-five volumes a minute. The book-making process proceeded through seven functionally specialized floors, housing a vast machinery and 300 females to operate its simple levers." In the thirty years prior to the publication of *Moby-Dick*, the volume of printing in America had "increased ten-fold." Women and domesticity were targeted as primary subjects produced by this publishing boom.[47] By 1860 the circulation of *Godey's Lady's Book* had reached 150,000. Other periodicals, gift books, and annuals produced since 1820 included titles such as *Lady's Cabinet Album*, *Lady's Casket Album*, *Ladies' Companion*, *The Ladies' Garland*, to list only a few. These, too, can be considered paper machines whose product is femininity.[48]

The infinitely reproducible women in Melville's "factory" do not simply make paper; the paper makes them. The rise of industrial production, the decline of handmade products, and the alienated labor that ensues are viewed by Melville as *metaphors* for the cultural and psychological predicament of women whose own cultural "labor" supports a machinery of stereotyping that executes them. Tartarus is an Ophelia factory. The discursive production of a particular kind of feminine character by the *industry of culture* enables those who "rule" the culture to paper over contradictions of class, labor, and gender.[49]

Let us conclude, then, that the political work of "The Tartarus of Maids" is to hint at complex links between industrial capitalism, the ideological role of literature, feminization, and the kind of tension that appears to be more private and narrowly psychological in "The Birthmark." The reduction of a woman to a "hand" (a "hand only"), the reading of the "hand" as a flaw or a curse, and the use of science to

drain the life from her "hand," especially after reading Melville's industrial tales, becomes complex, *socially* symbolic behavior to interpret.
Its symbolism and associations refer to an industrial and cultural *slight*
of "hands" that middle-class "common-sense" classifies as unrelated to
personal life.[50]

Hawthorne and especially Melville, I wish to suggest, saw that they
were related. By the 1840's and 1850's both domestic women and industrial workers, fair Una and "yron" Talus, were organizing to resist the
abuses of feminization and industrialization. Melville's "The Tartarus of
Maids" and "The Bell-Tower," in their representation of mechanized
"belle" construction and angel making, recognize a political unconscious
in "The Birth-mark" that underlies or at least coexists with signs that
on the surface may appear predominantly psychological and personal
(especially to twentieth-century middle-class readers). By criticizing the
cultural role played by patriarchal literary discourse, both Hawthorne
and Melville ask us to think about their culture's "supernatural machinery" as social and historical in nature.

Yet Melville's "Tartarus," like Hawthorne's "The Birth-mark," is
also a product of this ideological "machinery." Both stories reproduce
the victimization they attempt to criticize by imagining women only
as bloodless victims ("passive-looking girls"). The women workers who
spoke through *The Voice of Industry* and the middle-class women who
wrote for *The Una* were neither "whispering girls" (p. 217) nor damsels-
in-distress who relied on a Talus to drive their point home.

5

Sowing Dragons' Teeth

*Personal Life and Revolution
in 'The Scarlet Letter'*

I proposed earlier that Medusa, the original "decapitated surveyor," be read as a symbol of revolutionary potential in Hawthorne's fiction, an unfeminine power that Hawthorne paradoxically identified with (himself a decapitated surveyor) and was petrified to look at. When young Perseus, in Hawthorne's "The Gorgon's Head," pulls Medusa's snaky severed head from his "wallet," he gives birth to a revolution: King Polydectes and his court are petrified. The fantasy is that the manipulation of a mythically dangerous female head makes revolution possible. This male fear of unfeminine power had historical coordinates; for there is also, as I noted, a similarity between the three gorgons ("terrible monsters") and Hollingsworth's depiction of women's rights advocates ("imaginary monster[s]," "petticoated monstrosities"). It is another aspect of this similitude that I now wish to elaborate.

These sister-monsters are also portrayed by Hawthorne's narrator as "a very frightful and mischievous species of dragon." Their wings were "exceedingly splendid . . . pure, bright, glittering, burnished gold" and "when people happened to catch a glimpse of their glimmering brightness, aloft in the air, they seldom stopt to gaze, but ran and hid themselves as speedily as they could" (7: 13). Why this dread of winged "dragons"?

I suspect that here, as elsewhere, Hawthorne is expressing cultural anxieties about artistic or political women with a bite in corporeal terms and that a dread of *dragonism*, like a fear of female monstrosity, should be situated in the context of anxieties about the "venomous" female "tongues" wagging in conventions and in print by the late 1840's.

"During the early part of my life," wrote Sarah Grimké, the outspoken women's rights advocate, "my lot was cast among the butterflies of the *fashionable* world; and of this class of women, I am constrained to say, both from experience and observation, that their education is miserably deficient; that they are taught to regard marriage as the one thing needful, the only avenue to distinction."[1] The winged, unwed dragon sisters, armed to the teeth and not easily crushed, are the antithesis of the shrinking "butterfly" or the paper-winged "angel" in the house.

I offer historical speculations on this undomesticated species of dragonism because the dragon theme resurfaces provocatively in Hawthorne's revision of the myths of Cadmus and Jason, published just two years after "The Gorgon's Head," in *Tanglewood Tales* (1853). In these myths, male warriors who originate from the *mouth* of a dragon threaten civilization itself. There may be a link in Hawthorne's mind between cultural anxieties surrounding dragon women with "terribly long tusks" (7: 13), and crazed warriors who sprout full-grown from the teeth of a dragon. The myths of Jason and Cadmus, as we shall see, suggest that Hawthorne saw the ideology of middle-class domesticity as potent enough to maintain a clearly mythic social order threatened by dragons' teeth. I shall propose, as my argument proceeds, that Hawthorne's determination to uphold this mythic *impression* of social order, over against those who would "sow" dragons' teeth, should be the key to our reading of *The Scarlet Letter*.

Our first task is to begin by unpacking the popular middle-class assumptions informing the "dragon" myths of Jason and Cadmus. In both myths our intrepid heroes must sow broadcast the "dragon's teeth," which yield a crop of spellbound soldiers poised for battle: "bright objects sprouted higher," before Jason's very eyes, "and proved to be the steel-heads of spears" (7: 359). Barely human incarnations of Ahab's "madness maddened," these warriors collectively "had come into this beautiful world, and into the peaceful moonlight, full of rage and stormy passions, and ready to take the life of every human brother, in recompense of the boon of their existence" (7: 360). So "fierce and feverish" was this army of armored monomaniacs that they turned on one another to a man, in response to a stone thrown by Jason, and reaped "the only enjoyment which they had tasted on this beautiful earth!" But why should they revel so in self-slaughter and "lopping of arms, head, and legs" (7: 361), something neither adult nor child should enjoy? Hawthorne offers a clue to his young readers: "They never had women for their mothers" (7: 360). And mother, mind you, should make all the difference.

Cadmus, like Jason, throws a stone at the charging soldiers, who then, in a blind rage, turn on one another "until the ground was strewn with helmeted heads" (7: 260). Five dragon's-teeth men remain standing, and Cadmus discovers that with a little domestic magic they can be put to good use. Cadmus is on a futile quest for his sister Europa ("everybody's queen"), who had been kidnapped long ago by Jupiter disguised as a white bull. In her place he is given as his wife Harmonia, "a daughter of the sky." At this juncture Hawthorne's retelling converts wholesale into a fantasy of middle-class domestic magic. Together King Cadmus and Queen Harmonia dwell in a "palace" where they find "comfort," "but would doubtless have found as much, if not more, in the humblest cottage by the wayside." In time Cadmus and Harmonia sprout some "rosy little children (but how they came thither, has always been a mystery to me)." The most dramatic transformation, however, is in the five surviving dragon's-teeth soldiers, who help build Cadmus a city and now delight in playing grandads to his "little urchins" (7: 264). Thus we learn that the profitable alembic of domesticity and maternal influence is capable of transmuting bloody competitors into cooperative workers and sentimental guardians.

The adult contemporary middle-class reader of Hawthorne's myths would have smiled at the popular assumptions and values of the "cult of domesticity" that informed these mid-century revisions. Both mid-century myths, for instance, pay holy tribute in ways obvious and subtle to the magical socializing powers of middle-class mothers. Without mother's magic little girls might grow up unruled, perhaps even tainted by dragonism. In "The Golden Fleece," for example, one of Jason's "oarsmen" is a woman, Atalanta, "who had been nursed among the mountains by a bear." Unlike Zenobia, she is unsinkable, and, like Christ, could walk on water "without wetting more than the sole of her sandal." There are, nevertheless, grave domestic deficiencies in this exceptional woman. Having been suckled outside a nursery, and not by a mother, she has imbibed a "very wild" disposition and thus "talked much about the rights of women, and loved hunting and war far better than her needle" (7: 345). Zenobia suffered similar deprivation. Her too fertile mind, Coverdale explains in *Blithedale*, sprouted "weeds" because "she lacked a mother's care" (3: 189). Mother is entrusted with weeding out combative dragonisms.

In *The Girl's Book*, first published during the Depression of 1837, Lydia Hunt Sigourney's authoritative maternal tone exemplifies Mother's role as agent of conformity and social order: "Shew respect to magistrates, and to all who are in places of authority. There would be fewer mutinies and revolutions; if children were trained up in obedience." Seeming to forget that Washington headed a Revolutionary army, and leaving aside his legendary naughty proclivity to hack down cherry trees, she writes: "It was said of Washington, by his mother, that 'his first lesson was to obey.'"[2]

The agenda of the mid-century Harmonia, however, was not simply to inculcate habits of obedience but to socialize girls and boys to be *middle class.* "Mother" was a bourgeois construction viewed as essential to the social reproduction of middle-class identity. Before the middle of the nineteenth century child rearing after infancy had been the responsibility of the patriach, but, as historian Mary Ryan has observed, it gradually became the mother's job to impose "sweet control." She undertook to rule, not by corporal discipline, but by nurturing conscience so that the child "would become the emotional marionette of its parents, in a warm and morally salubrious environment devoid of all cause for rebellious expression." As Ryan describes it, mother's mission was to implant "petit bourgeois traits—honesty, industry, frugality, temperance, and, preeminently, self-control" in her wards. Harmonia's "emotional skills" were directed toward the social reproduction "of small families, conservative business policies, dogged work habits, and basic literary skills—that is, the attributes required of the owners of small shops and stores and an increasing number of white-collar workers."[3]

Ideally this ideological reproduction equipped boys for their eventual entry into the marketplace and girls for their adult role as emotional providers for the males who survived their labors in "the world." The capitalist marketplace was often portrayed in middle-class domestic tracts as a bloody battlefield where neither man nor woman, especially woman, would wish to go. Its portrayal was, in fact, often like the "dragon's teeth" clash witnessed by Jason and Cadmus. The Rev. E. H. Chapin sketched "the bitter world" of 1851 as a war zone in which man is "driven . . . back on himself" and where "anger, scorn, or calumny" excite him to "madness."[4] In 1865 Ruskin described the public sphere outside of the "queen's" garden as "torn up by the agony of men, and beat level by the drift of their life-blood."[5] Dragon's-teeth soldiers personify the middle-class fear of "change and chaos" discussed by Carroll Smith-Rosenberg. This hysteria, notes Mary Ryan, commodified and intensified by the flourishing publishing industry of the 1840's and 1850's, "cast suspicion on the ties between the family and the community and discouraged involvement in social and political organizations, especially on the part of the fragile female."[6] The therapeutic "magic circle" became the ideological solution. Without the softening influences of mother, home, and family, men on the make might regress into the army of uncontrollable monomaniacs witnessed by Jason and Cadmus, an army whose sole "enjoyment" resides in strewing the ground with "helmeted heads."

The ameliorative cultural project of domestic alchemy, as exemplified in Hawthorne's "The Old Manse," is that it promises to transform men in the way that it seems to transmute the trees in the apple orchard: it "humanizes" them. Dragon's-teeth warriors, once domesticated and mothered by the Queen Harmonias of America, pay off: they build cities and homes, and play with children. The socializing influences of domesticity and motherhood help make middle-class capitalist culture possible.

Thus it is intriguing that in *The Scarlet Letter* Hawthorne brings to life a "dragon's-teeth" child, Pearl, who, in accordance with the doctrine of the transmission of impressions, has imbibed (like Atalanta from her bear) the rebellious "turmoil" of her adulterous "mother's system." "She never created a friend," writes Hawthorne, perhaps also reflecting on unpacified tendencies in his own work, "but seemed always to be sowing broadcast the dragon's teeth, whence sprung a harvest of armed enemies, against whom she rushed to battle" (1: 95).[7] As Roger Chillingworth observes, with literary allusiveness, the "child's composition" is based on "no law, nor reverence for authority, no regard for human ordinances or opinions, right or wrong" (1: 134). Like an author unable to get a handle on her composition, Pearl's mother, Hester Prynne, "failed to win the master-word that should control this new and incomprehensible intelligence" (1: 93). "I hardly comprehend her!" (1: 203), Hester confesses to Dimmesdale. As a kind of creative principle the illegitimate Pearl is, like the undomesticated "dragon's-teeth" soldiers, combative, unfeminine, and unmotherly; indeed, she is singularly "hostile" toward the imaginary "offspring of her own heart and mind" (1: 95). In Pearl, then, Hawthorne incorporates aspects of the high-flying dragon women as well as the dragon warriors.

Hawthorne seems to hint that the enigmatic Pearl can serve vigilantly and even maliciously as a feminist conscience for Hester. Little Pearl proves to be a strict mistress when her mother exhibits stereotypical signs of feminine weakness or sentiment. When Hester, baffled by her "perverse" daughter, would "burst into passionate tears," the "dragon's-teeth" child "would frown, and clench her little fist, and harden her small features into a stern, unsympathizing look of discontent" (1: 92–93). But often Pearl's "perverse" behavior might be read as the quintessence of Hester's own determination to resist puritan authority. Pearl refuses to let her mother *pacify* herself by responding to her predicament in a conventionally feminine manner. She outlaws in her mother what Mary Ryan terms the "tear-jerking" responses cultivated by many mid-century sentimental novels.[8] Sometimes, "but this more rarely happened," Pearl would respond differently to her mother's show of sentiment: "she would be convulsed with a rage of grief, and sob out her love for her mother in broken words, and seem intent on proving that she had a heart, by breaking it" (1: 93). Yet these hysterics also seem contrived to agitate rather than pacify Hester and to proscribe weeping as an emotional outlet for her mother.

Unlike the self-destructive dragon's-teeth soldiers, much of Pearl's hostility is recognizably political and retributive: her "incoherent exclamations" and "witch's anathemas" (1: 94) are directed toward the puritans and their children. It is possible at times to view Pearl as an angry, nascent, dragon revolutionary, pitting her "ever-creative spirit" (1: 95) against the patriarchal authority of the puritans. Pearl's furious imagination converted the pine trees of the forest into puritan fathers and the "ugliest weeds" into their offspring, "whom Pearl smote down and uprooted, most unmercifully" (1: 95). In "The Custom House," the autobiographical preface to the novel, Hawthorne admitted that as Salem's Surveyor of Customs he was no "exterminating angel" (1: 14) who could threaten the "patriarchal body" of indolent hangers-on with dismissal. Pearl would have had no such compunction, for she, in her insurrection against puritan children, "resembled, in her fierce pursuit of them, an infant pestilence,—the scarlet fever, or some such half-fledged angel of judgment,—whose mission was to punish the sins of the rising generation" (1: 102–3). It is as if Pearl, a lawless "composition" born of adulterous lovers, personifies a transgressive dimension of Hawthorne's own "creative force" which allows him to rebel against his "stern and black-browed" puritan fathers who, in his own mind, rebuke him as "a writer of story-books!" (1: 10).

Considered in the context of the history of mid-century childrearing, Pearl's temperament is significant because she bears no signs of having internalized the authority that marks the young middle-class conscience-under-construction. If the role of the mid-century Harmonia is to socialize her child to provide "the vital integrative tissue for an emerging middle-class," Hawthorne represents Hester as a flop. Rather than writing a good middle-class novel about "a kind of portable parent" lodged deep "within the child's personality," Hawthorne has reversed the process and, if anything, gives us a Pearl whose rebellious conscience is lodged deep within her mother.[9] As Richard Brodhead notes, the project of maternal socialization "supplied an emerging group with a plan of individual nature . . . that it could believe in and use to justify its ways" and, furthermore, employ to promote its class specific norms as "American 'normality.'" Pearl rejects this middle-class "puritan" normality.[10]

Hawthorne, of course, did not have to wait for Max Weber to recognize that the "normality" prescribed by these puritans exemplified a protestant work ethic that nurtured the spirit of capitalism. Of the Election Day procession he writes, "Then, too, the people were countenanced, if not encouraged, in relaxing the severe and close application to their various modes of rugged industry, which, at all other times, seemed of the same piece and material with their religion" (1: 231). It is these nascent *middle-class* puritans who would, in Hawthorne's imagination, denounce him as an "idler" (1: 10).

But Hawthorne also identified with his stern puritan ancestors, whose administrative careers exemplified the "persecuting spirit." "And yet, let them scorn me as they will," he acknowledges, "strong traits of their nature have intertwined themselves with mine" (1: 10). "Neither cast ye your pearls before swine," we are advised in Matthew 6: 6. It may be that Hawthorne, like the defiant and adulterous mother of Pearl, on one level identifies with his rebellious dragon's-teeth progeny. As Sarah Hale noted in *Flora's Interpreter*, the "hawthorne" bush bears "flowers scarlet." Nevertheless, an "angel of judgment,—whose mission was to punish the sins of the rising generation" is certainly not Sigourney's shrinking middle-class angel in the house. This probably made Hawthorne uneasy.[11] Insofar as Pearl can be read as the personification of a creative and rebellious tendency in his own "composition," a scarlet force that subverts middle-class socialization, perhaps Hawthorne himself tried to impose "a tender, but strict control" over his dragon child, but found, like Hester, that the task was beyond his skill. Yet Hawthorne does succeed in reprogramming her (and perhaps his own writing in the same way).

Hawthorne converts Pearl as he did the surviving dragon's-teeth warriors: he domesticates her in the most theatrical of circumstances. The "scene" is the scaffold with the scarlet trio on stage: Rev. Dimmesdale, Hester, and Pearl. Dimmesdale, to the approbation of his daughter, appears to acknowledge his paternity in full view of his flock:

Pearl kissed his lips. A spell was broken. The great scene of grief in which the wild infant bore a part, had developed all her sympathies; and as her tears fell upon her father's cheek, they were the pledge that she would grow up amid human joy and sorrow, nor forever do battle with the world, but be a woman in it. (1: 256)

The public gathering of her family as a family "humanizes" Pearl, like the grotesque apple trees in Hawthorne's orchard. Now she can be daddy's little girl, if only for a moment, for daddy—in what seems to be a parody of mid-nineteenth-century sentimental fatherhood—is about to perform a death scene.[12] We see that Pearl is "human" and can know "joy" again because, like a good girl, she weeps.

Harriet Beecher Stowe put Topsy, the "naughty" slave girl, through a similarly theatrical ideological conversion in *Uncle Tom's Cabin* (1852), which Stowe began publishing in serial form only one year after the appearance of *The Scarlet Letter*. Topsy, who inherits Pearl's naughtiness without her politics, creates domestic havoc and is in need of reformation. Since it "grieves" Eva, the white angel of the house, that Topsy is "so naughty," Stowe's little evaporating evangelist takes it upon herself, enacting the role of the middle-class mother, to subdue Topsy with sentiment and guilt ("I shan't live a great while . . . be good, for my sake"). Stowe has Topsy respond to Eva's entreaty with a torrential downpour of tears. Stowe's language of redemption reveals its debt to an ethnocentric discourse of "dark continent" colonization: "Yes, in that moment, a ray of real belief, a ray of heavenly love, had penetrated the darkness of her heathen soul!"[13] Eva displays the redemptive power of middle-class femininity just as Hawthorne's reunited family on a scaffold manifests the transformative power of middle-class domesticity. Ostensibly both Pearl and Topsy are "humanized," but more particularly they are tamed through the act of crying.

Rebellious little Pearl, it can be argued, gets a bum rap from this "humanizing" sleight of hand. Pearl's tears, we are told, should be read as her "pledge that she would grow up amid human joy and sorrow" and, moreover, that she would not "forever do battle with the world, but be a woman in it." To qualify as a "woman" is to pledge to refrain from "battle with the world."

Hawthorne was not consistently disaffected with *male* revolutionaries who did "battle with the world." Perseus, wielding Medusa's head, carries out a revolution by petrifying the evil King Polydectes and his court and then trots home to mother. Jason, in pursuit of the golden fleece, is also seen in a glowing light as an avenging revolutionary who seeks "to punish the wicked Pelias for wronging his dear father, and to cast him down from the throne, and seat himself there instead" (7: 332). Nonetheless it is Medea whose powerful magic puts the dragon to sleep so that Jason can pull its teeth. Her power automatically makes her an object of suspicion: "These enchantresses, you must know, are never to be depended upon" (7: 364). Perseus and Jason (who would be stumped without the aid of Medusa and Medea respectively) are lionized as heroic social actors, while Pearl is sketched as an imaginative brat, a little girl "all in disorder" (1: 91).

Let us return to the scaffold and ask: does Pearl's tearful union with her family "humanize" her (no longer a dragon's-teeth child more predatory than human) or *feminize* her in the manner prescribed by so many writers on domesticity? I would argue for the latter, that Hawthorne's ideological pearl of wisdom for his middle-class female readers is that you cannot rebel and be feminine at the same time.[14] In this ideological equation, to lose your femininity is to surrender your humanity.[15]

Hester is subjected to the same politics of representation and sleight of hand as her Pearl. We know, for instance, that Hester's isolation has been a radicalizing process, enabling her to roam beyond the premises policed by the puritan fathers: "She assumed a freedom of speculation, then common enough on the other side of the Atlantic, but which our forefathers, had they known it, would have held it to be a deadlier crime than that stigmatized by the scarlet letter" (1: 164). Yet Hawthorne never divulges the "deadlier" contents of this scarlet "speculation."

Of course, Hester's manifestly radical accomplishment is the "fertility and gorgeous luxuriance of fancy" shown in the embroidery of her letter, which went "greatly beyond what was allowed by the sumptuary regulations of the colony" (1: 53). One of the merciless "female spectators" of Hester on the scaffold is correct to recognize in her embroidery a refusal to obey to the letter. Hester is aware that her ideological function is to serve as a living stereotype not simply of sinfulness or adultery but of "woman's frailty and sinful passion" (1: 79). By taking liberties with her letter, by showing skill, intelligence, creativity, and pride rather than shame, she is engaged in a semiotic battle with a puritan patriarchy that seeks to regulate biological and ideological reproduction.[16]

This ideological reproduction is at one point symbolized as a mirror. In Governor Bellingham's mansion Hester views herself in the breast-plate of standing armor, a "convex mirror" which exaggerates the size of her letter so as to render it "the most prominent feature of her appearance" and to obscure her "behind it" (1: 106). The "mirror" is reminiscent of Aylmer's daguerreotype of Georgiana, which, like the alchemist's fixating imagination, reproduces only the "hand" where her "cheek should have been" (10: 45). Bellingham's mirror can be read as a symbol of the way the puritan fathers would like Hester to view herself and her transgression. Hester's "voluptuous" art, if anything, functions to parody this "convex" puritan vision. It is significant that it is the dragon's-teeth child who directs Hester to gaze into the mirror. Hawthorne represents this as another sign of Pearl's impishness and naughtiness; yet Pearl's action signals to her mother exactly how the puritan fathers will try to contort her vision of herself in the interview which is to follow.

Hester does well as a cultural critic, given the fact that her author, that ambivalent descendant of puritan administrators, granted her merely one letter of the alphabet to work with. Only one letter makes it difficult for Hester to lead what Margaret Fuller aspired to and achieved, a "life of letters."[17] She remains a seamstress rather than a lecturess or an authoress.[18] Hawthorne has this woman of one letter earn her living, not without irony, by adorning the puritan patriarchy. Her embroidery distinguishes those "dignified by rank or wealth" from "the plebian" (1: 82) and thus helps legitimize the authority of the "new government" (1: 82) that censured her.[19]

However empowering Hester's revolutionary thoughts may be for her, Hawthorne makes her pay for them: as she gains in vision, she loses her "looks." When we first see the scarlet woman she is like a Lady of Shalott or a magnificent Medusa before being transformed into a gorgon: "She had dark and abundant hair, so glossy that it threw off the sunshine with a gleam" (1: 53). On the scaffold this woman of vision exhibited "a burning blush, and yet a haughty smile, and a glance that would not be abashed" (1: 52–53). Hester confines her "rich and luxuriant hair" (1: 163) in a cap and increasingly entertains radical thoughts.[20] Hawthorne has this intellectual activity wither her looks, all within seven years. It is difficult not to think of the way Hawthorne may have perceived his recently deceased friend, Margaret Fuller, when he writes of Hester: "All the light and graceful foliage of her character had been withered up by this red-hot brand, and had long ago fallen away, leaving a bare and harsh outline, which might have been repulsive, had she possessed friends and companions to be repelled by it" (1: 163).[21] Hester, like a queen, is now "majestic and statue-like"; but she is no longer, Lord help her, someone Hawthorne deems fit to cuddle: her "bosom" offers no "pillow of Affection" (1: 163).

Hawthorne explains that her "marble coldness . . . was to be attributed to the circumstance that her life had turned, in a great measure, from passion and feeling, to thought" (1: 164). Then we learn of her egregious "freedom of speculation." All that sexy hair stuffed under her cap makes Hester not only think too much, but lose her femininity (her humanity): "She who has once been a woman, and ceased to be so, might at any moment become a woman again if there were only the magic touch to effect the transfiguration" (1: 164). If Hester, when free to "speculate," has perforce "ceased" to be a "woman," then what is she? Hawthorne's sleight of hand (his own crafty "magic touch") is here installing ideological criteria for what qualifies a female to be a "woman." Hester deviates from Hawthorne's discursive construction of "woman."

Hawthorne constructs "motherhood" as Hester's redemption. This conventional middle-class faith in the saving grace of Motherhood can also be seen in Horace Greeley's quip about Margaret Fuller (who had been one of his most successful columnists): "A good husband and two or three bouncing babies would have emancipated her from a great deal of cant and nonsense."[22] Hawthorne may have felt that one "bouncing" baby should be enough to drive the dragonism ("cant and nonsense") out of a radical woman. If not for Pearl, he assures us, the scarlet mother "might have come down to us in history, hand in hand with Anne Hutchinson, as the foundress of a religious sect. She might, in one of her phases, have been a prophetess" (1: 165). Just as sewing clothing may well have diverted Hester from unambiguously sowing broadcast the "dragon's teeth" in other forms, so does child rearing, which gave "the mother's enthusiasm of thought . . . something to wreak itself upon" (1: 165).

Yet it seems as if Pearl, from birth, has fired up her mother's radical "enthusiasm of thought." Her "fierce" reactions to the "little Puritans" who scorn them "had a kind of value, and even comfort, for her mother; because there was at least an intelligible earnestness in the mood, instead of the fitful caprice that so often thwarted her in the child's manifestations" (1: 94). Pearl's "fitful caprice," by contrast, often operates to "thwart" her mother's "enthusiasm of thought." This would seem to present us with an enigma. If Pearl's only "discoverable principle of being" is, as Hester tells Dimmesdale, "the freedom of a broken law" (1: 134), and if she takes the lead in repelling "little Puritans" who torment the wearer of the scarlet letter, why then does Pearl demand that her mother refasten the scarlet badge of puritan authority to her bosom in the forest, and kiss it when Hester gives in? I shall suggest later that this "perverse" tormenting of her mother and this expression of allegiance to a symbol of puritan authority be read as the Dimmesdale side of Pearl.

Hawthorne, despite what appears to be conflicting evidence about the effect of Pearl on Hester, wants his readers to regard sewing and motherhood as fulfilling the cultural function later attributed by Oliver Wendell Holmes to the piano. In *Elsie Venner* Holmes profiles women as naturally secretive, resentful, and dangerous—ready to combust. They possess, for some unprobed reason, a "stormy inner life" that demands "free utterance" in "words or song." He gratefully concludes: "What would our civilization be without the piano?"[23] Hawthorne, by invoking the mid-century construction of middle-class motherhood, frames the question somewhat differently: what would our civilization be without the safety valve of "motherhood"?

Hawthorne's more fundamental question underlying this one is: what would our middle-class civilization be without feminized women? By "our civilization" both Holmes and Hawthorne mean a "civilization" based on the unquestionable primacy of patriarchal authority ("our"). Defeminized behavior, more than sexual transgression per se, is what Hawthorne sees as the "deadlier" (1: 164) threat to the puritan patriarchs as well as to the middle-class "civilization" of his own day.

Although Hawthorne chooses not to disclose the details of Hester's scarlet "speculation," his allusion to the comprehensiveness of her vision of the revolutionary task before her is telling:

As a first step, the whole system of society is to be torn down, and built up anew. Then, the very nature of the opposite sex in its long hereditary habit, which has become like nature, is to be essentially modified, before women can be allowed to assume what seems a fair and suitable position. . . . woman cannot take fair advantage of these preliminary reforms, until she shall have undergone a still mightier change; in which, perhaps, the ethereal essence, wherein she has her truest life, will be found to have evaporated. (1: 165–66)

In his Hutchinson piece of 1830 Hawthorne maintained that a "false liberality . . . mistakes the strong division-lines of Nature for arbitrary distinctions."[24] But here, twenty years later, Hawthorne acknowledges that women and men inhabit "opposite" gender roles, which, though they become "like nature," are not quite "nature" ("hereditary habit") and can be changed. The phrasing does not specify what authority will at long last "allow" women to take up what "*seems* a fair and suitable position" (emphasis mine); nor does it spell out this new "position." Nevertheless, the radicalism here is in Hawthorne's suggestion that there is a vital *connection* between sex roles and specific forms of society. If sex roles change, everything changes, for these roles legitimize, enforce, and symbolize the larger "system," however unfree and contradictory this "system of society" may be. Hawthorne's perception of a link between gender reform and social change is, as we have seen, also overt in Coverdale's paranoid representation of Zenobia's catastrophic feminism ("oversetting all human institutions"). Defeminization leads not only to unlearning assumptions about gender but to dismantling assumptions undergirding patriarchal bourgeois constructs of "civilization" and "humanity." In this respect Hawthorne may well have made a connection between the "dragon's" mouth and a powerful force issuing from it that did indeed menace "civilization" as he knew it and wanted it to be.[25]

Hawthorne, then, may not have just been ambivalent about female sexuality or procreativity, or simply ambivalent about poetical and political "monsters" who deviate from prescribed roles; he may have felt distinctly uneasy about his own apocalyptic vision that "the whole system of society" as he knew it *had* to be "torn down" to set things right. Here Hawthorne is thinking expansively about why "our civilization," which implies a particular power structure, relies on the binary classification of "opposite" sexes. His theorizing resembles that of historian Joan W. Scott on the ways in which sexual difference becomes "one of the recurrent references by which political power has been conceived, legitimated, and criticized." What is at issue in Hawthorne's novel and his culture is not solely the control of women's bodies, behavior, and thinking, but in a more encompassing sense the "consolidation" of middle-class power and identity: in Scott's words, "The binary opposition and the social process of gender relationships both become part of the meaning of power itself; to question or alter any aspect threatens the entire system." [26] Paulina Wright Davis, the pioneer women's rights advocate who edited *The Una* in the early 1850's, also recognized this when, in 1870, she averred that the women's rights movement was "intended from its inception to change the structure, the central organization of society." [27]

The fundamental inquiry for both Hawthorne and Scott is the ideological use of "the feminine in the political order." Once sexual difference seems "sure and fixed, outside of human construction," it can be used ideologically to naturalize and therefore legitimize other social relations, such as class divisions and the unequal distribution of wealth and power. This is what Melville was thinking about five years later in "The Tartarus of Maids," when he hinted that nature and feminized women workers were being transformed into signs intended to advertise the presence of the factory as a wholesome American institution. On the cutting edge of Hawthorne's middle-class consciousness was some awareness that, as Scott maintains, "the concept of class in the nineteenth century relied on gender for its articulation." [28]

Of course, Hawthorne's sketch of Hester's revolutionary vision ("the whole system of society is to be torn down, and built up anew") could have been a good deal more specific. For it may have been a theoretical *abstraction* of criticisms launched by the members of female reform and benevolent associations. Hester is herself a one-woman benevolent association in Salem, aiding the poor, ministering to the sick, and counseling abused and confused women. Concomitantly she is, all wrapped into one, exactly the kind of woman whom mid-century benevolent associations sought to assist: a seamstress, a fallen woman, and, at the outset, a prisoner.

Barbara Berg has advanced the thesis that in these associations, which flourished between 1830 and the 1850's, one can locate important origins of American feminism. The women who volunteered for these associations were middle-class and upper-class, and one lesson they learned (perhaps like Hester) as they moved out of their conventional "spheres" was that middle-class "motherhood" had indeed privatized them. "Many a woman is lost to society" once she becomes a mother, concluded one reformer in 1852.[29] Coming face to face with exploited seamstresses, starving widows, and prostitutes, these reformers began not only to develop a sense of sisterhood with such women but to criticize *specific* structural contradictions that accounted for their plight.

In 1839, the year Hawthorne began work as a weigher and gauger of coal and salt at the Boston Custom House, one woman, a member of the Boston Seaman's Aid Society, wrote about the socioeconomic predicament of seamstresses. Her vision of the relationship between gender and exploitation is more focused than the revolutionary vision that Hawthorne attributes to Hester. "The irresistible influence of the Government, by its agents, is brought to operate directly to beat down the price of wages on the only kind of labor which a considerable class of females in every large city can perform." The year before, another member of the society observed in their publication: "The only means of earning money for those who cannot go out to labor in families, nor take in washing, is by needlework." They blamed not only government, and employers, but men for allowing this to happen: it is, charged another member, "a shame and disgrace for any one, who writes himself a *man*, to make a fortune out of the handy-work of poor females!"[30]

Hawthorne was not oblivious to this and may have been cognizant of criticisms leveled by these associations. Two years after he left his Boston Custom House post and one month after he published "The Birthmark," he published "The Procession of Life" (1843). In this sketch he describes a "crowd of pale-cheeked, slender girls, who disturb the ear with their multiplicity of short dry coughs" (10: 209). They are seamstresses who suffer under the rule of "master-tailors and close-fisted contractors" (10: 210). But what these reformers grasped, perhaps more firmly than Hawthorne, was that the feminization that had prevented them in their middle-class homes from being aware of such laboring-class realities was also the feminization that, by prohibiting women from being trained in and taking up a range of employments, created an ever-present female underclass, a well-stocked labor pool of easily exploited and, due to socialization, often docile wage slaves. A New York reformer, well aware of the *economic* reasons why some women often became prostitutes, wrote in the *Advocate of Moral Reform* (1846): "Women are thus limited to a few employments, hence these are over-stocked with laborers." Another woman, writing for the same periodical in 1836, acknowledged that men speak "in extravagant terms on the excellence of women," but for her this now evoked the economic ramifications of such pedestal elevation and incited her to rock the belle-tower by demanding: "How is her labor requited?"[31]

In their criticisms there is a developing awareness that gender is a social construct. "Does the delicate mother fear that I would make her daughters masculine?" inquired one moral reform member in 1846. "Does she mean by masculine—thoughtful, judicious, wise, learned, independent, self-respecting—I plead guilty."[32] By the 1840's some reformers recognized that "masculine," as a construct, encompassed a congeries of activities and experiences that all human beings were entitled to share in.

These women of letters were discovering not that they could, in spite of censure from the clergy and elsewhere, retain their "humanity" even if they engaged in public reform, but that this process was enabling them to *redefine* humanity and to appropriate it for themselves and for the women they aided, perhaps for the first time. For some reformers this meant that their notion of "humanizing" would have to clash with the bourgeois notion of "humanizing" that had been part of their socialization as middle-class feminine women. Like Hester, many of these women had learned these lessons by helping "deviant" women and recognizing their sisterhood with them. But unlike Hawthorne, many of these women reformers were able to give their readers detailed reports of *how* gender socialization helps to produce and legitimize certain economic conditions inimical to laboring women and why, therefore, certain ideological and economic systems in a class stratified society should indeed in Hawthorne's words "be torn down, and built up anew."

Hawthorne's resistance to Hester's rather abstract vision of structural social change is not only political but emotional: the delicate femininity ("truest life") he reveres must evaporate in the change. The process of feminine evolution that produces Priscilla and other "true" women would be reversed, perhaps leaving us with the likes of the "man-like" Queen Elizabeth and Anne Hutchinson.

Hence Hawthorne proposes another solution. If woman embraces her role as Heart, he advises, these complex problems will "vanish." Hester's defeminized heart "had lost its regular and healthy throb, [she] wandered without a clew in the dark labyrinth of mind" (1: 166). A fastidious heaven will not award the sacred role of "prophetess" to "a woman stained with sin, bowed down with shame, or even burdened with a life-long sorrow" (1: 263). Instead heaven, in its "own time," will send an angel to the house. This "apostle" will bring revelation rather than revolution; not an "angel of judgment" or an "exterminating angel," but an angel of domesticity: "The angel and apostle of the coming revelation must be a woman, indeed, but lofty, pure, and beautiful; and wise, moreover, not through dusky grief, but the ethereal medium of joy" (1: 263).

Anne Hutchinson, Margaret Fuller, Hester, and Zenobia, all grounded by their politics and passion, were no angels. If Hester possesses wings, they are bedaubed wings of scarlet. Through a sleight of hand presented as Hester's "revelation," the scarlet woman is made to read herself as did Hawthorne, the nineteenth-century, middle-class son of the puritans, and to acknowledge that, stained "with a life-long sorrow," her domestic wings have forever been clipped.

Hawthorne managed to yank Hester's dragon's teeth with a sleight of hand even more subtle than that which had her bow to the cultural supremacy of the angel in the house. In "The Custom House" Hawthorne's statement of objective seems innocent enough: in "dressing up" Surveyor Pue's brief history, he has issued himself an artistic license to imagine "the motives and modes of passion that influenced the characters who figure in it" (1: 33). In doing so, I suggest, he contributes to the construction of a middle-class psychological "self" and that it is this we must continue to problematize as we did in Chapter 1.[33] This notion becomes essential to the way his reader is encouraged to imagine not only the "self," but power and social authority. *The Scarlet Letter* is one of a number of "puritan" texts in which Hawthorne psychologizes the wielding of cultural power. Hawthorne's insight that gender roles, though they are represented to seem "like nature," are not natural, becomes the theoretical road not taken. I shall argue that Hawthorne's critical consciousness of the discursive production of the gendered self is made subordinate to the idea that desire is the defining factor of the "self," that desire is at the root of the drive to possess cultural power.

From the first we are exposed to a number of mild double entendres that analogize writing with desire. In the intellectually sterile Custom House "lettered intercourse" (1: 27) is rare. The collection of official documents disappoints Hawthorne as "worthless scratchings of the pen" (1: 28). Hawthorne's "dressing up" of Dimmesdale's "motives and modes of passion," however, may well have gratified his own "scratchings" by way of compensation. For the writing and desire analogy is conspicuous in Hawthorne's description of Dimmesdale's triumphant all-nighter spent composing his Election sermon: daylight found him "with the pen still between his fingers" (1: 225). This presumably more fluid version of the sermon was inked with "an impulsive flow of thought and emotion," and in spite of the good minister's doubt that "Heaven should see fit to transmit the grand and solemn music of its oracles through so foul an *organ-pipe* as he" (1: 225) (emphasis mine).[34]

Religion is consistently represented as a substitutive form of sexual expression for Dimmesdale and even some of his flock. Dimmesdale's "popularity" as preacher of the Word reflected his great "intellectual gifts, his moral perceptions, his power of experiencing and communicating emotion"; but all of these qualities "were kept in a state of preternatural activity by the prick and anguish of his daily life" (1: 141). His guilt, appropriately termed "prick and anguish," and his sexuality, sublimated through the Word, make him an impassioned preacher. He ignites the faith of his flock with a "Tongue of Flame" (1: 142). Hot stuff, we learn, for the pubescent "virgins of the church grew pale around him, victims of a passion so imbued with religious sentiment that they imagined it to be all religion, and brought it openly, in their white bosoms, as their most acceptable sacrifice before the altar" (1: 142). They get turned on, and Dimmesdale himself gets turned on, by his confessions that "he was altogether vile, a viler companion of the vilest." "They heard it all"—but not quite all—"and did but reverence him the more" (1: 144). Dimmesdale's confessions, like Hawthorne's rendition of Hester's revolutionary vision, stay *abstract*. D. H. Lawrence knew this game; the itchy minister gets the same substitutive pleasure out of flagellating himself by preaching in public as he does by mortifying his flesh in private: "It's a form of masturbation."[35]

Dimmesdale seems like a lubricious lad liberated from the pages of antimasturbation tracts of the 1830's and 1840's penned by Sylvester Graham, John Todd, and the Fowler brothers. As we have seen in Chapter 1, phrenological and antimasturbation authors advised readers on how to decode signs of a libidinal interiority that their own texts constructed and implanted as natural. Hawthorne has done what these writers did in their "manuals": he has locked up desire inside the self, privileged it as the essence of the self, and designated it as the explanatory key to the allegory of behavior. Note the language of interiority used to describe Dimmesdale, whose "Tongue of Flame" has been relighted in the forest by Hester:

> Before Mr. Dimmesdale reached home, his inner man gave him other evidence of a revolution in the sphere of thought and feeling. In truth, nothing short of a total change of dynasty and moral code, in that interior kingdom, was adequate to account for the impulses now communicated to the unfortunate and startled minister. At every step he was incited to do some strange, wild, wicked thing or other, with a sense that it would be at once involuntary and intentional, in spite of himself, yet growing out of a profounder self than that which opposed the impulse. (1: 217)

Dimmesdale surrenders to an "inner" man, an "interior kingdom," a "profounder self." This model of sexual interiority governs how he and we as readers imagine character and conceive of liberation. His "revolution," by the by, seems less ambitious than Hester's. The scarlet woman's speculative freedom pushes her toward questioning why the architects of a power structure would want to create and enforce sexual difference as a strategy to legitimize their authority. Dimmesdale's "revolution in the sphere of thought and feeling," on the other hand, arouses him to be naughty in public and private whenever he can get away with it.

Hawthorne's construction of the naughty psychological self also provides the theoretical basis for a cultural theory. Not only is Dimmesdale naughty and repressed, so are the governing puritans in several of Hawthorne's puritan tales. In "The Maypole of Merrymount" (1836), "Endicott and the Red Cross" (1838), and "Main-Street" (1849), desire underlies the puritans' motives for enforcing cultural power. Hawthorne's cultural theory resembles Freud's in " 'Civilized' Sexual Morality and Modern Nervousness" (1908), in which the father of psychoanalysis encodes "civilization" as a form of necessary sexual repression, but advises that this repression be made less severe. "Our civilization is, generally speaking, founded on the suppression of instincts."[36] Puritan semiotic control is represented by Hawthorne as symbiotic with sexual control.

In "The Maypole of Merrymount," for instance, the puritan whipping post gratifies unacknowledged libidinal satisfactions not all that different from the sexual desires that the merrymounters are being whipped for celebrating around the maypole. Cultural conflict is thus translated into a sexual power struggle. William Bradford's *Of Plymouth Plantation* and Thomas Morton's *New English Canaan*, as seventeenth-century accounts of the puritan suppression of the merrymounters, stress economic and religious causes. Hawthorne, writing within the bourgeois "deployment of sexuality" described by Foucault, psychologizes their motives.

In "Main-Street" Hawthorne implicates his own ancestor as he depicts Ann Coleman being dragged and whipped through the streets "naked from the waist upward": "A strong-armed fellow is that constable; and each time that he flourishes his lash in the air, you see a frown wrinkling and twisting his brow, and, at the same instant, a smile upon his lips. He loves his business, faithful officer that he is, and puts his soul into every stroke, zealous to fulfil the injunction of Major Hathorne's warrant, in the spirit and to the letter" (11: 70). One can almost imagine Hawthorne smiling when writing *The Scarlet Letter* and musing self-critically whether he was putting "his soul into every stroke, zealous to fulfil the injunction of Major Hathorne, in the spirit and to the letter." Hawthorne gives us puritan authorities, seemingly bound to the logic of Freud's "projection," who get turned on by punishing in others impulses they would publicly deny in themselves.[37]

Of course, this twist was one way for Hawthorne to handle his own ambivalence about those iron-faced practical ancestors who in his imagination scoffed at him as a writer of mere "story-books." Hawthorne's "Freudian" joke is on them and their collective unconscious. The repression model gives him a means of controlling how interiority is imagined by his readers and authorizes him to assign his puritan fathers subterranean (sexual) "motives."

Hawthorne's assumptions about interiority in *The Scarlet Letter* often seem closer to Freud's than to Foucault's or Joan Scott's. This privatized model of the self and of culture competes with and perhaps towers over Hester's more politicized understanding of gender identity as a construction and culture as the site of political struggle. Hawthorne seems to marginalize, if not quite dismiss, the insights of Hester into social construction theory as the misleading lessons of a scarlet letter that "had not done its office" (1: 166).

The final scaffold scene allows Hawthorne to return us to what I take to be his principal ideological scheme. The Pearl who throws stones and utters "witch's anathemas" at her little puritan persecutors is expressing the antagonistic fertility and political rebelliousness of her mother. Of course, her "sowing" is at last domesticated. But Pearl has also inherited the naughtiness of her father. One day Hester gazed into the little imp's eyes and "fancied that she beheld . . . a face, fiend-like, full of smiling malice, yet bearing the semblance of features that she had known full well, though seldom with a smile, and never with malice in them" (1: 97). The Pearl who delights in tormenting her mother with guilt is, in part, daddy's little girl. Once Pearl is domesticated on the scaffold, she is something other than socially rebellious or perversely naughty. Hawthorne's real "pearl" of wisdom is that domesticity "humanizes" both the maternal political self and the paternal psychological self in Pearl.

Perhaps the domestic theme is also what Hawthorne deploys to "humanize" these two theoretical tendencies in his art. When domesticity "humanizes" the self, for example, an extended criticism of gender and social structure in one's writing is rendered superfluous. At the same time, this process of domestic "humanizing" presumably diminishes one's susceptibility to the psychological creatures lurking in the darker regions that one has figured within one's text.

To conclude, the fundamental ideological project of *The Scarlet Letter* seems contradictory but self-consciously so: Hawthorne reinforces *and* problematizes the middle-class ideology that domesticity "humanizes." One can argue persuasively that the former tendency prevails over the latter in the climactic "humanizing" of a teary-eyed and heart-inflated Pearl on the scaffold and in Hester's own ironclad acknowledgment that she is disqualified to be a ministering "angel" of celestial "revelation." Yet the text also allows us to question the authority of its narration by wondering whether Hester would have been at all interested in sentimental "revelation" anyway. If *The Scarlet Letter* sets out to affirm motherhood as that which saves Hester from becoming Anne Hutchinson, the scarlet mother remains, nevertheless, an unorthodox mother. To make matters more complex, the scarlet family winds up not on a pedestal but on a scaffold. The image, despite the middle-class domestic message we might draw from it, is way off balance.[38]

Hawthorne states in his preface that by leaving the Salem Custom House for Home and Hearth he was able to transform his "snow-images into men and women" (1: 36). Yet he seems to have converted his snow-images into what Mrs. Oliphant and other contemporary reviewers saw as an almost unrecognizable group of misfits. Because Hester shattered the feminine stereotype, she was seen by some reviewers to be as shocking as any other character in the novel. Indeed, in 1852 Charles Hale profiled Hawthorne's unsentimental heroines in terms that conjure Hawthorne's three "dragon" women in "The Gorgon's Head": "They are all weird, and as much a creation of his fancy as the three sisters in MacBeth are Shakespeare's. . . . We never fell in love with such. In truth, they are not lovable; they are incomprehensible, and full of mystery."[39]

Hawthorne's "romance" did not sit right as a reassuringly domestic novel because it was not intended to. One half-expects Hester, given the odd tilt of the book, to contest the official "humanizing" (feminizing) ideology of the narrative with a counterargument. This argument could easily be what Hawthorne certainly recognized while penning his sometimes kinky "romance": that transgression, given the puritan or mid-nineteenth-century middle-class context, is what potentially makes a woman fully "human" (begrimed with "dusky grief").

6 Cleaning House

From the Gothic to the Middle-Class World Order

Cleaning house and scrubbing out the scarlet was Hawthorne's major ideological project in the second of his three novels of the early 1850's, *The House of the Seven Gables* (1851). To help clarify what I mean by this, let us return briefly to Hawthorne's earlier effort to concoct an interior pest-control, "Egotism; Or, the Bosom Serpent" (1843).

The fall in "Egotism" is into a hyperpsychological allegorical vision of the self which sees snakes in the place of hearts. The sentimental iconography of the heart has been displaced. How you "figure" out your wife governs, by implication, how you imagine yourself and everyone else. If she seems to fall, as a "serpent" *with* a "bosom," then everyone "falls" (harbors snakes in bosoms). Yet there is redemption for Roderick. At the conclusion of the tale Hawthorne invokes the ideology of middle-class domesticity as a "humanizing" force to squelch this psychologized (snake-infested) model of the self that we also see broached in *The Scarlet Letter*.

As in *The Scarlet Letter* the solution to being "unhumanized" is to be domesticized. Slithering in the grass, the snake-possessed Roderick hisses, "Could I, for one instant forget myself, the serpent might not abide in me" (10: 282). At this critical juncture Rosina enters their garden saying gently, "Forget yourself, my husband . . . forget yourself in the idea of another!" Then she gives him the magic touch of feminine love and, "if report be trustworthy, the sculptor beheld a waving motion through the grass." Presto, Roderick is humanized! "Rosina!" he wails. "Forgive! Forgive!" (10: 283).

Rosina is, please note, not merely any woman; she is the "ideal of gentle womanhood" (10: 270). As the personification of domestic discourse, Rosina is none other than the angel in the house who has returned to reclaim home and garden as a prelapsarian Eden with no serpents allowed. When the "bosom friend" dismisses the "bosom fiend" as a "dark fantasy," she beams "a heavenly smile" (10: 283). It was she who "was indissolubly interwoven with that of a being whom Providence seemed to have unhumanized" (10: 270). As a figuration of ideal womanhood, Rosina redeems her dangerously self-referential allegorist from a figuration of the self that locks him into a psychologized way of seeing.

But Hawthorne leaves us with an unexamined contradiction. Domesticity is the solution, but it is also a probable cause of Roderick's ambivalent attachment to and identification with snakes. Roderick began to exhibit the symptoms of a serpent after Rosina separated from him. Yet early on we learn that "his shattered schemes of domestic bliss" were "wilfully shattered by himself" (10: 271). I have already suggested that Roderick's "envy" of Rosina lead to his stereotyping her as "the foulest of all created things." Her return as a domestic angel merely locks her into a different stereotype of sexual difference. At the conclusion, one stereotype of woman is magically endowed with the power to evict the other: the angel-with-a-bosom expels the serpent-with-a-bosom. When Rosina counsels Roderick to "forget yourself in the idea of another," she might as well have said, forget yourself in the idea of an "other."

As we shall see, it was important for Hawthorne to work on this "idea of" an other in another context, because as early as 1843 he thematizes what may have been his own effort to move out of a fiendishly creative psychologized allegorical vision and into a more conventionally domestic one. But to do so less contradictorily he would have to "humanize" Rosina herself without allowing her to lose her magic touch or her wings. The trick would be to naturalize the "other" as "other." This winged woman, *without* the bite, would function as the symbolic vehicle for his own narrative and figurative migration from a psychologized to a more sanitized domestic discourse with its own sentimental vision of the self.

Hawthorne's *Seven Gables* reworks a number of themes and images broached in "Egotism."[1] The most important similarity is that in the novel Hawthorne elaborates what is at stake in redeeming a domestic worldview from a gothic or psychological vision—what I have called pest-control. In both works Hawthorne is engaged in a monologue with himself and is writing about what kind of cultural discourse he wishes to employ and why.

Hawthorne's self-reflexivity is evident in the description of the house of the seven gables, itself a symbol of discourse. We learn that in the seventeenth century Colonel Pyncheon used his influence in the legislature to expropriate the property of Matthew Maule, a carpenter, in order to build his own house upon it. Hawthorne makes its façade suggestively literary: "Its whole visible exterior was ornamented with quaint figures, conceived in the grotesqueness of a Gothic fancy" (2: 11). (One might have said that Roderick's bosom fiend also was conceived with "Gothic fancy.") Its chief carpenter, it so happens, is none other than the son of the dispossessed and persecuted Matthew Maule, who, with help from the hue and cry of the land-grabbing colonel, had been executed for witchcraft. Yet Hawthorne remains chief architect of this grotesque "Gothic fancy," and it is clear that he sees it in part as a house of fiction, a structure symbolizing his own gothic conventions. Colonel Pyncheon's "common-sense" led him to dismiss the notion of some that his stately mansion was at risk having been built over "an unquiet grave" (2: 9). But "Gothic fancy" prevails as the commonsensical Pyncheon seemingly falls prey to the curse of the condemned "wizard," Maule, that "God will give him blood to drink!" (2: 8).

Hawthorne's use of the gothic is twofold. One strategy is to gothicize unjust social authority as a means of dismantling it. For example, he uses the gothic to criticize or parody the capitalist personality.[2] Judge Pyncheon, the mid-nineteenth-century capitalist descendant of the aristocratic Colonel Pyncheon, inherits his ancestor's "common-sense" and has no stock in "ghost stories" (2: 279). Yet he too is literally gagged with the same bloody ink. Hawthorne makes the gothic, as manifested in Maule's curse, the secret weapon of the working class. Even before the judge's own gothic demise, however, Hawthorne uses the gothic as a kind of x-ray vision to expose his hidden reality. He reconstructs the judge as a gothic edifice, like Poe's "House of Usher," in which there "may lie a corpse, half-decayed, and still decaying, and diffusing its death-scent all through the palace! The inhabitant will not be conscious of it; for it has long been his daily breath!" (2: 230). Sometimes, however, a "seer" can look through this "marble palace" of the self to "the hidden nook, the bolted closet, with the cobwebs festooned over its forgotten door, or the deadly hole under the pavement, and the decaying corpse within" (2: 230). The gothic interior, once constructed, haunts this greedy capitalist. Gothic conventions here serve the same function as Holgrave's daguerreotype, which "actually brings out the secret character" (2: 91) of Judge Pyncheon.[3]

Of course, the gothic "brings out" the "truth" it installs. Gothic conventions authorize Hawthorne the romancer, not unlike Maule the wizard, to inflict a psychological curse on those grasping mercantile monkeys whose sole desire is to accumulate "ill-gotten gold, or real estate" (2: 2). The gothic permits him to situate a tarn at the foundation of their so-called "real" estate and watch it sink. Just when unholy social authority thinks it has covered up cracks and contradictions, Hawthorne's avenging gothic, like a return of the repressed, rips them asunder.

Despite its serviceable conventions, the gothic is also a discourse that Hawthorne seeks to move beyond. Thus, its second function is to suggest a way of seeing that must be transcended. Hawthorne may well have been thinking about the fictional structures of his own grotesque "Gothic fancy" when the narrator observes that "The old house . . . had both the dry-rot and the damp-rot in its walls; it was not good to breathe no other atmosphere than that" (2: 174). Holgrave likewise condemns the house as oppressing his "breath with its smell of decaying timber" (2: 214). This gothic odor seems to have a peculiarly psychological effect on the occupants of the house and, as such, threatens to foul domesticity itself. With the malodorous seven gables in mind, the overwrought Clifford generalizes that "Morbid influences, in a thousand-fold variety, gather about hearths, and pollute the life of households. There is no such unwholesome atmosphere as that of an old home, rendered poisonous by one's defunct forefathers and relatives" (2: 261).

This "unwholesome atmosphere," whether fictional or architectural, can be especially deleterious for women. Hepzibah, for example, has become gothicized and emaciated like a Poe heroine, though lacking Ligeia's beauty or intelligence: she is "a tall figure, clad in black silk, with a long and shrunken waist" (3: 32). Her mind has contracted as well, for she "had grown to be a kind of lunatic, by imprisoning herself so long in one place, with no other company than a single series of ideas, and but one affection, and one bitter sense of wrong" (2: 174).

In several instances the narrator expresses the fear that the flower-like Phoebe will be blighted by the same gothic privatized fate. Poe's pastoral Berenice, once snared by the gothic, was shriveled up, buried alive, and had her teeth yanked in the bargain. The narrator's anxiety for Phoebe, however, is that she will endure etiolation, like Georgiana. If Phoebe had not been able to alight from the seven gables to enjoy other diversions, "we should soon have beheld our poor Phoebe grow thin, and put on a bleached, unwholesome aspect, and assume strange, shy ways, prophetic of old-maidenhood and a cheerless future" (2: 175). Even Hepzibah, herself a gothic parody, warns Phoebe not to "fling away" her "young days in a place like this. Those cheeks would not be so rosy, after a month or two. Look at my face!" (2: 74). Hawthorne sets up a contest between the power of Phoebe and that of this gothic structure. Will Phoebe, like Berenice or Madeline Usher, "fade, sicken, sadden, and grow into deformity, and be only another pallid phantom?" (2: 297). Will she be wilted by the gothic and inhale the malodorous and morbid atmosphere, or retain her "flower-fragrance" (2: 174) and sentimental charm? For Hawthorne this is tantamount to a battle between two discourses, two ways of seeing: gothic-psychological versus domestic.

Phoebe is no pushover. She has, like a best-selling domestic novelist, a homely version of the Midas touch. This domestic alchemist is able "to move in the midst of practical affairs, and to gild them all—the very homeliest, were it even the scouring of pots and kettles—with an atmosphere of loveliness and joy" (2: 80). Such qualities proved profitable, and perhaps Hawthorne hoped that her Midas touch, in lieu of Medusa's head, would line his wallet as well.[4] The cakes she baked to sell in Hepzibah's shop resembled "some of the bread which was changed to glistening gold, when Midas tried to eat it" (2: 100). She assures Hepzibah, "I am as nice a little saleswoman, as I am a housewife!" (2: 78).

Phoebe, like a good domestic novelist, possesses the power to feminize the house into a home, "that very sphere which the outcast, the prisoner, the potentate . . . instinctively pines after—a home!" She *situates* those she touches. In her "grasp, soft as it was, you might be certain that your place was good in the whole sympathetic chain of human nature" (2: 141). When Phoebe instinctively repels Judge Pyncheon's effort to plant his lecherous kiss on her lips, the narrator tells us that she had to "smother . . . her intuitions as to Judge Pyncheon's character" or else "the universe were thereby tumbled headlong into chaos" (2: 131–32). What Phoebe is unconscious of is her own symbolic role as a homemaker whose job is to prevent the psychological universe of men from tumbling "headlong into chaos." The homemaker is a psychological universemaker. True to her name she is the moon shining upon the domestic world order. Through Phoebe, Hawthorne is inventing a source of enlightenment as well as articulating the cultural uses of and need for a distinctively middle-class femininity.[5]

Hawthorne invents Phoebe to fumigate the malodorous damp rot and dry rot of the gothic. She is a disinfectant of the mind, a psychological deodorizer. Her aerosol qualities read like before-and-after advertisement copy for Lysol: "the heavy, breathless scent which Death had left in more than one of the bed-chambers . . . these were less powerful than the purifying influence scattered throughout the atmosphere of the household by the presence of one, youthful, fresh, and thoroughly wholesome heart. There was no morbidness in Phoebe" (2: 137). Nor apparently was there any sweat: "Fresh was Phoebe, moreover, and airy and sweet in her apparel; as if nothing that she wore . . . had ever been put on, before; or, if worn, were all the fresher for it, and with a fragrance as if they had lain among the rose buds" (2: 168).

Like an oxygen tank, Phoebe supplied Clifford, "her poor patient," with "purer air" and "impregnated it, too, not with a wild-flower scent— for wildness was no trait of hers—but with the perfume of garden-roses, pinks, and other blossoms." Her "wholesome" therapy was predicated on ignoring that which was "morbid in his mind and experience" (2: 143). Phoebe, like Rosina, breaks the circuitry of gothic introspection in the beleaguered male. Clifford, like Roderick, had been "compelled to inhale the poison" of his "own breath, in infinite repetition" (2: 143). This garden-variety therapist is able to release Clifford from "too close an introspection," the only thing, the narrator warns us, which can puncture that domestic bubble "called happiness" (2: 158). The narrative of how Phoebe sanitizes Clifford's emotions leads us from one set of conventions to another. Clifford's recuperation parallels that of Hawthorne's own discourse.

Till finally we realize who Phoebe is after all: the charmingly rural, upwardly mobile, middle-class angel in the house. Her genius for ignoring the complexity and depth of Clifford's shattered psychological state is praised as the "heaven-directed freedom of her whole conduct" (2: 143). As a symbol of domestic salvation she is tantamount to "a Religion in herself" (2: 168). Phoebe is nominated "angel" in several passages.[6] The narrator's initial profile of Phoebe represents her as "fresh" and "unconventional," but she is in fact an advice-book construct of domestic femininity, a convention to the core. Part of the convention is that she appear perfectly natural. Within the space of a few paragraphs we read, "Such a flower was Phoebe" (2: 143) and "She was real!" (2: 141). But her "rose buds" (2: 168) nature is as natural as the rose buds mechanically stamped on letter-writing paper piled high by the bleached factory operatives in Melville's "Tartarus." Phoebe's cultural mission is to serve as a convention. Clifford

> read Phoebe, as he would a sweet and simple story; he listened to her as if she were a verse of household poetry, which God, in requital of his bleak and dismal lot, has permitted some angel, that most pitied him, to warble in his house. She was not an actual fact for him, but the interpretation of all that he lacked on earth, brought warmly home to his conception; so that this mere symbol, or lifelike picture, had almost the comfort of reality. (2: 142)

Skimming "household poetry" and reading women are culturally inseparable: the former encodes the latter. Hawthorne is suggesting that Phoebe can be of far greater cultural and psychological use to the Cliffords of the world as a deodorized, discursive construct, a "lifelike" angel, than as a woman who sweats, smells, and suffers conflicts of her own. Phoebe's response on one occasion, "I am no angel, Uncle Venner" (2: 221), is like Priscilla's rejoinder to Coverdale, "there is substance in these fingers of mine. . . . Why do you call me a dream?" But neither Phoebe nor Priscilla develop any critical resistance to warbling like angels.[7]

Hawthorne reintroduces some of his monstrous women of the early 1840's to redeem them as Phoebe (scrubbing out the scarlet). As the "true New England woman" (2: 73–74) Phoebe is a safe indigenous flower, rather than the more ambiguous Italianate Rappacini variety. Phoebe knows enough not to fraternize with poisonous flowers, nor to stick her nose into their poisonous "leaves." She spends her days, quite properly, conversing with hens. Thus Phoebe's "sweet breath" contrasts powerfully with Beatrice Rappacini's ostensible breath of death. Phoebe, unlike Beatrice and Georgiana, is not sexy, and she is classified as "very pretty" rather than "beautiful" (2: 80). Since her desirability has been deodorized, both for Holgrave and the reader, one can safely read about "the virginal development of her bosom" (2: 141) and her maidenly blush signifying "womanhood" (2: 220). If Georgiana's blush drives Aylmer to distraction, one perceives right away that Phoebe's "bud is a bloom!" (2: 220). Phoebe can be represented as safely human because she has been veiled in flower and angel metaphors.

If men desire her, it will be a sanitized desire; they will desire her sweet-smelling qualities rather than her "poisonous" charm or her alluring "hand." Phoebe is Hawthorne's textual reconstruction of the kind of woman domestic advice books would have men desire. She harbors no "wildness" (2: 143), "no riddles" (2: 144), and no bosom fiends. Hester thinks too much and has suffered too much sorrow, and is thus disqualified for angelhood, whereas Phoebe is allowed to mature because when she does grow "thoughtful" (2: 143) she merely droops. Conceiving revolutionary thoughts and drooping are qualitatively different responses to mental maturation. Phoebe has no bite.

But Phoebe is more than an elaborated portrait of Rosina. She scrubs out the gothic and dispels dusky grief; however, unlike her predecessor, she clearly serves as an advertisement for middle-class domesticity and for the emerging middle class itself. What Hepzibah at first regarded as a fault in Phoebe, Hawthorne recodes as a middle-class virtue: "What a nice little body she is! If she could only be a lady, too!" (2: 79). Phoebe's failure to be a "lady" is a sign of her naturalness and femininity. "Instead of discussing her claim to rank among ladies," Hawthorne's narrator instructs us, "it would be preferable to regard Phoebe as the example of feminine grace and availability combined, in a state of society, if there were any such, where ladies did not exist" (2: 80).

Colonel Pyncheon's largesse consists of an egotistical show of wealth, whereas Phoebe's largesse is made manifest as a spritz of domestic "atmosphere." Phoebe's middle-class feminine qualities bear parallels to those Nancy Armstrong sees emerging in eighteenth-century English conduct books for women. The discursive construction of Phoebe's qualities in effect render "her capable of authorizing a whole new set of economic practices that directly countered what were supposed to be seen as the excesses of a decadent aristocracy."[8]

In the 1840's and early 1850's the "excesses of a decadent aristocracy" were much on Hawthorne's mind.[9] Hawthorne's sketch for children of "Queen Christina" (1842), for instance, is not simply an account of one woman's unconventional life as ruler of Sweden; it is a cautionary tale for "quiet little Emily" that pits the virtues of middle-class femininity against aristocratic perversions of gender. "If we have any little girls among our readers, they must not suppose that Christina is set before them as a pattern of what ought to be." Instead the tale is "profitable" inasmuch as it demonstrates "the evil effects of a wrong education" (6: 275). When Christina, the Swedish princess, failed to cringe, like a little girl should, at the discharge of a "cannon," her father, King Gustavus, delighted by her mettle, decided to award her the benefits of a boy's education. Like Queen Zenobia of Palmyra, Christina was instructed in the arts, sciences, and languages, and was taught how to hunt; but she was deprived of those far more seminal lessons which cultivate the "delicate graces and gentle virtues of a woman" (6: 281). Through Christina, as negative exemplar, Hawthorne seeks to replace the girlish fantasy of princess-in-a-castle with that of the middle-class girl by her hearth: "No little girl, who sits by a New England fireside, has cause to envy Christina in the royal palace at Stockholm" (6: 281).

The sentences mount against her. Like Hester on the scaffold, Christina, who ascended the throne at age six, ruled independently with a "fierce and haughty look" rather than "soft and gentle looks" (6: 282). When somewhat older she retitled herself King Christina because "queen" "implied that she belonged to the weaker sex" (6: 282). Perhaps her most egregiously unfeminine behavior became evident after she, still a young woman, abdicated. "She wore no gloves," we are informed, "and so seldom washed her hands, that nobody could tell what had been their original color" (6: 283). Imagining her dirty-handed is what truly shocks the "timid, quiet and sensitive" (and middle-class) Emily. "I never could have loved her. . . . It troubles me to think of her unclean hands!" Through Emily, who has a "love of personal neatness" (6: 283), Hawthorne's conduct-book tale espouses a fastidious middle-class femininity that recoils from the "bold and masculine character" attributed to Christina. The message is clear: not only can aristocracy corrupt, it can ungender little women. "Happy are the little girls of America," we are counseled, "who are brought up quietly and tenderly, at the domestic hearth, and thus become gentle and delicate women!" (6: 283). The middle-class home-and-garden enables little girls to grow naturally and thereby to blossom, like Phoebe, as "true" women.

Hawthorne was writing in a tradition of biographical conduct-literature for girls that both acknowledged and reproved assertive aristocratic women. Thus, in *Sketches of the Lives of Distinguished Females* (1833) by "An American Lady," we find recognition of Queen Zenobia's accomplishments, but also censure for her discontent "with a small kingdom": " 'Ambition, my dear children,' replied Mrs. Grenville, 'was the cause of her downfall.' "[10] Queen Elizabeth provides Mrs. Grenville's girls with a case study of the link between aristocratic and unfeminine behavior. Although "none ever surpassed Elizabeth" in her public role as Queen, in her forceful "private character" growing girls "have nothing left to admire." The republican and feminine response is meant to shape that of the reader's: "'How glad I am,' exclaimed Marion, 'that I am an American, and am not forced to kneel to any human being.'" Despite the admission that Queen Christina "was one of the most extraordinary women that perhaps ever existed," the lesson Mrs. Grenville wishes her girls to glean is expressed by the domestic platitude, "'woman shines but in her proper sphere;' and whatever may be her talents or education, qualities or situation, if she step beyond the boundaries of her sex, she becomes ridiculous and disgusting to every well-regulated mind."[11]

Here, too, a specifically middle-class political message is symbiotic with the lesson on proper feminine behavior. Mrs. Grenville, concluding with Queen Christina, announces that the sketches to follow will be of "women in private life, among whom there is found more piety, more true excellence, and more exalted models of what women should be, than is generally exhibited in the contaminating crowd of courts, in the palaces of Kings, on the thrones of empires."[12] Domestic propriety is the test of "true" womanhood.

Cautionary biographical studies were written for young women as well as for girls. In 1841 Sarah Hale published "An Evening's Conversation About Autographs" in Godey's. Young Ellen and her cousin Charles discuss which autographs of famous women they would most like to see. When Charles nominates Queen Elizabeth, his very proper cousin launches into a mild diatribe on behalf of sexual difference: "She should have been a man, for she really had great talents for government, and was, for those iron times, a very good sort of despot to her people. But I never can bear to think of her as one of my own sex; for there was scarcely a trait of womanly feeling or affection to love in her whole long career."[13] These gender presuppositions correspond to Hawthorne's in The Scarlet Letter when he refers to the "man-like Elizabeth" who "had been the not altogether unsuitable representative of her sex" (1: 50). In Hale's compendious Woman's Record (1855), dedicated gratefully to the "Men of America," she offers a more laudatory account of the scholarly Queen Christina than does Hawthorne, but she cautions that Christina "should be a warning to all those aspiring females, who would put off the dignity, delicacy, and dress of their own sex."[14] Given the strictures evident in sketches of this sort, it is not surprising that Hawthorne, especially in Blithedale, envisioned advocates of women's rights as both imperious aristocrats and rebels, who, like "Queen" Zenobia, transgressed middle-class feminine behavior.[15]

Two aristocratic "ladies" are brutally subdued in *The House of the Seven Gables* so that Phoebe can be put securely in their place as the middle-class, republican, feminine ideal. Hawthorne's narrator plays the role of a middle-class sansculotte in humiliating and humbling Hepzibah Pyncheon, "A lady—who had fed herself from childhood with the shadowy food of aristocratic reminiscences, and whose religion it was, that a lady's hand soils itself irremediably by doing ought for bread" (2: 37). This hatchet job is unrelentingly cruel. Hepzibah, forced to open her store, is seen from various points of view as an "aristocratic hucksteress" (2: 79), "a mildewed piece of aristocracy" (2: 54), and, the narrator himself striking below the belt, a "time-stricken virgin" (2: 34) who never "knew, by her own experience, what love technically means" (2: 32). Hawthorne uses Holgrave to formulate the moral Hepzibah must acknowledge: "These names of gentlemen and lady had a meaning, in the past history of the world," he lectures her, but now "they imply not privilege, but restriction!" (2: 45). With a "friendlier smile" the young radical concludes, "I will leave you to feel whether it is not better to be a true woman, than a lady" (2: 45).

Hepzibah converts to this discourse when, behind the counter, she recognizes that America's new aristocrats are the consumers. When "a lady, in a delicate and costly summer garb" floats by, the humbled Hepzibah muses, "Must the whole world toil, that the palms of her hands may be kept white and delicate?" (2: 55). Hawthorne's most venomous assault on this gothic aristocrat, however, is his representation of her as too grotesque to be termed merely ugly. A frightful Medusa figure, Hepzibah is made all scowl with no power. Thus Hawthorne's narrator acidly apologizes for introducing her as a heroine of romance, "not a young and lovely woman, nor even the stately remains of beauty . . . but a gaunt, sallow, rusty-jointed maiden, in a long-waisted silk gown, and with the strange horror of a turban on her head! Her visage is not even ugly" (2: 41). On this basis Hawthorne's narrator excuses Clifford, the lover of the beautiful, for feeling that he owes her "nothing" for her kindness: "so yellow as she was, so wrinkled, so sad of mien . . . and that most perverse of scowls contorting her brow" (2: 109). The shrunken spinster, undomestic, unbeautiful, and unloved ("technically" or otherwise), is shamelessly distorted in a funhouse mirror shaped by Hawthorne.

The other aristocratic "lady" to be savagely punished is the beautiful and proud Alice Pyncheon. Alice is the heroine of the story that Holgrave narrates to Phoebe. In his tale, Matthew Maule, grandson of the original Maule, is summoned before the arrogant Mr. Pyncheon to cut a deal if he will reveal the whereabouts of the Pyncheon land grant to vast northern territories. The scene is a bout between the supercilious aristocracy and the still resentful working class. Maule consents to entertain the possibility of a bargain on condition that Pyncheon involve his lovely daughter, Alice. To which Pyncheon rejoins: "What can my daughter have to do with a business like this?" (2: 200). This is precisely what Hawthorne wishes us to ponder.

"If ever there was a lady born," observes Holgrave's narrator, "and set apart from the world's vulgar mass by a certain gentle and cold stateliness; it was this very Alice Pyncheon" (2: 201). Alice's aristocratic femininity, Maule quickly realizes, plays a symbolic role in defining the "vulgar mass" as such. Her femininity, like her father's fine wines and paintings, helps construct, reinforce, and legitimize the very idea of the aristocracy as an order of being superior to the working class. Thus her femininity plays a subtle political role.[16]

Having been beckoned by her father, Alice gives, not sexual, but "artistic" approval of "the remarkable comeliness, strength, and energy of Maule's figure." Maule, however, does not relish being surveyed like a horse. It was "that admiring glance," admiring yet unthinkingly condescending, which "the carpenter never forgave" (2: 201). The transaction is rife with what Richard Sennett and Jonathan Cobb have called, in their book of that title, "the hidden injuries of class," all of which are magnified by the acutely defensive carpenter. Holgrave's narrative asides accentuate this barbed defensiveness: " 'Then, Mistress Alice,' said Matthew Maule, handing a chair—gracefully enough, for a craftsman—'will it please you only to sit down, and do me the favor (though altogether beyond a poor carpenter's deserts) to fix your eyes on mine!' " (2: 201–2). Maule makes Alice his mesmeric subject because he knows that Alice not only is her father's greatest treasure but *symbolically* sanitizes his apparent right to grab as much treasure as he can. Thus Maule takes revenge on her ladyhood as a symbolic means of waging class warfare.

Hawthorne, as in "The Birth-mark," self-consciously alludes to *The Tempest* to suggest the complexity of the problem. As worker, Maule is Caliban symbolically raping Miranda; but as mesmerist, he is Prospero righting a wrong. Maule-as-mesmerist is also a gothic author treating his heroine in a heavy-handed manner; and through him perhaps we can detect Hawthorne reflecting on his own occasional heavy-handedness. In certain respects Maule's "experiment" (2: 204) is a rewriting of

Aylmer's manipulation of Georgiana: "Alas, for the beautiful, the gentle, yet too haughty Alice! . . . A will, most unlike her own, constrained her to do its grotesque and fantastic bidding" (2: 208). The vindictive "stage-manager" (2: 189) manhandles his aristocratic puppet as Hawthorne manhandles Hepzibah. Submissive to every "grotesque and fantastic bidding" of her mesmeric "despot," the dejected and now humbled Alice is summoned to the bridal party of a "laboring-man," Maule himself, to pay her respects. The "penitent" Alice, showing true nobility, kisses his bride "with a smile, all steeped in sadness" (2: 210). Returning home, through snow and rain, Alice "wasted" away. In an epigraph worthy of "The Birth-mark," Holgrave moralizes, "He meant to humble Alice, not to kill her; but he had taken a woman's delicate soul into his rude gripe, to play with;—and she was dead!" (2: 210). Maule gnashes his teeth, of course, because his real battle is with the class structure rather than with an individual woman whose aristocratic graces help to symbolize and uphold it.[17]

At the conclusion of his tale Holgrave realizes that he has fallen in love with Phoebe Pyncheon, and we in turn recognize Phoebe's own hypnotic womanhood as a symbol of her emerging class. It is Phoebe's endearing susceptibility to his mesmerizing storytelling power that has thoroughly enchanted the "lawless" (2: 85) storyteller. During the course of the "romance" she has matured into a mid-century Harmonia capable of converting dragon's-teeth soldiers into profitable family men. Holgrave is the "placeless," liminal young man of advice-book fame, who, by his very liminality, "represents the threat of social disorder, the dangers of formlessness."[18] Phoebe, unlike her scarlet predecessor, demonstrates the "imperial power" that enables a mother "to lodge a kind of portable parent deep within a child's personality"; but here her socializing power is deployed to uplift Holgrave.[19] She degothicizes Holgrave, domesticizes him, and ushers him out of his identification with his working-class ancestors, the Maules, and into the rising middle class.[20] In "The Old Manse" domesticity is symbolized by the "cheerful coat of paint, and golden-tinted paper-hangings" that paper over an interior "blackened" with smoke and "the grim prints of Puritan ministers" whose "sooty fierceness" made them look like "bad angels" (10: 5). Domesticity replaces the gothic past with a purified present. Phoebe's conventional presence, rather than any intellectual persuasion, effects Holgrave's transformation. Phoebe could just as easily have proclaimed to Holgrave what Rosina promises Roderick: "The past, dismal as it seems, shall fling no gloom upon the future" (10: 283).

Catherine Sedgwick, the celebrated author of *Home* (1836) and domestic advice books and Hawthorne's Berkshires neighbor while he was writing his romance, praised " 'Little Phoebe' " as the one redeeming force within Hawthorne's gabled "Gothic fancy." This is not surprising since in *Home* she praised Mrs. Barclay for establishing "a disinfecting principle in the moral atmosphere of the house."[21] Her criticism of *Seven Gables* echoes Mrs. Oliphant's animadversions of Hawthorne's psychological case studies. "The book is an affliction," Sedgwick wrote. "It affects one like a passage through the wards of an insane asylum, or a visit to specimens of morbid anatomy." Hawthorne's "little Phoebe," as "the ideal of a New England, sweet-tempered, 'accomplishing' village girl" mitigates the horror of our overexposure to "the raw head and bloody bones" of her author's "imagination." Phoebe's domestic alchemy is likened to the "elixirs, cordials, and all the kindliest resources of the art of fiction" that we need to endure "the tragedy of life." What Sedgwick omits is an acknowledgment of her own middle-class identification with Phoebe's upwardly mobile political mission.[22]

In full recognition of his bosom friend, Holgrave becomes "Wholesome." Only then do we comprehend that Phoebe's main political role is not only to displace the aristocracy but to "humanize" the working class. She helps to recategorize the world as one divided, not into competing classes (Parker's "heads" and "hands"), but into "true" women and "true" men. Once this shift in categories is accomplished, the middle class can authorize its own range of social behaviors and practices as "natural" and "human," rather than as class specific. Phoebe unknowingly personifies the political and cultural agenda of the middle-class cult of domesticity, as analyzed by historian Nancy Cott: "In the attempt to raise a democratic culture almost all types of classification had to be rejected, except the 'natural' ones such as sex (and race). . . . The division of spheres supplied an acceptable kind of social distinction. Sex, not class, was the basic category."[23] In order to orchestrate this ideological category shift, advice-book proponents of middle-class domesticity had to construct the "common identity of the domestic 'American lady' (not the aristocratic lady) for all."[24] They had to construct a Phoebe. These constructs, as Sarah Grimké recognized, were "a kind of machinery, necessary to keep the domestic engine in order, but of little value as the *intelligent* companions of men."[25]

Phoebe's conversion of Holgrave to Wholesome is a double coup, for Holgrave is both a descendant of the gothic (Maule the "wizard" had an "evil eye") and a representative of trendy radical thought. Both the gothic and radicalism, especially Fourierism, cast shadows on the sunlight of the family. In "Egotism" Hawthorne registers the unsettling possibility that bosom serpents grow not only in the home but *because* of the home. Mid-century American gothic tales and Fourierist criticisms of domesticity suggested this as well.

Poe's "The Black Cat" (1843), published in the same year as "The Birth-mark" and "Egotism," is a gothic tale told by a monomaniac. In his compulsion to kill a black cat, the monomaniacal narrator instead buries his axe in the brain of his wife. Poe luridly hints that it was the wife he was after all along. When the police inspect his cellar, the killer, subject to a return of the repressed, is overtaken by the impulse to strike the wall that entombs his wife. At first he hears "the sobbing of a child," and then a "shriek, half of horror and half of triumph" emerged from the wife. It was the wail of the gothic black cat, of course, buried alive on her head. Poe's representation of masculinity-at-home flies in the face of the middle-class ethos of self-control, self-reliance, and self-making that the wife and home were expected to reproduce. This tale, we are told, is a "wild, yet most homely narrative," just a "series of mere household events."[26] Poe's gothic, in other words, is also domestic.

The ideology of the home as a unifying force in the culture is also shattered in Poe's "The Fall of the House of Usher" (1839), in which a house is split asunder. Overflowing with anatomical connotations its "fissure" reveals not sunshine but a "blood red moon."[27] Poe exhibits everything held sacred by the cult of domesticity through the lens of the gothic: romantic love turns to incest; Jacksonian individualism transforms into madness; and brothers, in their passion, bury their twin sisters before they have died. In "Gothic fancy" domestic disorder explodes from *within*. The gothic, whether featuring bosom fiends, buried women not yet deceased, or what Clifford terms "morbid influences," implies that much was hidden and troubled beneath the well-scrubbed surface of the middle-class home celebrated by Sedgwick.[28] The gothic, as Poe's fissure suggests, resists ending with "sentimental closure."[29]

Holgrave's original censure of "homes" reworks Thomas Jefferson's prescription for periodic revolution: "It were better that they should crumble to ruin once in twenty years, or thereabouts, as a hint to the people to examine into and reform the institutions which they symbolize" (2: 184). "To plant a family!" Holgrave exclaims to Phoebe, "The idea is at the bottom of most of the wrong and mischief which men do. The truth is, that, once in every half-century, at longest, a family should be merged into the great, obscure mass of humanity, and forget all about its ancestors" (2: 185). Such notions smacked of Fourierism, a philosophy Hawthorne mocked even as he showed signs of being influenced by it.[30] That Hawthorne connects antidomestic and antiproperty notions to the notorious Frenchman is clear, for Holgrave himself identifies Uncle Venner's passing criticism of families devoted to heaping up "property upon property" as reflecting "the principles of Fourier" (2: 156). The narrator notes that young Holgrave envisioned reform in the future and recognized "that . . . there are the harbingers abroad of a golden era, to be accomplished in his own life time" (2: 179). Contemporary readers might well have identified "harbinger" as the title of the Fourierist newspaper founded by Albert Brisbane in the early 1840's. Brook Farm itself became a Fourierist community shortly after Hawthorne's departure in 1841. Hepzibah is alarmed because Holgrave fraternizes with "community-men" as well as "reformers" (2: 84).

Brisbane and other Fourierists hammered away at the isolated family and criticized the capitalist community as a gathering of families in hostile competition with one another. "The system of isolated households is the offspring of Poverty," Brisbane maintained, "—and the Selfishness, Conflicts and Discords which it engenders." He contrasted the benefits of Fourieristic "Association" and reform to the privatized tendency "to look selfishly and indifferently at the frightful amount of wretchedness which surrounds us."[31] Fourier himself singled out the isolated home, "unsociability reduced to its simplest form," as a seedbed of "perverted" passions. His American followers, such as Marx Lazarus, posited a causal relation between increasingly private family affairs and tensions in the home.[32]

Phoebe purifies Holgrave of his unwholesome gothic or Fourierist doubts about the salubrious benefits of middle-class domesticity. Once Phoebeized, Holgrave warbles what he himself admits is a "conservative" (2: 315) tune. "Moonlight, and the sentiment in man's heart, responsive to it," he chirps, "is the greatest of renovators and reformers. And all other reform and renovation, I suppose, will prove to be no better than moonshine!" (2: 214). Phoebe, again true to her name, is that "Moonlight." With no trace of irony the domesticated Holgrave concludes, "The world owes all its onward impulse to men ill at ease. The happy man inevitably confines himself within ancient limits" (2: 306–7). This is not simply insight; Holgrave enunciates middle-class domestic ideology. The radical part of his mind has been lobotomized. Phoebe's Eden makes the uncertainty and struggle involved in social reform superfluous. An anonymous reviewer of *Seven Gables* recognized Phoebe's political agenda in 1855: "Surely this pretty creation of Mr. Hawthorne's must stand for the Middle Classes of Society, to whom has been committed by Providence the mission of social reconciliation; which, once completed, the disunited are joined, the unblest, blessed, and the 'wild reformer' becomes a Conservative after Heaven's own fashion."[33]

Holgrave's domestic revelation does not contest the capitalist structure parodied by Hawthorne's "Gothic fancy." Phoebe, the feminine embodiment of shopkeeper capitalism, is "as nice a little saleswoman, as I am a housewife!" As Nancy Cott observes, "the canon of domesticity did not directly challenge the modern organization of work and pursuit of wealth. Rather, it accommodated and promised to temper them."[34] Middle-class domestic discourse promoted the home as a private sphere of compensation for the stress of battling it out in the dragon's-teeth fields, but it also operated to funnel men back into the marketplace renewed and ready to fight.

In the early 1850's Stephen Pearl Andrews, an American anarchist influenced by Fourier, blasted this capitalist middle-class family as emotionally privatized and socially irresponsible: "The intense concentration of all the affections upon the little circles of immediate family relations and connections, instead of being a positive virtue, as has been assumed, is in fact only a virtue relatively to the existing falseness and antagonism of all the relations outside of the family. It is a secret and contraband hoarding of the affections, which corresponds to the concealment of wealth in those despotic and rapacious countries, where there is no security for property."[35] Clifford seems to be thinking in this same vein when, energized by the railroad, he blurts out: "A man will commit almost any wrong—he will heap up an immense pile of wickedness, as hard as granite, and which will weigh as heavily upon his soul, to eternal ages—only to build a great, gloomy, dark-chambered mansion, for himself to die in, and his posterity to be miserable in" (2: 263). His agitated polemic moves toward an awareness of how the ideology of the family is used to authorize possessive individualism and the accumulation of wealth. Describing the trend toward middle-class privatization as the nineteenth century progressed, John Demos notes, "each family would look after its own—and, for the rest, may the best man win."[36]

As ideologically invested as Hawthorne probably was in inflating Phoebe's power, he also may have had doubts about her capacity to buoy the freight of this middle-class *private* enterprise. Hawthorne's narrator, sounding far more like the narrator of *Pierre* (1852), Melville's radical critique of domesticity, at one point informs us: "In this republican country, amid the fluctuating waves of our social life, somebody is always at the drowning-point" (2: 38). Hawthorne, not unfamiliar with decapitation in the marketplace and drowning points, struggled for three months to bring *Seven Gables* to a "prosperous close" and assured his publisher that he did his utmost "to pour some setting sunshine" over the ending.[37] In *The Marble Faun* Donatello pours some "Sunshine," his family wine, for Kenyon. Its peculiar qualities sound remarkably like an exaggeration of those ascribed to the privatized middle-class woman within the 1850's ideology of domesticity: "this rare wine of our vineyard would lose all its wonderful qualities, if any of it were sent to market" (4: 224).[38] The eminently marketable sentimental "sunshine" gilding the "prosperous close" of *Seven Gables*, once consumed, functions to haze our view so that the "drowning point" becomes a vanishing point.

Phoebe's femininity serves both cultural and *political* purposes in Hawthorne's text and his culture. Through Phoebe, Hawthorne thematizes not the feminization of women but rather the feminization of class. As a personification of the middle-class ideology of domesticity, Miss Clean (unlike the previous year's Mrs. Scarlet) not only fumigates the psychological gothic, and, like Rosina, disinfects the beleaguered male mind, but, by "humanizing" aristocrats and working-class reformers, promulgates her own sweet-scented brand of social pest-control. She exemplifies the ideological uses to which the "feminine" was put by the middle class in its class struggle. As Fredric Jameson has observed, "Ideology is designed to promote the human dignity and clear conscience of a given class at the same time that it discredits their adversaries."[39] Phoebe helps construct and legitimize middle-class identity and power by naturalizing home (the middle-class "custom" house) as the greatest reform and the most desirable "human" community.

7

Disciplinary
Misrepresentation
Reconstructing Miriam's Hand

In one of the most suggestive passages in *The Marble Faun* (1860) Hawthorne broaches the paradigm of a female character who seems capable of contesting the designs of her male author, a narrative tension which, as we shall see, was central to Hawthorne's final "romance." On beholding Kenyon's sculpture of Cleopatra, Miriam, herself an artist who represents powerful women, is full of praise: "What a woman is this!" "Tell me," she goes on to inquire (bringing to mind both Pygmalion and Dr. Rappacini), "did she ever try, even while you were creating her, to overcome you with her fury, or her love? Were you not afraid to touch her, as she grew more and more towards hot life, beneath your hand?" (4: 127). The narrator reinforces this image of a defiant female character who shows signs of acting independently of her maker: "The fierce Egyptian queen had now struggled almost out of the imprisoning stone; or, rather, the workmen had found her within the mass of marble, imprisoned there by magic, but still fervid to the touch with fiery life" (4: 377). If we substitute imprisoning text for imprisoning stone, we can detect Hawthorne reflecting on his own narrative tendencies both to inscribe resisting female characters and to contain their resistance.

Having noted Hawthorne's thematic interest in this paradigm, I now wish, in a purely imaginative vein, to apply the paradigm elsewhere. Thus think back to the "brilliant glow," the "magic endowments," and the "almost fearful distinctness" of the crimson hand on Georgiana's cheek in "The Birth-mark." Recollect its "charm," "creative force," "mysterious" ambiguity, and how some masculine observers "contented themselves with wishing it away, that the world might possess one living specimen of ideal loveliness" (10: 38). Now imagine this solitary hand as the only visible member of a crimson woman, not unlike Kenyon's Cleopatra, who has been submerged beneath the white surface of the "ideal" feminine face. Despite her submersion she has made her mark below the surface as well as above, for the "grasp" of her other hand has "caught hold" of the "ideal" woman's heart. Then envision her struggling to climb out of this face.

Next suppose that she has been allowed to escape into Hawthorne's fictions and that her scarlet presence disrupts Hawthorne's representation of feminized faces.[1] Recall the fate of Georgiana's crimson hand. Aylmer designated it a "symbol of his wife's liability to sin, sorrow, decay, and death" (10: 39). Would this crimson woman, upon entering Hawthorne's narratives as a grown woman, also be emplotted to read herself—with her brilliance, creativity, and power—as "the fatal flaw of humanity" whose "perfection must be wrought by toil and pain"?

Suppose also that her "grasp appeared to have caught hold" of her author's heart as well as of his understanding. Imagine that Hawthorne became increasingly fascinated by her capacity to mar his representations of "ideal" loveliness until he was tempted to rethink his middle-class assumptions about "humanity" and "perfection." One wonders what Hawthorne's crimson woman would be like and what he would make her contend with.

To find out, I suggest that one need look no further than *The Marble Faun*, Hawthorne's final completed novel. Just after reading "The Birthmark" in March of 1843, Henry Wadsworth Longfellow wrote Hawthorne that he "should have made a Romance of it, and not a short story."[2] Hawthorne's last novel, perhaps even more than his earlier ones, offers evidence of his having taken his friend's advice. The full-grown crimson woman I have in mind in my imaginative musing is, of course, Miriam Schaefer, the artist who identified and perhaps identified with Cleopatra's "hot life, beneath" the "hand" of her maker. I shall argue that Hawthorne structures his narrative so that Miriam's defeminizing art and heretical notions, like Cleopatra's body, are simultaneously made visible and contained. Hawthorne's peculiar "romance" grows out of this tension. The result is a "romance" that chronicles a fall from feminization not so much in Hawthorne's *official* values as in his recognition of what his art must reconcile about itself.

Miriam, like Zenobia, is a name that conjures representations of a powerful woman from ancient times. In Hebrew "Miriam" signifies "bitterness" and thus is aligned with the "bloody" topoi of Miriam's artwork.[3] Miriam, the older sister of Moses, is celebrated in the Old Testament for leading the Israelite women in songs of victory after the parting of the Red Sea, although her social role was more significant. Sarah Hale, in *Woman's Record*, praises Miriam as a joint leader of her people with her brothers, Moses and Aaron. "In genius," Hale writes, "she was superior to all the women who preceded her; and in the inspiration of her spirit (she was a 'prophetess' or poet), none of her contemporaries, male or female, except Moses, was her equal."[4]

Alas, there was a "fall of Miriam" clouded by narrative ambiguity: "What her crime was is not fully stated, only that she and Aaron 'spake against Moses' because 'he had married an Ethiopian woman.'" The allegedly insubordinate Miriam was afflicted with leprosy until Moses interceded with God to forgive her. She lived in obscurity for her remaining nineteen years. Hale's cautionary lesson may have pinpointed the real transgression: "That she was too ambitious is probable, and did not willingly yield to the authority with which the Lord had invested her younger brother. . . . a warning is sounded against the pride and self-sufficiency which the consciousness of great genius and great usefulness is calculated to incite."[5]

Hawthorne's Miriam is portrayed as ambiguous, independent, and dangerous. Only near the conclusion of the "romance" do we learn that she is of "English parentage . . . with a vein likewise of Jewish blood" (4: 429). Perhaps this "vein," like Georgiana's crimson hand, threw "an ambiguity about this young lady, which, though it did not necessarily imply anything wrong, would have operated unfavourably as regarded her reception in society, anywhere but in Rome" (4: 20). In reference to her gripping self-portrait the narrator perhaps somewhat nervously speculates that "she might ripen to be what Judith was, when she vanquished Holofernes with her beauty, and slew him for too much adoring it" (4: 48).

It may be that Hawthorne was reminded of the Old Testament Miriam and began embodying his own version when he found his imagination absorbed by a young woman sitting across from him at a banquet given by the Lord Mayor of London in 1856.[6] This woman's complexion, like Miriam's (4: 48), was ambiguously "dark, and yet not dark, but rather seemed to be of pure white marble, yet not white." Her hair was "deep, raven black," yet "*not* raven black . . . it was hair never to be painted, not described." Confessing impotence, he admits, "my pen is good for nothing." The classificatory capacity of Hawthorne's pen, however, did prove good for something. Her "wonderful" hair was recognized as Jewish, and the "beautiful outline" of her nose "was Jewish too." Her ambiguity is re-examined through a stereotyping grid by aid of which she is plotted as Rachel, Judith, Bathsheba, and Eve, though not Miriam. She was "what Judith was; for womanly as she looked, I doubt not she could have slain a man." Hawthorne's desire rises in the guise of denial: "I never should have thought of touching her, nor desired to touch her; for, whether owing to distinctness of race, my sense that she was a Jewess, or whatever else, I felt a sort of repugnance, simultaneously with my perception that she was an admirable creature."[7] Add "desirable" to "admirable." If he "never should have thought of touching her," why mention it? These mixed emotions—desire, admiration, and repugnance—may provide a key to reading his representation of Miriam and her representations.

Hawthorne authorizes Miriam to dismantle the kind of stereotyping grid through which he himself plotted the English "Jewess." In praising Hilda's copy of Guido Reni's portrait of Beatrice Cenci, Miriam objects that, "Everywhere we see oil-paintings, crayon-sketches, cameos, engravings, lithographs, pretending to be Beatrice, and representing the poor girl with blubbered eyes, a leer of coquetry, a merry look as if she were dancing, a piteous look, as if she were beaten, and twenty other modes of fantastic mistake" (4: 65). Beatrice, who was, after all, famous (or notorious) for parricide in response to sexual abuse, has been exploited as a discursive construct—sensationalized or sentimentalized at the whim of the artist. Miriam shocks Hilda by problematizing Guido's canonical representation as a questionable patriarchal construct: " 'After all,' resumed Miriam, 'if a woman had painted the original picture, there might have been something in it which we miss now. I have a great mind to undertake a copy myself, and try to give it what it lacks" (4: 68). Miriam knows that every "copy" is in fact a reading based not on reality but on an earlier reading that invents the original. Her project is to snap this gendered chain of representation, however canonical it may be, by offering an alternative reading not based on the "real" Beatrice Cenci, for no such unmediated reality is available to her, but on a critical reinterpretation founded on her knowledge of the ways in which patriarchal artists conventionally misrepresent women. Perhaps Miriam would do to Guido's representation what Zenobia does to the mid-century construct of Shakespeare's Ophelia. As will become clear, this provocative probing of the ideology informing (mis)representation *invites* the reader to contest Hawthorne's narrator's representations as Miriam challenges Guido's, and to try to give the questionable narration which we get what it "lacks."

Hawthorne also authorizes Miriam to use her "lay figure" to show how women are afflicted by stereotypes. The "lay figure" appears as "a woman with long dark hair, who threw up her arms, with a wild gesture of tragic despair" (4: 41). Although this is no overt self-portrait, its "long dark hair" brings to mind Miriam's "black, abundant hair" (4: 48). Its description also may be hinting at Miriam's vulnerability underneath Hawthorne's own pen:

She means you no mischief, nor could perpetrate any if she wished it ever so much. It is a lady of exceedingly pliable disposition; now a heroine of romance, and now a rustic maid; yet all for show, being created, indeed, on purpose to wear rich shawls and other garments in a becoming fashion. This is the true end of her being, although she pretends to perform many parts in life, while really the poor puppet has nothing on earth to do. (4: 41)

Miriam has profiled not an isolated individual but a cultural predicament, "describing nine women out of ten in the person of my lay figure" (4: 41). It is not until the description has been completed that we learn that this "woman" is a "lay figure," an easily manipulated doll used by artists in place of a live subject. The "puppet" lady exhibits one of the requisite virtues of the "proper" lady or "true" woman, what Mary Poovey has termed "constructed helplessness."[8]

Sarah Grimké satirized the ideological production of this type of womanhood in 1838. She singled out the Eve of *Paradise Lost* as Milton's feminized puppet. "His Eve is embellished with every personal grace, to gratify the eye of the admiring husband; but he seems to have furnished the mother of mankind with just intelligence enough to comprehend her supposed inferiority to Adam, and to yield unresisting submission to her lord and master." With the authority of a Moses speaking for God, Milton "puts into Eve's mouth" his fantasy of total mastery over his happy idiot: "My author and disposer, what thou bidst, / Unargued I obey; so God ordains— / God is thy law, thou mine: to know no more, / Is woman's happiest knowledge and her praise."[9] In "Of Queen's Gardens" Ruskin invokes literary authorities to naturalize conventions of the feminine and asks defiantly: "Are Shakespeare and Æschylus, Dante and Homer, merely dressing dolls for us?"[10] Grimké, and perhaps Hawthorne, would have entertained this possibility.

Miriam's sketches "attempted" (4: 43) to depict women who imbrue their hands in an effort to resist being hung up as feminized "heroines of romance." "Over and over again," as the narrator tells us, "there was the idea of woman, acting the part of a revengeful mischief towards man. It was, indeed, very singular to see how the artist's imagination seemed to run on these stories of bloodshed, in which woman's hand was crimsoned by the stain" (4: 44).

Donatello views a sketch of "Jael, driving the nail through the temples of Sisera . . . as if Miriam had been standing by, when Jael gave the first stroke of her murderous hammer—or as if she herself were Jael, and felt irresistibly impelled to make her bloody confession, in this guise" (4: 43). Shortly before this description there appears a passage, not unlike one in *The Scarlet Letter*, on how sewing releases "what would otherwise be a dangerous accumulation of morbid sensibility" in women. What causes such a "dangerous accumulation" is not addressed. The cessation of sewing, by the same token, is interpreted by the narrator as a "sign of trouble" (4: 40). The correspondence between the sewing needle and Jael's "nail" is clear. Jael has stopped sewing and, like Hester Prynne, has put the ostensibly therapeutic needle to other uses. By likening Miriam to Jael, as the narrator does, we can also imagine the paintbrush symbolized by the "nail."

From the narrator's description of the sketch, it is obvious that Miriam highlights Jael's anger. Yet the narrator would have us interpret this portrayal of Jael's anger as botching her heroism. "Her first conception of the stern Jewess had evidently been that of perfect womanhood, a lovely form, and a high, heroic face of lofty beauty; but, dissatisfied either with her own work or the terrible story itself, Miriam had added a certain wayward quirk of her pencil, which at once converted the heroine into a vulgar murderess" (4: 43). If the narrator were Coverdale, we could argue that he is once again misinterpreting what he sees. I bring up Coverdale, a narrator whose reliability is at times made overtly dubious, because there is a very different way of reading how the narrator describes Miriam's sketch, and this alternative reading brings to mind Miriam's criticism of Guido and canonical male representations of Beatrice Cenci. I suggest we entertain the possibility that Miriam's "wayward quirk of the pencil" was deliberate and reflects her refusal to idealize or feminize Jael's action. In which case Miriam is redefining what it takes to be a "heroine." Perhaps Miriam was "dissatisfied," not with "the terrible story itself," but with pictorial reproductions of Jael as a "lovely" and uncomplicated representative of so-called "perfect" womanhood. Thus Miriam's sketch of Jael may indeed be putting into practice what she said she would like to do with Guido's Beatrice by painting what Beatrice "lacks" in the masters' versions of her—*anger*.

Hawthorne's description of Miriam's sketch of Judith also makes possible readings that are at odds with how the narration instructs us to read it. Judith's decapitation of Holofernes was a popular subject of the "old masters." Miriam's portrayal, rather suspiciously, goes astray. "Here, too, beginning with a passionate fury and fiery conception of the subject in all earnestness, she had given the last touches in utter scorn, as it were, of the feeling which at first took powerful possession of her hand" (4: 43–44). What this original "feeling" was we never learn; but what did result is most curious. Recall that Hawthorne titled himself (in caps) the DECAPITATED SURVEYOR in *The Scarlet Letter* and that in middle age, according to a sketch made in 1859 by his son Julian,[11] he sported a long, curlicued moustache: "The head of Holofernes (which by-the-by, had a pair of twisted mustachios, like those of a certain potentate of the day,) being fairly cut off, and screwing its eyes upward and turning its features into a diabolical grin of triumphant malice, which it flung right at Judith's face. On her part, she had the startled aspect that might be conceived of a cook, if a calf's head should sneer at her, when about to be popt into the dinner-pot" (4: 44). This representation seems to decree that any attempt on Judith's or Miriam's part to do away with the patriarchal head (even if "fairly cut off") will be futile. But the narration is troubling, for the sketch does not seem to portray Miriam's "utter scorn"; rather—and more visibly—it celebrates the decapitated surveyor's "utter scorn, as it were, of the feelings which at first took powerful possession of her hand."

Only a handful of women painters were usually cited in mid-nineteenth-century accounts of the history of painting. Among them was a woman who achieved fame (or notoriety) for her paintings of Judith, the seventeenth-century Italian artist Artemesia Gentileschi. As one critic put it, her Judiths "are endowed with the traits of that fuller humanity that has traditionally been allowed only to male characters."[12] In all likelihood, Hawthorne saw her Judiths in Florence and may have imagined Gentileschi as another model for Miriam.[13]

Mrs. Jameson, the popular art critic, was incensed by Gentileschi's painting of Judith. As noted earlier, Hawthorne borrowed Jameson's

Characteristics of Women (1832) from the Salem Atheneum twice in 1835, and there is little doubt that Sophia, a well-read female artist, was aware both of Gentileschi's controversial work and of Mrs. Jameson's publications on art. Nathaniel and Sophia met Mrs. Jameson in Rome in May 1858 and exchanged ideas on art and aesthetics. "She is a very sensible old lady, and sees a great deal of truth; a good woman too, taking elevated views of matters," wrote Nathaniel, "but I doubt whether she has quite the finest and highest perceptions in the world" (14: 208). Mrs. Jameson wrote that Gentileschi, though possessing "rare talent," nonetheless "belied her sex" in her painting and "wished then, as I do now, the privilege of burning it to ashes."[14] Two years later she referred specifically to Gentileschi's "Judith Decapitating Holofernes" (c. 1620) to reprove the artist as a "woman" not only for selecting such indelicate subject matter but for representing it with "atrocious fidelity and talent." Gentileschi stands out as the artist with the "most power" among all of the female painters reviewed by Mrs. Jameson. The others, unlike Gentileschi, "were *feminine* painters. They succeeded best in feminine portraits, and when they painted history they were only admirable in that class of subjects which came within the province of their sex."

It becomes evident, as her discussion of female painters proceeds, that Mrs. Jameson believes painting should express the natural differences between men and women and that there exist both a *feminine* aesthetic and a *feminine* subject matter. This is the aesthetic ideology that the nineteenth-century Miriam has "attempted" (4: 43) to defy in her sketches of Judith and Jael. Gentileschi's indelicate "power" is an embarrassment because it gives the lie to Mrs. Jameson's thesis that "the physical organization" of women must be altered "before we produce a Rubens or a Michael Angelo."[15] Mrs. Jameson's objective is nothing less than to use her writing on art to rhetorically produce the female artist's hand as *feminine*, so that, in all of its strokes, it will confirm and reproduce the ideology of sexual difference.

Mrs. Hale, in *Woman's Record*, acknowledges that Gentileschi's "Judith killing Holofernes . . . is a picture of deep and terrible passion," but Hale reassures her reader that the artist's "private life was excellent."[16] Not so excellent in her teenaged years, however, when she was raped "many, many times" by a colleague of her father's, Agostino Tassi, employed by him to teach her "perspective."[17] Perhaps neither Mrs. Jameson nor Mrs. Hale—nor Mr. Hawthorne—knew of this episode, although the rape was made public in a trial during which the veracity of Gentileschi's testimony was tested by "the torture of *sibille*, metal rings tightened by strings around her fingers."[18]

The version viewed by Mrs. Jameson in Florence shows Judith and Abra, her maid, straddled over Holofernes in a bed with his head almost sliding off the edge and his legs spread apart.[19] In her right hand Judith holds a vertical sword in the shape of a cross and in her left she has grasped Holoferne's hair and beard. The scene seems more like a castration (legs apart) than a rape. One wonders if the nineteenth-century commentators who knew of the rape suspected that Gentileschi was ritually beheading—or symbolically castrating—her art "master" in her representations of the slaying.[20] Hawthorne's narration seems to prevent Miriam from following in the unfeminine brushstrokes of an artist like Gentileschi (perhaps for the same reason that Hester was prohibited from following in the footsteps of Anne Hutchinson).

Miriam's "bloody" sketches incense Donatello, who "snatched up one sketch after another, as if to tear it in pieces" and "clasped his hands over his eyes" (4: 44). Hawthorne's Donatello may be simple-minded, but he knows unfeminine subject matter when he sees it. Our reading of his agitation becomes more complex, however, when we consider what Nathaniel and Sophia would surely have known: Donatello bears the name of the celebrated fifteenth-century Florentine sculptor, whose own bronze sculpture of Judith and Holofernes was famous. Donatello's Judith, hooded like a grim reaper, and draped in robes, like a judge, stands erect and somber before Holofernes, who sits passively at her feet (her left foot on his right wrist, her right foot on his groin) awaiting her sentence. The unstated irony in Hawthorne's representation is that his Donatello is shocked when a woman artist attempts to make art out of subject matter that his illustrious male namesake had converted into a "masterpiece." By implication, only the male artist, not the female, is permitted to portray powerful women.[21]

Comic though it is, can we read Miriam's sketch of Judith as an image of Hawthorne's anxiety over what this crimson force let loose in his narratives would like to do to him? If so, the narrator's curious misreading of the evidence of Miriam's sketches demonstrates how he attempts to contain this force: the artist "failed not to bring out the moral, that woman must strike through her own heart to reach a human life, whatever were the motive that impelled her" (4: 44). Read literally, this suggests that woman must impale herself "to reach a human life." This image fits not the historical subjects selected by Miriam but, rather, a popular mythological subject painted by Guido, Botticelli, Titian, and others: the suicide of Lucretia.[22] Lucretia, raped by Tarquin, stabbed herself in the heart to avoid living with the shame. The women portrayed by Miriam, whose circumstances and motivations are unlike Lucretia's, bloody their hands, not by striking through their own hearts, but by impaling or decapitating male craniums. The narrator seems to be leading us astray.

Neither Jael nor Judith is overtly strung up as a "heroine of romance" like the "lay figure"; on the other hand, neither is allowed to drive her point home without narrative sleight of hand to deflect it. Jael is disparaged as a "vulgar murderess," while Judith discovers that the joke is on her. Both Jael and Judith are consummately *political* women whose political actions on behalf of Israel are discredited by the narration.[23]

The lesson Miriam should learn from having "attempted" (dared) such sketches of "remarkable power" might be hinted in the narration of another sketch representing a sainted "decapitated surveyor" and Salome: "Miriam had imparted to the Saint's face a look of gentle and heavenly reproach, with sad and blessed eyes fixed upward at the maiden; by the force of which miraculous glance, her whole womanhood was at once awakened to love and endless remorse" (4: 44). What Hawthorne seems to be doing in these *interpretations* of Miriam's representations is participating in Mrs. Jameson's ideological project: the rhetorical disciplining of the female artist's hand. Yet, by allowing his reader to envision Miriam's sketches and thus to contest the authority of his narrator's readings of them, Hawthorne self-consciously compromises this feminizing project. Hawthorne is, in effect, enabling his reader to view Miriam, like Cleopatra, struggling out of the "imprisoning stone," but still "imprisoned there by magic."

Miriam's art is not all "bloody" minded. Although she lives in a decaying palace that exhibits no signs of a "happy fireside" or "domestic enjoyment" (4: 38), Miriam, like the "humanized" Pearl, seems to yearn for the hearth and would ostensibly prefer sewing to impaling male craniums. In fact, she illustrates domestic scenes as well as "stories of bloodshed." She explains apologetically to Donatello that her bloody images "are ugly phantoms that stole out of my mind; not things that I created, but things that haunt me" (4: 45). Her conventional domestic scenes are as self-referential as her bloody ones. They portray a figure, who resembles Miriam, steeped in "deep sadness" (4: 46) and always on the outside looking in. The narrator praises her scenes for "idealizing a truer and lovelier picture of the life that belongs to woman" (4: 46). Domestic scenes, flower paintings, landscapes, miniatures, and portraits, rather than historical scenes (like Judith and Jael), were the subjects that women, such as Sophia Hawthorne, were encouraged to paint in mid-century America if they wished to sell their wares.[24]

But Miriam's homey scenes, which she also calls her "trifles" (4: 45), are narrated in such a way that their sentimental significance is rendered problematic. In the first place, these domestic reveries are blatantly *conventional* images of romance or maternal yearning: "There was a drawing of an infant's shoe, half-worn out, with the airy print of the blessed foot within" (4: 45). Second, the narrator complicates our reading of these "subtly idealized" (4: 45) stereotypes by adding that Miriam's domestic sketches edit out "hard and dusty facts" that could have "inspired" (4: 46) radically different visions. Miriam's "sketches intimated such a force and variety of imaginative sympathies as would enable Miriam to fill her life richly with the bliss and suffering of womanhood." Again the narrator turns the screw when he adds: "however barren it might individually be" (4: 46). Sentimental images of women are thus meant to provide a satisfaction that renders individual barrenness inconsequential, simply part and parcel of the "bliss and suffering." Hawthorne, in other words, undercuts the credibility of domestic femininity even as he celebrates it.

He undercuts Hilda as well. Hilda is the middle-class feminized angel in the text.[25] At times she reads like a caricature of Phoebe (herself part caricature). Hilda has not merely a "feminine mind" (4: 57), she fetishizes femininity. When Miriam asks Hilda if she ever worships the Virgin, whose shrine she maintains so vigilantly on her rooftop, Hilda responds: "She was a woman once. Do you think it would be wrong?" This middle-class daughter of the puritans can do so because she reveres the Virgin as "true" woman rather than as a Catholic representative of God. "It has for me," she confesses, "a religious significance" (4: 112).

She also shows devotion to the works of the great male canon and, like a mirror, strives to "reflect" the "immortal pencils of old" (4: 57).[26] Like a fastidious housekeeper, Hilda has the chloric vision that sees through the grime of time to the original intention of the "master" and restores this in her copy.[27] Hilda, "endowed with a deep and sensitive faculty of appreciation" (4: 56), is a male fantasy, a medium, like Priscilla, rather than a creator herself. She does what Aylmer wants Georgiana to do—"locates creativity . . . in the Masters."[28] Before her own transformation takes place, Hilda is unable to see the spirituality of the Old Masters as an effect produced by the deployment of conventions. This naïveté is the basis for her "devout sympathy" (4: 375). Her original sketches, like Miriam's domestic scenes, lacked "the reality which comes only from a close acquaintance with life, but so softly touched with feeling and fancy, that you seemed to be looking at humanity with angel's eyes" (4: 55).

Hawthorne problematizes "angel's eyes" on a number of counts at the same time that he pays homage to them. Both Miriam and Kenyon liken their obsessive friend to St. Hilda, a seventh-century Scottish princess and abbess. St. Hilda, who frowned upon the tonsure of priests as heathenish, bordered on being a parody of orthodoxy. The venerable Bede commended her "strict observance of justice, piety, chastity." The key word is "strict."[29] Hawthorne has Hilda wield an uncompromising sword. Even Kenyon, who fetishizes her, admits to Hilda that he has "been perplexed to conceive how such tender sympathy could coexist with the remorselessness of a steel blade! You need no mercy, and therefore know not how to show any!" (4: 384). Unlike her Catholic namesake, the New England angel is grossly deficient in "charity." Paradoxically, Hilda's "steel blade" associates her, rather than Miriam, with the executions rendered in Miriam's bloody hand sketches. Her stainless steel spirituality, not unlike Aylmer's (who dreams of surgical blades), is manifested as a moral arrogance which denies that the "alloy of earth" (4: 354) is a human attribute. Hilda's intolerance is distant from the acceptance informing the wisdom of Hester's moving plea to Dimmesdale: "Let God punish! Thou shalt forgive!" (1: 194). It may be that Hilda appears not simply upright but often laughably uptight because Hawthorne himself was becoming uptight about the conformity his representative of middle-class femininity personified.[30]

Hilda's remorseless moral swordsmanship is even more curious when one considers that in several ways she resembles Hawthorne's wife, Sophia. The artist community of Rome dubs Hilda the "Dove" (4: 56), an appellation that Nathaniel reserved for Sophia in his love letters of the early 1840's. Before marrying Hawthorne, Sophia Peabody had gained some reputation and income of her own as a copyist of classic paintings. At her sister Elizabeth's home and bookstore at West Street in Boston, "Sophia was given her own upstairs studio room. Her copies of old master paintings were displayed for sale in the parlor."[31] In August 1841, almost a year before their wedding, Hawthorne wrote to Sophia that it would be "no trouble" to him if she relinquished her painting and sculpting, despite the fact that everybody "thinks it of importance." His sense of what made Sophia important was explicit: "It is not what you do," he pleaded, "but what you are, that I concern myself about."[32] Yet sales of her copies enabled her to buy secondhand bedroom furniture for the Old Manse in 1842. She also helped support the family in 1849 by selling painted fire screens and lampshades[33] while Nathaniel was (un)employed writing *The Scarlet Letter*.

Like Hilda, Sophia exhibited a technical "command of hand," which, the narrator adds somewhat condescendingly, "is an endowment separate from pictorial genius, though indispensable to its exercise" (4: 57). Sophia's notion of aesthetic value was also, like Hilda's, bound up with assumptions about female purity. In 1858 she praised Raphael's Madonna in terms that remind one of "The Birth-mark": "It is a sacred face of maternity—woman, without a shadow of earth upon her, with something of the delicate tints of Fra Angelico's angels." By contrast, she saw Titian's Venuses as "not goddesses—not womanhood—not maternity—not maidenhood, but nude female figures."[34]

Although Sophia excelled as a copyist, it appears that she had a deeper urge to create. When she did create, as this letter of 1832 to her sister suggests, the "female complaints" that often afflicted her subsided:

What do you think I have actually begun to do? . . . Nothing less than *create* and do you wonder that I lay awake all last night after sketching my first picture. . . . I have always determined not to force the creative power but wait till it mastered *me* and now I feel as if the time had come and such freedom and revelry of spirit does it bring![35]

Yet, as art historian Josephine Withers notes, Sophia conformed to the cultural stereotype of the middle-class woman encouraged to be "artistic" but not an "artist." One sad encounter with William Ellery Channing illustrates the cultural constraints Sophia may have found overwhelming:

Dr. Channing said, "Miss Sophia," upon which I roused me and looked at him; but his face was buried in his hands. . . . He went on to say he had been reading about some females who would be painters—and that it was said they were generally wanting in strength, or as Fuseli said, "There was no *fist* in it." I tried to respond to his very kind notice of little me—; but I found that no thought could find expression, and so I sunk away into my shell again.[36]

This exchange may have been the basis for the narrator's observation that young Hilda required "a darker and more forcible touch, which would impart to her designs the relief they needed" (4: 55). Hilda's "hand" is too inexperienced and too feminized.

The relationship between Miriam and Hilda also bears similarities to the close friendship between Margaret Fuller and Sophia in the early 1840's. Recall that Sophia composed her sonnet "To a Priestess of the Temple Not Made with Hands" for Fuller, whom she once idolized. Sophia, of course, participated in Fuller's "conversations" when she moved to Boston to live with her sister Elizabeth in 1840. The proposed topic of that season's "conversations," to be held in Elizabeth's bookstore on West Street, was "The Fine Arts."[37] Sophia's involvement in these "conversations" may have been in the back of Hawthorne's mind when the narrator praises Hilda's acceptance of her own limitations as a copyist: "this feeble girl" (4: 60) chose "to be the handmaid of those old magicians, instead of a minor enchantress within a circle of her own" (4: 61). Comments on Miriam's connection to Donatello recall Hawthorne's mocking of Fuller's marriage to Count Ossoli. Kenyon, for instance, "was startled to perceive how Miriam's rich, ill-regulated nature impelled her to fling herself, conscience and all, on one passion, the object of which, intellectually, seemed far beneath her" (4: 280).

Bearing these biographical correspondences in mind, the intensity of Miriam's bond with Hilda is suggestive. The more than sisterly love between the two women is jeopardized when Hilda catches Miriam and Donatello red-handed. By chance Hilda observes the involvement of her two friends in the murder of Miriam's model, whom Miriam had accused of contaminating and persecuting her. Hilda prefers to remain out of touch with Miriam lest she as a witness be polluted by her knowledge. Miriam beseeches Hilda, heart in hand:

> "You were to me a younger sister; yes, dearer than sisters of the same blood; for you and I were so lonely, Hilda, that the whole world pressed us together by its solitude and strangeness. Then, will you not touch my hand? Am I not the same as yesterday?"
> "Alas! No, Miriam!" said Hilda.
> "Yes, the same—the same for you, Hilda," rejoined her lost friend. "Were you to touch my hand, you would find it as warm to your grasp as ever." (4: 207)

But Hilda taboos Miriam as a polluted woman or a leper now only capable of contaminating others. "If I were one of God's angels," Hilda explains, "with a nature incapable of stain, and garments that never could be spotted, I would keep ever at your side, and try to lead you upward" (4: 208).

To be caught red-handed is to imperil the purity of one's feminization. As in *Blithedale* we see Hawthorne show both apprehension of and fascination with the powerful woman who transmits impressions to the pale maiden. This transmission of impressions is literalized when Hawthorne allows us to catch Hilda herself red-handed. Unbeknownst to Hilda, a young Italian artist rapidly sketches her as she daydreams of Miriam after having recognized her tabooed friend's resemblance to da Vinci's "Joanna of Aragon." The finished portrait "represented Hilda as gazing with sad and earnest horrour, at a blood-spot which she seemed just then to have discovered on her white robe" (4: 330). Being caught red-handed herself suggests that Hilda is denying, through her rejection of her friend, her own capability of responding as Miriam did and that she is projecting that "bloody" fear onto Miriam. This fear of herself makes Miriam untouchable.

Nor should we ignore other "bloody" connotations. Hawthorne may be hinting that Hilda's obstinate urge to remain "the stainless maiden" and to deny her moral coming of age is futile. The scene also recalls the sexual innuendo of Poe's Madeline Usher emerging from the crypt to embrace her twin brother Roderick with "a low moaning cry" and "blood upon her white robes."[38] Hawthorne may be suggesting that Miriam is responsible for Hilda losing her moral virginity and for inseminating her stainless mind with the conflict and ambiguity that breeds an experienced woman and a woman artist.

Hawthorne's English publishers gave the "romance" the apt title, *Transformation*.[39] Yet Hawthorne was disappointed by this selection (one of his own original suggestions).[40] Perhaps their title hit too close to home. Hawthorne, not without some conflict, may have been disclosing the "transformation" not only of his four characters but of his own sense of his art.

The scene of Hilda's bloody impression also calls to mind the debate between Miriam and Kenyon over Hilda's unblinking reverence for Guido's painting of the Archangel Michael battling Satan. Miriam argues that if her friend's "soul were less white and pure—she would be a more competent critic" (4: 183–84) of Guido's interpretation. By admiring Guido's proclivity to idealize Michael, Hilda no doubt identified with the Archangel, for recall that her own conscience is figured as a "steel sword." Hilda reproduces the artist's *distortion* of moral vision.

In Miriam's dirtier and bloodier version, "A full third of the Archangel's feathers should have been torn from his wings; the rest all ruffled, till they looked like Satan's own! . . . the battle never was such child's play as Guido's dapper Archangel seems to have found it" (4: 184). Not only must Michael struggle in Miriam's rendering, as the conflict intensifies it becomes difficult and perhaps impossible to tell the two contenders apart. Miriam sees Michael's engagement in conflict as a catalyst for his own inevitable transformation. "'For Heaven's sake, Miriam,' cried Kenyon, astonished at the wild energy of her talk, 'paint the picture of man's struggle against sin according to your own idea! I think it will be a masterpiece'" (4: 184).

As his comment suggests, Kenyon has been partly hooked by Miriam's defeminized art. Miriam, like Fanny Fern, seems capable of casting off what Hawthorne termed the "restraints" of "decency." Indeed, she contests middle-class assumptions about spiritual development as well as patriarchal representations of womanhood. This poses another challenge to Kenyon's assumptions. "I tremble at my own thoughts," Miriam tells Kenyon, "yet must probe them to their depths." Thinking of her complicity with Donatello in the murder of the model who tormented her, she muses: "Was the crime—in which he and I were wedded—was it a blessing in that strange disguise? Was it a means of education, bringing a simple and imperfect nature to a point of feeling and intelligence, which it could have reached under no other discipline?" (4: 434).

For Kenyon, and perhaps the elusive Hawthorne as well, these are indeed "unfathomable abysses" (4: 434). "It is too dangerous, Miriam!" protests Kenyon: "I cannot cannot follow you!" (4: 435). Yet follow her he does when a few chapters later he frames the question for Hilda: "Did Adam fall, that we might ultimately rise to a far loftier paradise than his?" To which Hilda testily rejoins: "Oh, hush!" (4: 460). Miriam proposes that transgression and the guilt which ensues is what humanizes the pastoral Donatello and, more generally, that the same principle of moral development obtains for mankind. This concept, rather interestingly, threatens to supplant the middle-class idea, so dear to Hawthorne and no doubt to Sophia too, that domesticity is what "humanizes" mankind. Within Miriam's heretical frame of reference the domestic humanizing mission of a Phoebe Pyncheon is as unreal as the contest between Satan and "Guido's dapper Archangel." The transgression that disqualified Hester Prynne to be the "prophetess" who would champion women's rights is here elevated to the spiritual status of that which qualifies us and educates us to be human.

Miriam goes so far as to suggest that the one representative of domestic femininity in the novel, Hilda, needs an infusion of transgression to humanize her, or a stain of blood on her conscience to turn her into a woman: "As an angel, you are not amiss; but, as a human creature, and a woman among earthly men and women, you need a sin to soften you!" (4: 209). Miriam's criticism sounds remarkably similar to the Man of Fancy's appraisal of the fictional "dream-woman" he inscribed in his "visionary youth," who, to his more mature literary eyes is seen as "a sort of wax-figure of an angel, a creature as cold as moonshine, an artifice in petticoats, with an intellect of pretty phrases and only the semblance of a heart."

It would be fallacious, however, to dissociate Hawthorne from Hilda's view of art, morality, and femininity.[41] Hawthorne, for instance, goes to great pains to make being a "copyist" into a virtue of true womanhood if not true artistry. "The handmaid of Raphael, whom she loved with a virgin's love! Would it have been worth Hilda's while to relinquish this office, for the sake of giving the world a picture or two which it would call original; pretty fancies of snow and moonlight; the counterpart, in picture, of so many feminine achievements in literature!" (4: 61). Hawthorne recoils from sentimental pap perhaps as much as he does from Miriam's bloody-minded feminist art. Nevertheless, it is arguable that Hawthorne tips the scales in Miriam's favor as a woman artist with a sting. Yet he makes her contend with his narrative shenanigans from beginning to end.

From the first it is insinuated that Miriam had been sexually or criminally tainted by her devilish model who, like a shadow, follows her everywhere. Charging that Miriam's "white hand had once a crimson stain," her model proceeds to examine it: " 'It looks very white,' said he; 'but I have known hands as white, which all the water in the ocean could not have washed clean!' " " 'It had no stain,' retorted Miriam bitterly, 'until you grasped it in your own!' " (4: 97). Thus Miriam is made to enter the world of the "romance" as a woman artist somehow, like Beatrice Cenci and Lucretia, tainted by her own victimization, and in some sense this is supposed to spoil her. The analogy to Lucretia is apposite, for the narrator has Miriam tell her model, in suicidal desperation: "Might not a dagger find my heart? . . . Would not poison make an end of me? Will not the Tiber drown me?" (4: 94). But Hawthorne once again wishes his reader to evaluate this particular interchange as one would a conversation between Zenobia and Westervelt not heard by, yet fantasized by, Coverdale. Hawthorne *undercuts* the authority of the narration by calling attention to its artifice: "In weaving these mystic utterances into a continuous scene, we undertake a task resembling, in its perplexity, that of gathering up and piecing together the fragments of a letter, which has been torn and scattered to the winds. . . . If we insert our own conjectural amendments, we perhaps give a purport utterly at variance with the true one" (4: 92–93). Hawthorne *wants* his readers to catch his narrator in the act and to focus on narrative sleights of hand.

To see this is to begin to understand that Hawthorne also wants his readers to view him as obligated to plot against Miriam because of what he has made her represent. In Old Testament terms, Miriam must be afflicted with a kind of leprosy for the threat she represents. Like Georgiana's birthmark itself, Miriam is allegorized as the bearer of "sin, sorrow, decay, and death." "The story of the Fall of Man! Is it not repeated in our Romance of Monte Beni?" (4: 434) Miriam asks Kenyon. Earlier, seeking forgiveness from Donatello, she laments that "it was my doom, mine, to bring him within the limits of sinful, sorrowful mortality!" (4: 320). Thus Miriam is emplotted to read herself as Eve. She assumes responsibility for nothing less epic than the fall of man.

But Hawthorne uses Miriam to transform this fall of man into a mode of redemption. The question is whether Hawthorne then buys this idea of redemption. Perhaps his authorial conflict is disclosed in one of Miriam's references to Donatello: "He will not listen to the whisper of his heart, telling him that she, most wretched who beguiled him into evil, might guide him to a higher innocence than that from which he fell" (4: 283).

Miriam's heretical theory is that it is transgression and repentance rather than domestic alchemy that humanizes humankind.[42] This vision of humanity bases itself upon a view of women at odds with the stereotype of the middle-class "angel." The sole representative of middle-class femininity in Hawthorne's romance is the character most in need of humanizing, whatever the agency. Hawthorne associates Hilda's uptight, middle-class femininity not only with an aesthetic, but with a particular view of sin and humanity. When Miriam wonders if Donatello will someday recognize that she "might guide him to a higher innocence than that from which he fell," Hawthorne might be thinking about not only his own "fall" from a conventional middle-class view of "humanizing" but his fall from the middle-class ideology of feminization as cultural redemption.

I wonder if, when Hawthorne wrote *The Scarlet Letter*, he began with a nexus of threatening ideas that were attached to notions of unconventional womanhood and, as such, had to be dressed up in the clothes of an adulteress.[43] If so, *The Marble Faun* may have originated in the same fashion. Hawthorne's scarlet artist is a defeminized character capable of demystifying patriarchal representations of women and putting her own images of women who resist in their place. As we have seen, one can make a case that Hawthorne's narrator sometimes distorts these images in his *interpretation* of them. Yet Hawthorne allows his reader to view his narrator's efforts to restrain Miriam, like Cleopatra, within the "imprisoning stone." His chief strategy for contending with Miriam's critical powers, which so fascinated and disturbed him, was to make her the polluted Eve who introduces mortality, sin, and the "fall." Still, he allows his defeminized crimson woman to articulate this "fall" as a redemption. Hilda, the young "copyist," rather than holding up as an ideological alternative to Miriam's vision of womanhood and humanity, is clearly undergoing an initiation into adulthood that she shudders to acknowledge.

Hilda does marry Kenyon, however. The sculptor blissfully embraces what he misreads as Hilda's "white wisdom" (4: 460), which at this point in the narrative evokes visions of nothing so much as a blank canvas. When Kenyon broaches Miriam's heretical concept of redemption, Hilda's sharp reply, true to her "true womanhood" and true to her class, is as telling as Kenyon's response: " 'Oh, hush!' cried Hilda, shrinking from him with an expression of horrour which wounded the poor, speculative sculptor to the soul" (4: 460).

A shrinking but uncompromising voice advocating "white wisdom" in Hawthorne may have responded "Oh, hush" as well. *Transformation*, written and published in England before being retitled for American consumption, is in some ways Hawthorne's most complex and contradictory criticism of middle-class feminization. It was the last "romance" he completed, five years before the end of his life.

Coda

Hawthorne, the Disturbing Influence, and the Process of Class Formation

Hawthorne was not unproductive between the publication of *The Marble Faun* in 1860 and his death in 1864; but in terms of fiction he became, in the words of Richard Brodhead, "a copyist: drafting and redrafting works that never did get made, because he could no longer stand toward them as their maker."[1] What he often drafted and redrafted was the theme of the frustrated alchemist. In *Septimius Felton: Or the Elixir of Life*, his most concerted attempt to write a novel, several scenes hark back to the preoccupations of his "grotesque" postnuptial allegories. Perhaps the most bizarre is one in which Septimius discovers that he has inherited an "ancient English script" containing "rules of life and moral diet, not exactly expressed in the document." Hawthorne lists twenty-two "rules of life and moral diet" reminiscent of taboos prescribed by health, diet, and sex reformers such as Sylvester Graham. One prohibition stands out:

Kiss no woman if her lips be red; look not upon her if she be very fair. Touch not her hand, if thy finger-tips be found to thrill with hers ever so little. On the whole, shun woman, for she is apt to be a disturbing influence. If thou love her, all is over, and the whole past and remaining labor and pains will be in vain. (13: 105)

In this passage the thrilling woman, perhaps another manifestation of a crimson force in Hawthorne's fiction ("If thou love her, all is over"), is *tabooed* ("Touch not her hand") as threatening to male purity, labor, and alchemical success.

The specific "disturbing influence" in this rambling and revealing narrative is Sybil Dacy, who is determined to take revenge for Septimius's murder of her brother, but who purposefully—recalling Georgiana and Beatrice—poisons herself. She is dubbed "brain-touched," although it becomes evident that this eighteenth-century woman has in fact been "touched" by concerns debated by mid-nineteenth-century feminists. Sybil professes an alchemical interest in attaining immortality to ascertain "whether there is or no, some deadly curse on woman, so that she has nothing to do, and nothing to enjoy, but only to be wronged by man and still to love him, and despise herself for it;—to be snaky in her revenges" (13: 171). The emphasis on enforced inactivity marks this "snaky" curse as distinctly middle- or upper-class. Woman's "curse" is also enunciated in terms that reiterate contemporary notions about middle-class "female complaints": "Women, so feeble and crazy in body," says Sybil, summing up her gender, "fair enough sometimes, but full of infirmities, not strong, with nerves bare to every pain, ailing, full of little weaknesses, more contemptible than great ones" (13: 171). Overcome by this ineluctable biological curse, Sybil contemplates advising women to "kill their female children as fast as they are born" (13: 171).

Thus it is Sybil, rather than the alchemist, who is written up by Hawthorne to "shun woman" by categorizing her as "contemptible" and to stereotype women (including herself) as a "disturbing influence." Sybil is made to *biologize* this cultural curse and to perceive her social position ("nothing to do") as what Hawthorne earlier termed "rules of life" rather than alterable circumstances imposed on her by her society. Grimké, Fuller, and contributors to *The Una* and *The Lily* would very likely have disputed aspects of the ideology recited by Sybil, and have gone on to challenge, as did Grimké of Milton, the motives of Sybil's "author and disposer."

What Hawthorne has condensed in one conflicted character is a feminized subject who biologizes her cultural oppression, a privatized subject who renders invisible her social positioning, and a psychologized subject whose consciousness is governed by a variant of altruistic projection ("to be wronged by man, and still love him, and despise herself for it"). This adds up to a psychologically vulnerable *political* subject. Perhaps Hawthorne became aware that if he was not killing, he was certainly enfeebling his female characters "as fast as they were born" in his final attempts to write a novel.

In the preceding chapters I have argued that what is at stake in rethinking passages such as Sybil's rendition of woman's curse is more expansive than biographical speculations about Hawthorne's ambivalence toward women or textual explications of the tensions defining Hawthorne's aesthetic. Such biographical and literary considerations must be theorized as cultural ones and reassessed in the context of mid-nineteenth-century social processes and ideological patterns. Here we have focused on feminization (of women), privatization, and the emergence of a middle-class psychological discourse. Feminization, privatization, and the discursive configuration of a middle-class psychological self, rather than a "machine in the garden," are key historical processes in several of Hawthorne's "psychological" allegories and in his novels. Yet it must be borne in mind that this middle-class "emotional revolution" was causally connected to the industrial and commercial revolution that accounts for the presence of machine-in-the-garden imagery in other mid-century texts.

I have shown throughout my discussions of these texts that Hawthorne's fictions are not only implicated in these related historical processes, all integral to the development of middle-class consciousness, but that Hawthorne often proves critical of the ideological role that his writing plays in these processes. He is a product, agent, and critic of an emerging middle-class interiority, and is aware that his participation in reproducing the forms of subjectivity of his class is political.

That Nathaniel and Sophia Hawthorne were representatives of their class is clear from their journals recounting their stay at the Old Manse, a consummately middle-class "Eden." Recall that it was her Irish Catholic maid, Mary O'Brien, whom Sophia "summoned" to draw her bath at "half past six" on the morning of December 7, 1843, so that she could peruse the *Democratic Review* in it (with no hint of irony). Of Mary O'Brien, Sophia wrote (with humanizing zeal): "My purpose is to cultivate her particularly on Sundays, as the best use I can make of the day. But she does not accomplish much, because it tries her to sit still & stupefies her to be in a warm room at a long time." O'Brien took the heat for almost two years. Their next Irish Catholic domestic servant withstood this humanizing for only a month or less. In January 1845, Sophia noted with relief, they were able to afford "the luxury of an *American* & a *Protestant* maid." To return to Laura Wexler, quoted above in the Introduction, middle-class sentimental discourse "aimed at the subjection of different classes and even races who were compelled to play not the leading roles but the human scenery before which the melodrama of middle-class redemption could be enacted."[2] Mary O'Brien was scenery in Eden.

Even if Phoebe is unaware of her middle-class "humanizing" mission in *Seven Gables*, Hawthorne permits his reader to see that she is engaged in a *political* mission. Phoebe is essential, as a symbol of middle-class femininity, to the reproduction of an acceptable class interiority. Sybil, too, is positioned within this role, but the "rules of life and moral diet" implanted in her render her incapable of recognizing the systemic relationship between this reproductive agenda and her strained predicament. In this instance Hawthorne mystifies the construction of feminized womanhood and obfuscates its symbolic and ideological significance within the rise of the middle class.

The *House of the Seven Gables*, more than any other of his narratives, sketches, journals, or letters, clarifies that at the base of Hawthorne's plotting of womanhood is his plotting on behalf of the middle class. In *Seven Gables* Hawthorne represents constructions of gender and interiority as intimately tied to the cultural reproduction of middle-class identity. Hester Prynne's abstract revolutionary vision is barely concrete enough to suggest this systemic connection: when women break out of middle-class feminine roles (or even appear as if they might do so), they threaten to sabotage the ideological machinery that molds them as symbols who legitimize middle-class subjecthood. The scarlet mother qualifies as a "disturbing influence" because she jams the machinery of social reproduction symbolically through her adultery. But she would have been far more "disturbing," as Hawthorne interjects, if the puritan fathers had known of her "deadlier" (1: 164) revolutionary thoughts.

If I may, in closing, point to one area in the study of American literature, cultural history, gender, and class that requires more expansive historical and theoretical rethinking, it is this: we now have a grasp of the structural relationship between the nineteenth-century industrial revolution and capitalist class formation, but we need to theorize and historicize the political relationship between the emergence of a rigidly gendered, somewhat privatized, psychologized nineteenth-century consciousness and the determinative process of class formation.[3] In a novel like Dickens's *Hard Times* (1854) it is easy to see the relationship between mid-nineteenth-century social transformations in the workplace and at home because they resemble one another. Bounderby rationalizes work in his factory and endeavors to drain his "hands" of their humanity in the process. And Gradgrind, possessed by utilitarian zeal, rationalizes his family and prohibits any expression of sentimental subjectivity. There is no "political unconscious" to make visible because the brutal power relationships are evident. Dickens delineates how one emerging class oppresses another for its profit and how it utilizes its capitalist ideology to do so. If the historical importance of Dickens's novel can be summarized as his sentimental critique of a possessive individualism that clearly arises from antagonistic relations within industrial capitalism, the historical significance of some of Hawthorne's fiction can be described as his criticism of and participation in an emerging class discourse of psychological and gendered individualism whose ideological "alchemy" often works to cover up its origins within antagonistic social relations. We must rethink Hawthorne's preoccupation with gender, privatized spaces, and a psychological self in political terms, for if the forms of subjectivity that he is at turns illuminating, mystifying, legitimizing, and contesting also play a part in the ideological production of a *class*, then these forms of subjectivity must be reevaluated as not strictly "personal" or "domestic" but as integral to a *power* relationship in which one class sought to establish cultural and economic hegemony over another.

Reference Matter

Notes

Complete authors' names, titles, and publication data for sources cited in short form in the notes are given in the Bibliography, pp. 221–40.

Introduction

1. See Crews, *Sins of the Fathers*, especially pp. 10–11, 274, 277. For Crews's first recantation, see *Out of My System*. Also see his later collection of recantations, *Skeptical Engagements*. My own views on the problems of using Freud to "explain" Hawthorne have to do with history rather than Crews's skepticism about the empirical basis of psychoanalysis; I will elaborate on this in Chapter 1. See Jeffrey Steele: "Especially during the American Renaissance we observe a darkening of languages of the self as the irrational and the physical take on an increasingly important role in visions of the psyche" (*Representation of the Self*, p. 137). Steele, like Crews, does not try to offer historical explanations for why this was the case.

2. Henry James is quoted in Colacurcio, *Province of Piety*, p. 3. Some seminal contributions to the theorizing of the history of personal life which have had an enormous influence on my understanding of the scope of history include Norbert Elias's studies (originally published in 1939) *The History of Manners* and *Power and Civility*, volumes 1 and 2 respectively of *The Civilizing Process*; Philippe Ariès, *Centuries of Childhood: A Social History of Family Life*; Eli Zaretsky, *Capitalism, the Family, and Personal Life*; Michel Foucault, *An Introduction*, vol. 1 of *The History of Sexuality*; Richard Sennett, *The Fall of Public Man: On the Social Psychology of Capitalism* and his "Destructive Gemeinschaft"; Howard Gadlin, "Private Lives and Public Order: A Critical View of the History of Intimate Relations"; Stephanie Coontz, *The Social Origins of Private Life: A History of American Families, 1600–1900*; John D'Emilio and Estelle Freedman, *Intimate Matters: A History of Sexuality in America*; John Demos, *Past, Present, and Personal*; Jack Larkin, *The Reshaping of Everyday Life 1790–1840*; Michelle Per-

rot, ed., *From the Fires of Revolution to the Great War*, vol. 4 of *A History of Private Life*.

3. Blumin, *Emergence*, pp. 64, 33, 18, 12, 137, 107.

4. Hawthorne, *American-Notebooks*, in *Works: Riverside Edition* 4: 220–22.

5. Ripley is quoted in Frothingham, *George Ripley*, p. 307. Charles Lane, a member of the community, once described its most "praiseworthy" objective as the rendering of "the labor of the hands more dignified and noble, and mental education more free and loveful" ("Brook Farm," p. 357). Hawthorne soon became disenchanted with a middle-class "reform" that romanticized manual labor, especially when he found that such labor made him too weary to write. Hawthorne's *The Blithedale Romance* (1852) can be read as a critique of Brook Farm as a middle-class, pastoral, playacting inadequate to the social contradictions that it ostensibly sought to ameliorate.

6. Blumin, *Emergence*, pp. 190–91. M. P. Ryan, *Cradle*, pp. 190–91, 238, 241. Nancy Cott's study of women's reasons for wishing to separate from their husbands cited in eighteenth-century divorce petitions shows only a slight shift from strictly financial reasons, like inadequate support, early in the 1700's, to affective ones, such as loss of love, in the latter half of the century ("Eighteenth-Century Family and Social Life," p. 123; also see Cott, "Divorce"). For a sweeping view of shifts in late-eighteenth- and early-nineteenth-century conjugal relations, consult Shorter, *Making of the Modern Family*, especially pp. 228–29.

7. Demos, "Oedipus and America," pp. 28–29, 33, 27. Coontz, *Social Origins*, pp. 88, 34, 100, 155. On the narrowing of the range of occupations available to women from 1800–40, see Lerner, "The Lady and the Mill Girl."

8. Zaretsky, *Capitalism*, pp. 76, 120.

9. Stallybrass and White, *Politics and Poetics*, p. 192.

10. R. Johnson, "Cultural Studies," p. 44.

11. Weedon, *Feminist Practice*, pp. 82–83.

12. Coontz, *Social Origins*, pp. 101–2.

13. For an excellent analysis of this see Schnog, "Inside the Sentimental."

14. Wexler, "Tender Violence."

15. For an extended historical analysis of "Hawthorne's life in American letters," see Brodhead, *School of Hawthorne*.

16. Stallybrass and White, *Politics and Poetics*, p. 193.

17. From Gramsci's "The Study of Philosophy," *Selections from the Prison Notebooks*, p. 324 (as quoted in Paul Gilroy, "Cultural Studies and Ethnic Absolutism").

Chapter 1

1. Sophia Hawthorne, "Journal," p. 7.

2. In comparing these tales to Hawthorne's earlier ones, Nina Baym observes, "Where women in the earlier group of stories were, apparently, inadver-

tently caught up and victimized by the man's obsession, woman herself is now the obsession" ("Thwarted Nature," p. 65).

3. John C. Willoughby discusses Hawthorne's self-referential "horticultural metaphors" in " 'The Old Manse' Revisited," especially pp. 50–51.

4. Privacy is idealized in this introductory piece, but in fact Sophia's "voluminous correspondence" reveals "a constant stream of family and friends' visits" (McDonald, " 'The Old Manse' and Its Mosses," p. 107).

5. Hawthorne quoted in Julian Hawthorne, *Hawthorne and His Wife* 1: 238.

6. Ariès, *Centuries of Childhood*, pp. 40, 386, 413. Also see Ariès, "The Family and the City," p. 32; Weeks, *Sex, Politics, and Society*, p. 97.

7. M. P. Ryan, *Empire of the Mother*, p. 33.

8. Ruskin, "Queen's Gardens," p. 91.

9. West, "Hawthorne's Magic Circle," pp. 314, 318.

10. Hawthorne, *American-Notebooks*, in *Works: Riverside Edition* 4: 84.

11. M. D. Bell, *Development of the American Romance*, p. 130.

12. For some classic examples of the psychological approach see: D. H. Lawrence, *Studies in Classic American Literature* (1923); Leslie A. Fiedler, *Love and Death in the American Novel* (1960); Frederick Crews, *The Sins of the Fathers* (1966) and Michael Davitt Bell, *The Development of the American Romance* (1980). "The Birth-mark" has even attracted the interest of psychoanalytic publications: see Proudfit, "Eroticization."

13. Colacurcio, *Province of Piety*, pp. 494, 4, 2, 487; Colacurcio quotes his own marginalia: "My God—Hawthorne is Perry Miller" (p. 1). For another example of a trenchant historicist critique of the abuse of psychological approaches to Hawthorne's tales see Budick, "The World as Specter."

14. See Colacurcio's discussion of the seventeenth-century historical dimension of Hawthorne's tale in *Province of Piety*, pp. 251–82. "History," writes John Berger, "constitutes the relation between a present and its past" (Berger et al., *Ways of Seeing*, p. 11). The puritan history Hawthorne allegorizes and reimagines is not merely a thing of the past, but necessarily the relation between Hawthorne's present and this past.

15. See Leo Marx's 1964 classic, *The Machine in the Garden*.

16. See "The Procession of Life" (Apr. 1843), "The Celestial Railroad" (May 1843), "The New Adam and Eve" (Feb. 1843), "The Intelligence Office" (Mar. 1844), "The Christmas Banquet" (Jan. 1844), and "Earth's Holocaust" (May 1844). Of the 31 pieces Hawthorne published between 1837 and 1845, 22 appeared in the *Democratic Review*, a periodical founded to champion the Democratic Party and its Jacksonian platforms.

17. See Walker, *Critical Pronouncing Dictionary* 1: 176, and S. Johnson, *Dictionary*.

18. Julian Hawthorne, *Hawthorne and His Wife* 1: 225.

19. Mellow, *Hawthorne in His Times*, p. 164.

20. See *The Tempest* 1.2.316. Richard Bernheimer suggests that the wild

man addresses "the impulses of reckless self-assertion which are hidden in all of us, but normally kept under control" and "man's instincts and desires . . . which normally make their compromise with the demands of reality" (*Wild Men*, pp. 3, 121). It is likely that Hawthorne had *The Tempest* in the back of his mind if not open on his desk when writing "The Birth-mark."

21. See Barker-Benfield, *Horrors*, pp. 91, 101. Also see Alain Corbin, "The Secret of the Individual" in Perrot, ed., *Fires of Revolution*: "dreams have a history" (p. 518). On the branding of slaves from colonial times to the early nineteenth century see Jordan, *White over Black*, pp. 51, 60, 107, 112, 233, 366.

22. *McDowall's Journal* 1 (Feb. 1833): 11.

23. Ibid., p. 9.

24. On the fate of McDowall and *Fanny Hill*, consult Boyer, *Urban Masses*, p. 20.

25. Quoted in Barker-Benfield, *Horrors*, p. 108.

26. S. Freud, *Dora*, p. 67; "'Civilized' Sexual Morality and Modern Nervousness" (1908), in *Sexuality*, p. 26.

27. Brown, *Life Against Death*, pp. 158, 157, 163.

28. S. Freud, "Obsessive Acts," pp. 23–24.

29. Melville, *Moby-Dick*, p. 248.

30. Fenichel, *Theory of the Neuroses*, p. 289. Also consult Ferenczi, "Embarrassed Hands" and "Washing-Compulsion and Masturbation" (especially p. 311), in *Further Contributions*.

31. Rosenberg, "Sexuality, Class, and Role," especially pp. 137–38. On the mid-century advice book industry, see Walters, *Primers for Prudery*.

32. Todd's *Student Manual* is quoted in Barker-Benfield, *Horrors*, p. 170; also see Barker-Benfield, "The Spermatic Economy." Graham, *Lecture*, p. 88; Graham also writes of a compulsive offender who, when his hands become too unruly, consented "to be manacled" (p. 183).

33. J. DuBois, *Marriage Physiologically Discussed*, p. iv.

34. Graham, *Lecture*, p. 87. Also see Becklard, *Know Thyself*, which catalogs signs of masturbation ranging from "pimples and blotches" (p. 14) to "the blanched cheek" (p. 11). On the mid- and late-nineteenth-century anxiety over "plague spots" (more signs of self-pollution) see Haller and Haller, *Physician and Sexuality*, pp. 105, 204, 223.

35. Foucault, *Use of Pleasure*, pp. 11, 5.

36. Georgiana was not the first to have a hand imprinted on her face in mid-century representations. In the 1830's and 1840's, the artist George Catlin portrayed Native American males ("Calibans") with large hands painted across their faces. He exhibited his work in Boston, New York, and other cities in 1837. See Hassrick, *Catlin Book of American Indians*, p. 111 ("The Cheyenne," Pawnee, 1832) and p. 94 ("Strong Wind," Chippewa, 1843) and see p. 23 for information on Catlin's exhibitions.

37. *The Tempest*, 5.1.275–76; 5.1.50–51. *Moby-Dick*, p. 249.

38. A. Freud, *Writings*, pp. 126, 133.

39. Withycombe, *Dictionary of English Christian Names*, pp. 128–30, 39.

40. S. Freud, *Dora*, p. 136.

41. Crews, *Sins of the Fathers*, p. 25. Crews does not develop a detailed reading of the tale, but occasionally refers to it in passing.

42. Foucault, *An Introduction*, p. 131.

43. Stallybrass and White, *Politics and Poetics*, p. 197.

44. H. N. Smith, *Democracy*, p. 14.

45. Fetterley, *Provisions*, p. 26.

46. Tompkins, *Sensational Designs*, p. 198.

47. Anonymous review of *Twice-Told Tales* in *The Boston Miscellany of Literature* 1 (Feb. 1842): 92. My reading of reviews has been guided by Faust, "Hawthorne's Contemporaneous Reputation." Also see the copious collection of reviews reprinted in W. Cameron, *Hawthorne Among His Contemporaries*.

48. Anonymous review of *The Scarlet Letter* in *Graham's Magazine* 36 (May 1850): 346.

49. Duyckinck, "Nathaniel Hawthorne," pp. 323, 324.

50. C. Hale, "Nathaniel Hawthorne," p. 179.

51. Botta, *Hand-book*, p. 537.

52. Tuckerman, "Nathaniel Hawthorne," p. 344.

53. Quoted in Colacurcio, *Province of Piety*, p. 3.

54. F. Jameson, *Political Unconscious*, p. 62.

55. Lasch, *Culture of Narcissism*, p. 88.

56. Barker-Benfield, *Horrors*, p. 99.

57. Weedon, *Feminist Practice*, pp. 82–83.

58. Stallybrass and White, *Politics and Poetics*, p. 192. Nina Baym describes the female "force" that men repress in many of Hawthorne's stories as "woman's ability to create life." This life-giving force also serves as a metaphor for woman as artist and social actor. See Baym's wide-ranging discussion, "Hawthorne's Women," especially p. 253.

59. Hawthorne, *English Notebooks*, pp. 88–89.

60. Ovid, *Metamorphoses* 10: 243–97.

61. Gubar, "'The Blank Page,'" pp. 292–93. See also Arner, "Pygmalion in 'The Birthmark.'" And see Ruskin, "Queen's Gardens," p. 90: man "is eminently the doer, the creator" whereas women's "intellect is not for invention or creation, but for sweet ordering, arrangement, and decision."

62. For some astute comments on the politics of feminizing Nature see Homans, *Women Writers*, p. 13.

63. "Birthmark" is not in John Walker's *Critical Pronouncing Dictionary*, Dr. Johnson's *Dictionary*, Webster's *American Dictionary*, or W. Turner's *School Dictionary*, nor does "birthmark" have its own entry in the *OED*. (Interestingly, *Webster's Ninth New Collegiate Dictionary* [1985] dates "birthmark" from 1580 but gives no further information.) See Shakespeare, "Rape of Lucrece," ll. 536–37.

64. Hooper, *Lexicon Medicum*, p. 96; I am grateful to Dr. John Mulliken of

the Harvard Medical School for pointing out that the birthmark was also called a *naevus* and for recommending that I refer to Hooper.

65. Steven Youra reads Aylmer's as the hand that wrote "mortality" in " 'The Fatal Hand.' "

66. See Bush, "Bosom Serpents"; Van Leer, "Roderick's Other Serpent."

67. McDowall, *McDowall's Journal* II (May 1834): 34. The narrator says of Roderick's crusade: "Still, the city could not bear this apostle" (10: 278).

68. George Monteiro discusses medieval emblems of Envy with a snake emerging from its mouth in "Hawthorne's Emblematic Serpent." Bram Dijkstra points out the gynandrous characteristics of Medusa, "with her bouffant of snakes, paralyzing eyes, and bestial proclivities," in fin-de-siècle European representations (*Idols of Perversity*, pp. 309–10).

69. See M. P. Ryan, "Femininity and Capitalism," p. 159. Ryan quotes from domestic conduct books to suggest that the middle-class domestic woman was perceived as a kind of symbolic bosom.

70. Holmes, *Elsie Venner*, p. 278.

71. In the mid-century "bosom friend" denoted a wax or cotton stuffing that a woman would put beneath her dress to enlarge the appearance of her bodice; see Halttunen, *Confidence Men*, p. 73.

72. M. Douglas, *Purity and Danger*, pp. 98–99. Also see Hastrup, "Semantics of Biology"; Sanday, *Female Power*.

73. Smith-Rosenberg, "Sex as Symbol," pp. 245, 226. Also see Stephen Nissenbaum's brilliant study, *Sex, Diet, and Debility*, p. 129.

74. Barker-Benfield, *Horrors*, p. 290.

75. For an exemplary analysis of the ideological significance of changes in eighteenth- and nineteenth-century medical representations of the female body that seek to establish a biological foundation for sexual difference, see Laqueur, "Orgasm."

76. See Young, *Hawthorne's Secret*, pp. 59–62, 67–68.

77. Evans, *Abuse of Maternity*, pp. 26–27, 30, 28.

78. Grattan quoted in Calhoun, *Social History*, p. 160.

79. On Sophia's miscarriage in February, 1843, see Mellow, *Hawthorne in His Times*, p. 219. On pathological representations of the female body that appear in nineteenth- and twentieth-century medical discourses see Martin, *The Woman in the Body*, especially p. 87.

80. Rogin, *Fathers and Children*, p. 71. Dr. Edward H. Dixon, in the 1840's, still believed that female hysteria is "intimately connected with uterine derangements" and observed that the etymology of hysteria derives from Greek for womb. He also hinted, however, that this hysterical dis-ease may be causally related to domestic derangements: "certain females will pretend hysteric attacks" to exert control over their lives (*Woman, and Her Diseases*, pp. 100, 131, 140). On this topic see Smith-Rosenberg, "Hysterical Woman"; Smith-Rosenberg and Rosenberg, "The Female Animal," especially pp. 336–38. On "Mother" as "hysterical passion" see S. Johnson, *Dictionary*; Webster, *American Dictionary*, p. 543; Walker, *Critical Pronouncing Dictionary*, p. 347.

81. Ann Douglas Wood, "'Fashionable Diseases,'" p. 10. Baym, *Woman's Fiction*, p. 313.

82. Knowlton is quoted in Showalter and Showalter, "Victorian Women and Menstruation," p. 40. Rowe, *Important Disorders*, pp. 27–28. Rowe is also quoted in an excellent article on the subject by Smith-Rosenberg, "Puberty to Menopause," p. 29. Also see Blake, "Women and Medicine."

83. Williams, *Language of America*, p. 31. Adair, *American Indians*, p. 123. Many seventeenth- and eighteenth-century French priests, traders, and scientists recounted pollution rituals among northeastern tribes; see Axtell, ed., *Indian Peoples*, especially p. 60 from David Zeisberger's *History of the North American Indians* (1780). For some contemporary accounts see Catlin, *Letters and Notes*, p. 168; Ellis, *Polynesian Researches*, especially 4: 385–86 and 1: 128–29.

84. M. Douglas, *Purity and Danger*, p. 162.

85. On blood as a metaphor for women's writing, see Gubar, "'The Blank Page,'" pp. 296, 304. On "The Birth-mark" and menstruation imagery, see Lesser, *Fiction and the Unconscious*, pp. 88, 94; Fetterley, "Women Beware Science: 'The Birth-mark,'" pp. 22–33 in *Resisting Reader*, especially p. 25. Lesser's narrow but interesting psychoanalytical reading proposes that the "crimson stain symbolizes sexuality." In a note he suggests (following the advice of a friend) that the hand represents "female sexuality—that is . . . a castration symbol." What Lesser hints but does not seem able to say is that the "bloody hand" may be read psychoanalytically as a sign that sets off a chain of association in the minds of Aylmer and the "fastidious women" that leads to menstruation. Fetterley, in her provocative chapter, draws on Lesser's reading and does more than hint, although she too does not use the word menstruation.

86. Hawthorne quoted in Warren, *American Narcissus*, p. 191.

87. "The Heroine's Hand."

88. "Fashion Plates," p. 57. Stowe's letter to the editor appeared in the "Editor's Table," *Godey's* 26 (Jan. 1843): 58. Hale wrote in the "Editor's Table," *Godey's* 26 (May 1843): 249–50.

89. Shakespeare, in his portrayal of Prospero's coercive alchemy, questioned the morality of his own "alchemical" power to manipulate an audience through his art; see Egan, *Drama*, pp. 90–119. In his *Defence of Poesy* (1595) Sir Phillip Sidney celebrates the literary alchemist whose "invention" "doth grow in effect into another Nature, in making things either better than Nature brought forth, or, quite anew, forms such as never were in Nature." Like the alchemist working with lead, the poet transforms the "brazen" to "deliver a golden" (*Prose and Poetry*, pp. 108–9). Or in Aylmer's words, the alchemists have sought "the universal solvent by which the golden principle might be elicited from all things vile and base." Shelley's *Defence of Poetry* (1821), first published in 1840, also endows poetry with alchemical properties. Poetry, he writes, "transmutes all that it touches. . . . Its secret alchemy turns to potable gold the poisonous waters which flow from death through life." This immortalizing alchemy "adds beauty to that which is deformed" and "makes beautiful that which is distorted" (pp.

580, 561). In his final efforts to write a novel in the early 1860's, Hawthorne became obsessed with the theme of men searching for the alchemical elixir of life. Alchemical success may have been associated in Hawthorne's mind with writing the immortal work (immortalizing one's "hand" through literary fame).

90. M. D. Bell, *Development of American Romance*, p. 149.

91. Benjamin quoted in F. Jameson, *Marxism and Form*, pp. 70–71. Benjamin also observed, "In the nineteenth century allegory abandons the outside world, only to colonize the inner" (p. 73).

92. Tocqueville, *Democracy in America* 2: 240–41.

93. Sigourney, "Home," pp. 13–14.

94. Lazarus quoted in Stoehr, *Free Love*, p. 83.

95. Letter quoted in Rothman, *Hands and Hearts*, p. 64; also see pp. 56, 65.

96. Stanton quoted in E. C. DuBois, *Feminism and Suffrage*, p. 28.

97. M. P. Ryan, *Cradle*, pp. 235, 188; *Empire of the Mother*, p. 23.

98. Millicent Bell points out that "The Oval Portrait" probably influenced "The Birth-mark" (*Hawthorne's View of the Artist*, p. 81).

99. Poe, "The Oval Portrait," *Complete Tales and Poems*, pp. 290–92. Also see Christina Rossetti's poem on a similar theme, "In An Artist's Studio" (1856). Elizabeth Cady Stanton could easily have been commenting on Poe's tale when, in 1852, she wrote that "so long as man denies woman's identity with himself, he has no data to go upon in judging her.—He might as well attempt a sketch of the peculiar characteristics of Satan or Gabriel; he must, in either case, draw upon his imagination for the whole of it" ("The Wife").

100. Poe, "Berenice," *Complete Tales and Poems*, pp. 643–46. For an astute reading of "Berenice" see Dayan, *Fables of Mind*, pp. 135–58.

101. M. P. Ryan, *Cradle*, p. 148.

102. On formal relationships between allegory and obsession, read Angus Fletcher's chapter on "Psychoanalytic Analogues: Obsession and Compulsion," pp. 279–303 in *Allegory*.

103. For overviews of Spenser's influence on Hawthorne see Stewart, "Hawthorne and *The Faerie Queene*"; Himelick, "Hawthorne, Spenser, and Christian Humanism"; Jones, "Hawthorne and Spenser."

104. F. O. Matthiessen relates Hawthorne's predilection to employ allegory to "the Christian habit of mind that saw the hand of God in all manifestations of life" (*American Renaissance*, p. 243). An awareness of this puritan background is essential, but, as I suggest, other cultural roots of Hawthorne's preoccupation with allegory also require study.

105. Also relevant to an understanding of this context are the mid-century advice books, profiled by Karen Halttunen, that adumbrated a "sentimental typology of conduct" to encourage young men to decode character in the urban "world of strangers" populated with confidence men and painted women. Halttunen discusses the middle-class preoccupation with the "moral language of physiognomy" (*Confidence Men*, pp. 40–41).

106. On Spurzheim's trip to Boston see the early history of phrenology by R. W. Haskins, *History and Progress of Phrenology*, pp. 82, 118. Sophia is quoted in Stoehr, *Hawthorne's Mad Scientists*, p. 281; see Stoehr's chapter on "Physi-

ognomy and Phrenology," pp. 64–102. Also see Davies, *Phrenology Fact and Science*.

107. Soler, *Phrenology*, p. 23.

108. Fowler, *Fowler on Matrimony*, p. 45; see prefaces for figures on book sales.

109. Fowler, *Amativeness*, p. 45. For background on the Fowler brothers, consult M. B. Stern, *Heads and Headlines*.

110. See, for example, an anonymous, untitled essay in *The American Phrenological Journal and Miscellany* 2 (1840): 576. After advising his reader to beware the "Xantippe" (shrew) who "may rouge and powder her face" and the "fair infidel" who "may play the outward devotee to perfection," the author bestows his pity on the "anti-phrenologist" who lets slip the "guiding staff through the quicksands of courtship and marriage."

111. Neal, "The Young Phrenologist," pp. 157–69. Richard Sennett, whose emphasis is on Europe, concludes that the "inflation" of details into signs of motives and feelings signals trouble in the nineteenth-century bourgeois family (*Fall of Public Man*, p. 179).

112. M. D. Bell, *Development of American Romance*, p. 137. On Hawthorne's psychological (rather than ideological) use of allegory to criticize characters who allegorize others also consult J. O. Rees, Jr., "Hawthorne's Concept of Allegory"; Grunes, "Allegory Versus Allegory."

113. Tompkins, *Sensational Designs*, pp. 163–67. Lydia Sigourney's "The Father" (1834) is an earlier example of sentimental writing that both expresses and is critical of the feminine "ethic of submission"; see Fetterley, *Provisions*, pp. 105–6. The "ethic of submission" was produced through advice books as well as literature. Rev. E. H. Chapin, for example, counseled the middle-class wife as follows: no matter what "head-long impulses may drive him [the husband], and 'fierce passions' shake him like a reed," woman, with "the touch of the 'soft hand' that rested upon his head in his youthful prayer" must strive to "check and calm him." This exhortation on behalf of domestic therapy soon twists into a sanction for something more disturbing. Although the wretch "who crushes with a polluted hand that affection that has entrusted him" is denounced, the submissive wife is urged to bear her cross in private. Like Georgiana, woman must "anoint the hands that have abused her . . . like Christ washing the disciples feet" (*Duties*, pp. 134, 63). In Melville's *Pierre Or, the Ambiguities* (1852), Isabel, a caricature of the submissive lover, offers to "go blind for thee, Pierre; here, take out these eyes, and use them for glasses." Isabel vies with Lucy for the affection of Pierre by offering to "sell her hair; have these teeth pulled out . . . some way I will earn money for thee!" (pp. 374, 391).

114. Gay, *Bourgeois Experience*, p. 444. For a critique of the proposition that Freud's theories about psychological relations within the family are "timeless," see Mark Poster: "Before the formation of the connection between romantic love and monogamy, before the nuclear family, extended families and kinship structures were dominant and these were integrated into larger social structures. A true psychological history of the family would concern itself with the nature of these differences and hence with the limits of the Freudian model based on

the Oedipus complex. . . . [Freud] extends the nuclear family, with its privatiza-tion of love and sex, as the norm of all family structures" (*Critical Theory of the Family*, p. 37).

115. M. P. Ryan, *Cradle*, p. 185.

116. It has been argued that Hawthorne's preoccupation with represent-ing psychological relationships should be situated in the context of early- and mid-nineteenth-century psychology. After all, Thomas Upham, author of *Ele-ments of Mental Philosophy* (1831) and *Outlines of Imperfect and Disordered Mental Action* (1840), was Hawthorne's teacher at Bowdoin. And Hawthorne borrowed Dugald Stewart's *Philosophical Essays* (1811), Thomas Brown's *Lectures on the Philosophy of the Human Mind* (1822), and David Hartley's *Observations of Man* (1801) from the Salem Atheneum. Allan Gardner Smith assesses the influ-ence that such early psychology texts probably had on Hawthorne in his short monograph *The Analysis of Motives*, pointing out a number of correspondences between passages from these texts and Hawthorne's writings. However, he also concludes that Hawthorne's study of guilt and "isolation" are original and that his study of obsession is (by modern notions) more sophisticated ("Where the psychologists describe, Hawthorne analyses," p. 104). Hawthorne, unlike the psychologists he drew on, developed a concept of the *unconscious*. Although Smith roots his discussion in the history of psychology, he nonetheless seems to envision this history as a teleological discovery of an unconscious self that we are now more adept at comprehending. He does not historicize "psychol-ogy" itself as a category whose sociological emergence is connected to other transformations in the culture.

117. See, for example, Philip Young's *Hawthorne's Secret* on *The Scarlet Let-ter*: "The subtlety, penetration, and modernity of its psychological understand-ing . . . is astonishing. (With Chillingworth, Hawthorne sketches the portrait of a psychiatrist, and in accounting for Dimmesdale's malady he lays down the basic principle of psychosomatic medicine, generations before it existed. . . .)" (p. 34). For another ahistorical discussion of Hawthorne's "pre-Freudian ideas" in *The Scarlet Letter*, see Adams, "Pathography."

118. F. Jameson, *Political Unconscious*, p. 64. Also see his *Marxism and Form*: "What if the Freudian raw material (. . . dreams, slips of the tongue, fixations, traumas, the Oedipal situation, the death wish) were itself but a sign or symptom of some vaster historical transformation? In this context, the Freud-ian typology of the mental functions may be seen as the return of a new type of allegorical vision" (p. 27). The historical connection I am suggesting between Hawthorne's symbolic system and Freud's (focusing on the historical conditions of possibility) is much like the connection that Jameson makes between Conrad and Sartre's existentialism: "It should be clear that I am neither suggesting an in-fluence of Conrad on Sartre, nor, inversely, making a case for Conrad as Sartre's precursor"; rather, we "ought to direct our attention first to the similarity of the social structures and historical conditions in which, as symbolic gestures," their works are "meaningful" (*Political Unconscious*, p. 259). Also see Mitterauer and Sieder, *European Family*, especially pp. 59–61. Mitterauer, whose focus is on

Austria, demonstrates both the historical and the class specificity of Freud's *privatized* assumptions about the family. There are also many similarities between nineteenth-century American and German gender roles; see Hausen, "Family and Role-division," especially pp. 55–56.

119. See Crews, *Sins of the Fathers*, "Afterword," pp. 273–86.

120. Demos, "Oedipus and America," pp. 27, 33, 37, 34, 37.

121. Ibid., p. 36. Jameson, Foucault, Poster, Mitterauer, Demos, and I are *not* recycling Freud's acknowledgment that, as Henri Ellenberger put it, the "great writers" were "his masters." What Ellenberger omits in his account of "Freud's sources" is a history of personal life that helped to produce Freud's sources. See Ellenberger, *Discovery of the Unconscious*, p. 540.

122. Erlich, *Family Themes*, see pp. 13, 42, 44, 73, 118, 132–33. See Mintz's provocative synthesis of the history of family life and biography, *Prison of Expectations*.

123. For some astute remarks on the emergence of the novel and middle-class privatization see D. A. Miller, *The Novel and the Police*, pp. 82–83.

124. Dana, "Domestic Life," in *Writings*, p. 441.

125. Dana, *Paul Felton*, see pp. 268, 272–73, 324, 361. See S. Freud, "Certain Neurotic Mechanisms in Jealousy, Paranoia, and Homosexuality" (1922), in *Sexuality*.

126. Simms, *Confession*, pp. 133, 179, 143. For a brilliant reading of Dana's *Paul Felton* and Simms's *Confession* see D. B. Davis, "Jealousy and the Immoral Wife," pp. 179–209 in *Homicide*. Also see Barrett and McIntosh, *The Anti-Social Family*, pp. 51–52, on the deleterious effects of privatization on the personality structure of the child.

127. Dana and Simms show us a heated-up psychological version of what historian Stuart Blumin has termed the "domestic privatism" of the middle class, but few healthy signs of "intraclass sociability" to counter this retreat (*Emergence*, p. 257).

128. Halttunen, *Confidence Men*, p. 4. Also see Kett, *Rites of Passage*, pp. 105–7; Susman, " 'Personality' and the Making of Twentieth-Century Culture," pp. 271–85 in *Culture As History*.

129. Michael Davitt Bell discusses the idea of Hawthorne's literary contribution to "psychological realism" but seems to regard it as Hawthorne's insight into *the* self rather than a middle-class ideological construction whose emergence should be situated in the context of related discursive developments and other determinative social transformations. See Bell's excellent essay "Arts of Deception," especially p. 46.

130. Oliphant, "Modern Novelists," pp. 562–65.

131. Smith-Rosenberg, "Davey Crockett," p. 90. In his study of sex roles in mid-century utopian communities, Louis J. Kern has endeavored to account for the "ordering" of personal life (and its ensuing disorder) as a complex emotional response to social change (*An Ordered Love*, pp. 38–39). David Brion Davis has suggested that themes of tension between the sexes in "sub-classic" mid-nineteenth-century fiction be decoded historically as symbolic of larger social

pressures: "Popular writers expressed their fear of change in specifically sexual terms. . . . Social disorganization could be represented in its ultimate form of sex and death" (*Homicide*, p. 209). Larzer Ziff has proposed that we consider reversing "the more familiar critical procedure" (psychoanalysis) and suggests that the representation of sexuality in Hawthorne's writings is "itself symbolic of other concerns," but this idea is not fully explored (*Literary Democracy*, pp. 136–37).

132. On the mid-century publishing industry and the formation of middle-class identity, see James D. Hart's chapter on "Home Influence," pp. 85–105 in *The Popular Book*.

Chapter 2

1. Hawthorne used these encyclopedias (although we have no record of his borrowing the volumes containing the entry on "naevus"). See Kesselring, "Hawthorne's Reading," pp. 178–79. Hawthorne borrowed volume 10 of the *Encyclopaedia Britannica* on June 12, 1835, and volume 18 on Oct. 19, 1827, from the Salem Atheneum. He borrowed various volumes of Rees's *Cyclopaedia* in 1827, 1829, and 1830.

2. "Imagination" in Society of Gentlemen, *Dictionary*, pp. 1738–39.

3. Huet, "Living Images," p. 74. Also see Gilbert and Gubar, "Horror's Twin: Mary Shelley's Monstrous Eve," pp. 213–47 in *Madwoman in the Attic*. Although he does not develop the idea of Georgiana-as-monster, the correspondence A. G. Lloyd Smith makes between Frankenstein's monster and Georgiana ("the monster [who] already exists") are fascinating (*Eve Tempted*, p. 99).

4. Giovanni's anxiety about Beatrice resembles mid-century anxieties about the seductive "influence" of confidence men and painted women as described by Halttunen, who quotes from Rev. David Magie, *The Spring-time of Life, or, Advice to Youth* (1853): their influence on unsuspecting young men was "like poison, taken into the physical system, and will be sure, sooner or later, to reveal its bitter results" (*Confidence Men*, see pp. 4, 13). Giovanni is, on his own in Padua, like the liminal, uprooted young men of the mid-century to whom so many advice books were directed.

5. See Kesselring, "Hawthorne's Reading," p. 190. On Oct. 4, 1837, either Nathaniel or his sister Elizabeth borrowed from the Salem Atheneum Sir Walter Scott's *Demonology and Witchcraft* (1831); on p. 51 Scott relates traditions that equate witches and poisoners. Margaret Hallissy discusses Sir Thomas Browne and other possible sources for Hawthorne's ideas about poison and poisonous women in "Hawthorne's Venomous Beatrice."

6. Shelley, *Valperga*, p. 51.

7. On advice book representations of the public sphere as "poisonous," see Cott, *Bonds of Womanhood*, p. 68.

8. For a provocative reading of some of the sexual imagery here see Fryer, "Beatrice Rappacini: The Literary Convention as Allegory," pp. 40–47 in *The Faces of Eve*. Also see Leverenz, *Manhood*, p. 239.

9. The first quote is from Eaton, *Botanical Grammar and Dictionary*; the second, from *Encyclopaedia Britannica* (1797).

10. [Dr. Ray], "Decandolle's Botany," pp. 35–39. Also see Gray, "Dr. Lindley's Natural System of Botany," p. 300.

11. On the anxiety that monsters may be the originals, see [Dr. Ray], "Decandolle's Botany," pp. 46–47; Daniels, "The Deluge of Facts," in *American Science*, especially p. 117. Russel Blaine Nye also provides a useful introduction to the importance of the Baconian method and classification to mid-century American science in *Society and Culture*, pp. 237–58. Also see Foucault's suggestive chapter on "Classifying" (he also discusses "monsters"), pp. 125–65 in *The Order of Things*.

12. Pliny quoted in Delaney, Lupton, and Toth, eds., *The Curse*, p. 7. Yet several mid-century medical authorities regarded Pliny's suspicion that the "catamenial fluid was poisonous" a "most ridiculous opinion"; see Michael Ryan's *Manual of Midwifery* (1835), p. 30; and William P. Dewees's *Treatise on the Diseases of Females* (1826), pp. 62–63. Philip Young cites these "ancient superstitions" as relevant to Georgiana and Beatrice, for Hawthorne was well trained in the classics at Bowdoin (*Hawthorne's Secret*, p. 62). While Hawthorne was editing *The American Magazine* in May, 1836, his sister Elizabeth borrowed Philemon Holland's 1601 translation of Pliny (Kesselring, "Hawthorne's Reading," p. 189).

13. For medical texts, see M. Ryan, *Manual of Midwifery*, p. 29; Pancoast, *Ladies' New Medical Guide*, p. 157. On menstruous plants, see Lindley and More, eds., *Treasury of Botany* 2:735 (also cited in OED).

14. Ruskin, "Queen's Gardens," pp. 116, 109, 91.

15. Davidoff and Hall, *Family Fortunes*, pp. 191–92.

16. Halttunen, *Confidence Men*, pp. 86–87.

17. On women authors see Ann Douglas: "Such names, flirting coyly with suggestions of vegetative process, are decorative advertisements of luxury items. Even while they flatter the authors' femininity, they define it as superfluous; they are purely fictional" (*Feminization of American Culture*, pp. 222–23).

18. S. J. Hale, *Flora's Interpreter*, p. v.

19. Ibid., p. iii.

20. The letter was quoted by Hale in her regular column "Editor's Table," *Godey's* 24 (May 1842): 286.

21. Hawthorne quoted in Chevigny, *The Woman and the Myth*, p. 161.

22. Hawthorne quoted in Wade, *Margaret Fuller*, p. 111.

23. Chevigny, *The Woman and the Myth*, p. 161.

24. Wade, *Margaret Fuller*, pp. 4–7.

25. Emerson quoted in Chevigny, *The Woman and the Myth*, p. 24.

26. Ibid., pp. 67, 74, 216.

27. Ibid., p. 231.

28. Fuller quoted in Blanchard, *Margaret Fuller*, p. 191.

29. Channing quoted in ibid., pp. 58–59.

30. Weld's edition of Winthrop's *A Short Story of the Rise, reign, and ruine of*

the *Antinomians, Familists & Libertines* is excerpted in Hall, ed., *Antinomian Controversy*, pp. 214, 263, 262. Anne Kibbey suggests that anxieties about female "monstrosity" may have been a displacement of anxiety about the 1637 war with the Pequots in her chapter on "1637: the Pequot War and the Antinomian Controversy," pp. 92–120 in *Interpretation of Material Shapes*. Also see Schutte, " 'Such Monstrous Birth' "; Barker-Benfield, "Anne Hutchinson."

31. E. Johnson, *Wonder-Working Providence*, pp. 132–33.

32. Hawthorne, "Mrs. Hutchinson," *Works: Riverside Edition* 4:168–69. The piece originally appeared in the *Salem Gazette*, Dec. 7, 1830. See A. Turner, *Hawthorne: A Biography*, pp. 55–57.

33. See Baym, *Women's Fiction*. As cited by Judith Fetterley, Helen Papashvily's *All the Happy Endings* (1956) estimates that "of the two-hundred-odd works of fiction produced by Americans between 1779 and 1829, 'better than a third were written for or by women' " (*Provisions*, p. 5).

34. Quotations on Wright in Eckhardt, *Fanny Wright*, pp. 185, 258, 3. Also consult O'Connor, *Pioneer Women Orators*, pp. 47–53.

35. *McDowall's Journal* 1 (Feb. 1833): 9.

36. Wright, *Course of Popular Lectures*, p. 25.

37. Gage quoted in Calhoun, *Social History*, p. 124.

38. Stille quoted in Barker-Benfield, *Horrors*, p. 85.

39. "Critical Notices," pp. 266–67.

40. Poe, *Autography*, pp. 171, 149.

41. Fern, "American Female Literature." One anonymous critic for *The Lily* noted that the domestic position of the woman writer was acutely vulnerable: "A literary *woman* must not neglect the smallest tithe of her multifarious duties, or she is condemned without judgement or mercy" ("Woman's Rights," p. 28).

42. Tharp, *Peabody Sisters*, p. 161. Also see Greenwood, *Greenwood Leaves*. Greenwood and Hawthorne had the same publisher. She paraded herself "stark naked" with sketches such as "Heart Histories," "Destiny in a Rose-Bud," and "A Spring Flower Faded." For an account of Hawthorne's and Sophia's contempt for Greenwood's literary clichés, see Hull, " 'Scribbling' Females."

43. Hawthorne quoted in Pattee, *Feminine Fifties*, pp. 110–11. Also see H. N. Smith, "Scribbling Women."

44. For a useful study of Hawthorne's relationship to his mother, sisters, and wife, see Gloria Erlich's chapter on "The Inner Circle: Hawthorne's Women," in *Family Themes*, especially pp. 66–103.

45. Hawthorne, "Mrs. Hutchinson," *Works: Riverside Edition* 4: 168–69.

46. Hale, *The Lecturess*, p. 21.

47. Ibid., p. 8.

48. Hawthorne proposed the three titles in a letter he wrote to Evert Duyckinck on Feb. 22, 1846; quoted in Willoughby, " 'The Old Manse' Revisited," p. 53.

49. Leland S. Person, Jr., has pointed out language in Nathaniel's courtship letters to Sophia which suggests his sense that he has been impregnated

by her (*Aesthetic Headaches*, pp. 103–4). The general thrust of his interesting (but ahistorical) close readings of Hawthorne's tales and novels is that "Hawthorne embodied his deepest creative impulse in his strongest female characters" (p. 172).

50. Ruskin, "Queen's Gardens," p. 102.

51. See Morgan, *The Puritan Family*, pp. 40, 48–49, 53, 78; Gadlin, "Private Lives and Public Order," p. 38. Also see Demos on the "little commonwealth" vs. the nineteenth-century "hothouse" ("Oedipus and America," p. 28).

52. Coontz, *Social Origins*, p. 189.

53. D'Emilio and Freedman, *Intimate Matters*, pp. 73, 82, 84.

54. See M. P. Ryan, *Womanhood in America*, p. 79.

Chapter 3

1. Allen, *Woman's Place*, p. 5.

2. M. P. Ryan, "Femininity and Capitalism," p. 151.

3. Hawthorne, *English Notebooks*, p. 89.

4. See Cott, "Passionless"; Berg, *The Remembered Gate*. Berg quotes from Hawthorne's *Our Old Home* (1863): "Foreigners who visit this country [comment] that American ladies have, almost without exception, a delicacy of complexion and appearance, connoting almost a sickness" (p. 112). Other reports on America's pallid women are on pp. 112–13.

5. Coontz, *Social Origins*, p. 98.

6. Reviewers in the 1850's saw Priscilla as, in the words of one critic, "one of those pretty phantoms with which Mr. Hawthorne occasionally adorns his romances," a "pretty-looking ghost." This critic goes on to chide Hawthorne for failing to make the effort to embody Priscilla: "A very few lines will indicate a spectre, when it would take an entire month to paint a woman." If Hawthorne continues to give his readers "shadows," soon his "imitators will inundate their books with skeletons" (anonymous review of *The Blithedale Romance* in *The American Whig Review* 16 (Nov. 1852): 417–24; the quote is on p. 421.

7. See Smith-Rosenberg, "From Puberty to Menopause," p. 27; also Barker-Benfield, "The Spermatic Economy."

8. Clarke, *Sex in Education*, pp. 62, 63. On pale women also see Buchan, *Domestic Medicine*, p. 330. Paleness was read as a sign of the progress of civilization; cf. Dr. Dio Lewis, *Our Girls* (1871): "The fragile, pale young woman with a lisp, is thought, by many silly people, to be more a *lady*, than another with ruddy cheeks and vigorous health. . . . There exists, somehow in the fashionable world, the notion that a pale and sensitive woman is feminine and refined, while one in blooming health is masculine and coarse" (quoted in Cogan, *All American Girl*, p. 7).

9. Welter, "Female Complaints," pp. 57–70 of *Dimity Convictions*, p. 57.

10. Grimké, *Letters*, pp. 33, 22.

11. "Sydney Smith vs. T. S. Arthur."

12. Fuller's remark on overgrown children is quoted by Welter, "Coming of Age in America: The American Girl in the Nineteenth Century," in *Dimity Convictions*, p. 12. For Fuller's view of *Godey's* see A. Douglas, *Feminization of American Culture*, p. 323.

13. Ward, "The True Woman," reprinted in *The Story of Avis*; see pp. 269–72.

14. Fetterley, *Resisting Reader*, p. 22. Also see M. P. Ryan: "Significant sex segregation cut an especially deep rift through American life in the nineteenth-century, dividing culture, society, and even human emotions into male and female domains" (*Cradle*, p. 191).

15. Berger et al., *Ways of Seeing*, pp. 46–47.

16. See Banner, *American Beauty*: she comments on social powerlessness and beauty on pp. 13–14; quotes the 1852 *Godey's* on p. 10; quotes Stowe on p. 47; reports on arsenic and painting faces on pp. 41, 4; quotes Hawthorne on pp. 57, 305.

17. James, *Diary*, p. 95.

18. Douglas, *Feminization of American Culture*, pp. 153, 2. Poe also writes of female death as a romantic ideal: "The death, then, of a beautiful woman is unquestionably, the most poetical in the world" (*Letters*, p. 38).

19. See Owens, "Posing," p. 7.

20. Oliphant, "Modern Novelists," p. 564.

21. R.H.N., "American Authorship—Hawthorne," p. 506. George Eliot felt that Hawthorne's narrative decision not to let Zenobia "come out of her struggle in regal triumph" exhibited his "lack of moral earnestness" (quoted in A. Turner, *Hawthorne: A Biography*, p. 241).

22. Review of *The Blithedale Romance*, *American Whig Review* 16 (Nov. 1852): 417–424; see p. 419.

23. *Hamlet* 3.1.142.

24. Kesselring, "Hawthorne's Reading," p. 184.

25. A. Jameson, *Characteristics of Women*, pp. 130–33. Mrs. Jameson's sentimentalizing simply reproduces the Queen's narrative of Ophelia's death; she tells Ophelia's brother, Laertes, that the drowning maiden "chaunted snatches of old times, / As one incapable of her own distress." Until finally her clothes, "heavy with drink, / Pull'd the poor wretch from her melodious lay, / To muddy death" (*Hamlet* 4.7.179–84): Ophelia, shrouded by the Queen's "melodious lay," sinks in a swamp of poetic conventions. The "pastoralization" of Zenobia's death also parallels the transformation of mourning into an Arcadian excursion in what Ann Douglas terms "The Rural Cemetary Movement": "The cemetary functioned not like experience but like literature; it was in several senses a sentimental reader's paradise" (*Feminization of American Culture*, p. 253). Also see Halttunen on the theatricality of middle-class mourning rituals in the 1850's (*Confidence Men*, pp. 124–52).

26. A. Jameson, *Characteristics of Women*, pp. 131, 72, 74.

27. Showalter, *The Female Malady*, pp. 60, 86, 81, 79. Also see Showalter's "Representing Ophelia."

28. Ward, "The True Woman," p. 272. And see Brodhead, "Veiled Ladies."

29. Owens, "The Medusa Effect." Also see Vickers, "'The Blazon of sweet beauty's beast.'"

30. See Shriber, "Justice to Zenobia."

31. John Harmon McElroy and Edward L. McDonald play detective and accuse Coverdale of murdering Zenobia in "The Coverdale Romance." Beverly Hume takes the narrative evidence they discuss to suggest that Coverdale is Hawthorne's mid-century portrait of an aggressive madman in "The Case against Hawthorne's Coverdale."

32. Ovid, *Metamorphoses* 1: 20–32.

33. Chevigny, *The Woman and the Myth*, p. 27.

34. Eckhardt, *Fanny Wright*, p. 258.

35. Conway, *Life of Nathaniel Hawthorne*, p. 140.

36. C. Hale, "Nathaniel Hawthorne," p. 180.

37. Chevigny, *The Woman and the Myth*, pp. 87, 133, 231–32. Chevigny also cites Edna Dow Cheney's testimony of Fuller's influence: "Although I believed that I should learn from her, I had no idea that I should esteem, and much more, love her" (p. 230). For a different emphasis on Fuller see Eakins's chapter "Self-Culture: Margaret Fuller and Hawthorne's Heroines," pp. 49–79 in *New England Girl*.

38. Chevigny, *The Woman and the Myth*, pp. 160, 419, 416. In trying to account for Hawthorne's ambivalence toward Fuller, Mason Wade suggests that Hawthorne may have been shocked by her frankness and passion, jealous of her greater renown (her reviews of Hawthorne helped build his reputation), and perhaps even jealous of her influence on Sophia in the early years of his marriage: "It would be natural, too, for him to resent the admiration that his Sophia paid the Sybil of the Conversations" (*Margaret Fuller*, p. 108). Wade observes many similarities between Fuller and Zenobia, but also notes that Zenobia was a beautified version of her: "Beauty was a conventional and necessary attribute of the heroine of a novel" (p. 115).

39. Anthon, *Classical Dictionary*, p. 1405. On Hawthorne's use of Anthon see McPherson, *Hawthorne as Myth-Maker*, p. 38.

40. "What Says History of Woman?" *The Lily*.

41. Child, *Brief History*, p. 30.

42. Grimké, *Letters*, pp. 32–33. A. Jameson, *Celebrated Female Sovereigns*, p. 59.

43. Ware, *Zenobia* 2: 87, 32. Ware's novel is discussed (not in relation to Hawthorne) by Ann Douglas in *The Feminization of American Culture*, p. 138; this reference encouraged me to reread *Blithedale* in light of Ware's earlier work. Since then David S. Reynolds has suggested a connection between the two novels in his wide-ranging *Beneath the American Renaissance* (p. 379).

44. Ware, *Zenobia* 1: 89, 143.

45. George Eliot's comments on Fanny Wright, a Zenobia of sorts, apply equally well to Ware's heroine: her "passionate, ideal nature demanded an epic life" in preference to the "many-volumed romances of chivalry and the social conquests of a brilliant girl" (quoted in Eckhardt, *Fanny Wright*, p. 3).

46. Here Ware may have followed the lead of Boccaccio, who sketches Zenobia as having intercourse with her husband only for purposes of procreation in order to serve the state; see Boccaccio, *Concerning Famous Women*, p. 228.

47. Ware, *Zenobia* 2: 36, 144.

48. Anthon, *Classical Dictionary*, p. 1405.

49. Ware, *Zenobia* 2: 278–79.

50. Boccaccio, *Concerning Famous Women*, pp. 226, 229.

51. Child, *Brief History*, p. 31.

52. On Hawthorne and sympathy, see Hutner, *Secrets and Sympathy*.

53. S. Freud, "Medusa's Head" (1922), pp. 212–13 in *Sexuality*. Also see Ferenczi, whose psychoanalytic reading that "the head of Medusa is the terrible symbol of the female genital region" accords with Freud's, but he adds, "The fearful and alarming starting eyes of the Medusa head have also the secondary meaning of erection" (*Further Contributions*, p. 360).

54. See Hertz, "Medusa's Head," p. 40, on the French revolution and figurations of revolutionary women as Medusa. For a critique of Hertz's tendency to psychologize, see Catherine Gallagher, "More About 'Medusa's Head,'" pp. 55–57.

55. Here too the parallel, not only between Fuller and Zenobia, but between Fuller and Hester comes into play. As one critic notes, Fuller's defense of Mazzini and the Italian revolution marked her as "an ardent revolutionary supporting the overthrow of the most prominent political-religious leader in the world"; both Hester and Fuller "were associated with the ideas of temptation and revolution, with the figures of Eve and liberty"; and both gained a new vision, perhaps like Hawthorne, by, in the eyes of their public, losing their heads (L. Reynolds, "Revolutions Abroad," p. 66). Sacvan Bercovitch also connects Hester's revolutionary thoughts, fear of social revolution, and American anxieties about European and American female revolutionaries: "There is every reason to assume that [Hawthorne] was deliberately evoking what social commentators had just designated the first major symptom of the 'red plague of European revolutions . . . on these shores.' I refer to the Women's Rights Convention at Seneca Falls in 1848" ("Hawthorne's A-Morality," p. 5).

56. In his tales Hawthorne mainly offers us constructs of the "true woman" rather than the "real woman." On the advice book construct of "true womanhood" see Welter, "The Cult of True Womanhood" (also collected in Welter, *Dimity Convictions*). On the literary and advice book construct of "real womanhood" see Cogan, *All American Girl*.

Chapter 4

1. Cott, *Bonds of Womanhood*, p. 69. In addition to Cott's historical account of this systemic relationship, see M. P. Ryan, "Femininity and Capitalism," p. 152.

2. Leyda, ed., *Melville Log* 1: 380.

3. In *Moby-Dick* Ahab's "birthmark" is white, like the whale he hunts. Like Georgiana's bloody hand, Ahab's "rod-like mark" prompts speculations about its origins and meanings, the last of which supposes that this "birthmark" extends from crown to sole (p. 169). Rather than a handsome woman, we find a "handsome sailor" in *Billy Budd*. Billy's handsome "mysteriousness," like Georgiana's "charm," gets him into deadly trouble with men. The explicit link here is the flaw: "like the beautiful woman in one of Hawthorne's minor tales, there was just one thing amiss in him. No visible blemish, indeed, as with the lady; no, but an occasional liability to vocal defect. . . . Billy was a striking instance that the arch interferer . . . slip[s] in his little card, as much as to remind us—I too have a hand here" (pp. 19–22). Billy's striking handsomeness and his striking hand lead to his downfall. On the complex relationships between the novels of Hawthorne and Melville see Brodhead, *Hawthorne, Melville, and the Novel*.

4. I am grateful to Richard Brodhead for suggesting long ago that I consider the relationship between these two tales. See Mumford, *Herman Melville*, p. 236; Rogin, *Subversive Genealogies*, p. 207. "The Bell-Tower" and "The Tartarus of Maids" are cited in the text by page number from *Great Short Stories of Herman Melville*.

5. On the "empire of necessity," see Rogin, *Subversive Genealogies*, p. 207. Mumford notes that mid-century "industrialism was a value in itself: people encouraged it as the patrons of the Renaissance encouraged art, not doubting that the activity was a great one, and made for a higher civilization" (*Herman Melville*, p. 65). See for example, the article "Modern and Ancient Works" in *Scientific American* 4 (Feb. 1849): "A spinning jenny does more good for a country than a palace, and a steam engine confers more benefit than a temple. We do not disparage the Fine Arts by any means . . . but these are only secondary triumphs of genius" (p. 165). Also consult Fenton, "The Bell-Tower."

6. Marvin Fisher makes the connection between Bannadonna's bell and the Liberty Bell in his suggestive reading of "The Bell-Tower" in *Going Under*, p. 102. My readings of this tale and "Tartarus" have benefited from Fisher's literary and historical insights.

7. Also see Melville's *Pierre*, p. 110: "a smile is the vehicle of all ambiguities."

8. Poe, "The Fall of the House of Usher," *Complete Tales and Poems*, p. 241.

9. Spenser, *Faerie Queene* 5.1.12.

10. On the ideology of the "belle" see Banner, *American Beauty*, pp. 93, 100, 103–5. Also see a mild criticism of "our fashionables" by Sarah J. Hale, "New Year At Home."

11. For example, see an anonymous review of Hawthorne's tales (probably written by Evert A. Duyckinck) in which Hawthorne is portrayed as an artisan who casts metals: "Many costly ingredients, many rude ones, like rings and crucifixes tumbled in with masses of ore in the casting of some old church bell, have been melted down and purified together before there is music in the heart" ("Nathaniel Hawthorne," p. 378). In "The Artist of the Beautiful" (1844) Hawthorne used machinery as a trope for writing (making it Owen Warland's "esthetic passion"). Several years before, in 1839, the *Godey's* editor compared tales to "mechanical contrivances": "The smaller ones are often more complicated and more ingenious than those of greater dimensions" (S. J. Hale, "Tales.") Also see Dr. Elder, who wrote in *The Una*: "The writer having the control of his machinery, enlists the highest feelings in the plot of his story, and takes care to gratify them fully in the issue, making the mechanism work out the best wishes of the heart" ("The Truth of Fiction," p. 5). Hawthorne himself, in sending a draft of *Blithedale* to the reviewer E. P. Whipple, wrote: "Should you spy ever so many defects, I cannot promise to amend them; the metal hardens very soon after I pour it out of my melting-pot into the mould" (quoted in A. Turner, *Hawthorne: A Biography*, p. 237).

12. For an account of the development of Davis's commitment to women's rights in Utica, see M. P. Ryan, *Cradle*, pp. 226–29. Also see O'Connor, *Pioneer Women Orators*, pp. 85–86.

13. P. W. Davis, "The Myth of Una."

14. Letter to the Editor, *The Una* 1 (Apr. 1853): 38.

15. The first critic is Caroline Healy Dall, "Charlotte Bronte Nicol, Or Currer Bell"; the second is A. H. Price, "Reasons Why Woman Should Define Her Own Sphere."

16. Linn, "Marriage the Only Resource," p. 2.

17. For an account of how Una was identified in the mid-century with "true womanhood," see Herbert, "Nathaniel Hawthorne, Una Hawthorne." Considering Herbert's subtle argument that Hawthorne's daughter, Una, refused to live up to the construct of femininity imposed by her name, perhaps Melville, who often visited the Hawthornes when they lived in the Berkshires, also had Hawthorne's Una in mind as one who was molded within a belle tower.

18. See D. Reynolds, *Beneath the American Renaissance*: "By 1860 it was estimated that of the 48,900 operatives in American woolen factories, 41 percent were women; of the 118,920 workers in cotton factories, a staggering 62 percent were women" (p. 352).

19. *Illiad* 8.10–14.

20. Spenser, *Faerie Queene* 2.12.6. Also see Lydia Maria Child's description of the Tartar women in her *Brief History of the Condition of Women*: "The Tartar women in general perform a greater share of labor than the men; for it is a prevailing opinion that they were sent into the world for no other purpose but to be useful and convenient slaves to the stronger sex" (pp. 162–63).

21. See Leyda, *Melville Log* 1: 103. The character of papermaking had

changed considerably over the first half of the nineteenth century. In 1829 only 6 of the 60 paper mills in Massachusetts had papermaking machines; in the rest paper was manufactured by hand. Even in this phase papermaking was turning into big business. By 1845, when the number of paper mills in Massachusetts had grown to 89, there were only 2 hand-operated mills left in America (Hunter, *Papermaking*, pp. 357, 360).

22. Weston, "Papermaking in Berkshire County," p. 22.

23. J. E. A. Smith, *History of Berkshire County*, p. 664.

24. Marx, *Capital*, p. 233; in addition, see p. 256. Also see a fine study of Marx's tropes by Stanley Edgar Hyman, *The Tangled Bank*. Marx, Hyman observes, rhetorically portrayed capitalists as "ghouls" who were busy " 'coining children's blood into capital' " (p. 134).

25. For the full text of the Nov. 17(?), 1851, letter to Hawthorne, see Melville, *Letters*, p. 144.

26. For phenomenological readings of body imagery in Hawthorne and Melville see S. Cameron, *The Corporeal Self*. None of what follows is brought up by Cameron, whose readings of body imagery are ahistorical and largely asocial. Reading body imagery outside of history can be revealing, as Cameron's book demonstrates, but misses subtle meanings inscribed by specific historical and cultural conditions.

27. Parker, "Thoughts on Labor," p. 503.

28. "How have you risen?" Orestes Brownson asked in his fiery essay "The Laboring Classes" (1840): "By the productive industry of your own hands? . . . One rises from the class of proletaries only by making those, he leaves behind, the lever of his elevation" (p. 463).

29. Larcom, *Idyl of Work*, pp. 141–42. Also see Larcom's *New England Girlhood*, especially her responses to machinery: pp. 182, 183, 223, 229.

30. Parker, "Education of the Laboring Classes," p. 94. For a poem about "crushed" hands, see Foner, ed., *Factory Girls*, p. 91.

31. For more extensive coverage of the representation of labor as "hands" and the connections between this historical symbol and Hawthorne's "The Birth-mark" and "The Artist of the Beautiful" as well as Melville's "Tartarus," see Joel Pfister, "Hawthorne and the History of Personal Life" (Ph.D. diss., Yale University, 1985), pp. 14–15 ("The Birth-mark"), pp. 134–45 ("The Birth-mark" and "Tartarus"), pp. 146–95 ("Artist"). I was pleased to find that Nicholas K. Bromwell's essay " 'The Bloody Hand' of Labor: Work, Class, and Gender in Three Stories by Hawthorne" (1990) also reads "The Birth-mark" (as well as "The Artist of the Beautiful" and "Drowne's Wooden Image") in reference to the contemporary "bloody hand" of labor. We use many different historical sources to reach our conclusions, which also differ in emphasis.

32. See Everett, "American Manufactures" (1831), in *Orations and Speeches* 2: 69, 70; "On the Importance of Scientific Knowledge: To Practical Men, and On the Encouragements to Its Pursuit" (n.d.), in *Orations and Speeches* 1: 248; "The Importance of the Mechanic Arts" (delivered 1837), in *Orations and*

Speeches 2: 248; "Accumulation, Property, Capital, Credit" (delivered 1838), in *Orations and Speeches* 2: 295. The metaphor was "in the air." For more quotes from politicians that employ magic as a metaphor for industrialization, see Siracusa, *A Mechanical People*, p. 72.

33. Abbott, "The Armory at Springfield," pp. 145, 141, 146. Also see Abbott's "The Novelty Works," especially p. 274 for his personification of machinery. And see the anonymous article "American Machinery.—Matteawan" in *Scientific American*. Also see L. Marx, *The Machine in the Garden*, especially chap. 4.

34. See Kasson, *Civilizing the Machine*, pp. 64, 100.

35. Eisler, ed., *Lowell Offering*, pp. 56–57.

36. Kasson, *Civilizing the Machine*, p. 56.

37. Spenser, *Faerie Queene* 3.12.19–22.

38. See "How Steel-Pens Are Made" in *Harper's* (1853): "We are given at once into the charge of an intelligent guide" (p. 691).

39. The notion of the maids as "white slaves" was explored by Marvin Fisher in his seminal article, "Melville's 'Tartarus' "; see his superb analysis of the paper-making machine as mechanical birth process on p. 97. Jay Leyda has noted that when Melville visited the "Old Red Mill" in 1851, Elizabeth, his wife, was pregnant; thus it is perhaps not surprising that he hinted at such analogies through his puns and images (*Melville Log* 1: 403–4). Melville developed such associations just when female midwives (such as the unemployed nurse who catches paper) were being discredited and gynecology was emerging as a special subject of study for (male) doctors. In 1855 Dr. J. Marion Sims, who had experimented on female slaves, established the first hospital for the treatment of women's "disorders" in New York City, the year Melville published "Tartarus"; see Barker-Benfield, *Horrors*, p. 89 and, on midwives, pp. 61–71. Also on midwives see Gordon, *Woman's Body*.

40. Fisher, "Melville's 'Tartarus,' " p. 97.

41. Rogin, *Subversive Genealogies*, p. 204.

42. Letter to the Editor, *Una* 1 (June 1853): 74. Price, "Reasons Why Woman Should Define Her Own Sphere," p. 9.

43. Eisler, *The Lowell Offering*, p. 58.

44. Stearns, "Early Factory Magazines," pp. 704, 701, 687.

45. Spenser, *Faerie Queene* 3.12.31.

46. See McGaw, "The Sources and Impact of Mechanization," pp. 319, 327, 334, and " 'A Good Place to Work.' " For McGaw's remarks on women suffering snapped tendons and paper cuts, see "Technological Change and Women's Work," especially p. 98.

47. M. P. Ryan, *Cradle*, pp. 115, 34–35, 42.

48. See Berg, *The Remembered Gate*, pp. 300–301.

49. If on one level Hawthorne recognizes his own complicity as a literary alchemist, so does Melville, who in his first-person narrative can be loosely identified with the "seedsman" who travels to Tartarus to save money on "en-

velopes" for his "seeds." Melville acknowledges that he too profits from the uniform production of such blank "envelopes."

50. Yet, as Stuart Blumin points out (when discussing the relation between changing attitudes toward work and the historical emergence of middle-class personal life), "the increasing clarification of the boundary between manual and nonmanual worlds" was what "made the idea of a new and ascending middle-class plausible" (*Emergence*, p. 137).

Chapter 5

1. Grimké, *Letters*, pp. 46–47. On "butterflies" see Berg (*The Remembered Gate*, pp. 98–99), who quotes from "Young Ladies at Home," *Golden Keepsake* (1851): the author criticizes "female characters who spend their time and talents in as useless a manner as possible and with the same superficial appearance as the painted butterfly." In addition note Fanny Fern's "The Women of 1867," reprinted in *Ruth Hall*: "A woman—but not necessarily a butterfly—not necessarily a machine, which, once wound up by the marriage ceremony, is expected to click with undeviating monotony till Death stops the hands" (p. 344). In Hawthorne's "The Artist of the Beautiful" (1844), Owen Warland's mechanical butterfly can be read as a miniature technological substitute for a shrunken "angel" in the house.

2. Sigourney, *The Girl's Book*, p. 47.

3. M. P. Ryan, *Cradle*, p. 232; *Empire of the Mother*, p. 52; *Cradle*, p. 161; *Empire of the Mother*, p. 57; *Cradle*, p. 238.

4. Chapin, *Duties*, p. 15.

5. Ruskin, "Queens' Gardens," p. 115.

6. M. P. Ryan, *Empire of the Mother*, p. 39.

7. See Larry J. Reynolds's "Revolutions Abroad," (pp. 46–47, 59–60); Reynolds suggests that Hawthorne may have read Margaret Fuller's dispatches to the *New York Tribune* in 1849 about the Italian Revolution and borrowed the image from her: "Every struggle made by the old tyrannies . . . only sows more dragon's teeth," she wrote.

8. M. P. Ryan, *Cradle*, p. 17.

9. M. P. Ryan, *Empire of the Mother*, pp. 18, 51.

10. Brodhead, "Sparing the Rod," p. 77.

11. For the story of how Hawthorne's daughter's occasionally unfeminine autonomy made him uneasy, see Herbert, "Nathaniel Hawthorne, Una Hawthorne," especially pp. 292–95. Una may have been the model for Pearl, and her father refused to allow her to read *The Scarlet Letter*.

12. Dimmesdale, who does not fit the pedagogical mold of the seventeenth-century father, seems to parody mid-nineteenth-century sentimental fatherhood on stage. See Demos, "The Changing Faces of Fatherhood," pp. 41–67 in *Past, Present, and Personal*.

13. Stowe, *Uncle Tom's Cabin*, p. 410.

14. David Leverenz develops the gender politics of Pearl's pacification: the kiss "pacifies her. . . . Now Pearl gains her narrator's praise for returning to femininity" (*Manhood*, p. 269). For Larry J. Reynolds, Pearl's pacification is also paid off with upward mobility: "In what seems to be a reward for her docility she marries into European nobility (thereby accomplishing a restoration of the ties with aristocracy her maternal relatives once enjoyed)" ("Revolutions Abroad," p. 65).

15. For a clever reading of Pearl's "humanizing" worked out within the terms of Hawthorne's discourse, see Ragussis, "Family Discourse," especially p. 885.

16. Amy Schrager Lang points out that Hester's letter "ties the liberation of the creative, the generative, impulse to lawlessness" ("An American Jezebel: Hawthorne and *The Scarlet Letter*," in *Prophetic Woman*, p. 167.)

17. Blanchard, *Margaret Fuller*, p. 46.

18. See Sarah J. Hale's *The Lecturess*: "Mother . . . I try to make other women do something more than sew" (p. 17). Also see Ware's *Zenobia*, in which Zenobia, on the verge of being defeated, asks herself rhetorically: "Should I have done better to have sat over my embroidery, in the midst of my slaves, all my days, than to have spent them in building up a kingdom?" (2: 142). Fanny Fern points to the significance of the needle as a symbol of domesticized woman when parodying the patriarchal ideology which predicted that Stowe's *Uncle Tom's Cabin* would be a flop: "You see you had no 'call,' Mrs. Tom Cabin, to drop your babies and darning-needle to immortalize your name. . . . Women should have their ambition bounded by a gridiron, and a darning needle" ("Mrs. Stowe's *Uncle Tom*," in *Ruth Hall*, p. 256).

19. See Pease, *Visionary Compacts*, pp. 89, 91. Yet her embroidery, as Pease notes, might also be read not "as a form of repentence but [as] public restatements of her private relationship with Arthur" (p. 91).

20. As Judith Fetterley points out, "the containment of Hester constitutes a primary action of the text. Although flashes of Hester's power occur and reoccur, they serve essentially to rationalize the systematic reduction of her power: her sexuality is imprisoned beneath her drab clothing and severe cap; her artistry is diverted from rebellious self-expression into the works of charity; her maternal force is converted into the ineffectual fumblings of a mother with a 'bad' child whom she cannot control" (*Provisions*, p. 26). Yet by containing her hair in a cap, Hester seems able to break away from the way the townspeople see her and the way she has been taught to see herself.

21. Francis E. Kearns makes parallels between Hester and Fuller's advocacy of female prisons, her "conversations" with women, and her cultural role as a "prophetess" ("Margaret Fuller as a Model for Hester Prynne"). As I noted earlier, Larry J. Reynolds also notes the correspondence of their revolutionary thoughts in "Revolutions Abroad," p. 66.

22. Greeley quoted in A. Douglas, *Feminization of American Culture*, p. 339.

23. Holmes, *Elsie Venner*, p. 341.

24. Hawthorne, "Mrs. Hutchinson," *Works: Riverside Edition* 4: 168.

25. On Hawthorne's "liberal" representation of Hester's radicalism ("fear of process run amok," p. 649) see Bercovitch, "A-Politics." David Stineback offers a useful discussion of the radicalism underlying Hawthorne's concerns with gender in "Gender, Hawthorne, and Literary Criticism."

26. Scott, "Gender: A Useful Category" pp. 1072–73.

27. Davis quoted in M. P. Ryan, *Cradle*, pp. 228–29.

28. Scott, "Gender: A Useful Category," p. 1073.

29. Berg, *The Remembered Gate*, p. 248.

30. Ibid., pp. 168, 171.

31. Ibid., pp. 206, 204–5.

32. Ibid., p. 207.

33. For a discussion of how the novel both reflects and participates in one aspect of this construction, see Brodhead, "Sparing the Rod." Brodhead's analysis of shifts in modes of disciplinary punishment in the middle-class leads him to suggest that "Hawthorne's whole project in *The Scarlet Letter* could be thought of as an attempt to weigh the methods and powers of a newer against an older disciplinary order, by juxtaposing a world of corporal correction (embodied by the Puritans' punishment of Hester) and a world of correction-by-interiority (embodied in Chillingworth and Dimmesdale)" (p. 78). The Foucauldian outcome seems to be something like the institutionalization of a peculiarly middle-class superego.

34. On sexual imagery in *The Scarlet Letter*, see Michael Davitt Bell, "Arts of Deception," p. 49; Bell notes Hawthorne's irony in making Dimmesdale oblivious to the sexual pun on "organ-pipe."

35. Lawrence, *Studies*, p. 90.

36. S. Freud, " 'Civilized' Sexual Morality and Modern Nervousness," in *Sexuality*, p. 25.

37. Freud observes that socially prescribed "punishment will not infrequently give those who carry it out an opportunity of committing the same outrage under colour of expiation. This is indeed one of the foundations of the human penal system and it is based, no doubt correctly, on the assumption that the prohibited impulses are present alike in the criminal and in the avenging community" (*Totem and Taboo*, p. 72).

38. For David Leverenz, Hawthorne "seems fully aware that his readers will accept Hester only while she suffers for her sin. . . . Yet though he silences Hester with values he and his audience hold dear, he makes his readers uncomfortable with those values. . . . His narrative continuously invokes and undermines prevailing conventions of womanhood and manhood" (*Manhood*, p. 277).

39. C. Hale, "Nathaniel Hawthorne," p. 179.

Chapter 6

1. Four of the five main characters live, like Roderick, in an "antiquated residence" in decline. Hepzibah and Clifford Pyncheon, like Roderick, enter-

tain aristocratic pretensions but have been humbled by a fall in fortune. Scipio, a black servant who appears in both "Egotism" and Holgrave's tale of Alice Pyncheon, believes that Roderick's serpent was an inherited "peculiarity" (10: 282). The inheritance of punishment for wrongdoing from one generation to the next is one of the more famous themes in the novel. Judge Pyncheon's prototype may well have been the "ambitious statesman," stung by Roderick, whose bosom harbors nothing less than a ravenous "boa constrictor" (10: 275).

2. For a perspective on eighteenth-century gothic as a "historical symptom" and nineteenth-century New England gothic as "moral parable or sociocultural analysis," see Buell, *New England Literary Culture*, pp. 352–53.

3. Donald A. Ringe provides a good survey of Hawthorne's gothic themes in *American Gothic*, pp. 152–76.

4. See Michael T. Gilmore's chapter, "The Artist in the Marketplace: The House of the Seven Gables," in *American Romanticism*, pp. 102–12. Hawthorne, of course, rewrote the story of Midas as "The Golden Touch" in *A Wonder Book* (1852) (actually published in 1851). Midas's "golden touch" kills his daughter and thus destroys his domestic happiness (perhaps also the risk faced by domesticity in a burgeoning mid-nineteenth-century capitalist marketplace).

5. Mary Ryan describes the relationship between household sanitizing and the formation of middle-class identity in mid-century Utica, N.Y.: "Those shining window panes and whitewashed gates, no less starched white collars, gave a material expression to the formation of the American middle-class" (*Cradle*, p. 203).

6. In response to Uncle Venner's analogy that Phoebe works like one of "God's angels," the narrator adds: "Angels do not toil, but let their good works grow out of them; and so did Phoebe" (2: 82). This ideological use of the angel convention recodes actual domestic labor as the effortless expression of feminine angelhood. Yet Phoebe's practical skills make her closer to a stereotype of the "real womanhood" ideal proliferated by advice books as opposed to the stereotype of the "true woman" also represented in advice books. The construct of the "real woman" is discussed by Cogan, *All-American Girl*, pp. 1–61.

7. Hawthorne read Coventry Patmore's long-winded poem "Angel in the House" with "unusual pleasure and sympathy" and met Patmore and his "angel" in 1858: "Mr. Patmore seems to acknowledge her as the real Angel in the house, although he says she herself ignores all connection with the poem. It is well to do so, and for her husband to feel that the character is her real Portrait; and both, I suppose, are right" (*English Notebooks*, pp. 619–20).

8. Armstrong, *Desire and Domestic Fiction*, pp. 20, 73. Also see Armstrong and Tennenhouse's introduction to *Ideology of Conduct*. Mid-century criticisms of an American "aristocracy" were in the air. As Francis J. Grund pointed out in his satirical *Aristocracy in America* (1839), "a wealthy overgrown [American] *bourgeoisie*" not only emulated the pretensions of European aristocracy but was more extreme in its prejudices against the "industrious masses over whom it strives to elevate itself." Like Judge Pyncheon, it endeavors to "disguise" this

enmity "by cunning and soft speeches, or an hyperbolical affectation of republicanism" (pp. 10, 145). In apparent opposition to "aristocracy" of all kinds, the American middle class represented its version of domesticity (and by implication the economic practices that supported it) as truly republican. On the American "aristocracy" and its relation to the emerging middle class see Blumin, *Emergence* pp. 234, 236, 244, 246. Also see Coontz, *Social Origins*, p. 161.

9. On this anti-aristocratic theme also see Hawthorne's "Oliver Cromwell" (6: 251–60). "Queen Christina" and "Oliver Cromwell" appeared in *Biographical Stories for Children*, first published in 1842 and reprinted in 1851 as *True Stories from History and Biography*.

10. *Sketches*, p. 35.

11. Ibid., pp. 51–55.

12. Ibid., p. 58.

13. Sarah J. Hale, "An Evening's Conversation About Autographs," *Godey's* 22 (Apr. 1841): 146–49, see p. 146. Also see Hale's earlier "Evening's Conversation About Autographs," *Godey's* 21 (June 1839): 256–59.

14. S. J. Hale, *Woman's Record*, p. 262.

15. Margaret Fuller was of course ridiculed as "Queen Margaret" by Sophia in 1844. Fuller actually became an aristocrat, the Marchioness d'Ossoli, at the very moment she aided the Republican cause in the Italian Revolution. The last writing completed by the Marchioness was reputed to have been "On the Revolution in Italy"; see S. J. Hale, *Woman's Record*, p. 667.

16. Alice's ideological role is wholly accepted by Pyncheon's slave, Scipio, who takes umbrage at Maule's reference to her: " 'He talk of Mistress Alice!' cried Scipio, as he returned from his errand. 'The low carpenter-man! He no business so much as to look at her a great way off!' " (2: 188). Obviously Holgrave (and of course Hawthorne) wishes us to note the irony of this view.

17. Walter Benn Michaels recognizes this scene as both a business transaction and a rape; see "Romance and Real Estate," in *Gold Standard*, pp. 107–8.

18. Halttunen, *Confidence Men*, p. 24.

19. M. P. Ryan, *Empire*, pp. 33, 51.

20. Halttunen, *Confidence Men*, p. 29. As Halttunen points out, the middle class saw itself as upwardly liminal.

21. C. M. Sedgwick, *Home*, p. 28.

22. Sedgwick's comments on *The House of the Seven Gables* quoted in Cowie, *Rise of the American Novel*, p. 211. For a brief critique of the "upper-middle-class" ideology underlying the assumptions of Sedgwick's *Home*, see D. Reynolds, *Beneath the American Renaissance*, pp. 354–55.

23. Cott, *Bonds of Womanhood*, p. 98. Also see Bell Gale Chevigny's insightful essay, "To the Edges of Ideology," in which she states: "The ideology of gender not only concealed its basis in social inequity, it also contradicted the ideology of class even as it was used to support it. For only by insisting on essential *differences* in gender could men pursue supposedly *universal* values of economic freedom and individual development" (p. 181). Also consult Stephanie

Coontz: "The assignment of one behavior pattern and image to all women allowed men to be defined not by their class but by their non-femininity" (*Social Origins*, p. 218).

24. Cott, *Bonds of Womanhood*, p. 99.

25. Grimké, *Letters*, p. 48.

26. Poe, "The Black Cat," *Complete Tales and Poems*, pp. 230, 223. On the bourgeois ethos see M. P. Ryan, *Cradle*, pp. 154, 161.

27. Poe, "The Fall of the House of Usher," *Complete Tales and Poems*, p. 245. See Michael Davitt Bell's comments on anatomical symbolism in *Development of the American Romance*, p. 111.

28. Karen Halttunen points out that the Gothic elements of Henry Ward Beecher's "The Strange Woman" (1844), an attack on prostitution, made it a "nightmarish inversion of the Victorian cult of domesticity" ("Gothic Imagination and Social Reform," p. 116).

29. Davidson, *Revolution and the Word*, p. 225; and see her observation about Charles Brockden Brown's gothic: the gothic "asked precisely those questions that bourgeois ideology labored to suppress" (p. 237). Also consult E. K. Sedgwick, *Coherence of Gothic Conventions*, pp. 140–75.

30. On his parents' contempt for Fourierism, see Julian Hawthorne, *Hawthorne and His Wife* 1: 268–69. On Brook Farm and Fourierism, see Curtis, *Season in Utopia*, especially "The Change to Fourierism," pp. 162–226. Also see the chapter on "Associationism" in Stoehr, *Hawthorne's Mad Scientists* (pp. 147–61).

31. Brisbane, "Practical Organization" and "Association." Also see Brisbane, "Defects of the System."

32. See Riasonovsky, *Teaching of Charles Fourier*, p. 149. On Lazarus, see Stoehr, *Free Love*, p. 86.

33. The review appeared in *Tait's Edinburgh Magazine* (Jan. 1855) and is quoted in Milton R. Stern Introduction (to *The House of the Seven Gables*), p. xxx.

34. Cott, *Bonds of Womanhood*, p. 69.

35. Andrews, *Love, Marriage, and Divorce*, pp. 49, 50. On "egotism," "individualism," and the increasingly privatized American family, see also Tocqueville, *Democracy in America* 1: 293.

36. Demos, *Past, Present, and Personal*, p. 39.

37. Hawthorne quoted in Gilmore, *American Romanticism*, pp. 107–8.

38. Also recall that on the scaffold Hester's hair "threw off the sunshine with a gleam" (1: 53). In his "Introductory" to *Tanglewood Tales* Hawthorne notes the following of Eustace Bright's rewriting of several violent Greek myths: "How were they to be purified? How was the blessed sunshine to be thrown into them?" (7: 179). "Sunshine," once "thrown into" the Cadmus myth, transformed it into a domestic tale suitable for middle-class children. Phoebe is, as she herself recognizes, the embodiment of "sunshine" (2: 110, 214–15, 297). And Holgrave's "truth"-revealing daguerreotypes rely on "sunshine" (2: 91, 92,

94). I am indebted to Jennifer Levine, who developed the domestic significance of Donatello's "sunshine" during a seminar discussion on *The Marble Faun* in the fall of 1988.

39. F. Jameson, *Marxism and Form*, p. 380.

Chapter 7

1. Early in his career Hawthorne mused on how a story can shape "itself against his intentions"; see Ragussis, "Family Discourse," p. 880.

2. Mellow, *Hawthorne in His Times*, p. 223.

3. Comay and Brownrigg, *Who's Who in the Bible*, p. 267.

4. S. J. Hale, *Woman's Record*, p. 49.

5. Ibid. In *Golden Keepsake* (1851) one contributor questioned whether the reputations of Miriam, Deborah, and Hannah had been "brought into disrepute" because these women transgressed their "appointed bounds"; quoted in Berg, *The Remembered Gate*, p. 248.

6. See Erlich, *Family Themes*, pp. 93–94.

7. Hawthorne, *English Notebooks*, p. 321.

8. Poovey, *Proper Lady*, p. 243. The mesmerized Alice Pyncheon becomes the "lay figure" of Maule.

9. Grimké, *Letters*, p. 90.

10. Ruskin, "Queen's Gardens," p. 87.

11. Mellow, *Hawthorne in His Times*, pp. 368–69.

12. Garrard, *Artemisia Gentileschi*, p. 7.

13. Of course, my argument by no means hinges on the very real possibility that Gentileschi provided Hawthorne with one model for Miriam. Hawthorne visited Florence and saw representations of Judith at the Uffizi Gallery and the Pitti Palace, although he makes no reference to Artemisia Gentileschi's Judiths (nor does Sophia in *Notes in England and Italy*). On June 13, 1858, he saw Allori's version, and two days later at the Uffizi he commented on Bardone's; see his *Italian Notebooks* (14: 314–15, 318). The Allori version (1616–20) is interesting, because it was believed to represent the artist's head as Holofernes and his former mistress as Judith (actually this was true of his 1613 version in Hampton Court). Hawthorne's version, however, inverts the power relationship: the mistress (who resembles Hawthorne's description of Miriam) is humbled. On the Allori paintings see Garrard, *Artemisia Gentileschi*, p. 300.

14. A. Jameson, *Characteristics of Women*, p. 35. Sophia Hawthorne's knowledge of art and art critics is evidenced in *Notes in England and Italy* (which does not recount her visit with Mrs. Jameson). In his *Italian Notebooks* Nathaniel notes that Mrs. Jameson visited them on May 9, 1858, and that Una and her governess, Miss Shepard, "are full of her books, just now" (14: 206).

15. Jameson's comments quoted from *Visits and Sketches* (1834) in Holcomb, "Anna Jameson on Women Artists," pp. 15, 19.

16. S. J. Hale, *Woman's Record*, p. 325.

17. See Garrard, "Artemisia and Susanna," pp. 163, 162. Also see Murray and Murray, *Penguin Dictionary of Art*, p. 156; Artemisia is not awarded an entry under her own name but is discussed below the entry for her father, Orazio.

18. Garrard, *Artemisia Gentileschi*, p. 21. Also see Parker and Pollock, *Old Mistresses*; p. 21.

19. Garrard, "Artemisia and Susanna," p. 163; *Artemisia Gentileschi*, p. 313.

20. See Shearman, "Cristofano Allori's 'Judith,' " p. 8.

21. See Grassi, *Donatello*, plates 166 and 167.

22. See Pepper, *Guido Reni*, plates X, 113, 130, 206; Lightblown, *Sandro Botticelli*, plate 55; Wethey, *Paintings of Titian*, plate 37. I am indebted to Elizabeth Milroy for her insights into Donatello's "Judith" and paintings of Lucretia.

23. On Hawthorne's anti-Semitism, see Roulston, "Hawthorne's Attitude Toward Jews."

24. See Cogan, *All American Girl*, p. 257; she quotes from Virginia Penny, *How Women Make Money, Married or Single in All Branches of the Arts and Sciences, Professions, Trades, Agricultural and Mechanical Pursuits* (1862). Also see Penny, *Employments of Women*, in which she quotes an unnamed authority: "Women succeed in painting portraits; also, in painting flowers and fruit; very few have tried historical paintings" (p. 79).

25. Hilda seems to be a caricature of the "passionless" woman described by Nancy F. Cott in "Passionless."

26. As Richard Brodhead observes, "Hilda is the bearer of a militant high-cultural spirit. . . . [She] belongs to a historical transformation of art into an object *of* reverence . . . an object whose use is to reinforce the attitude of deference in general" (*School of Hawthorne*, pp. 73–74).

27. Nina Baym has pointed out the genteel "miniaturizing impulse" of Hilda's copies which idealize only the *details* of the patriarchal masterpieces (*Shape of Hawthorne's Career*, p. 242). This framing of detail, interestingly, is reminiscent of Aylmer's idealizing obsession with the part rather than the whole.

28. See Brodhead, "Introduction," p. xxi.

29. On St. Hilda, see A. Jameson, *Legends of the Monastic Orders*, p. 64.

30. Brodhead reads Hilda as symbolic of "the cultural forces that worked to erect a severely hierarchical high-cultural order in America from the 1850's on. . . . She personifies the related forces that worked to make the appreciation of high artistic culture seem like the final test of human adequacy" ("Introduction," p. xx).

31. I quote from Mellow, *Hawthorne in His Times*, p. 175. See also Stewart, *Hawthorne: A Biography*, p. 36.

32. Quoted in Julian Hawthorne, *Hawthorne and His Wife* 1: 236. Sophia's journal entry for Dec. 29, 1843, reads: "A grey morning. My dear husband advised me so strongly not to paint as I did not feel very bright, that I yielded, not against my will, but much against my purpose. He wanted me to sit with him too & that was too tempting. I did not do much" ("Journal," p. 18). The

Christmas entry reads: "I should have painted as it was sunny; but my lord asked me to sit with him Christmas day & I was only too glad to do so" (p. 16). Other entries from the journal (Dec. 1, 1843–Jan. 5, 1844) record that she did paint, but often had to overcome nervousness to do so. On Jan. 2, for example: "I had a fine time painting" (pp. 21–22).

33. On the purchase of furniture, see Mellow, *Hawthorne in His Times*, p. 203. On fire screens and lampshades, see Tharp, *Peabody Sisters*, pp. 188–89; the lampshades sold for $5 apiece, and the fire screens went for $10.

34. Sophia Hawthorne, *Notes in England and Italy*, pp. 352–53.

35. Tharp, *Peabody Sisters*, p. 55.

36. Withers, "Artistic Women," p. 332. Also see Sophia's account of Washington Allston reviewing one of her first creative works: "I stood behind him trembling like a sinner. Mary [her sister] whispered, 'Tell him you painted it in perfect ignorance' and like a parrott, said I, 'Mr. Allston, I painted it in perfect ignorance' " (Tharp, *Peabody Sisters*, p. 57). I am indebted to Rebecca Rossen's superb seminar paper, "The Artist's Wife," for reminding me of this quote and for its research and argument.

37. Mellow, *Hawthorne in His Times*, pp. 174–75.

38. Poe, "Fall of the House of Usher," *Complete Tales and Poems*, p. 237.

39. Mellow, *Hawthorne in His Times*, p. 518.

40. A. Turner, *Hawthorne: A Biography*, p. 346.

41. At one point Hawthorne actually suggested to Ticknor that the title of the novel be *St. Hilda's Shrine*, ibid., p. 346.

42. Even the narrator seems to concur with this theory on occasion. Donatello's "sorrow and remorse," we are told, transform him into a "man of feeling and intelligence" (4: 320).

43. Making a case for Hawthorne's radicalism in creating Hester, Myra Jehlen writes, "No amount of penitence on Hester's part can undo his act in having invented her" (*American Incarnation*, p. 136).

Coda

1. Brodhead, *School of Hawthorne*, p. 80.

2. Sophia Hawthorne, "Journal," pp. 4, 24. Wexler, "Tender Violence." As Nina Baym notes, profiling the period between 1790 and 1870, "the rapidly expanding middle class increasingly imposed its expectations on ever-larger numbers of women in towns and cities" ("Portrayal of Women," p. 211).

3. Some of the most provocative theoretical work in this area can be found in the writings of Nancy Armstrong and Joan Scott respectively. Myra Jehlen makes important distinctions between the nineteenth-century American and European middle classes and their literary productions in "The Novel and the Middle Class in America," in Bercovitch and Jehlen, eds., *Ideology and Classic American Literature.*

Bibliography

Abbott, Jacob. "The Armory at Springfield." *Harper's New Monthly Magazine* 5 (July 1852): 145–61.
———. "The Novelty Works." *Harper's New Monthly Magazine* 2 (May 1851): 721–34.
Adair, James. *The History of the American Indians*. London: Edward and Charles Dilly, 1775.
Adams, Michael Vannoy. "Pathography, Hawthorne, and the History of Psychological Ideas." *Emerson Society Quarterly* 29 (3rd Quarter 1983): 113–26.
Allen, Elizabeth. *A Woman's Place in the Novels of Henry James*. London: Macmillan, 1984.
"American Machinery,—Matteawan." *Scientific American* 5 (Apr. 1850): 253.
Anderson, Michael. *Approaches to the History of the Western Family, 1500–1914*. London: Macmillan, 1980.
Andrews, Stephen Pearl. *Love, Marriage, and Divorce, and the Sovereignty of the Individual; A Discussion between Henry James, Horace Greeley, and Stephen Pearl Andrews and a Hitherto Unpublished Manuscript: Love, Marriage, and the Condition of Women*. Ed. Charles Shively. Weston, Mass.: M & S Press, 1975.
Anthon, Charles. *A Classical Dictionary*. New York: Harper, 1848.
Ariès, Philippe. *Centuries of Childhood: A Social History of Family Life*. Trans. Robert Baldick. New York: Vintage, 1962.
———. "The Family and the City in the Old World and the New." In Virginia Tufte and Barbara Myerhoff, eds., *Changing Images of the Family*. New Haven, Conn.: Yale University Press, 1979.
Armstrong, Nancy. *Desire and Domestic Fiction: A Political History of the Novel*. New York: Oxford University Press, 1987.
Armstrong, Nancy, and Leonard Tennenhouse, eds. *The Ideology of Conduct: Essays on Literature and the History of Sexuality*. New York: Methuen, 1987.

Arner, Robert D. "The Legend of Pygmalion in 'The Birthmark.'" *American Transcendental Quarterly* 14 (1971): 68–71.

Axtell, James, ed. *The Indian Peoples of Eastern America: A Documentary History of the Sexes.* New York: Oxford University Press, 1981.

Banner, Lois. *American Beauty.* New York: Knopf, 1983.

Barker-Benfield, G. J. "Anne Hutchinson and the Puritan Attitude Toward Women." *Feminist Studies* 1 (Fall 1972): 65–96.

———. *The Horrors of the Half-Known Life: Male Attitudes Toward Women and Sexuality in Nineteenth-Century America.* New York: Harper Colophon, 1977.

———. "The Spermatic Economy: A Nineteenth-Century View of Sexuality." In Michael Gordon, ed., *The American Family in Social-Historical Perspective.* New York: St. Martin's, 1978.

Barrett, Michèle, and Mary McIntosh. *The Anti-Social Family.* London: Verso, 1982.

Baym, Nina. "Hawthorne's Women." *Centennial Review* 15 (Spring 1971): 250–72.

———. "Portrayal of Women in American Literature, 1790–1870." In Marlene Springer, ed., *What Manner of Woman: Essays on English and American Life and Literature.* New York: New York University Press, 1977.

———. *The Shape of Hawthorne's Career.* Ithaca, N.Y.: Cornell University Press, 1976.

———. "Thwarted Nature: Nathaniel Hawthorne as Feminist." In Fritz Fleischmann, ed., *American Novelists Revisited: Essays in Feminist Criticism.* Boston: G. K. Hall, 1982.

———. *Woman's Fiction: A Guide to Novels by and About Women in America.* Ithaca, N.Y.: Cornell University Press, 1978.

Becklard, Eugene. *Know Thyself: The Physiologist, or Sexual Physiology Revealed.* Boston: Bela Marsh, 1859. Reprinted in Charles Rosenberg and Carroll Smith-Rosenberg, eds., *Sex, Marriage and Society.* New York: Arno, 1974.

Bell, Michael Davitt. "Arts of Deception: Hawthorne, 'Romance,' and *The Scarlet Letter.*" In Michael J. Colacurcio, ed., *New Essays on 'The Scarlet Letter.'* Cambridge, Eng.: Cambridge University Press, 1985.

———. *The Development of the American Romance: The Sacrifice of Relation.* Chicago: University of Chicago Press, 1980.

Bell, Millicent. *Hawthorne's View of the Artist.* New York: State University of New York Press, 1962.

Bercovitch, Sacvan. "The A-Politics of Ambiguity in *The Scarlet Letter.*" *New Literary History* 19 (Spring 1988): 629–54.

———. "Hawthorne's A-Morality of Compromise." *Representations* 24 (Fall 1988): 1–27.

Bercovitch, Sacvan, and Myra Jehlen, eds. *Ideology and Classic American Literature.* Cambridge, Eng.: Cambridge University Press, 1987.

Berg, Barbara. *The Remembered Gate: Origins of American Feminism: The Woman and the City, 1800–1860.* New York: Oxford University Press, 1978.

Berger, John, Sven Blomberg, Chris Fox, Michael Dibb, and Richard Hollis. *Ways of Seeing*. Harmondsworth, Middlesex: Penguin, 1979.

Bernheimer, Richard. *Wild Men in the Middle Ages: A Study in Art, Sentiment, and Demonology*. Cambridge, Mass.: Harvard University Press, 1952.

Blake, John B. "Women and Medicine in Antebellum America." *Bulletin of the History of Medicine* 39 (Mar.–Apr. 1965): 79–123.

Blanchard, Paula. *Margaret Fuller: From Transcendentalism to Revolution*. Reading, Mass.: Addison-Wesley, 1987.

Blumin, Stuart. *The Emergence of the Middle Class: Social Experience in the American City, 1760–1900*. Cambridge, Eng.: Cambridge University Press, 1989.

Boccaccio, Giovanni. *Concerning Famous Women*. Trans. Guido A. Guarino. New Brunswick, N.J.: Rutgers University Press, 1963.

Botta, Anne C. Lynch. *Hand-book of Universal Literature*. New York: Derby & Jackson, 1860.

Boyer, Paul. *Urban Masses and Moral Order in America, 1820–1920*. Cambridge, Mass.: Harvard University Press, 1978.

Brisbane, Albert. "Association." *New-York Tribune*, Mar. 2, 1842.

———. "Defects of the System of Isolated Families." *New-York Daily Tribune*, July 11, 1842.

———. "Practical Organization of Association." *New-York Daily Tribune*, May 17, 1842.

Brodhead, Richard H. *Hawthorne, Melville, and the Novel*. Chicago: University of Chicago Press, 1977.

———. Introduction to *The Marble Faun*. New York: Penguin, 1990.

———. *The School of Hawthorne*. New York: Oxford University Press, 1986.

———. "Sparing the Rod: Discipline and Fiction in Antebellum America." *Representations* 21 (Winter 1988): 67–96.

———. "Veiled Ladies: Toward a History of Antebellum Entertainment." *American Literary History* 1 (Summer 1989): 273–94.

Bromwell, Nicholas K. " 'The Bloody Hand' of Labor: Work, Class, and Gender in Three Stories by Hawthorne," *American Quarterly* 42 (Dec. 1990): 542–64.

Brown, Norman O. *Life Against Death: The Psychoanalytical Meaning of History*. Middletown, Conn.: Wesleyan University Press, 1977.

Brownson, Orestes. "The Laboring Classes." *Boston Quarterly Review* 3 (Oct. 1840): 450–512.

Buchan, William. *Domestic Medicine: or, a Treatise on the Prevention and Cure of Diseases by Regimen and Simple Medicine*. Charleston, S.C.: John Hoff, 1807.

Budick, E. Miller. "The World as Specter: Hawthorne's Historical Art." *PMLA* 101 (Mar. 1986): 218–32.

Buell, Lawrence. *New England Literary Culture: From Revolution Through Renaissance*. Cambridge, Eng.: Cambridge University Press, 1986.

Bush, Sargent, Jr. "Bosom Serpents Before Hawthorne: The Origins of a Symbol." *American Literature* 43 (May 1971): 181–99.

Calhoun, Arthur W. *A Social History of the American Family*, Vol. 2, From

Independence to the Civil War. New York: Barnes & Noble, 1960.

Cameron, Sharon. *The Corporeal Self: Allegories of the Body in Melville and Hawthorne*. Baltimore, Md.: The Johns Hopkins University Press, 1981.

Cameron, Walter. *Hawthorne Among His Contemporaries: A Harvest of Estimates, Insights, and Anecdotes from the Victorian Literary World and an Index*. Hartford, Conn.: Transcendental Books, 1968.

Catlin, George. *Letters and Notes on North American Indians*. Ed. Michael McDonald Mooney. New York: Clarkson N. Potter, 1975.

Chapin, E. H. *Duties of Young Women*. Boston: George W. Briggs, 1851.

Chevigny, Bell Gale. "To the Edges of Ideology: Margaret Fuller's Centrifugal Evolution." *American Quarterly* 38 (Summer 1986): 173–201.

———. *The Woman and the Myth: Margaret Fuller's Life and Writings*. Old Westbury, N.Y.: Feminist Press, 1967.

Child, Lydia Maria. *Brief History of the Condition of Women*, vol. 1. New York: C. S. Francis; Boston: J. H. Francis, 1845 [1835].

Clarke, Edward H. *Sex in Education*. Boston: Osgood, 1875.

Cogan, Frances B. *All American Girl: The Ideal of Real Womanhood in Mid-Nineteenth Century America*. Athens: University of Georgia Press, 1989.

Colacurcio, Michael J. *The Province of Piety: Moral History in Hawthorne's Early Tales*. Cambridge, Mass.: Harvard University Press, 1984.

Comay, Joan, and Ronald Brownrigg. *Who's Who in the Bible*. New York: Bonanza, 1980.

Conway, Maurice. *Life of Nathaniel Hawthorne*. London: Walter Scott, 1985.

Coontz, Stephanie. *The Social Origins of Private Life: A History of American Families, 1600–1900*. London: Verso, 1988.

Cott, Nancy F. *The Bonds of Womanhood: 'Woman's Sphere' in New England, 1780–1835*. New Haven, Conn.: Yale University Press, 1977.

———. "Divorce and the Changing Status of Women in Eighteenth-Century Massachusetts." *William and Mary Quarterly* 33 (Oct. 1976): 586–614.

———. "Eighteenth-Century Family and Social Life Revealed in Massachusetts Divorce Records." In N. F. Cott and Elizabeth Pleck, eds., *A Heritage of Her Own: Toward a New Social History of American Women*. New York: Simon and Schuster, 1979.

———. "Passionless: An Interpretation of Victorian Sexual Ideology, 1790–1850." In N. F. Cott and Elizabeth H. Pleck, eds., *A Heritage of Her Own: Toward a New Social History of American Women*. New York: Simon and Schuster, 1979.

Cowie, Alexander. *The Rise of the American Novel*. New York: American Book, 1951.

Crews, Frederick. *Out of My System: Psychoanalysis, Ideology, and Critical Method*. New York: Oxford University Press, 1975.

———. *The Sins of the Fathers: Hawthorne's Psychological Themes*. Rev. ed. Berkeley: University of California Press, 1989 [1966].

———. *Skeptical Engagements.* New York: Oxford University Press, 1986.

"Critical Notices." *Southern Literary Review* 8 (July 1853): 255–88.

Curtis, Edith Roelker. *A Season in Utopia: The Story of Brook Farm.* New York: Russell and Russell, 1971 [1961].

Dall, Caroline Healy. "Charlotte Bronte Nicol, Or Currer Bell." *The Una* 3 (July 1855): 104.

Dana, Richard Henry. *Poem and Prose Writings.* Philadelphia: Marshall, Clark; Boston: Russell, Odiorne, 1833.

Daniels, George. *American Science in the Age of Jackson.* New York: Columbia University Press, 1968.

Davidoff, Leonore, and Catherine Hall. *Family Fortunes: Men and Women of the English Middle Class, 1780–1850.* Chicago: University of Chicago Press, 1987.

Davidson, Cathy N. *Revolution and the Word: The Rise of the Novel in America.* New York: Oxford University Press, 1986.

Davies, John D. *Phrenology Fact and Science: A Nineteenth-Century American Crusade.* New Haven, Conn.: Yale University Press, 1955.

Davis, David Brion. *Homicide in American Fiction, 1798–1860: A Study in Social Values.* Ithaca, N.Y.: Cornell University Press, 1968 [1957].

Davis, Paulina Wright. "The Myth of Una." *The Una* 2 (Feb. 1854): 212–13.

Dayan, Joan. *Fables of Mind: An Inquiry Into Poe's Fiction.* New York: Oxford University Press, 1987.

Delaney, Janice, Mary Jane Lupton, and Emily Toth, eds., *The Curse: A Cultural History of Menstruation.* New York: E. P. Dutton, 1976.

D'Emilio, John, and Estelle Freedman. *Intimate Matters: A History of Sexuality in America.* New York: Harper & Row, 1988.

Demos, John. "Oedipus and America: Historical Perspectives on the Reception of Psychoanalysis in the United States." *The Annual of Psychoanalysis* 6 (1978): 23–38.

———. *Past, Present, and Personal: The Family and the Life Course in American History.* New York: Oxford University Press, 1986.

Dewees, William P. *A Treatise on the Diseases of Females.* Philadelphia: H. C. Carey and I. Lea, 1826.

Dijkstra, Bram. *Idols of Perversity: Fantasies of Feminine Evil in Fin-De-Siècle Culture.* Oxford: Oxford University Press, 1986.

Dixon, Edward H. *Woman, and Her Diseases. From the Cradle to the Grave.* New York: Chas. H. Ring, 1847.

Douglas, Ann. *The Feminization of American Culture.* New York: Avon, 1977.

Douglas, Mary. *Purity and Danger: An Analysis of Concepts of Pollution and Taboo.* London: Routledge and Kegan Paul, 1979.

DuBois, Ellen Carol. *Feminism and Suffrage: The Emergence of an Independent Women's Movement in America 1848–1869.* Ithaca, N.Y.: Cornell University Press, 1978.

DuBois, Jean. *Marriage Physiologically Discussed.* New York: Printed for the Booksellers, 1839. Reprinted in Charles Rosenberg and Carroll Smith-Rosenberg, eds., *Sex, Marriage and Society.* New York: Arno, 1974.

Duyckinck, Mr. "Nathaniel Hawthorne." *The Literary World* 6 (Mar. 1850): 323–25.

Eakins, John Paul. *The New England Girl: Cultural Ideals in Hawthorne, Stowe, Howells, and James.* Athens: University of Georgia Press, 1976.

Eaton, A. *A Botanical Grammar and Dictionary.* Albany, N.Y.: Websters and Skinners, 1828.

Eckhardt, Celia Morris. *Fanny Wright: Rebel in America.* Cambridge, Mass.: Harvard University Press, 1984.

Egan, Robert. *Drama Within Drama: Shakespeare's Sense of His Art.* New York: Columbia University Press, 1975.

Eisler, Benita, ed. *The Lowell Offering: Writings by New England Mill Women (1840–1845).* Philadelphia: J. B. Lippincott, 1977.

Elder, Dr. "The Truth of Fiction and Its Charm." *The Una* 1 (Feb. 1853): 5.

Elias, Norbert. *The History of Manners.* Vol. 1 of *The Civilizing Process.* Trans. Edmund Jephcott. New York: Pantheon, 1978.

————. *Power and Civility.* Vol. 2 of *The Civilizing Process.* Trans. Edmund Jephcott. New York: Pantheon, 1982.

Ellenberger, Henri F. *The Discovery of the Unconscious: The History and Evolution of Dynamic Psychiatry.* New York: Basic Books, 1970.

Ellis, William. *Polynesian Researches during a Residence of Eight Years in the Society and Sandwich Islands,* 4 vols. London: Fisher, Son, & Jackson, 1831.

Encyclopaedia Britannica, or, Dictionary of the Arts, Science, and Miscellaneous Literature. Ed. Colin Macfarquhar and George Gleig. 18 vols. Edinburgh: A. Bell & C. MacFarquhar, 1797.

Erlich, Gloria. *Family Themes in Hawthorne's Fiction: The Tenacious Web.* New Brunswick, N.J.: Rutgers University Press, 1984.

Evans, Elizabeth. *The Abuse of Maternity.* Philadelphia: J. B. Lippincott, 1875.

Everett, Edward. *Orations and Speeches on Various Occasions,* 3 vols. Boston: Little, Brown, 1860.

"Fashion Plates." *Godey's* 26 (Jan. 1843): 56–57.

Faust, Bertha. "Hawthorne's Contemporaneous Reputation." Ph.D. diss. University of Pennsylvania, 1939.

Feidelson, Charles, Jr. "The Scarlet Letter." In Roy Harvey Pearce, ed., *Hawthorne Centenary Essays.* Columbus: Ohio State University Press, 1964.

Fenichel, Otto. *The Psychoanalytic Theory of the Neurosis.* New York: Norton, 1945.

Fenton, Charles A. "'The Bell-Tower': Melville and Technology." *American Literature* 23 (May 1951): 221–24.

Ferenczi, Sandor. *Further Contributions to the Theory and Technique of Psycho-Analysis.* London: Hogarth, 1950.

Fern, Fanny, [Sara Payson Parton]. "American Female Literature." *The Una* 2 (Aug. 1854): 329.
———. *Ruth Hall and Other Writings*. Ed. Joyce W. Warren. New Brunswick, N.J.: Rutgers University Press, 1986.
Fetterley, Judith. *The Resisting Reader: A Feminist Approach to American Fiction*. Bloomington: Indiana University Press, 1978.
———, ed. *Provisions: A Reader from 19th-Century American Women*. Bloomington: Indiana University Press, 1985.
Fiedler, Leslie A. *Love and Death in the American Novel*. New York: Stein and Day, 1975.
Fisher, Marvin. *Going Under: Melville's Short Fiction and the American 1850's*. Baton Rouge: Louisiana State University Press, 1977.
———. "Melville's 'Tartarus': The Deflowering of New England." *American Quarterly* 23 (Spring 1971): 79–100.
Fletcher, Angus. *Allegory: The Theory of a Symbolic Mode*. Ithaca, N.Y.: Cornell University Press, 1975.
Foner, Philip S., ed. *The Factory Girls*. Urbana: University of Illinois Press, 1977.
Foucault, Michel. *An Introduction*. Vol. 1 of *The History of Sexuality*. New York: Vintage, 1980.
———. *The Order of Things: An Archaeology of the Human Sciences*. New York: Vintage, 1973.
———. *The Use of Pleasure*. Vol. 2 of *The History of Sexuality*. New York: Vintage, 1986.
Fowler, O. S. *Amativeness: Or Evils and Remedies of Excessive and Perverted Sexuality with a Phrenological Exposition*. New York: Fowler and Wells, 1847.
———. *Fowler on Matrimony: Or, Phrenology and Physiology Applied to the Selection of Congenial Companions for Life*. New York: O. S. and L. N. Fowler, 1845.
Freud, Anna. *The Writings of Anna Freud*. Vol. 2, *The Ego and the Mechanisms of Defence*. New York: International Universities Press, 1966.
Freud, Sigmund. *Dora: An Analysis of a Case of Hysteria*. Ed. Philip Rieff. Trans. James Strachey. New York: Collier, 1963.
———. "Obsessive Acts and Religious Practices." In *Character and Culture*. Ed. Philip Rieff. Trans. James Strachey. New York: Collier, 1963.
———. *Sexuality and the Psychology of Love*. Ed. Philip Rieff. Trans. James Strachey. New York: Collier, 1963.
———. *Totem and Taboo: Some Points of Agreement Between the Mental Lives of Savages and Neurotics*. Trans. James Strachey. New York: Norton, 1950.
Frothingham, Octavius Brooks. *George Ripley*. Boston: Houghton, Mifflin, 1882.
Fryer, Judith. *The Faces of Eve: Women in the Nineteenth Century American Novel*. New York: Oxford University Press, 1976.
Gadlin, Howard. "Private Lives and Public Order: A Critical View of the History of Intimate Relations in the United States." In George Levinger and

Harold Rausch, eds., *Close Relationships: Perspectives on the Meaning of Intimacy*. Amherst: University of Massachusetts Press, 1977.

Gallagher, Catherine. "More About 'Medusa's Head.'" *Representations* 4 (Fall 1983): 55–57.

Garrard, Mary D. "Artemisia and Susanna." In Norma Broude and M. D. Garrard, eds., *Feminism and Art History*. New York: Harper and Row, 1982.

———. *Artemisia Gentileschi: The Image of the Female Hero in Italian Baroque Art*. Princeton, N.J.: Princeton University Press, 1989.

Gay, Peter. *The Bourgeois Experience: Victoria to Freud*. Vol. 2, *The Education of the Senses*. New York: Oxford University Press, 1984.

Gilbert, Sandra M., and Susan Gubar. *The Madwoman in the Attic: The Woman Writer in the Nineteenth Century Literary Imagination*. New Haven, Conn.: Yale University Press, 1979.

Gilman, Charlotte Perkins. *The Yellow Wallpaper*. Brooklyn: Feminist Press, 1973.

Gilmore, Michael. *American Romanticism and the Marketplace*. Chicago: University of Chicago Press, 1985.

Gilroy, Paul. "Cultural Studies and Ethnic Absolutism." Unpublished manuscript.

Gordon, Linda. *Woman's Body, Woman's Right: A Social History of Birth Control in America*. New York: Penguin, 1976.

Graham, Sylvester. *A Lecture to Young Men on Chastity*. Boston: Light and Stearns, Crocker and Brewster; New York: Leavitt, Lord, 1837.

Gramsci, Antonio. *Selections from the Prison Notebooks*. Ed. and trans. Quintin Hoare and Geoffrey Nowell Smith. New York: International Publishers, 1971.

Grassi, Luigi. *All the Sculpture of Donatello*, vol. 2. Trans. Paul Colacicchi. New York: Hawthorn, 1964.

Gray, Asa. "Dr. Lindley's Natural System of Botany." *American Journal of Science and Arts* 32 (1837): 290–303.

Greenwood, Grace [Sarah Jane Clarke Lippincott]. *Greenwood Leaves: A Collection of Sketches and Letters*. Boston: Ticknor, Reed, and Fields, 1850.

Grimké, Sarah. *Letters on the Equality of the Sexes and the Conditions of Women*. New York: Burt Franklin, 1970 [1838].

Grund, Francis J. *Aristocracy in America: From the Sketch-Book of a German Nobleman*. New York: Harper, 1959 [1839].

Grunes, Dennis. "Allegory Versus Allegory in Hawthorne." *American Transcendental Quarterly* 32 (Fall 1976): 14–19.

Gubar, Susan. "'The Blank Page' and the Issues of Female Creativity." In Elaine Showalter, ed., *The New Feminist Criticism: Essays on Women, Literature, and Theory*. New York: Pantheon, 1985.

Hale, Charles. "Nathaniel Hawthorne." *To-day: A Boston Literary Journal* 38 (Sept. 1852): 177–81.

Hale, Sarah J., *Flora's Interpreter: Or, the American Book of Flowers and Sentiments*. Boston: Marsh, Capen, and Lyon, 1832.

———. *The Lecturess: Or, Woman's Sphere*. Boston: Whipple and Dannell, 1839 [1838].

———. "New Year at Home." *Godey's Lady's Book* 20 (Jan. 1840): 2.

———. "Tales." *Godey's* 18 (Jan. 1839): 47.

———. *Woman's Record*. New York: Harper, 1855.

Hall, David, ed. *The Antinomian Controversy, 1636–1638: A Documentary History*. Middletown, Conn.: Wesleyan University Press, 1968.

Haller, John S., Jr., and Robin M. Haller. *The Physician and Sexuality in Victorian America*. Urbana: University of Illinois Press, 1974.

Hallissy, Margaret. "Hawthorne's Venomous Beatrice." *Studies in Short Fiction*, 19 (Summer 1982): 231–39.

Halttunen, Karen. *Confidence Men and Painted Women: A Study of Middle-Class Culture in America, 1830–1870*. New Haven, Conn.: Yale University Press, 1982.

———. "Gothic Imagination and Social Reform: The Haunted Houses of Lyman Beecher, Henry Ward Beecher, and Harriet Stowe." In Eric J. Sundquist, ed., *New Essays in Uncle Tom's Cabin*. Cambridge, Eng.: Cambridge University Press, 1986.

Hart, James D. *The Popular Book: A History of America's Literary Taste*. New York: Oxford University Press, 1950.

Haskins, R. W. *History and Progress of Phrenology*. Buffalo: Steele and Peck; New York: Wiley and Putnam, 1839.

Hassrick, Royal B. *The George Catlin Book of American Indians*. New York: Watson-Guptill, 1977.

Hastrup, Kirsten. "The Semantics of Biology: Virginity." In Shirley Ardener, ed., *Defining Females: The Nature of Women in Society*. London: Croom Helm, 1978.

Hausen, Karin. "Family and Role-division: The Polarisation of Sexual Stereotypes in the Nineteenth Century—an Aspect of the Dissociation of Work and Family Life." In Richard J. Evans and W. R. Lee, eds., *The German Family: Essays on the Social History of the Family in Nineteenth- and Twentieth-Century Germany*. London: Croom Helm, 1981.

Hawthorne, Julian. *Nathaniel Hawthorne and His Wife: A Biography*, 2 vols. Cambridge, Mass.: Printed at the University Press, 1884.

Hawthorne, Nathaniel. *The English Notebooks by Nathaniel Hawthorne: Based Upon the Original Manuscripts in the Pierpont Morgan Library*. Ed. Randall Stewart. New York: Modern Language Association of America, 1941.

———. "Phrenology." *The American Magazine of Useful and Entertaining Knowledge* 2 (Apr. 1836): 337.

———. "The Science of Noses." *The American Magazine of Useful and Entertaining Knowledge* 2 (Mar. 1836): 268.

————. *The Works of Nathaniel Hawthorne: Riverside Edition*, vols. 4, 6. Boston: Houghton Mifflin, 1882.

Hawthorne, Sophia. "A Sophia Hawthorne Journal, 1843–1844." Ed. John J. McDonald. In C. E. Frazer Clark, Jr., ed., *The Nathaniel Hawthorne Journal, 1974.* Englewood, Colo.: Microcard Editions, 1974.

————. *Notes in England and Italy.* New York: Putnam's, 1875.

Herbert, T. Walter, Jr.. "Nathaniel Hawthorne, Una Hawthorne, and *The Scarlet Letter*: Interactive Selfhoods and the Cultural Construction of Gender." *PMLA* 103 (May 1988): 285–97.

"The Heroine's Hand." *Godey's Lady's Book* 4 (Feb. 1832): 109.

Hertz, Neil. "Medusa's Head: Male Hysteria Under Political Pressure." *Representations* 4 (Fall 1983): 27–54.

Himelick, Raymond. "Hawthorne, Spenser, and Christian Humanism." *Emerson Society Quarterly* 21 (1st quarter 1975): 21–28.

Holcomb, Adele M. "Anna Jameson on Women Artists." *Woman's Art Journal* 8 (Fall 1987): 15–24.

Holmes, Oliver Wendell. *Elsie Venner: A Romance of Destiny.* Boston: Houghton Mifflin; Cambridge, Mass.: Riverside, 1891.

Homans, Margaret. *Women Writers and Poetic Identity: Dorothy Wordsworth, Emily Brontë, and Emily Dickinson.* Princeton, N.J.: Princeton University Press, 1980.

Homer. *Iliad.* Trans. Robert Fitzgerald. Garden City, N.Y.: Anchor/Doubleday, 1974.

Hooper, Robert. *Lexicon Medicum, or Medical Dictionary.* New York: Harper, 1841.

"How Steel Pens Are Made." *Harper's New Monthly Magazine* 7 (Oct. 1853): 691–92.

Huet, Marie-Hélène. "Living Images: Monstrosity and Representation." *Representations* 4 (Fall 1983): 73–87.

Hull, Raymona E. " 'Scribbling' Females and Serious Males: Hawthorne's Comments from Abroad on Some American Authors." In C. E. Frazer Clark, Jr., ed., *Nathaniel Hawthorne Journal, 1975.* Englewood, Colo.: Microcard Editions, 1975.

Hume, Beverly. "Restructuring the Case Against Hawthorne's Coverdale." *Nineteenth-Century Fiction* 40 (June 1985): 387–99.

Hunter, Dard. *Papermaking: The History and Technique of an Ancient Craft.* New York: Knopf, 1943.

Hutner, Gordon. *Secrets and Sympathy: Forms of Disclosure in Hawthorne's Novels.* Athens: University of Georgia Press, 1988.

Hyman, Stanley Edgar. *The Tangled Bank: Darwin, Marx, Frazer and Freud as Imaginative Writers.* New York: Atheneum, 1962.

James, Alice. *The Diary of Alice James.* Ed. Leon Edel. New York: Penguin, 1973.

Jameson, Anna. *The Characteristics of Women, Moral, Poetical, and Historical.* New York: John Wiley, 1833.

————. *Legends of the Monastic Orders.* London: Longman, Brown, Green, and Longmans, 1850.

———. *Memoirs of Celebrated Female Sovereigns*. New York: Harper, 1840.

Jameson, Fredric. *Marxism and Form: Twentieth-Century Dialectical Theories of Literature*. Princeton, N.J.: Princeton University Press, 1974.

———. *The Political Unconscious: Narrative as a Socially Symbolic Act*. Ithaca, N.Y.: Cornell University Press, 1980.

Jehlen, Myra. *American Incarnation: The Individual, the Nation, and the Continent*. Cambridge, Mass.: Harvard University Press, 1986.

Johnson, Edward. *Wonder-Working Providence, 1628–1651*. Ed. J. Franklin Jameson. New York: Scribner's, 1910.

Johnson, Richard. "What Is Cultural Studies Anyway?" *Social Text* 16 (1986): 38–80.

Johnson, Samuel. *A Dictionary of the English Language*, 2 vols. Dublin: Thomas Ewing, 1775.

Jones, Buford. "Hawthorne and Spenser: From Allusion to Allegory." In C. E. Frazer Clark, Jr., ed., *The Nathaniel Hawthorne Journal 1975*. Englewood, Colo.: Microcard Editions, 1975.

Jordan, Winthrop D. *White over Black: American Attitudes Toward the Negro, 1550–1812*. Baltimore, Md.: Penguin, 1969.

Kasson, John. *Civilizing the Machine: Technology and Republican Values in America 1776–1900*. Harmondsworth, Middlesex: Penguin, 1977.

Kearns, Francis E. "Margaret Fuller as a Model for Hester Prynne." *Jahrbuch für Amerikastudien* 10 (1965): 191–97.

Kern, Louis. *An Ordered Love: Sex Roles and Sexuality in Victorian Utopias—the Shakers, the Mormons, and the Oneida Community*. Chapel Hill: University of North Carolina Press, 1981.

Kesselring, Marion. "Hawthorne's Reading, 1828–1850." *Bulletin of the New York Public Library* 53 (Apr. 1949): 55–71, 121–38, 173–94.

Kett, Joseph. *Rites of Passage: Adolescence in America, 1790 to the Present*. New York: Basic Books, 1977.

Kibbey, Anne. *The Interpretation of Material Shapes in Protestantism: A Study of Rhetoric, Prejudice, and Violence*. Cambridge, Eng.: Cambridge University Press, 1986.

Lane, Charles. "Brook Farm." *The Dial* 4 (Jan. 1844): 351–57.

Lang, Amy Schrager. *Prophetic Woman: Anne Hutchinson and the Problem of Dissent in the Literature of New England*. Berkeley: University of California Press, 1987.

Laqueur, Thomas. "Orgasm, Generation, and the Politics of Reproductive Biology." In Catherine Gallagher and T. Laqueur, eds., *The Making of the Modern Body: Sexuality and Society in the Nineteenth Century*. Berkeley: University of California Press, 1987.

Larcom, Lucy. *An Idyl of Work*. Boston: James R. Osgood, 1875.

———. *A New England Girlhood: Outlined From Memory*. Gloucester, Mass.: Peter Smith, 1973 [1889].

Larkin, Jack. *The Reshaping of Everyday Life 1790–1840*. New York: Harper & Row, 1988.

Lasch, Christopher. *The Culture of Narcissism: American Life in an Age of Diminishing Expectations*. New York: Warner, 1979.

Lawrence, D. H. *Studies in Classic American Literature*. New York: Viking, 1972 [1923].

Lerner, Gerda. "The Lady and the Mill Girl: Changes in the Status of Women in the Age of Jackson, 1800–1840." In Nancy F. Cott and Elizabeth Pleck, eds., *A Heritage of Her Own: Toward a New Social History of American Women*. New York: Simon and Schuster, 1979.

Lesser, Simon O. *Fiction and the Unconscious*. Boston: Beacon, 1957.

Leverenz, David. *Manhood and the American Renaissance*. Ithaca, N.Y.: Cornell University Press, 1989.

Leyda, Jay, ed. *The Melville Log: A Documentary Life of Herman Melville 1819–1891*, 2 vols. New York: Gordian Press, 1969.

Lightblown, Ronald. *Sandro Botticelli, Life and Work*, vol. 1. Berkeley: University of California Press, 1978.

Lindley, John, and Thomas More, eds., *The Treasury of Botany: A Popular Dictionary of the Vegetable Kingdom*, 2 vols. London: Longmans, Green, 1866.

Linn, Lizzie. "Marriage the Only Resource." *The Una* 3 (Jan. 1855): 1–3.

Martin, Emily. *The Woman in the Body: A Cultural Analysis of Reproduction*. Boston: Beacon, 1987.

Marx, Karl. *Capital: A Critique of Political Economy*. Vol. 1, *The Process of Capitalist Production*. Ed. Frederick Engels. New York: International Publishers, 1967.

Marx, Leo. *The Machine in the Garden: Technology and the Pastoral Ideal in America*. New York: Oxford University Press, 1976 [1964].

Matthiessen, F. O. *The American Renaissance: Art and Expression in the Age of Emerson and Whitman*. New York: Oxford University Press, 1941.

McDonald, John J. "'The Old Manse' and Its Mosses: The Inception and Development of *Mosses from an Old Manse*." *Texas Studies in Language and Literature* 16 (Spring 1974): 77–108.

McDowall's Journal. Jan. 1833–Dec. 1834.

McElroy, John Harmon, and Edward L. McDonald. "The Coverdale Romance." *Studies in the Novel* 14 (1982): 1–16.

McGaw, Judith. "'A Good Place to Work.' Industrial Workers and Occupational Choice: The Case of Berkshire Women." *Journal of Interdisciplinary History* 10 (Autumn 1979): 227–48.

———. "The Sources and Impact of Mechanization: The Berkshire County, Massachusetts, Paper Industry, 1801–1885 As a Case Study," Ph.D. diss., New York University, 1977.

———. "Technological Change and Women's Work: Mechanization in the Berkshire Paper Industry, 1820–1855." In Martha Moore Trescott, ed., *Dynamos and Virgins Revisited: Women and Technological Change in History*. Metuchen, N.J.: Scarecrow, 1979.

McPherson, Hugo. *Hawthorne as Myth-Maker: A Study in Imagination*. Toronto: University of Toronto Press, 1969.

Mellow, James R. *Nathaniel Hawthorne in His Times*. Boston: Houghton Mifflin, 1980.

Melville, Herman. *Billy Budd and the Piazza Tales*. Garden City, N.Y.: Anchor, 1973.

———. *Great Short Works of Herman Melville*. Ed. Warner Berthoff. New York: Harper & Row, 1969.

———. *The Letters of Herman Melville*. Ed. Merrell R. Davis and William H. Gilman. New Haven, Conn.: Yale University Press, 1960.

———. *Moby-Dick Or, The Whale*. Ed. Charles Feidelson, Jr. Indianapolis: Bobbs-Merril, 1964.

———. *Pierre Or, The Ambiguities*. New York: New American Library, 1964.

———. *Typee: A Narrative of the Marquesas Islands*. London: J. M. Dent; New York: E. P. Dutton, 1921.

Michaels, Walter Benn. *The Gold Standard and the Logic of Naturalism: American Literature at the Turn of the Century*. Berkeley: University of California Press, 1987.

Miller, D. A. *The Novel and the Police*. Berkeley: University of California Press, 1988.

Mintz, Steven. *A Prison of Expectations: The Family in Victorian Culture*. New York: New York University Press, 1983.

Mitterauer, Michael, and Reinhard Sieder. *The European Family: Patriarchy to Partnership from the Middle Ages to the Present*. Trans. Karla Oosterveen and Manfred Horzinger. Oxford: Basil Blackwell, 1982.

"Modern and Ancient Works." *Scientific American* 4 (Feb. 1849): 165.

Monteiro, George. "Hawthorne's Emblematic Serpent." In C. E. Frazer Clark, Jr., ed., *The Nathaniel Hawthorne Journal, 1973*. Englewood, Colo.: Microcard Editions, 1973.

Morgan, Edmund S. *The Puritan Family: Religion and Domestic Relations in Seventeenth-Century New England*. New York: Harper & Row, 1966.

Mumford, Lewis. *Herman Melville*. New York: Literary Guild of America, 1929.

Murray, Peter, and Linda Murray. *The Penguin Dictionary of Art and Artists*. Harmondsworth, Middlesex: Penguin, 1983.

N., R. H. "American Authorship—Hawthorne." *Southern Quarterly Review* 7 (Apr. 1853): 486–508.

"Nathaniel Hawthorne." *Democratic Review* 16 (Apr. 1845): 376–84.

Neal, John. "The Young Phrenologist." *The Token and Atlantic Souvenir*. Boston: Charles Bowen, 1836.

Nissenbaum, Stephen. *Sex, Diet, and Debility in Jacksonian America: Sylvester Graham and Health Reform*. Westport, Conn.: Greenwood, 1980.

Nye, Russel Blaine. *Society and Culture in America, 1830–1860*. New York: Harper & Row, 1974.

O'Connor, Lillian. *Pioneer Women Orators: Rhetoric in the Ante-Bellum Reform Movement*. New York: Vantage, 1952.

Oliphant, Margaret. "Modern Novelists—Great and Small." *Blackwood's Edinburgh Magazine* 77 (May 1855): 554–68.

Ovid. *Metamorphoses*. Trans. Mary M. Innes. Harmondsworth, Middlesex: Penguin, 1982.

Owens, Craig. "The Medusa Effect or, the Spectacular Ruse." In Barbara Kruger. *We Won't Play Nature to Your Culture*. London and Basel: ICA and the Kunsthalle, 1983.

————. "Posing." In C. Owens et al., *Difference: On Representation and Sexuality*. New York: The New Museum of Contemporary Art, 1985.

Pancoast, Seth. *The Ladies New Medical Guide*. Philadelphia: John E. Potter, 1890.

Parker, Rozsika, and Griselda Pollock. *Old Mistresses: Women, Art and Ideology*. New York: Pantheon, 1981.

Parker, Theodore. "The Education of the Laboring Classes." In Parker, *Social Classes in a Republic*. Ed. Samuel A. Eliot. Boston: American Unitarian Association, 1907.

————. "Thoughts on Labor." *The Dial* 1 (Apr. 1841): 497–519.

Pattee, Fred Lewis. *The Feminine Fifties*. New York: D. Appleton-Century, 1940.

Pease, Donald E. *Visionary Compacts: Renaissance Writings in Cultural Context*. Madison: University of Wisconsin Press, 1987.

Penny, Virginia. *The Employments of Women: A Cyclopaedia of Woman's Work*. Boston: Walker, Wise, 1863.

Pepper, Stephen D. *Guido Reni: A Complete Catalogue of His Works with an Introductory Text*. New York: New York University Press, 1984.

Perrot, Michelle, ed. *From the Fires of Revolution to the Great War*. Vol. 4 of *A History of Private Life*, Phillipe Ariès and Georges Duby, gen. eds. Trans. Arthur Goldhammer. Cambridge, Mass.: Harvard University Press, 1990.

Person, Leland S., Jr. *Aesthetic Headaches: Women and Masculine Poetics in Poe, Melville, and Hawthorne*. Athens: University of Georgia Press, 1988.

"Phrenology Applied." *Phrenological Almanac* (1840).

Poe, Edgar Allan. *Autography*. *The Complete Works of Edgar Allan Poe*, vol. 15. Ed. James A. Harrison. New York: AMS, 1965.

————. *The Complete Tales and Poems of Edgar Allan Poe*. New York: Modern Library, 1965.

————. *The Letters of Edgar Allan Poe*. Ed. John Ward Ostrom. Cambridge, Mass.: Harvard University Press, 1948.

Poovey, Mary. *The Proper Lady and the Woman Writer: Ideology as Style in the Works of Mary Wollstonecraft, Mary Shelley, and Jane Austen*. Chicago: University of Chicago Press, 1984.

Poster, Mark. *Critical Theory of the Family*. New York: Seabury, 1980.

Price, A. H. "Reasons Why Woman Should Define Her Own Sphere." *The Una* 1 (Feb. 1853): 10.

Proudfit, Charles L. "Eroticization of Intellectual Functions as Oedipal Defence: A Psychoanalytic View of Nathaniel Hawthorne's 'The Birthmark.'" *International Review of Psychoanalysis* 7 (1980): 375–83.

Ragussis, Michael. "Family Discourse and Fiction in *The Scarlet Letter*." *ELH* 49 (1982): 863–88.

[Ray, Dr.] "Decandolle's Botany." *North American Review* 37 (Jan. 1834): 32–63.

Rees, Abraham, ed. *Cyclopaedia: or, a New Universal Dictionary of Arts and Sciences*, 39 vols. London: Longman, Hurst, Rees, Orme, and Brown, 1819.

Rees, John O., Jr. "Hawthorne's Concept of Allegory: A Reconsideration." *Philological Quarterly* 54 (Spring 1975): 494–510.

Reynolds, David S. *Beneath the American Renaissance: The Subversive Imagination in the Age of Emerson and Melville.* New York: Knopf, 1988.

Reynolds, Larry J. "*The Scarlet Letter* and Revolutions Abroad." *American Literature* 57 (Mar. 1985): 44–67.

Riasonovosky, Nicholas V. *The Teaching of Charles Fourier.* Berkeley: University of California Press, 1969.

Ringe, Donald A. *American Gothic: Imagination and Reason in Nineteenth-Century Fiction.* Lexington: University Press of Kentucky, 1982.

Rogin, Michael Paul. *Fathers and Children: Andrew Jackson and the Subjugation of the American Indian.* New York: Vintage, 1975.

——. *Subversive Genealogies: The Politics and Art of Herman Melville.* New York: Knopf, 1983.

Rosenberg, Charles E. "Sexuality, Class, and Role." *American Quarterly* 25 (May 1973): 131–53.

Rossen, Rebecca. "The Artist's Wife: The Art and Lives of Women Artists in Nineteenth-Century America." Unpublished manuscript.

Rossetti, Christina. "In an Artist's Studio." In *The Poetical Works of Christina Georgina Rossetti.* Ed. William Michael Rossetti. London: Macmillan, 1906.

Rothman, Ellen K. *Hands and Hearts: A History of Courtship in America.* New York: Basic Books, 1984.

Roulston, Robert. "Hawthorne's Attitude Toward Jews." *American Transcendental Quarterly* 29 (Winter 1976): 3–8.

Rowe, George Robert, M.D. *On Some of the Most Important Disorders of Women.* London: John Churchill, 1844.

Ruskin, John. "Of Queen's Gardens." In Ruskin, *Sesame and Lilies.* New York: John Wiley, 1865.

Ryan, Mary P. *The Cradle of the Middle Class: The Family in Oneida County, New York, 1790–1865.* Cambridge, Eng.: Cambridge University Press, 1981.

——. *The Empire of the Mother: American Writing About Domesticity.* Special issue of *Women and History* 2/3 (Summer/Fall 1982).

——. "Femininity and Capitalism in Antebellum America." In Zillah Eisenstein, ed., *Capitalist Patriarchy and the Case for Socialist Feminism.* New York: Monthly Review Press, 1977.

——. *Womanhood in America: From Colonial Times to the Present.* New York: New Viewpoints, 1979.

Ryan, Michael. *A Manual of Midwifery, or Compendium of Gynaecology and Paidonosology.* Burlington, Vt.: Smith and Harrington, 1835.

Sanday, Peggy Reeves. *Female Power and Male Dominance: On the Origins of Sexual Inequality*. Cambridge, Eng.: Cambridge University Press, 1981.

Schnog, Nancy. "Inside the Sentimental: The Psychological Work of *The Wide Wide World*." *Genders* 4 (Mar. 1989): 11–25.

Schutte, Anne Jacobson. " 'Such Monstrous Birth': A Neglected Aspect of the Antinomian Controversy." *Renaissance Quarterly* 38 (Spring 1985): 85–106.

Scott, Joan W. "Gender: A Useful Category of Historical Analysis." *American Historical Review* 91 (Dec. 1986): 1053–75.

Scott, Walter. *Demonology and Witchcraft*. London: John Murray, 1831.

Sedgwick, Catherine Maria. *Home*. Boston: James, Munroe, 1841 [1836].

Sedgwick, Eve Kosofsky. *The Coherence of Gothic Conventions*. New York: Methuen, 1986.

Sennett, Richard. "Destructive Gemeinschaft." In Robert Bocock, Peter Hamilton, Kenneth Thompson, and Alan Walton, eds., *An Introduction to Sociology*. Brighton, U.K.: Harvester, 1980.

——. *The Fall of Public Man: On the Social Psychology of Capitalism*. New York: Vintage, 1978.

Sennett, Richard, and Jonathan Cobb. *The Hidden Injuries of Class*. New York: Vintage, 1973.

Shakespeare, William. "The Rape of Lucrece." In *The Complete Works of William Shakespeare*. Ed. Lyman Kittredge. Boston: Ginn, 1936.

——. *The Tempest*. Ed. Frank Kermode. London: Methuen, 1975.

Shearman, John. "Cristofano Allori's 'Judith.' " *Burlington Magazine* 121 (Jan. 1979): 3–10.

Shelley, Mary W. *Valperga: Or, the Life and Adventures of Castruccio, Prince of Lucca*. London: W. B. Whittaker, 1823.

Shelley, Percy Bysshe *A Defence of Poetry*. In James Harry Smith and Edd Winfield, eds., *The Great Critics*. New York: Norton, 1951.

Shorter, Edward. *The Making of the Modern Family*. New York: Basic Books, 1975.

Showalter, Elaine. *The Female Malady: Women, Madness, and Culture in England, 1830–1980*. New York: Pantheon, 1986.

——. "Representing Ophelia: Women, Madness, and the Responsibility of Feminist Criticism." In Patricia Parker and Geoffrey Hartman, eds., *Shakespeare and the Question of Theory*. New York: Metheun, 1985.

Showalter, Elaine, and English Showalter. "Victorian Women and Menstruation." In Martha Vincus, ed., *Suffer and Be Still: Women in the Victorian Age*. Bloomington: Indiana University Press, 1973.

Shriber, Mary Suzanne. "Justice to Zenobia." *New England Quarterly* 55 (Mar. 1982): 61–78.

Sidney, Philip. *Sir Philip Sidney's Selected Prose and Poetry*. Ed. Robert Kimbrough. San Francisco: Rinehart, 1969.

Sigourney, Lydia Hunt. *The Girl's Book*. New York: Robert Carter, 1853 [1837].

———. "Home." *The Happy Home and Parlor Magazine* 5 (1857): 13–14.

Simms, William Gilmore. *Confession or the Blind Heart: A Domestic Story.* New York: Redfield, 1856 [1841].

Siracusa, Carl. *A Mechanical People: Perceptions of the Industrial Order in Massachusetts 1815–1880.* Middletown, Conn.: Wesleyan University Press, 1979.

Sketches of the Lives of Distinguished Females. New York: J. and J. Harper, 1833.

Smith, Allan Gardner. *The Analysis of Motives: Early American Psychology and Fiction. Costerus* 27–29 (Aug. 1980): 78–124.

Smith, A. G. Lloyd. *Eve Tempted: Writing and Sexuality in Hawthorne's Fiction.* London: Croom Helm; Totowa, N.J.: Barnes and Noble, 1984.

Smith, Henry Nash. *Democracy and the Novel: Popular Resistance to Classic American Works.* New York: Oxford University Press, 1978.

———. "The Scribbling Women and the Cosmic Success Story." *Critical Inquiry* 1 (Sept. 1974): 47–70.

Smith, Joseph Edward Adam. *History of Berkshire County, Massachusetts, with Biographical Sketches of Prominent Men,* vol. 1. New York: J. B. Beers, 1885.

Smith-Rosenberg, Carroll. "Davey Crockett as Trickster: Pornography, Liminality, and Symbolic Inversion in Victorian America." In Smith-Rosenberg, *Disorderly Conduct: Visions of Gender in Victorian America.* New York: Oxford University Press, 1985.

———. "The Hysterical Woman: Sex Roles and Role Conflict in 19th-Century America." *Social Research* 39 (1972): 652–78.

———. "Puberty to Menopause: The Cycle of Femininity in Nineteenth-Century America." In Mary Hartman and Lois Banner, eds., *Clio's Consciousness Raised: New Perspectives on the History of Women.* New York: Octagon, 1976.

———. "Sex as Symbol in Victorian Purity: An Ethnohistorical Analysis of Jacksonian America." *American Journal of Sociology* 84 (Special Summer Supplement, 1978): 212–47.

Smith-Rosenberg, Carroll, and Charles Rosenberg. "The Female Animal: Medical and Biological Views of Woman and Her Role in Nineteenth-Century America." *Journal of American History* 60 (Sept. 1973): 332–56.

Society of Gentlemen. *A New and Complete Dictionary of Arts and Sciences,* 4 vols. London: W. Owen, 1763.

Soler, Mariano Cubi I. *Phrenology: A Lecture.* Boston: Marsh, Capon, Lyon, and Webb, 1840.

Spenser, Edmund. *Faerie Queene, Spenser Poetical Works.* Eds. J. C. Smith and E. de Selincourt. Oxford: Oxford University Press, 1970.

Stallybrass, Peter, and Allon White. *The Politics and Poetics of Transgression.* Ithaca, N.Y.: Cornell University Press, 1986.

Stanton, Elizabeth Cady. "The Wife." *The Lily* 4 (Jan. 1852): 3.

Stanton, Elizabeth Cady, Susan B. Anthony, and Matilda Joslyn Gage, eds. *History of Woman Suffrage.* 6 vols. Rochester, N.Y.: Charles Mann, 1889.

Stearns, Bertha Monica. "Early Factory Magazines in New England: The *Lowell Offering* and Its Contemporaries." *Journal of Economic and Business History* 2 (Aug. 1930): 685–705.

Steele, Jeffrey. *The Representation of the Self in the American Renaissance.* Chapel Hill: University of North Carolina Press, 1987.

Stern, Madeline B. *Heads and Headlines: The Phrenological Fowlers.* Norman: University of Oklahoma Press, 1971.

Stern, Milton R. Introduction to *The House of the Seven Gables.* New York: Penguin, 1981.

Stewart, Randall. "Hawthorne and *The Faerie Queene.*" *Philological Quarterly* 12 (1933): 196–206.

———. *Nathaniel Hawthorne: A Biography.* New Haven, Conn.: Yale University Press, 1961.

Stineback, David. "Gender, Hawthorne, and Literary Criticism." *Mosaic* 18 (Spring 1985): 91–100.

Stoehr, Taylor. *Free Love in America: A Documentary History.* New York: AMS Press, 1979.

———. *Hawthorne's Mad Scientists: Pseudoscience and Social Science in Nineteenth-Century Life and Letters.* Hamden, Conn.: Archon, 1978.

Stowe, Harriet Beecher. *Uncle Tom's Cabin: Or, Life Among the Lowly.* Ed. Ann Douglas. New York: Penguin, 1981 [1852].

Susman, Warren I. *Culture as History: The Transformation of American Society in the Twentieth Century.* New York: Pantheon, 1984.

"Sydney Smith vs. T. S. Arthur." *The Lily* 3 (Aug. 1851): 62.

Tharp, Louise Hall. *The Peabody Sisters of Salem.* Boston: Little, Brown, 1950.

Tilt, Edward John. *On the Diseases of Menstruation and Ovarian Inflammation.* New York: Samuel S. and William Wood, 1851.

Tocqueville, Alexis de. *Democracy in America*, 2 vols. Trans. Henry Reeve. New York: Schocken, 1974.

Tompkins, Jane. *Sensational Designs: The Cultural Work of American Fiction, 1790–1860.* New York: Oxford University Press, 1985.

Tuckerman, Henry T. "Nathaniel Hawthorne." *Southern Literary Messenger* 17 (June 1851): 344–49.

Turner, Arlin. *Nathaniel Hawthorne: A Biography.* New York: Oxford University Press, 1980.

Turner, William. *The School Dictionary Designed for the Use of Academies and Common Schools in the United States.* Hartford, Conn.: H. and F. J. Huntington, 1829.

The Una. Feb. 1853–Oct. 1855.

Van Leer, David. "Roderick's Other Serpent: Hawthorne's Use of Spenser." *Emerson Society Quarterly* 27 (2nd quarter, 1981): 73–84.

Vickers, Nancy. "'The Blazon of Sweet Beauty's Beast': Shakespeare's *Lucrece.*" In Patricia Parker and Geoffrey Hartman, eds., *Shakespeare and the Question of Theory.* New York: Methuen, 1985.

Wade, Mason. *Margaret Fuller: Whetstone of Genius.* New York: Viking, 1940.

Walker, John. *A Critical Pronouncing Dictionary and Expositor of the English Language*, 2 vols. New York: Collins and Hannay, 1825.

Walters, Ronald G. *Primers for Prudery: Sexual Advice to Victorian America.* Englewood Cliffs, N.J.: Prentice-Hall, 1974.

Ward, Elizabeth Stuart Phelps. "The True Woman." In *The Story of Avis.* Ed. Elizabeth Hardwick. New Brunswick, N.J.: Rutgers University Press, 1985.

Ware, William. *Zenobia: Or the Fall of Palmyra*, 2 vols. New York: C. S. Francis; Boston: J. H. Francis, 1838.

Warren, Joyce. *The American Narcissus: Individualism and Women in Nineteenth-Century American Fiction.* New Brunswick, N.J.: Rutgers University Press, 1984.

Webster, Noah. *An American Dictionary of the English Language.* New York: S. Converse, 1829.

Weedon, Chris. *Feminist Practice and Poststructuralist Theory.* Oxford: Basil Blackwell, 1987.

Weeks, Jeffrey. *Sex, Politics and Society: The Regulation of Sexuality since 1800.* London: Longman, 1981.

Welter, Barbara. "The Cult of True Womanhood: 1820–1860." *American Quarterly* 18 (Summer 1966): 151–74.

———. *Dimity Convictions: The American Woman in the Nineteenth Century.* Columbus: Ohio University Press, 1976.

West, Harry C. "Hawthorne's Magic Circle: The Artist as Magician." *Criticism* 16 (Fall 1974): 311–25.

Weston, Byron. "History of Papermaking in Berkshire County Massachusetts, U.S.A." In *Collection of the Berkshire Historical and Scientific Society*, vol. 4. Pittsfield, Mass.: Press of the Sun Printing Co., 1894–97.

Wethey, Harold E. *The Paintings of Titian*, vol. 3. London: Phaidon, 1975.

Wexler, Laura. "Tender Violence: Domestic Fiction and Educational Reform." In Shirley Samuels, ed., *The Esthetics of Sentiment.* New York: Oxford University Press, forthcoming.

"What Says History of Women?" *The Lily* 3 (Apr. 1851): 31.

Williams, Roger. *A Key Into the Language of America.* London: Gregory Dexter, 1643.

Willoughby, John C. "'The Old Manse' Revisited: Some Analogues for Art." *New England Quarterly* 46 (Mar. 1973): 45–61.

Withers, Josephine. "Artistic Women and Women Artists." *Art Journal* 35 (Summer 1976): 330–36.

Withycombe, E. G. *The Oxford Dictionary of English Christian Names.* Oxford: Oxford University Press, 1977.

"Woman's Rights." *The Lily* 3 (Apr. 1851): 28.

Wood, Ann Douglas. "'The Fashionable Diseases': Women's Complaints and Their Treatment in Nineteenth-Century America." In Mary S. Hartman and Lois Banner, eds., *Clio's Consciousness Raised: New Perspectives on the History of Women.* New York: Octagon, 1976.

Wright, Fanny. *Course of Popular Lectures.* New York: Arno, 1972.

Young, Philip. *Hawthorne's Secret: An Un-Told Tale*. Boston: David R. Godine, 1984.

Youra, Steven. " 'The Fatal Hand': A Sign of Confusion in Hawthorne's 'The Birth-mark.' " *American Transcendental Quarterly* 60 (June 1986): 43–51.

Zaretsky, Eli. *Capitalism, the Family, and Personal Life*. New York: Harper Colophon, 1979.

Ziff, Larzer. *Literary Democracy: The Declaration of Cultural Independence in America*. New York: Viking, 1981.

Index

In this index an "f" after a number indicates a separate reference on the next page, and an "ff" indicates separate references on the next two pages. A continuous discussion over two or more pages is indicated by a span of page numbers, e.g., "57–60." *Passim* is used for a cluster of references in close but not consecutive sequence.

Library of Congress Cataloging-in-Publication Data

Pfister, Joel.
  The production of personal life : class, gender, and the
psychological in Hawthorne's fiction / Joel Pfister.
      p.   cm.
  Includes bibliographical references and index.
  ISBN 0-8047-1947-0 (alk. paper) :
  ISBN 0-8047-1948-9 (pbk. : alk. paper) :
  1. Hawthorne, Nathaniel, 1804–1864—Knowledge—Psychology.
2. Hawthorne, Nathaniel, 1804–1864—Political and social views.
3. Middle classes in literature.   4. Psychology in literature.
5. Sex role in literature.   I. Title.
PS1892.P74P45   1992
813'.3—dc20   91-16686
                                                        CIP

⊗ This book is printed on acid-free paper.

The Third Letter

To Marie
Thanks for
Patient Service
Fred Ramm
6-6-96

The Third Letter

Frank Ramirez

Cliffhanger
Press
Oakland, California

Typeset by Design, Type & Graphics

Published by
Cliffhanger Press
P.O. Box 29527
Oakland, California 94604-9527

Manufactured in the United States of America

Library of Congress Cataloging-in-Publication Data

Ramirez, Frank, 1954-
    The Third Letter / Frank Ramirez.
        p. cm.
    ISBN 0-912761-33-4 (alk. paper) **(pbk.)**
    I. Title.
PS3568.A445T47   1990
813'.54—dc20

First Edition

To Jennie

1.

Ellie says L.A. is an exemplar of the twenty-first century world, an anticipation of a future paradigm, an eschatological working model of an *ekklesia-cum-oikonomaia*. Ellie's my boss. She really talks that way.

It was during breakfast at the Manor that the subject came up. I was feeling so good I was willing to listen to anything. The smell of the breakfast Maggs was cooking had floated to the second floor, drawing me out of bed and to the window of my rooms in Ellie's mansion. From my perch in Belle Eyrie L.A. looked good. The wind had blown away the haze, and looking south across the basin I could see for miles.

Downstairs, breakfast was as good as it smelled. I smiled at Ellie and Miranda.

Ellie was feeling well. She was getting around without her walker. She was dressed for the day in a flowered dress, the morning papers spread out before her. Two sharp blue eyes danced out of a thin, dried-apple-doll face. She returned my smile.

That leaves Miranda Devlin, her handler, if you will, feeling grumpy and useless. Then Miranda made a comment about the 'good old days', and that's what got Ellie started.

"The good old days," retorted Ellie, "were based on backbreaking labor and the existence of a class of serfs. No, I am not speaking of the Middle Ages, I'm referring to the first half of the twentieth century. I was there, please recall. It is only recently that we have been able to refine leisure for all classes of society."

"Yeah, that's right," I piped in.

Murrie arched her eyebrows. "What do you know about it, Manny?"

"You can see it everywhere. The video stores, for instance—"

Miranda snorted, but Ellie interupted. "Allow Mr. Padilla to continue. I suspect he has anticipated me."

"Well," I said, a little more uncertain of myself. I'm not used to Ellie taking my side. "Drive down to Watts, to South Central Los Angeles, to East L.A.—"

"I'd rather not," said Miranda.

"Ms. Devlin, *please*," said Ellie, with emphasis.

"Thank you," I continued. "My point is, drive down there—keep the windows up and the door locked, of course—and you'll find video stores. Every one of those mini malls owned by the Koreans has one, along with a chicken place, a laundry, and a donut shop. Now you know the good folks from Beverly Hills and Santa Monica are not driving to those neighborhoods to rent *Kung Fu Katy, Nazi Machine Guns From Hell,* and *Psychotic Halloween Chain Saw Phantasm V* for ninety-nine cents. I have to assume that even in the poorest parts of town people own VCRs. Things are bad there—damn bad—but we live better than kings compared to what I've read of the old days."

"Thank you, Mr. Padilla," said Ellie. "An apt metaphor."

Then she started in on that business about L.A. being the exemplar and all the rest. Her point was that in the decades ahead more and more of the world's population would become interdepedent, allowing people to prosper in previously hostile environments, that cities and nations would move away from special-ization and emphasize versatility in their economies. Moreover, creative ethnic mixtures might defuse na-tionalistic fervor. Miranda challenged her on that one, but Ellie's point was that L.A. didn't suffer from a second city syndrome, nor did Angelenos tend to look down on other parts of the state or country. They're just not rivalry-oriented. (We'll see if she still feels that way the next time the Dodgers meet the Yankees in the series.)

We toss around our share of words over the breakfast table. Why not? We got a right. There's a lot of words floating out there, spoken, broadcast, and published.

They process lots of those words down here. Steamy bedrooms, seamy deals, streaming streets. Fat books of a thousand pages and more that you can't put down because you didn't know people really did things like that.

They don't call it literature and you won't see it reviewed in the *New Yorker,* but the supermarket racks get emptied and filled and emptied again, and the people writing the garbage make an awful lot of money.

Ellie thinks it's great. It reminds her of Shakespeare. She says the "real" writers of his era looked down on him because he made a lot of money, but that pleasing the masses has to count for something.

Not that she reads the Hollywood novels. Heaven forbid. But she approves of them. At a distance.

Which is how this whole mess got started. The mess with Nick Patterson, which you heard so much about.

I hadn't read any of Nick Patterson's books, but the catch phrase was everywhere. You couldn't escape it. So when our boss had finished her sermon, Miranda Devlin took another bite of her tea and toast and scowled. She wanted no part of Maggs' patented Ham 'n Eggs Tobasco Breakfast Quiche. I turned to her and said, "What's the matter, Murrie? You look like you got your Third today."

Blame Johnny Carson, if you have to blame anyone. On the tube late the night before he'd said "You're great folks, a great crowd—not like last night's crowd. Hoo, boy, it was a bad crowd."

He arched his eyebrow and waited. The audience took its cue and as one chanted—"How bad was it?"

"Hnnn," he groaned, stretching his closed lips across his teeth and rolling his eyes. "Let me tell you, folks, this crowd was so bad they were the kind of folks who send the Third Letter—*First!*"

It brought the house down.

Ellie looked up with a question in her eyes. It's a rare day when I have the jump on her so I said, "The Third, Ms. Kaufman. You know, the Third Letter."

Deliberately Ellie took a delicate bite of her quiche, and a sip of her orange juice. I smiled. I knew it. She hadn't heard of Nick Patterson's books. Which meant she hadn't seen Matthew James play the main character Jason Argo on "The Furies", the series based on the books.

I knew that Ellie would consult Miranda later and in private, and no doubt by dinner would have read *Damned If You Will, Requiem For A Starling,* and the most recent, *Winter's Son*. Then she'd lead the table conversation to Greek Mythology, refer to them as a source book for inspiration, point out several examples through the ages, then tout Patterson's books as a moderately successful update of an idea grounded in the thirst for justice, which would roll like a river of gravy over the potatoes Maggs was planning for dinner.

Then she'd turn to me and say in a gentle tone, "And what is your opinion, Mr. Padilla?"

To which I would have no reply since I hadn't read a one of them.

So I said, "Everyone's talking about it. Women leaving for work tell their husbands, 'Don't open any letters.' Kids chant, 'I got my First, I got my Second, you can have my Third.' Don't tell me you haven't—"

"Nick Patterson," said Ellie, her smile only tickling the ends of her lips. "Five novels in four years, *genre* detective, centered around the adventures of a dedicated civil libertarian named James Argo. His adversary is the mysterious star chamber styling itself The Furies. This dreaded sword of Damocles operates by giving the victim fair warning in the form of three letters which explain exactly when, where, and how the execution will take place. The Furies, as portrayed, have an interesting codicil which demands cessation of hostilities should the riddle of the letters be solved. James Argo solves the puzzles, but is sometimes unable to prevent the death of his client. This lends suspense to what would otherwise be another literary parlor game. Noted actor Matthew James plays the embattled Argo in a faddishly popular series."

She paused to take another bite. Murrie was choking on her toast.

"Otherwise, Mr. Padilla, I remain totally unacquainted with the subject. Will you have another slice?" she added, reaching for the quiche.

"I guess I've been given *my* First. Congratulations, Ms. Kaufman," I said. "I'm surprised. In the past you've told me you prefer your books aged a good five years or so. I didn't know you'd read his books."

Ellie was just about finished, so she pushed her plate back and began to rise. Miranda, who's a little compulsive, was up in a moment to help her.

"As you well know," said Ellie, waving Miranda away, "There have been few novels written since 1930 that have given me pleasure, *The Greater Trumps* and *The Lord of the Rings* being two major exceptions. I have not read Mr. Patterson's books, but it was necessary for Ms. Devlin to read them for me, as Mr. Patterson will be one of the guests at our little soiree next weekend."

"Pardon me?" I started.

"She's talking about the TV debate they're taping here next week," intruded Miranda. "The one about the California Literati. He's one of the authors we've invited."

"He is?"

"He is," said Miranda.

"Oh," I answered, "and it's next week?" Then I lied, "That's too bad. I'm sorry about missing the taping when I'm out of town next week because I know you'll do fine without me. Oh well. Murrie, you did tell Ms. Kaufman about my vacation days?"

"What the hell are you talking about?" she spluttered. "You didn't arrange for any vacation days next week! You're not getting out of this that easy."

"I think your memory's slipping, Miranda. I distinctly remember telling you about my planned trip to Sonora, you know, the old country. You said you'd tell El—Ms. Kaufman first chance you got. I left it in your hands."

"This is ridiculous." She turned to Ellie. "This is ridiculous," she repeated. "There was no such request."

"Mr. Padilla," said Ellie, "You might be interested in knowing that your friend, John Ronald, of the *Herald,* is coming."

"He is? Say 'Hi' for me, will you?" I said. Murrie gave me a sour look. "What's the big deal?" I continued. "I figure you'll do fine without me anyway. The last taping—when was it? About a year ago?— went off without a hitch, and you thought I was in the way. After the fuss you made last year I decided to take part of my vacation during the next one. Look, I've got errands this morning so if you'll excuse me..."

"What are you trying to pull?" asked Murrie. "Hey, don't you know this Patterson guy?"

"Not really."

"You do. I heard you bragging about it once to that friend of yours, Angie, about a year ago, when she was reading one of the books. You said you went to school together."

"Right. I passed him in the hallway a few times. He was a class ahead of me. Big deal."

"I get it," continued Murrie. "You were bragging to Angie, and now you're afraid she'll discover you were exaggerating. I knew I didn't forget any vacation."

"All right," I lied again. "You caught me. Now if it's all the same to you, I'd rather skip the taping next week."

"Mr. Padilla," said Ellie. "I will take every measure to sidestep any possible embarrassment, but I am afraid your presence is necessary, even vital, to our anticipated enterprise." She turned and walked to the kitchen door, shaking off Miranda's proffered help.

"Have the workmen arrived?" she then asked of no one in particular. "We must complete the plumbing in the blue guestroom before the day of the taping."

The two of them were gone.

I was starting to leave myself when Maggs, the cook, who had sat quietly listening to the exchange, called my name.

"Manny, get your butt over here."

Despite her blindness, Maggs has the disconcerting habit of staring right at you when she wants your attention. Since she's the one who puts meals on the table, I obeyed.

"Yeah?"

"Give me your hand," she said. "No, don't walk away. Just give it."

I stuck my hand in one of her strong mitts. She said the word, "Patterson." Then she grunted.

"Thought so." She released my fingers. "You been lying to Miss Ellie again, haven't you?"

"How did you know?"

"Your skin crawls when you lie, Manny. So you knew this Patterson fellow pretty good, didn't you? Want to talk about it?"

"No."

She shrugged. "Then I got work to do. You stay out of trouble, you hear?"

"As well as you."

"Damn little chance of that," she muttered as she walked away. "Damn little chance of that."

2.

I tried to beg off again. Ellie still insisted she needed me for the taping. The guests would arrive Tuesday evening for the banquet open to photographers and newsmen, followed by a round table discussion to set some of the parameters for the panel the next day. The round table itself would be filmed in case some of the bon mots were better than the planned discussion a day later.

It sounded boring to me, and I told her so. No go. Ellie's been wealthy for decades so she does what she wants.

"But what do you need me for?" I pleaded.

"Your presence is necessary," she offered, "if for no other reason than to serve drinks."

Ellie and Miranda were busy most of the day in the new guest wing. I'm not impressed by Ellie's penchant for construction, but the   new wing meant that the house wasn't swimming with sawdust. The disadvantage is that the new guest wing is totally separate from the house, so we have to step out the side entrance of the hall, and walk about fifty yards on the sidewalk or twenty on the grass to get to the first of the apartments.

They are nice. There are five of them—blue, green, grey, beige, and yellow. Each has its own phone and kitchenette. I was a little worried, though. Ellie'd had so much fun overseeing contruction she'd need something else as stimulating to take its place, and she was already eyeing my floor. My room is off limits—it's in my contract—but if she got to work on the elevator and stairwell at the same time I could see myself climbing a rope ladder to my room for weeks.

Maybe I could soften her up tomorrow. I told Ellie after dinner I was going out driving, and that I could be found at Angie's house in Duarte.

My truck and I had the streets of L.A. to ourselves. It was if I had stumbled into a post-holocaust Los Angeles. The silence was eerie. Most of the lights in the homes were out. Only the furtive gleams from darkened rooms hinted there might be life within. Here and there a dog walked its territory.

There was a reason L.A. was empty. The Lakers were playing a seventh game that night. All right-thinking folks were at home, glued to their sets. I'd have liked to have joined them, but I couldn't. I was too nervous. I can't watch. Yes, it is only a game, but what a game. I had suffered through seasons of disappointment at the hands of that team back east, and in my heart I still expected disaster in the playoffs every spring. So when the championship series begins each year, I simply stop watching until the last two minutes of each game. It makes me something of a social pariah, but it saves me layers of stomach lining.

For awhile I wondered if I'd make it in time for the last couple of minutes. I was tempted to tune in to find out how much time was left, but if I did that I'd want to know the score, and I'd listen to the crowd to try to discover what had happened, and I'd stop watching the road and—

My route took me south on Westwood from Sunset Avenue and through the UCLA campus. As I drove past student housing I saw figures hidden in alleys, under cars, and behind lamp posts. Stock-still they stood, then suddenly they would spring towards dorm windows to stuff envelopes into the unsuspecting victims' rooms, paint guns in their back pockets. The Three Letter Societies were springing up on campuses all over the country. Someone out there was getting his Second or her Third Letter that night. By convention, the "execution", a splotch of paint delivered to the forehead, had to follow in five hours. I flashed my brights and sent them running.

When I thought I'd wasted enough time, I caught the San Berdoo and dashed east for Angie's house, hoping to join her brothers in the living room and watch the ending of the game.

I was tuned to the FM station, where the DJ was too cool to care about the Lakers. Three hundred and sixty-four days of the year I thought of him as a jerk, but tonight he was my guardian angel.

Except that after playing "Car Strips in June" the DJ said, "And here's a quick note for you Neanderthals who still care what happens to the Lak—"

I jammed my finger turning the radio off, and drove the rest of the way in grieved silence.

As it turned out, I made it to Angie's with two and a half minutes to spare. Someone threw a beer at me as I jumped over the couch. I caught it on the fly and let the cushions absorb the shock of my landing. A Coop-a-Loop sent Angie's four brothers cheering, and I suspected at once that we were ahead. They were too happy for a tense game.

They were about to flash the score on the screen when Angie plopped down on my lap and said, "Hi, Manny. When did you get here?"

"Just now. Do you suppose—"

"And how is Ellen Kaufman?"

"She's fine. So's Murrie and Maggs. Look, I just want to see the score so could you—"

"How is the restaurant, you ask? It was a nice day at the restaurant. Not a single crisis, the salsa was hot, the flan stayed cool. We did a good business today. I left Jesse in charge."

As she spoke she settled deeper and deeper into my lap. Angie hasn't put on much weight since her roller derby days, but she was muscular then and she's muscular now and I'm just not that big of a guy. I tried to wrestle her off my lap, but it was useless. Any woman who used to be able to deck Mad Mary of the Detroit Demons isn't going to have any trouble with me.

So I shouted, "Julio, what's the score?"

"It's mumfle mumfle," he said, drowned out by the shouting and cheering from another basket.

The Lakers won, but I never saw it. Angie's mom had been in the kitchen, and when she came out she made Angie get up and served up a platter of *taquitos* and *guacamole*.

"Mama!" I said, rising to hug her.

"Manuelito," she answered, kissing me on the cheek. "There's *menudo* in the kitchen," she whispered, as if no one else could smell the heavenly aroma. Mama smacked Angie over the side of the head and shook her finger in Angie's face. She's from the old school and expects Angie to serve her brothers and me. It hasn't worked yet. I'm glad.

Outside the streets had exploded with noise. Kids were on the sidewalks screaming and waving. Cars filled the streets, honking, cruising at about five miles an hour. I could hear fireworks from neighborhood backyards. Car stereos two blocks away shook my fillings. I looked out Angie's window. Incredibly, there were already souvenir sellers hawking their wares.

Someone was yelling in the street, "Celtics got their Third! Celtics got their Third!"

Basketball made this town. With all this company, however, I knew no one else was going to be made tonight, so we settled in to an evening of talking too loud and drinking too much. Soon everyone was sitting in front of a steaming bowl of *menudo,* and hot tortillas were thrown from the stove to the table. There were tupperware bowls of oregeno and chili flakes and chopped onions and lemon wedges. Chuy and Beto, brothers both, began arguing over who was going to get some of the *pata,* which personally I can do without. The old tabletop gleamed from the steam. Brown bottles were pulled from the ice box and opened.

A little later Beto and I started pushing the furniture away from the television. The couch's upholstery was a little dusty, and I sneezed a couple of times, but it was still holding up well. That was where Angie and I settled a little later, while her brothers tuned in the news to watch the highlights again and again and again.

"Angie," I said. "I need your help. You got to cover for me."

"What is it this time?"

"Her nibs, what else? She's got me lined up to help out with a taping next week at the Manor. You know the routine. Writers show up for dinner, I got to do the serving and chauffering. Then they stay overnight, and I got to make sure they all have enough toilet paper, and find out who stole the soap from their shower."

She glowered darkly. "Are any of the writers women?"

Sensing suspicions I could exploit, I answered, "Two of them, and one of them's a real babe. I'm sure she'll need soap for her shower, maybe even a rubdown, and you know me, I'm putty in Ellie's hands. So could you cover for me? Doesn't one of your aunts need pancreatic surgery or something? Or aren't we moving one of your cousins to Silver City?"

"Well, I guess," she said. She loves Ellie and hates lying to her, but she will.

"I hope so. It'd be a real favor."

"Writer's conference, eh? I'll call her in the morning. Who else is going?"

"A couple of biggies, including that Nick Patter—"

"Nick Patterson!? Forget it."

"Forget what? You're going to call Ellie, aren't you?"

"You can open my Third, Manny," she glowered. "Nick Patterson's going to be there and I'm supposed to cover for you? You're getting me an autograph, Manny. Wait, wait," she jumped away from the table and disappeared. I could hear her rummaging in the next room.

"What's *that* all about?" asked Chuy.

I shrugged. "Maybe she's a Celtics fan."

"Oh, hey, before I forget, I'm taking a computer course at the J.C."

"Oh, really?" I said.

"Yeah," Chuy replied. "You know, like an intro course. Anyway, I know it's baby stuff to you, but could you look over my assignments some time? Give me some advice?"

"Sure. Sure," I said.

In a moment Angie had returned with a stack of five dog-eared books.

"I want his signature on all of these, and I want him to sign them to my name. My full name."

"Shall I have him sprinkle some fairy dust on them while he's at it?"

"Just do it."

"I've got a better idea," I said. "How about *you* go in my place? You know all about serving dishes and scrubbing toilets and—"

"The guys from Lennox Station are having their party at the restaurant that night. I *have* to be there. I want to make a good impression. They might start dropping in for coffee and *pan* on their rounds."

"Then I'll watch your place and you take my—"

"Manny, I thought you knew this Patterson guy. You told me you were buddies once."

"That was a long time ago, Angie. Back in high school we used to pal around. I'm not sure he'll even remember me." I was lying again. "And it has nothing to do with Nicky. Nick. It's just the last time I got sucked into one of these round tables Miranda worked my butt off and Ellie was too busy to notice."

"Well, I'm not covering for you and that's that." She paused. "But maybe after the sheriffs are gone I can spell you for a while. You'll be up later than us, won't you?"

"When do you expect the police party to break?"

"Midnight or one," she said.

"You're probably right," I sighed. I gave in. "All right," I said.

"And you'll get the autographs for me?"

"I'll do my best. Now what's that smell?"

I knew perfectly well what that smell was. Mama, like most moms, believed women had no right to leisure. She wouldn't be satisfied until we'd stuffed ourselves sick. At that moment she was making Mexican hot chocolate—a heady, sugary brew. I leaned over and saw her standing over the stove, breaking chunks of the confection into the warm milk, stirring all the while as she brought the drink to a hot perfection.

"Hey, Mama!" I called, "do you think there's a chance your lazy daughter can get me a cup of your perfect chocolate?"

I ducked.

3 .

There was no way I was going to get out of it. Come Tuesday I kept my mind off the bad business by helping Maggs in the kitchen. She does quite well by herself, thank you, but she knew I wasn't happy about this.

If I'd been planning the meal for a group of newshounds and writers I'd've slapdashed a trough of beans and a barrel of brew. However, it's a fact that the more important the folks coming over, the less you need to feed them. After a fancy dinner you always got to stop for a burger on the way home.

So Maggs and I were deboning chicken breasts and smashing them paper thin so we could wrap them around a core of proscuitto ham and provolone cheese. Right before dinner time Maggs would be rolling them in garlic and bread crumbs and flash frying them—but I'd be gone by then, forced to entertain the arriving guests.

Shortly after five I changed into slacks, a sports coat, and tie. Then I settled down to wait.

The first to arrive were the gentlemen and ladies of the working press. The one camera crew spent some time in the parlor, where the discussion would take place, setting up the cams and taking light readings. They also intruded into the dining room—rarely used by us since we ate at the round table at one end of the kitchen—and prepared to tape portions of the dinner for the evening news.

John Ronald from the *Herald* was one of the earliest. He is perhaps my only friend that Miranda likes. I think it's that ruddy face and thick mustache set atop his broad frame. I figure him for a good six-three or four. Normally we have a lot of catching up to do, but I could tell from his expression he couldn't get out of this assignment either. What was there to talk about, after that? Nicky was going to be here tonight. We shook hands and mumbled pleasantries, and I allowed myself to be distracted by another arrival shortly thereafter.

Fifteen minutes past the hour, and it was time for the guests of honor to arrive. Writers never pass up a free feed. But in L.A. arriving on time can be the kiss of death, socially. It means you have nowhere else to go, nothing else to do. It means you know and care what time it is.

Calliope Metropoulos, of neo-Western fame ("The Avocado Kid", "High Noon on Hoover", "The Return of The Avocado Kid") arrived, a bare ten minutes late. She stepped gingerly over the threshold, aware that she was the first, and anxious over the fact. Her lank, stringy hair was plastered over her scalp. She had developed a pot belly since her arrival in L.A., and a 'peasant blouse', unknown in these parts since the early seventies, displayed her pendulous charms freely. We didn't know each other, but she plastered a wet kiss on my cheek, but only because I averted my lips at the last second.

"Manuel, is it?" she said, with a high pitched laugh. "Where's that Ellen Kaufman? I can't wait to meet her. Is she here? She's read my stuff, hasn't she?"

"She'll be down later," I said, ignoring the question. No use lying this early in the evening. "If you'd like to sit down in the parlor and wait for the oth—"

"So this is the Grand Hall I've read about." She stamped to the center of the room, well aware of the cameras that followed her. Hands on hips, she stared up the thirty feet to the top of the dome and harumphed.

"What's that supposed to be? If it's supposed to be an imitation of a Greek Orthodox mosaic then I'm sorely disappointed. I'm Greek, you know. Third generation. Who'd you hire to plaster that monstrosity?"

It is not an imitation. It is the thing itself. And how that Eastern European government came to donate the dome is another story.

Fortunately the doorbell rang again and I had to run answer. John and a reporter from *Just Folks* magazine converged on her and began to ask questions.

I opened the door to Derrick Gleason. He peered down over his bow tie in a puzzled fashion, but I am given to understand that's his expression for just about everything. He's written something called *Halycon Daze* which I've never read but is supposed to be popular. He now lives in L.A. but he writes about somewhere else.

"I believe I am expected here at Ellen Kaufman's home," he said, slowly, almost apologetically.

"Yeah. Sure. Come in." We shook hands and I led him to the parlor. He seemed quite happy to stand in the middle of the room with a glass of water, nearly ignored. "This is—quite homey," he said, as I left to answer the door yet again. "Sort of reminds me of the Aunt Bertha's sitting room back home in Halycon, Indiana."

But I lost the rest as I ran to answer another, more insistant, ring. The door opened in my face and sent me back a step as Lou Mercer barrelled into the room.

He'd have seemed fat for a tall man, and he wasn't very tall. Barely my height, he was easily a hundred pounds overweight. Thick hair bristled over the edge of his tank top, which itself was covered by a greasy army jacket. Shapeless black slacks ended in old sandals. He wore a stylish three days' worth of beard over his pallid complexion. He was our token New Yorker.

They called him a poet. He'd written something called *Shout and Twist* about twenty years ago, and he was quite the thing back East. I'd tried on three different occasions to start the poem, but I'd never gone past line eighty or so.

"I'm here!" he shouted, stomping about. As he stepped away I saw he wore low riders. Why do some men think we want to see the top of their bottom? "Home Olga! What's going on here? Where's Kaufman? Where's dinner?"

"Welcome," I said, smiling. (That's my job). "Would you like to sit down in the parlor?"

"Is that where the drinks are?"

"Yes."

"Then what's keeping you, *garçon?*"

"This way, then," I pointed, but he'd noticed the reporters, so he elbowed his way to Calliope, put his arm around her, and began to declaim for their benefit. She had to ask John Ronald for the name of the sideshow, and that led to a little shouting match, all of it captured on film. To make a point Lou reached into a pocket for a cigar and stuck it in his mouth. I pulled it out.

"House rules," I stated. "Just like it said in your invitation."

He glowered at me and reached for it. I smiled. His hand stopped. We stared.

I had the advantage. I learned my stare from Paddington Bear. "Wouldn't want to offend the host," he said evenly, when he saw I wasn't about to back down.

I plopped the cigar in his pocket. "Word of honor, I assume," I concluded, turning away.

Janet Austin arrived.

She's as striking in person as on the back cover of her books. Her almost almond eyes were set against high cheekbones. Her dark blue suit blended into the near indigo of her skin. She and I were the only ones wearing ties. She offered her hand as I entered.

"Ms. Austin," I said. "This is a pleasure." And it was. I'd read all her books, the entire "Elocutionist" series. Miranda doesn't like them but what does she know?

She smiled and I melted. Angie who? "You're very kind," she said, in a rich contralto. "It's an honor to be here among this—" she caught sight of her compatriots, and with I assume must have been unaffected *noblesse oblige,* said, "—gallant company."

"Janet!" shouted Lou Mercer, dragging Metropoulos with him. He put his arms round her and mussed up her suit. Some not so deeply buried male instinct made me want to plug him.

"You obviously know each other so an introduction would be unnec—" I began.

"Never met the woman in my life," roared Lou. "But I recognize her. Janet, this is Calliope Metropoulos. You've heard of her. Who else is supposed to be here?"

"Derrick Gleason is in the parlor right now," I answered.

"That worm!" shouted Lou. "What the hell you want *him* for? Takes him a year to sweat out a sentence. And where is that woman, Kaufman? Isn't it a little *rude* to leave your guests standing around?"

"She'll be here. Resting up no doubt," I noted.

"He's in the parlor?" asked Janet with a gleam in her eye. "I've always wanted to meet him. Can you take me to him?"

Austin broke my heart by giving Derrick Gleason a warm handshake in the way of greeting.

"Mr. Gleason—"

"Derrick, please," he interupted.

"Derrick," she acquiesced. "I had to come to the dinner, if only to meet you. I've been waiting forever for this chance."

"J-Janet, You may not believe it, but I've been hoping to meet you."

"You're being polite, Mr. Gl—Derrick. A writer of your stature..."

I poured a couple of apple juices, then stepped to the side of their little love feast.

Maggs had planned dinner for about an hour after the scheduled start so all the guests would be there. There was still no sign of our fifth, however.

John Ronald sidled over to me and nudged my gut.

"She's quite a looker, isn't she?"

I didn't want Janet Austin referred to as a 'looker', but I wasn't in the mood to argue. I shrugged.

"I tried to get out of this too," he continued. "Did you?"

"Yeah," I shrugged. It was a subject I wanted to avoid.

Derrick and Janet started singing a duet, a song Derrick had made popular through his radio hour. I noticed that when he sang he had a tendency to close his eyes.

Folks always want to know where the action is, and we were soon joined by the other two writers and Sid Sidey, the telejournalist who'd be the moderator tomorrow. Lou Mercer knew the song also, it seemed, because he joined in, attempting, as always, to dominate the scene. The cameras were rolling and he knew it. Soon he was changing the lyrics. Poetry of his own, I imagine.

He was wasting his time. Derrick and Janet sang, gazing into each other's eyes, and we were the rest of us stage props.

Ellie appeared.

I don't know how she does it, but when she wants to she can enter in the most unobstrusive manner. Murrie hovered next to her shoulder, gazing with disdain at the intruders. She counts me in that category. Maggs she barely tolerates.

Lou's stomach prevented him from making a full bow, but he tried. He then approached Ellie, arms extended for a hug. I froze. The very idea appalled me. Miranda tensed. She'd have tackled him before he got a mitt on Ellie.

It wasn't necessary. There's something—invulnerable—about Ellie. She simply stood and stared, smiling, at Lou. He stopped as if flattened by an invisible barrier.

"How wonderful to meet you all," she said, when she was ready. She seemed stronger than she'd been in days. Her hand barely rested on the arm of a chair. "I've been looking forward to this gathering with great anticipation. Each of you has so much to offer. I welcome also my friends from the print and visual media. Without you this meeting would be impossible. It is the custom of our household to cement new friendships with good food. Ms. Magdalene, our resident genius, has prepared an exceptional repast. If you will follow me..."

There is something marvelous about the way she simply *commands*—Ellie insists she merely commends. I leaned over to Miranda and whispered, "Aren't we short a guest?"

"Ms. Kaufman preferred we eat on time. Maggs has put a lot of work into dinner."

"Suits me."

Together we re-entered the hall and headed towards the dining room. The fading sun darkened the room. The halogen lamp was shining from below and sparkling off the Hagia Sophia mosaic.

As a group we had travelled halfway to dinner when the bell rang. I ran to open the door.

There he was. Nick Patterson. He wore a pinstripe suit with a thin tie. His shoes shone with a high gloss. Every hair of his head had been expertly trimmed to a fashionable length. His face was as I remembered from high school—the archetype of a leading man. He smiled and his perfect teeth sparkled.

"Sorry I'm late," he said, breezily. "Thanks for your patience."

I looked from face to face. From the expressions on our four other guests I reached a tentative conclusion—that each of them, like John Ronald and myself, had a personal reason to either fear, detest, or loathe the man.

4.

It couldn't have lasted more than a moment. I wish I'd had a camera. Janet's eyes were narrowed. Derrick's lips were compressed. Lou's eyebrows were furrowed. Calliope—

Calliope's expression was one of deep and distant amusement, colored with a touch of disdain.

John Ronald looked at me and I at him. I think we both saw that moment from our youth again, that terrible second when helplessly we stood and watched as Nick bared his teeth and—

But Ellie was smiling, a Mandarin, hands folded at her waist. She was speaking:

"I am sure you are not late, Mr. Patterson. We are all early."

The moment passed. Smiles were the rule as everyone shook hands all around. Everyone, that is, except John and myself. We slipped off to the dining room. Maggs was glowering.

"I've been waiting thirty seconds. Where *is* everybody?" she asked.

"Here," I answered, as they entered. Quickly I directed all to their places, held Ellie's chair as she seated herself, then began to serve. Music drifted out of the stereo. Ellie had selected a set of soft English folk ballads.

It's Ellie's rule that everybody eats. That means if a construction crew is working a little late, they're expected to stay for dinner. In this instance it meant there were places set for the working members of the press.

Derrick Gleason stared at his plate in wonderment. Delicately his fork touched the stuffed chicken breast. Woefully he shook his head, then allowed the implement to rest atop one of the seared new potatoes.

"What's the matter?" asked Janet carefully. "The chicken is delicious. Aren't you going to have a bite?"

"It's *too* good," Derrick said slowly. "I'm almost afraid that if I eat it, someone from my past, not my parents, perhaps, but one of their friends, will come here, shake their heads sadly, and walk away."

"Sir?" asked Ellie, smiling.

"In my home town you didn't do this sort of thing to a chicken. This is the way a, well, a pentecostal might eat chicken. All fire and garlic. Roast beef was safer, less likely to lead you down the primrose path that led through premarital sex to that ultimate degradation—dancing."

Calliope Metropoulos smiled, then choked on something. She waved away help as her eyes teared and she gulped down her water. I refilled her glass but she was fine.

"Sorry," she said, embarrassed. "I'm all right."

"You were about to say something," said Janet Austin.

"Yes. But it wasn't worth getting all choked up about. Sorry. No, I was just going to say that Gleason and I are alike in that one respect."

"What respect is that?" asked Derrick, surprised.

"We both write about what we know. About our own towns, our own backgrounds."

That was a stunner. I don't think there was a one of us who thought of Calliope as one of the beautiful people who populated her books, popping in and out of beds, drinking heavily, living hard, dying young. She continued, "I don't think I could write about Halycon Junction, or whatever you call it, any more than you could write about Hollywood."

Derrick nodded numbly, still trying to figure out the significance of the point, and in his confusion, he cut off and ate a portion of the chicken. Deliberately he chewed and swallowed, with a look that made it clear than he had somehow let down his ancestors and that if he ended up stuck in Tinseltown, well, it was no more than he deserved.

"I wonder," said Ellie, "if we are begining to touch, even now, upon that question which concerns us tonight and tomorrow."

"And that is?" interrupted Lou.

"I refer, of course, to the seeming dichotomy between popular writing and art. Does one define art by popularity, or does one preclude the other? The two of you, for instance, both write extraordinarily popular fiction. Does that make you artists?"

Calliope answered "Yes."

Gleason said, "I always imagined that art was something that Fred Bellows, who owned the general store, did on his Sundays off. He would set up his easel by the side of the pond, and try to paint the ducks. But they wouldn't stay put. And of course if he held still so as to not startle the mallards, well, then he couldn't get any painting done."

"Of course in my books," said Janet, jumping in, "I make no pretence of presenting a realistic story. The puzzle story depends on a framework of manners. They're very stylized. Otherwise the complexities of the world make puzzle solving impossible. I suppose it's a weakness to my work."

Calliope came to her defense. "I used to think that when I first read your books. I though you were letting down other—ah, what is it you people are calling yourselves nowadays?"

"Humans," whispered Janet, almost too softly to be heard.

"Never mind," said Calliope, ignoring the reply. "You know what I mean. That was during my Realism phase. Now I understand your work. I realize there's a yearning for justice, an unfulfilled hunger, and books like yours feed that hunger. We demand the stock characters, the parallel plots. We demand the author play a fair game with us. We demand at least a chance to solve the puzzle, and we are far more delighted to discover we were wrong but that the protagonist was right."

But no one was paying attention to Lou, and that was impermissable. He stopped shoveling food long enough to say, "Permit me to disagree—"

"As if we could stop you," muttered Nick Patterson. It was the first thing he'd said since the introductions.

"—but I refuse to try to penetrate another man's—person's mysticism," hollered Lou. "This whole idea that the populace knows anything about art is a fallacy. It takes an expert who studies for years to tell the good from bad. The popular taste is subject to the vagaries of emotion. People respond to the work because they 'liked' it, or because it scared them, or moved them, or excited them, or aroused them, or angered them."

"Whereas the proper function of art is—?" asked Ellie.

"Well, it needs to break new ground, it needs to ride the cutting edge, the new wave. It must be bold, make a statement, it must—"

"—be beautiful?" I suggested.

"Bah! What is beauty? That's an emotional response."

"Your work cannot be accused of that transgression," noted Patterson.

"What?"

"Come on, Lou, you're covering up for the fact that only highbrow prigs would ever buy your books, and if it wasn't for the fact that some college professors get kickbacks from the texts, your books would all be gathering dust in a publisher's cellar. Even so, I hardly consider forced reading on the part of pimply freshmen a definition of art."

For a moment Lou was too enraged to speak. He stood up and waved his fists over his head. Then, "I do not forget, Nick, I do not forget what your words to the publisher have done to my career!" Catching himself, his face reddened. Then, in a more controlled tone of voice, he said, "But even if we take as a definition of art those books which most accurately reflected reality, a utilitarian definition at best, where would that leave your novels? Third Letter? Bah! What have your letters to do with reality? Who can ever claim to have received a Third Letter?"

"As a matter of fact—" said Nick, then stopped. Lou didn't notice.

"Your artifice cannot support the structure of this too real world. Your books are worse than popular. They are—trivial!"

"And they are read! What's more important than that? I'm not talking money here," said Nick firmly, but calmly. "This is my challenge to oblivion, my gauntlet cast to eternity. I am more than a blade of grass, or flower of the field. I am a voice, thin and reedy and transient, but a voice that even if only for a little while is heard. I write in clear English sentences. If that's a crime, then shoot me."

I jumped when he said that. John did too.

There was an embarrassed silence. Calliope said, "Oh, really," which was followed by a few nervous giggles.

Derrick pursed his lips and shrugged. "All right," he said. "Next time I'll just shut up and eat my chicken."

Lou rose, turned to Ellie and bowed. "My apologies. I have been rude to my host. Hostess."

"Not at all," said Ellie. "My guests are free to speak their mind, as long as they grant me this same privilege. Some of you have made interesting points. I hope you will remember them tonight and tomorrow when the cameras are rolling. *And* can express them in a less personal fashion. *Argumentum ad hominem* is spectacular, but not conclusive."

"Now there, you've proved my point," said Lou. "Thank you. You are a genius."

"I had not meant to validate anyone's viewpoint at this early stage," said Ellie. "Perhaps if you would elaborate–"

"Ah, but see? A personal attack such as you refer to is an appeal to the ignorant masses, precisely *because* they are ignorant. But a reasoned attack necessitates you ignore the rabble, the *canaglia,* and speak only to the *cogniscenti.*"

"What the hell are you talking about now?" asked Patterson in a tired voice.

"Not what," yelled Lou, "but where. And where is right over your head."

"And who's stooping to *Argumentum ad—*"

"Bah, I am stating facts. You are ignorant. Your books are stupid. They are not based on fact. The only thing that commends them in the public's eye is the fact that they make money, and because they make money people buy them. Now my books—"

"—have been untainted by a breath of suspicion in that regard."

"I am finding this rather tiresome," said Janet Austin. "I think most of us would agree."

Ellie said nothing. She doesn't mind a good argument as long as she's not involved. Of course when she doesn't agree with you there's no argument.

"Besides," continued Patterson. "You're arguing in circles, saying my books are popular because they make money. Before I could make money, one of my books had to be accepted by the populace before it became generally popular."

"People on the West Coast buy anything," said Lou. "They read anything. Like cows chewing their cud—they want regurgitated words that tread the same path over and over and over. No new ground. No vanguard."

"And no obscurity," continued Patterson.

But Derrick was talking to Janet. "Now these vegetables are too fresh, too crisp. They're almost sinful. I bet the apple that Eve took a bite into was this fresh. That's why back home we used to lay the vegetables to rest. We used to boil them, and send all their texture and taste and nutrition back to the Maker. It was proper respect for the hard life. I remember the first time Samuel Thorndike came back from college for Christmas. I was a sophomore then. He'd put on ten pounds, at least ten pounds. And he'd gained it all on salads and vegetables. And Sammy told us of a world where the green things were alive, and crisp and full of vitamins. The thought of actually having something to chew—well I remember how our parents used to discourage us from eating something directly from the garden in its pristine, almost holy state..."

He gazed dreamily into space, until Calliope reached across the table and nudged his elbow.

"So what happened to Sammy?" she urged.

"One day, he was standing in the middle of the fields, munching on a raw radish. He was wincing with the pleasure, when suddenly Earl the mailman, who'd been working the same route nigh on thirty-five years, runs up to him, waving a special delivery letter. Says to Sammy, 'You're a going to have to sign for it, you are.' Well, Sammy doesn't know anyone who can write, at least not living around those parts, so naturally he's interested, and he tears the thing open and—" Derrick looked directly at me and winked, "—and he read:"

"'Consider this message rehearsed
'And read it for batter or wurst.
'You masticate flora.
'It's not hunky-dora.
'Consider this Letter your First.

"And it was signed: 'Sincerely, the Vegetable Liberation Front.'"

Nick stared at him for a moment, his lips wanting desperately to tighten in anger. He then exploded in laughter.

5 .

Ellie says civilized society is based on eating. Eating isn't the glue that holds society together. It is the thing itself.

"That was the problem with the *refrigeraria* in the early Christian world," she was saying after dinner. "It wasn't just a form or imitation of worship. It was the primary exercise of worship."

"A chilling subject," observed Calliope. My opinion of her went up a notch.

"What exactly is a *refrigeraria*?" asked Ms. Austin. I had by this time convinced myself she was more than human. She had toyed with her meal, leaving most of it uneaten. Everyone else had gladly accepted the seconds that Maggs cooked during our firsts.

"It was a meal that commemorated the passing of a loved one. The whole family gathered—"

"Morbid," interupted Lou. "Reminds me of Spain and Hemingway. That would be one invitation I'd be glad to miss."

Ellie smiled.

It is my observation that people aren't as bright after a good dinner. They're full, and the blood rushes from the brain to the stomach. They think they're witty, and they're as prone to laugh as yawn, but it takes a good half hour before the conversation picks up.

Not this crew, however. Things were no more harmonious when we adjourned to the parlor for coffee and cameras. Ellie sipped from what passed for tea in her book. A carafe of water was set in the middle of a table, surrounded by glasses. The cameras were rolling, hoping for a few tidbits from this informal prelude to the morrow's activites. Miranda sat at Ellie's feet, watching the guests for any sign of weapons. She's the suspicious sort.

Ellie's tactic in such situations is to defuse hostilities by scattering attention.

It seemed to be working. A discussion on pre-Constantinian worship is not particularly conducive to controversy. There's nothing like time to lend perspective.

So Ellie responded to Lou by saying, "Hardly morbid. It was a time for celebration, remembrance, and joy. The family existed not in the present but in the past, and through the children playing nearby, into the future."

"So food was shared in a symbolic way," concluded Calliope.

"No," said Ellie. This is her favorite part of this excursus. She likes to watch the reactions of her listeners. "Food was shared literally. Sarcophagi were built with a hole through which a portion of the dinner might be poured."

She let her audience chew on that for a moment before she continued. "Of course a favorite ancestor's anniversary would require a large feast, with the full extended family present. And since a particularly important martyr's family included every local communicant, some of the *refrigeraria* became feasts of some two or three days standing. Each remembrance, whether large or small, was worship, communion, what you will. This was a threat to the established clergy, who were unnecessary to the worship. With the fusion of church and state that accompanied the Constantinian abberation, the situation became untenable. The laity was quite jealous of its prerogative. Things came to a head when two hundred priests burst into a full blown bacchanalian *refrigeraria* with the intent to break it up—and none emerged."

"What happened?" asked Nick, after a moment's silence.

"Heads rolled. Literally. The rite was suppressed with the execution of celebrants. It took years."

"What did you mean when you referred to the meal as communion?" asked Derrick slowly.

"Communion in the early church was eating—like a potluck at the corner Methodist Church. It had nothing to do with ritual."

"That explains it," said Derrick, lips pursed into a satisfied expression.

"Explained what?" I asked, never one to resist a straight line.

"It explains why my Aunt Bertha's lemon pie was so divine. When your fork punctured the crust and the steam was released into the air, it was as if a breath of Eden, a breeze from paradise drifted through the room, calling, 'You, you, this is too good for you.'"

There were a few chuckles, and a broad smile from Janet, but Ellie can hit the curve ball.

"Exactly," Ellie was saying. "That piece of pie was communion—not because it was pie, but because it was made by your Aunt Bertha. It was the visible evidence of an invisible bond. I am put in mind of a passage in one of your own books, Mr. Gleason. It was a remembrance of communion in your house church. The loaf had to be made by a relative—the smells of dinner were directly associated with the quality of worship. That is why I insist eating is civilization."

I think Derrick was startled by Ellie's observation. Humilty can be aggressive. You can hold center stage with diffidence, and courtesy requires that others pay attention.

"I liked that part of the book," Janet Austin said. "It read so easily. I imagine it was written easily also."

"Before Mr. Gleason might comment," said Ellie, "I would like to make the observation that ease of reading has nothing to do with the ease of writing. Mr. Lewis—Clive Staples Lewis—labeled the phenomenon 'The Personal Heresy'. The latter may be defined as the belief that one can reach conclusions regarding the autorial process and draw biographical conclusions simply by reading the *oeuvre.*"

Derrick Gleason coughed gently, pushed his horn-rimmed glasses back from the tip of his nose and said, "Well put, Ms. Kaufman. That was one of the most difficult passages to write. I must have rewritten that section seven or eight times. I find that difficult to live with, to be honest. As children we were expected to perform effortlessly the daily tasks of our existance—after the manner of our elders, of course. Never mind that their expertise at any number of trivial or even useless tasks was the result of years of practice. We were expected to emerge from the womb with the ability to drive a hammer, insulate an attic, or bake an apple pie. That's probably why no one ever explained the facts of life to us. Perfection was expected to come naturally."

Nick Patterson cleared his throat and leaned back in his chair. It was obvious he was used to gesturing with a pipe in hand, but that was out of the question in Ellie's house. "Speaking for myself," he said, "prose comes easily. I have little patience for those who complain of artistic difficulties. It's a job, like any other."

"Prose," muttered Lou. "Bah. Prose is *passe*. Poetry is raw, poetry is alive, poetry bleeds, it slaps us awake, destroys our pretty dreams and makes us see life as it really is."

"Let me not to the marriage of true minds admit impediments," smiled Ellie, but nothing impeded Patterson, who ignored them both.

"The process of writing lends itself to mystery only because so very few people actually try it. Mysticism clouds the fact that you simply choose your goal, and achieve it."

"I don't believe you," said Calliope. "That's a lot of hot air. The phone rings. Ideas play themselves out. On second glance what seemed to be magnificent needs extensive rewriting. Pens run dry. Disks become scarce. There are barriers."

"People create their own barriers," said Patterson suavely. "That's what I believe. We create our own worlds. Success and failure are both illusions. Most people choose failure, and are content with it. We choose what sort of soap bubble we create. It's a danger to take life too seriously."

"Mr. Patterson," said Ellie dryly. "You are the product of an accident of birth. No, hear me out, sir. Had you been born elsewhere, it is likely you would not consider hunger an illusion, success and failure soap bubbles. There are those who are born in the street, are raised there, and die never having slept beneath a roof in their meager count of years. There are children who are born to drug addiction, to whom the idea of self-determination is impossible. Their worlds were created for them."

"Nevertheless, Ms. Kaufman," said Nick, "I am because I choose..."

"You are an ass," growled Lou Mercer, "and a fool." He rose, and his worn coat dropped off his arms. The thin material of his short-sleeved white shirt was pierced by the bristling hairs of his arms and back.

Nick smiled, rose, and leaned against the mantle. One eyebrow arched. The actions were the sort of thing you saw in a bar, right before a brawl. A slightly acrid odor drifted through the parlor.

"Ahem," I said. "Gentlemen? Here?"

The two antagonists stared at each other, Lou through wide angry eyes, Nick under arched and amused brows. Lou took two heaving breaths in silence—near silence, I guess. I could hear the gentle hum of the cameras. Then his shoulders relaxed, he smiled, and stuck out a sweaty arm. Nick grabbed the hand at the end of it and they shook, side by side, leering for the photographers.

Lou took two steps away, then turned and charged, arms outstretched, roaring. Nick barely moved. Lou did most of the moving. He flew a beautifully tight arc across the room, to land in a heap in the one blank spot on the carpet. Lou stared stunned, as did just about everyone else in the room. Nick's suit wasn't mussed. At last he said, "A fair go, I'd say. A fair go."

Ellie stood and clapped her hands once.

"Enough," she said.

Lou rose unsteadily and faced Ellie. He bowed low. "My humble apologies," he said. "I have disgraced myself. I will leave now."

"Ridiculous. We have serious work to do here and you are essential to our intentions. Your work is diametrically opposite in form and intent to Mr. Patterson's. Ms. Metropoulos, Ms. Austin, Mr. Gleason, all of you have accomplished something different in the world of arts and letters, and it is at my pleasure you spend this evening here. Let us, however, spar with words and not fisticuffs."

Lou nodded once, and took a seat, out of breath and still a little bonkers. The press was loving it. Some of this was going to be on the eleven o'clock news.

There was an embarrassed silence, but it didn't last long. None of those present were the kind who could keep their peace. In groups of two and three reporters and participants began to converse. John Ronald sidled over to me and cut me off before I could corner Janet. Nick got her instead. I made the best of it, and John and I began to compare notes.

"Is this going to work?" he asked me. "I knew you artistic types took things seriously, but—"

"—what's a mother to do?" I answered. "I've never seen anything like it. There's something going on there. Hidden agenda, I mean."

"Go to the head of the class, Manny. I tell you what. When I go home tonight I'm going to call a buddy of mine in New York who writes book reviews, and see if he's heard anything about a blood feud between these two."

"Don't forget the time difference. You'd better wait until morning."

"Right. I'll wait til three, four AM. It'll be six or seven then."

Suddenly there was the sound of a slap. Nick was still standing, smiling, but his left cheek was red. Janet was running from the room. Again everyone was snapped into silence. Nick shrugged.

"Go figure," he said.

"Mr. Patterson," said Ellie quietly. "You seem to have a talent."

"I didn't do anything," said Nick. "It wasn't my fault." I shivered. The same words he'd uttered back in high school.

John Ronald paled. He'd been there too. A wave of nausea swept over me as the dike that held back hell threatened to buckle. The memory was returning—that stunned look.

Ellie simply said, "Sir."

Conversation resumed, much more fitfully than before. John poured himself a glass of ice water and drained it. Neither of us felt like talking. Nick had disappeared.

I decided I'd best leave. Winking at Ellie, who was holding court with a member of the print media, I stepped into the hall, caught a glimpse of two figures, and ducked behind a pillar.

It was dark. Night had fallen and the light shining off the mosaic of the dome created muted shadows. I hadn't been observed.

Janet Austin was staring into the eyes of Nick Patterson. Nick tried to put his hands on her shoulders, but she swatted them away. A physical bunch we'd invited.

"I'm telling you—" she hissed. I could barely hear her.

"Tell me, then."

"I don't care how you treat the others, just keep your hands off Derrick."

"Why?" He was laughing. "What's he to you?"

"Just back off."

"Why should I?"

"You owe me."

Silence.

"You can't hold that over my head forever," he said at last. "Sooner or later you'll blurt it out anyway. And they won't believe you. Not after all these years. You should have spoken up then."

"You owe me."

Silence.

"He's a wimp. Who cares?"

"Keep away from him."

"Sure," said Nick. "Sure, I will. Promise. Cross my heart. That good enough for you?"

6 .

As quietly as I could I snuck back to the parlor, opened, then slammed the door. Having made my presence known I re-entered the room and walked past the couple, who were standing and pointedly not talking to each other.

"Manny," said Nick, when I was two steps past them.

"Hello, Nick," I said, turning awkwardly to face them.

"Do you two know each other?" asked Janet. Right then that was the last thing I wanted to admit.

"We went to the same high school years ago," I answered.

"In that case, don't let me get in the way of a reunion."

Before I could protest, she was gone. Nick and I stood, looking at each other.

"So," he said at last.

"So," I said in reply.

"So what do you know?" he continued. "Do you ever see any of the old gang?"

"Why?"

"I don't know," he answered. "School spirit. The memory of The Game. You know, the whole bunch of us should get together once in awhile."

I shrugged. "Never thought about it, to be honest."

"So," he said, as casually as he could. "Do you ever hear from Susan?"

"Susan?"

"Susan Delgado. Don't tell me you don't remember, Manny."

"Of course I remember. Why would you bring up Susan after all these years?"

"No reason. Just an example of how we drift apart sometimes." He paused. "You don't happen to have her number, do you?"

"No," I said. "Can't say that I do."

"Well look, Manny, it's good to see you after all these years. Maybe we can talk some more in just a few minutes. I have to look into something."

He walked past me, back towards the parlor and the laughter of voices. I waited half a minute, then followed.

The conversation had livened up as I entered. Murrie was talking, and it took me a couple of moments to catch her drift.

"—about what you know," she was saying. "I agree, to an extent, but you can run far afield when it comes to using your personal experience. Take Marlowe—"

I looked to Ellie. This is one of their few areas of disagreement. Marlowe is Miranda's personal favorite.

"One might say he did not live long enough to garner the personal experience to be a great writer, but without question university politics, the tumult of daily London life, and his term as a secret service agent gave him the materials for the Macchiavelian vision of his well-known—"

"Not well known to me," interupted Calliope, ignoring Miranda's stare. "But you're right about personal experience. I like to think that every incident in *Sunset Cowboys* is based on my private life, one way or another. And I mean *every* incident."

"I can well believe that," grumbled Lou. "That mindless procession of sweaty bodies pressed between grimy sheets—"

"And don't forget they did it on the genuine Armenian leather of a new model *Kudakan*," muttered Derrick Gleason.

"—bespeaks of a limited and monomaniacal experience. There is a dreary sameness to that parade of tawdry trysts and politic pandering."

"Chop it up and it's poetry," quipped Nick.

Calliope clapped. "So you've read it."

"Twice," admitted Lou.

"I think personal experience, or the lack of it, is why my books are criticized as academic puzzles or parlor games," said Janet quietly. "I really do," she continued to Derrick's expression of protest. "Nothing's ever happened to me. I grew up in a happy home—"

"I thought you grew up in South Central Los Angeles," said Calliope.

"Well, yes," said Janet, guardedly. "But we were happy in those days. That was before the shooting and the drugs and the violence. And in those days we didn't know anyone better off than ourselves. I spent my time reading books. I skipped dating, then graduated from a women's college with a degree in English and a minor in History. I have a hard time writing about real villains. Some say I can't. I don't even want to try. That's why I admire Derrick's books so much. Nothing ever happened to him either, but he's done so much with it."

"Reading constitutes experience," noted Derrick. "Consider Tolkien. *The Lord of the Rings*. That novel was born of his love for words and their genesis. Was he ever chased by *Nazgul*? I think not. But—"

The discussion was finally turning exactly into what Ellie'd had in mind when she'd organized the meeting. Then Nick spoke. "I'd like to go back to Janet's comment regarding parlor games," he said, commanding the attention of all present. I knew Nick. Something was up.

"There are those who think that parlor games are unreal. There are times when they take on a life of their own. They can be a matter of life and death."

"And you, perhaps," said Calliope, "intend to illustrate this point?"

"I intend to personify it," he answered, reaching into his suit and pulling out two sheets of paper, which he held up for all to inspect. It was evident at a glance that someone had pasted magazine letters on sheets of ruled notebook paper.

"Don't tell me," groaned Sid Sidey. He was one step ahead of the rest of us. Miranda looked sharply for the culprit. The media had instructions to record, not participate. I suspect that was her rule, not Ellie's.

Nick chuckled. "That's right. This," he said dramatically, "was delivered two weeks ago to the day. It's my First. And this other sheet was delivered one week ago to the day. It is my Second. That means that some time today I should receive my Third. After that—" he paused, "I'm finished."

"This is some kind of joke," said Lou.

"Probably," said Nick. "But I haven't been able to penetrate it. Indeed, I had hopes this august company might succeed where I have failed. I must admit I'm rather embarrassed. Although I suspect this is the work of a fan who wants to one-up me." He turned to Ellie. "May I share these, Mrs. Kaufman?"

"It might be amusing," answered Ellie, who hasn't been a Mrs. since her third husband died.

"Before I read these, let me mention that they are nothing at all like the examples in my books. I spend a lot of time on those letters, writing clearly yet allusively. I rely on misdirection, yet I am painstakingly fair. It is possible to solve the puzzle before the hero does. These letters, on the other hand, seem quite obscure. In fact, they are rather amateurish. In addition, some words seem to be misspelled. I'm not sure if that is through ignorance or the fact that some letters were harder to find at the moment than others. The spacing is so irregular that some of them may have fallen off. Let me read them now, then we'll pass them around."

This is the text of the first letter.

Act Now. To Reach the Goal of
Third letter decipherment You must literally
fllow the trac set by the mode. It is possible to decipher anything.
A nervous tic shortly betrays. The Aracnid seeks release at all costs, even locjaw.
Cordiall, Jack.
Certes.

"Oh," said Janet softly, when he was through. She was the first to reach for the letter. She stared at it thoughtfully for a moment, then passed it on.

Before she even took a glance Ellie turned to the newsmen and asked, "Do any of you recognize the font?"

Sid Sidey snatched it from Lou, and several huddled around. It was John Ronald who said, "The letters have been taken from advertisements, so they would appear uniformly the same in many different periodicals."

But another added, "I think from the size though, we're talking about the *Digest*, or a magazine of that size."

"That's interesting," said Nick. "Let me read the second one."

This is what the Second Letter said.

The WAC dealt in healing. Receive the Cavern's bounty.

Action leads to aches. The Knight Parcfal Cornered the grail.

Clean We wipe the slate.
Clean we bare Our souls.
Ciao
The tic should reappear
Yours,
Billy.

When he read 'Billy' I jumped. Really I did. Nick showed no emotion, however, when one of the reporters asked, "Who's this Billy?"

"Damned if I know," Nick replied. I shook my head in disbelief. John Ronald looked at me, disgust in his eyes. The three of us had known a Billy. Yes we had.

I couldn't make any sense of it at all. Neither did anyone else, as far as I could tell. I was rather disappointed. Angie had talked to me about the letters on TV and they were rather clever. I hated to admit it, but Nick was a hell of a writer. There was one, I remember, that had a clear meaning in English, but phonetically one could piece together Welsh from the text. Angie had memorized that one. This seemed gibberish.

"How were these delivered?" asked Ellie.

"They were thrust under the door of my house in Malibu."

"What time of day?"

"Night. I discovered them both late in the evening while I was checking my doors before bed."

"Both letters?"

"Yes."

"So tonight someone should be delivering a Third Letter under your door tonight."

"I'd think so," said Nick. "That's one of the reasons I came here, to be honest. The joke isn't funny. It isn't even well done. All the same, I don't care to be there for the forfeit. My guess is that some college students intend to toilet-paper my house. As a matter of fact I've hired extra security to watch the place tonight. But I don't care to have my photo taken with them, or to give them any extra publicity.

"All the same, I'd like to be able to say I'd anticipated them before the fact."

It was my turn to pipe up. "I wonder if it'd be worth while to go to his house and get the Third Letter."

Nick shrugged. "I don't give out my address too often. As a matter of fact, I'm surprised someone found me. I'm not listed in any directory and my mail goes to a post office box on Sunset, far from my home. I did my best to mask the purchase of this house. My neighbors are not aware of my identity and I have not had one caller since I moved there three years ago."

"You seem awfully sure of all that," said Miranda dryly.

"I used to be," said Nick ruefully. "Until this. I think I resent the invasion of privacy more than any implied threat."

"I get to ask the obvious question," said Calliope merrily. "Do you have any enemies that would like to kill you?"

I'll give Nick credit. Not a trace of any inward emotion revealed itself.

"Not that I'm aware of. Maybe a few editors. There's not a writer alive who hasn't antagonized his editor."

That brought a few chuckles. Janet raised her hand, forgetting this was no school, and said, "Does anyone know you're here? Is there a chance the Third Letter will be delivered here?"

That got everyone's attention.

Nick turned to Ellie. "What kind of publicity preceeded this little love feast?"

She thought for a moment, then turned to Miranda for confirmation. "If I remember correctly, Ms. Devlin, there was a little paragraph in the *Times'* Calendar section, I believe. Page two. Every paper in the area received a press release, but I don't believe anyone else touched the story. They were waiting for the event to occur. Which is not to say that the story did not go out over the wire and will not appear in an out-of-state paper." She smiled graciously at the media assembled.

"But if someone was observant, they could find out," said Nick. "Perhaps the Third Letter *will* make its appearance here tonight." He looked around the room. "Anyone want to change rooms with me?"

The laughter was a little forced.

Maggs had slipped out unobserved, but she was back, with a large blackberry cobbler in hand. That was my cue to run out and get the plates, and when I returned Murrie and I quickly served dessert to all assembled.

Everyone switched chairs in the process of rising to receive their plate, so when I was left standing with my own piece of cobbler I noticed with delight that Janet was seated by herself on the couch, and that there was no other spot open. Shrugging as if to show it made no never-mind to me, I eased my hams into the empty spot and nodded to Janet. She smiled back.

"I hadn't counted on this," she said. "Had you?"

"Counted on what?" I laid my dessert on the coffee table so I could inch a little closer.

"This little mystery. I find it quite exciting. And," she lowered her voice, "a little too pat. Are you sure that Ellen Kaufman didn't plan this?"

"She planned the meeting if that's what you mean."

"No. I mean, did she plan this little mystery? Did she plan the fight?"

"I'm sure she didn't plan the fight." That wasn't her style, I thought to myself. I used the excuse of confidentiality to get close enough to speak near her ear. She had nice ears. She had nice everythings.

"As for the letters, I don't think so. But I wouldn't put it past her."

"She's amazing. She's been around forever. I mean, my mother grew up admiring her during her suffragette days. She had a scrapbook. Has. When she heard I was coming here she insisted I get an autograph on her old copy of the *Alice* commentary. Do you think Ms. Kaufman would mind?" She put her hand on my knee when she asked.

"She'd love it. But you know, getting back to this letter business, if she was behind it, she might not tell me, and if she told me, I might not tell you. Orders, you know."

She looked slightly disappointed.

"That's too bad. I was counting on some inside information."

"Well, I've got lots of that," I said, trying to heal our sudden rift. "You can't live with Ellen Kaufman without being privy to a lot of strange goings on. Let me tell you, I've learned enough to fill books."

"Like what?"

"All sorts of useful things," I said, wondering what I could say to keep her interest. "Like how to murder someone, for instance. We've had plenty of experience with that, I'm afraid. She and Police Detective Herman Schmoller go way back."

"Detective Schmoller?" she said, with a touch of wonder. "The one you see on the news whenever there's a big murder?"

"That's the one. Ms. Kaufman was his godmother. And you know she's been helping him in an unofficial capacity for decades. Thanks to her, I've seen a lot of it. Poisons, blunt instruments, firearms, faked accidents, you name it, and she's solved it. You see enough and you can almost plan the perfect crime yourself."

"How exciting! I wish I lived here. Can I tell you a secret? It was my fantasy when I was a little girl that I'd grow up and work in this mansion. What's Miranda Devlin like? She looks sweet. How long will she work here, do you suppose?"

"She's on her last legs. Look at her smile. You'd never know, would you. She's an inspiration to us all, the way she puts a good face on her illness. If I were you I'd put in an application tomorrow."

I'd have been more than glad to introduce Murrie to a body bag. At that moment, however, two events intervened.

First of all a shadow loomed over the two of us. We looked up. To Janet this newcomer meant nothing.

She smiled. I coughed down my surprise as Angie, hands on hips, stood over me, a bundle wrapped in a brown paper bag stuffed under her arm. "What have we here, loverboy?" she asked.

However, whatever mayhem Angie had planned was upstaged when Ellie said gently, "If everyone feels he or she has had a fair chance at the puzzle I'd like to announce a solution."

7.

"No!" bellowed Lou Mercer. "No. *I've* got the solution, and I want to tell it."

Perhaps he was expecting some objection, because he waited for a moment. None was forthcoming, and he ended up looking a little foolish as we waited for his words of wisdom.

"Okay," he said. "Here it is. I got to thinking it over, and I realized that the whole point of these letters was to let Nick Patterson take center stage. He made them up. Now we're playing his game. Only I'm not."

Nobody said anything in the way of objection, least of all Patterson, who leaned against the wall, his arms folded, his suit still unwrinkled. The only flaw in the picture was the faint red on his cheek from Janet's blow.

"You can't say I'm playing the game," Lou continued, "just because I realized what was going on. I'm not looking for a solution." He cleared his throat. "Anyway, that's what I think."

"Thank you, Mr. Mercer," said Ellie sweetly. "Does anyone else have any ideas?"

"Well," said Janet meekly, "a couple of items caught my eye. It does seem like gibberish, but I wondered—well, could I have those pages back? Who has them right now?"

Derrick Gleason looked up from the sheets, with his perpetually puzzled expression.

"Here they are, love. To be honest, they remind me of—oh, am I stealing your thunder, Janet? I think it is *your* turn."

"No," she said. "Please. Go ahead."

"Well, it's not really a solution, but I couldn't help but be reminded of a Bob Dylan song. He was a Minnesota boy, you know. Not any song in particular, but just the feeling you got when you listened to some of the albums from the second half of the sixties. A lot of allusive lines that might or might not mean anything. Sort of reminds me of those first days of FM, which seemed almost illegal because the stations were so hard to tune in. In the midst of all that static we discovered that songs didn't have to be two and a half minutes long. You could have songs of five minutes, six minutes, even, well, epics, of ten or twelve minutes! The revelation was a shock. It was almost like a gospel, a message, that music might mean something. Of course, deep down, the message might still be 'I Want To Hold Your Hand.'"

"Excuse me," said Miranda. "I wonder if this is leading to a solution or anything?"

"Well, no, not as such. Perhaps you might consider this a prelude, a prolegomenon, if you will, to a solution."

"So considered," said Ellie. "Ms. Austin?"

"Okay," said Janet. "I guess I was concentrating on the first letter. It mentions something about a nervous tic betraying something, and lockjaw, and a spider. I was wondering if there some some sort of poison from a spider that causes lockjaw?"

"Interesting," said Ellie. "Does the second letter shed any light?"

"I don't know," said Janet. "But it seems vaguely religious. Could a fanatic religious group be blackmailing him before the tic reappears?" She made a face. "It really isn't as good as the letters in the books."

Angie by this time has seated herself between Janet and me, and was looking over her shoulder at the letters.

"Are these supposed to be real or what?" she asked. The guests looked at her with a puzzled expression. "Oh," she said. "I guess some of you don't know me. I'm a friend of Manny's. Call me Angie."

"Angie!" said Lou, rising to shake her hand. "What a damn delightful surprise! Angelica Del Monica!" He turned around and looked at everyone else, as if he expected them to rise and pay homage. "You were my favorite on the Thunderbirds. I never missed them on TV in the old days. Such thunder, such fire, such art!" He was waving his arms around wildly, a gleam in his eye. "The magic of motion, gliding around the banked track, a set script, with danger lurking at every turn. The modern morality play, America in miniature." Angie looked over her shoulder, but no, he was speaking to her. Nor was he releasing her hand. Effortlessly she spread her fingers wide, and his fingers fell away. She's got strong hands. Lou turned to Ellie.

"Why didn't you tell me she was invited?! Now our brave company is complete."

Angie nervously cleared her throat. "Actually, I just sort of popped in to get an autograph from Nick Patterson." She rose and picked up the paper bag.

She fumbled within and five books spilled out.
Awkwardly she picked them up, straightened herself,
and turned to Nick. "I wonder if later, perhaps, when
you've got more time, you might sign these? They're
hardcovers, not paperbacks."

"I'd be glad to," said Nick smoothly, taking the
books under his arm. "I'm pleased to meet a friend of
an old friend of mine. Manny and I go way back."
That drew a couple of startled looks from the participants. "You look familiar. Did you go to Pontius Pilate
High School?"

"Pardon me?" she asked.

"Excuse me. That was the in-joke at St. Peter the
Pilot High School. Manny and I and John Ronald," he
said, pointing at the reporter, "went there these many
years ago."

"Oh. Well, no, I didn't go there. I met Manny later.
I'm not anybody, really, but it's an honor to—"

"Not anybody!" shrieked Lou. "This is Angie of the
Thunderbirds! Green and Yellow uniform, blinding
speed, brutal power, she's famous."

"I don't want to be the killjoy," said Murrie, which
was a lie. She lives for that. "I seem to recall that we're
examining a little puzzle, or whatever you'd like to call
it, and that Ms. Kaufman was going to solve it."

"Perhaps it might be more appropriate to say I have
decoded the message. I cannot claim to have solved
any puzzle," said Ellie. She turned to Angie. "I want to
welcome you officially. I was given to understand you
would not be joining us until much later, but you are of
course always welcome."

"The police left early," said Angie. "They'd just
started on the nachos when this call came through and
they all had to leave. We'll have to have the dinner
another time."

"Welcome again." Ellie stood, smoothing her dress. "I suppose I could be wrong, but consider the First Letter. The second sentence seems to make it clear that the goal is not deduction but decipherment. The latter is tied to a literal solution." Ellie loves alliteration. "The Third Letter is the key to each of the novels. Literally, the third letter is 'C', so I—"

"Oh Gosh!" said Janet suddenly, staring at the sheets. "Oops. I'm sorry. Me and my big mouth."

"Quite all right," said Ellie. "Perhaps you would consent to share our little discovery."

"If you take the first letter after each 'C' you can spell out a message. –The first letter says:" and she spoke slowly as her eyes scanned each line, "This - is - no - jay oh kay, oh, I've got it, joke. 'This is no joke.' That's the message. And the second one reads—oh." She put the page down.

"Would you like some assistance?" asked Ellie. Murrie snatched the pages away before Janet could reply. After a glance he turned to Ellie and said, "It doesn't work."

"It works," said Ellie. "Actually, quite clever. You were about to tell me there is no 'W' after the last 'c', but the 'iao' in Ciao takes its place. The message of the Second Letter is 'Death follows'."

8.

Everyone was talking at once, and no one said a thing I could understand, except Angie, who turned to me and whispered, "I haven't forgotten your making googoo eyes at that dark-eyed bimbo."

"Now come on," I answered. "Janet needed some advice. We were discussing plot lines."

"Janet! So you know her name. What else do you know about her?"

"I know her last name too. Austin. Janet Austin."

"Oh," she said, the anger suddenly drained from her voice. "That's Janet Austin? Do you think we can get her autograph, too?"

By this time some semblance of order had been restored, and Ellie was speaking to Nick.

"You intimated earlier you had made no contact with the authorities. Is that true?"

"Yes."

"I should advise you to call them now."

"I would not accept such advice. I don't need the publicity."

"Even so. My personal contacts in the LAPD are discreet. You have my assurance."

"Thank you," said Nick. "But no. I'm not afraid. I don't wish to give the hunter the satisfaction of watching me cower."

"But how will they know," I asked, "that you've brought in the police unless you take out an ad? 'No one here but us chickens!'"

"The press is present," said Nick. True, true, I thought.

"More importantly," he continued, "all of *you* are present."

That gave us all something to chew. Lou bolted the news the quickest, and said, "Are you suggesting one of us is somehow involved in this farrago?"

"I'm not eliminating the possibility. We received our invitations a month ago and they listed all the members of tonight's party."

Angie took her turn. I was proud of her. "Before you could even begin to suspect somebody here you'd have to know about some kind of motivation that someobody here would have. Right?"

Nick bowed slightly. "Exactly."

Janet drew up her to her full height of five-foot-two. Hands on hips she turned to Nick and said, "I, for one, have had enough of this. You don't have to manipulate every situation to your benefit. If you want to be some kind of hero and ignore this alleged threat, that's your business, but these faceless allegations are just the sort of thing I've come to expect from you."

"Ms. Devlin," said Ellie, "would you agree we have had enough excitement for a single evening?"

"Wholeheartedly."

"Then let us agree to put a bookmark on the night and begin again in the morning, after breakfast, which will be at eight A.M. sharp. I want to thank all of our journalists present, and wish them a good evening. I invite you to breakfast, and, failing that, to join us here in the parlor at nine."

Ellie has the ability to douse everyone with cold verbal water when she wants, and somehow her presence was dampening some of the anger that had surfaced. We hadn't exactly adjourned, but it was obvious we were done for the night.

It normally fell to me and Murrie alone to get our guests settled. Since Angie had popped in she decided she could help too, and neither of us minded.

You'd have thought Angie and Janet were old friends by the way Angie took her by the arm and offered to help her get settled in the guest wing. Murrie was taking Lou Mercer in tow. I turned about the room and suddenly realized Calliope hadn't said a word for quite awhile.

"Excuse me," I said. "May I help you to your—"

"Pardon me?" she asked.

"I said, 'Can I help you to your room?'"

"Hmmm? Oh, sure. Yes." She rose, and seemed to refocus. "That would be nice. Sorry. I was thinking. I mean, I was getting sleepy."

"Hey, Manny," called out John Ronald. "I'll catch you later."

"Hold on!" I shouted. "I'll be right back. Let me say good-bye to John."

"That'll be fine. I need a drink of water anyway."

While the gentlemen from Channel 8 wrestled with their minicams, John, a card carrying member of the print media, simply folded his steno pad, and walked to the door. There he turned and spoke.

"Nick looks good," he said simply.

"Who'd a thunk it?"

"Yeah. I don't know." He ran his fingers through his hair, which showed no signs of thinning, and stared over my shoulder. "I didn't think it would be this bad, getting a look. I thought the years..." he trailed off.

"It was worse than I thought it would be," I answered. "Funny thing. He asked about Susan."

"Susan? Why?"

"Beats me."

"Me too," he agreed, then sighed. "If I think about it too long, I'll start caring. Hey, I gotta go."

"Hi guys," said Nick Patterson, who seemed to appear out of nowhere. "So what's new?"

I didn't quite start, but I came close. "Hi, Nick," I said.

"So," he said. "Here we are. The three musketeers, wouldn't you say? Just like old times."

I shrugged. He went on. "I didn't see you guys at the reunion."

"Musta missed it," said John.

"You ever hear from anyone from the old days? Any of the gang from the AV club? Boy, those were good times. Or Susan, for instance? Did you ever hear from Susan?" he continued.

"Not since high school," said John. "Look, Nick, I gotta—"

"Just wondering," said Nick. "Just thought you might have heard from her."

"No, I haven't," said John firmly. " I gotta go."

"You do, huh?" He seemed for the first time at a loss for words. "I thought we might share a couple of drinks. Talk about each other. I mean, you're married now, aren't you? Got kids?"

"Divorced twice," said John wearily. "Ancient history. Look, Ms. Kaufman said it was time for the media to go. That's me."

"Ah, she's not going to care if some old friends get together and—"

"Nick," said John, softly, cutting him off, "no."

Nick turned to me. I looked past him.

And John turned and left without another word. I watched his broad back as he walked away, cutting across the grass to his car parked against the street. The interior lamp of his Honda briefly bathed him in light until he shut his door. The engine flared up, he unclinched the wheels, and sped up the hill.

Nick was gone.

I felt like a heel, but I was a prisoner of the past, as sure as Nick.

I walked back and found Calliope. She was reading titles on a shelf in the parlor. "I'm ready if you are," I said. She nodded and followed.

Calliope was getting the Green Room. I fumbled with the keys and unlocked the door. Her bags had been desposited earlier.

Quickly I glanced to make sure there were enough towels. "Sorry, no ice machine," I said, "But there's bottled water in the refrigerator, and a fair supply of treats in the freezer and cupboard. Phone here for local and long distance calls. This directory contains all the numbers you'll need here at the Manor, including mine if you need more ice, or the other guests if you want to bother them. Is there anything you need in particular?"

"Company," she said, a little too breezily. "I'll leave the door open."

"Not a wise idea," I said, ignoring the implication. "Even in this neighborhood."

"Then I'll leave it unlocked, for when you check the doors." She was standing between me and escape. "Knock once if you feel like it. Or maybe just surprise me."

There was something about her, well, rank sexuality that left me speechless. Her hands rested on her hips. At some point she had managed to undo her blouse's top two buttons. I swallowed.

"Wake up call?" I asked, slipping past her. "No? Then I'll see you at breakfast."

Murrie was in the process of leaving Lou in the Blue Room, and Angie was waving cheerfully to Janet in the Yellow Room. We walked back together to the parlor, where Angie and Miranda together assisted Nick, while I led Derrick to his quarters.

Nick was keyed for Grey, so Derrick and I unlocked the Beige Room. He gingerly tapped the bed, evidently found it acceptable. I guess he was played out, because he had absolutely nothing to say. He smiled that tight smile of his and waved weakly as I departed.

I climbed to my room, vaulting the steps three at a time. Throwing myself back on the bed, I glanced at the clock—1:30 A.M. I was beat, but still too up to go to sleep. I rose and turned on the television, found the news channel, when there was a knock at the door.

Obviously, Angie intended to spend the night, which was all right with me. She switched channels without asking, and then rummaged through my small refrigerator, pulling out a bottle of orange juice. Then we settled into bed together.

For about five minutes, anyway. My phone rang.

"Hello?" I asked

"Mr. Padilla. This is Ellen Kaufman."

"Yes?"

"I must apologize for intruding at this late—this early hour, but I need your assistance."

"No problem, Ms. Kaufman. What can I do for you?"

"I smell cigar smoke. It is coming through my window from the guest rooms below."

"No problem. Do you want a head on a platter or do they get a warning first?"

"A word to the wise will suffice."

She hung up. I shrugged, smiled, and pulled on my pants. Angie arched an eyebrow, but with my job I never really punch out.

It wasn't hard to pin down the culprit. I could smell the cigar from the street, and it only took a second to determine it was coming from the Blue room. Lou Mercer. Good. The lights were extinguished. Great. He was probably smoking in bed. I stepped up to his door and knocked gently.

There was no response. I took a deep breath and knocked a little louder. No reply.

I banged as loudly as I could, throwing in a kick while I was at it. "Open Up!" I shouted.

"Go away!" roared Lou.

"Go away!" yelled Calliope simultaneously.

Oh.

I paused. No question but that this was an awkward situation. It was still possible to redeem it, however, if I grabbed the tiger by the—oh, forget it.

"Put out the cigar!" I shouted. Another pause.

Then, "Sorry, okay."

There was giggling coming from the doorway of the Brown Room. Derrick and Janet, she in her stockinged feet, stood arm and arm together, watching my discomfiture. Derrick raised a glass to me.

"Well done, sirrah. The smell was starting to get to us."

Janet giggled again. I took a long bow, then departed.

For a minute I worried that I might have locked myself out of the manor, but though I'd forgotten my key, the door had not quite latched. I pushed it gently, and was inside.

Angie and I were left alone for awhile.

Some time after that, however, and here I admit I should have checked the time, I heard a noise.

Angie didn't hear the noise. She had stepped into the necessary only a moment before. I heard the sound again, so I opened my door and stuck my head in the hallway. The front door was opening, and closing. There were voices, whispering voices.

Quickly I pulled on a pair of shorts and tiptoed downstairs. I had no idea who might have entered at that hour, but I was sure they had no business being inside.

It turned out they were as quiet as I because I nearly stumbled into them as I slipped through the darkened front chamber. I drew back behind a pillar and watched as the two of them embraced.

"I told you," whispered Nick Patterson, wearing a pair of pink silk pajamas, "that I could get in just about anywhere. Shall we raid the kitchen?" He drew her closer. Calliope Metropoulos remained unaware of Nick's chosen irony.

Calliope was wearing a gauzy negligee. It clung to the sweat on her thighs. Her hair was matted at odd angles. She was standing on the tips of her toes, kissing his chin. He was staring out into space. He might have heard me. I stood still. He spoke.

"What do these others know?" he was saying. "Kudos? Who's kidding who? I'll take large stacks of cash to the applause of the so-called cultured any day?"

"I agree. I know they look down on my books," said Calliope, "but I stopped reading reviews years ago. Now I just cash checks."

"That's why I find clowns like Mercer so laughable, with their cant about credos. I don't know what Art is. I can't see it, I can't taste it or touch it."

"He makes me sick," said Calliope.

"We'll just have to stick together, won't we? Satisfied with your look around or is there anything you'd like to do while we're here?"

"No. I admit it. You can break in when you want. Now let's get out before we wake someone up."

With one motion Nick lifted Calliope and carried her to the door. With his elbow he nudged it open ever so quietly—then slammed it. I jumped.

Maybe he'd known I was there and this was his way of rubbing my nose in it. With Nick you could never tell. I started to go back up the stairs when I literally stepped into Miranda.

It was like walking into a stone wall. I took a step back to catch my balance and used a few choice words.

"What are you doing here?" we both said, as one. She was wearing her blue robe, which is about the thickest thing she owns.

"I was investigating a noise."

"So why'd you slam the door?"

"I didn't slam the door."

"Who did?"

"One of our guests. He—they were getting a look around. I think it was supposed to be a joke."

"Who?" she asked.

"Does it matter?" I asked. "I think they heard me. That's why they left. Here, get out of the way. I want to get some sleep."

Miranda eyed me suspiciously as I walked around her.

"Okay," I said, annoyed. "I confess. I was visiting the servants' quarters. Please don't tell Angie."

I didn't turn on the lights as I entered my room. Angie was back in bed.

"Where were you?"

"I heard a noise. Didn't you hear a noise?"

"Yeah, a second ago."

"This was before that."

"Oh. Okay," she mumbled.

"Go back to sleep," I said.

After awhile we did go back to sleep.

I was asleep, deep deep asleep, when the phone rang again. Angie groaned. "I should've driven home," she muttered. "I'd a got more sleep."

I glanced at the clock again. It was now 3:35 A.M.

9 .

I should've let it ring. I should've let Murrie answer it. It would have served her right.

But Angie gets real grumpy when she's awakened by the phone, so I rolled over and pulled it off the hook.

"Hello?" I asked.

"Manny? Good. I was hoping you'd answer."

"Who *is* this?"

"Nick. Look—"

"This doesn't sound like Nick," I said.

"Dammit, something's wrong, Manny. Get down here."

"What's this all about?" I asked suspiciously.

"Hurry," he said, speaking as I spoke. "Hurry, Manny. I need you."

The line went dead.

"Who was that?" asked Angie blearily.

"Nick Patterson."

"What'd he want?"

"I don't know. Me, I guess."

"You don't have to go, do you?" she asked me.

"It's my damn job."

It took me a second to find some shorts and slacks, and to fumble with a pair of shoes. There had to be a shirt somewhere. I didn't bother to turn on any lights. I didn't even grab a flashlight. I stumbled my way to the front door and walked across the wet grass to Nick's door.

My cuffs were soaked as I pulled out my master key. I knocked once but there was no answer. I knocked again. While I waited , I looked up . Mars had stumbled into the pre-dawn sky, and Orion was taking pot shots at him. The streets were still, and along guest row all the lights were out, for what that was worth.

So I jammed in the master key and fiddled with it for a second. It stuck for a moment, then turned. I entered Nick's room. I could see nothing in the dim light that seeped in from the street.

"Nick?" I called. "Nick, what's the big deal?"

I stepped on a piece of paper. Bending over, I picked it up and held it up to the street light outside. It was a letter.

I had a funny feeling, and I reached behind to turn on the light. It took me a moment to find it and switch it on.

Nick was there. He was fully dressed in a suit I hadn't seen earlier that evening. He looked good, stretched out on a perfectly made bed, although his jaw hung slackly and his eyes were rolled back. He looked dead.

Suddenly I had no feelings. Maybe I should have run, but I knew what to do. I stepped over to the body and placed my fingers on his neck. There was no pulse. He had a watch on the dresser. I held its dial under his nostrils. No fogging. I gently bent over him.

There was an odd smell, a nutty smell. I looked on the far side of the bed. There was a glass lying on its side, a fluid spilled on the carpet. A second glance around the room revealed an opened bottle of mineral water.

A flicker caught my eye. There was something burning in the bathroom. I ran in. The papers in the bottom of the trash can were nearly ashes. I doused the fire in the shower, burning my hand in the process. Then I got a look.

I had no business doing that. Let's be clear on that. Fishing through the damp ashes I found two scraps of paper. They seemed to be envelopes. The first was in the best shape. Nick's name and return address, a post office box, was in the corner. It was addressed to:

SUSAN DELGADO B...

26...

The rest had been destroyed. Stamped between the address and return address were the words "Refused — Return To Sender."

The second was in someone else's handwriting and consisted solely of the return address. It read:

...AM BENTO...

...S LANE...

...LMS SPR...

I stuffed them in my pocket and walked back to the body.

Then I saw the stack of Angie's books. I reached over and opened them. I don't know why. They were all signed. At least he'd done one damn thing right in his life.

I picked up the phone to call Ellie when everyone tried to come in.

There was Lou, in an absurd dressing gown, open to the waist and barely covering his buns in back. Derrick Gleason was wearing a pair of checked pajamas. Calliope was now wearing a thick, furry gown, and Janet Austin was clothed in a deep blue robe.

"Stop!" I shouted.

We stood silently. Then Lou said, "I got a phone call, maybe thirty seconds ago. Nick Patterson. He said to rush over. He said you were threatening him. He hung up before I could say anything."

"I got the same call," said Calliope, breathless. "Only half a minute ago. He sounded funny, but it was him."

Janet and Derrick exchanged glances. "Did you two get the same call?" I asked. They nodded. "Half a minute ago?" They nodded. "You rushed over here, all of you?"

I looked at my hand. I realized I still had the letter. I wanted to get a look at it, but there was one more thing to do.

"Let's all stand right here while I make a phone call. You all watch me, okay?"

They nodded. They were looking at Nick. They were jumping to conclusions.

I dialed without looking. Three rings and an answer.

"Yes?"

"Hello, Ms. Kaufman. Sorry to wake you, but we have a problem." I paused but she didn't respond so I plowed ahead. "About five minutes ago I got a call from someone that sort of sounded like Nick so I rushed downstairs and found him dead. He seems to have received his Third Letter. I am holding it in my hand. Our four other guests each received a call, virtually simultaneously, from someone that sort of sounded like Nick telling them to come immediately, and that I was—threatening him?" They nodded. "So here we are. Together. I don't suppose I should leave this room, for now. Would you call Detective Schmoller for me?"

"Yes, Mr. Padilla. Thank you for the phone call. I will be down as I may."

"Give John Ronald a call. He deserves a scoop. His home number's on the disk. Give Angie a call too. She's in my room."

Ellie hung up.

"So," I said. No one said anything, so I figured I'd better do the talking. "Ah, someone got to Nick, it looks like. My guess is poison. Bottle here on the counter. Glass here, on this side, where you can't see it, spilled contents. He sure looks nice, doesn't he? In a few minutes the police will arrive and start asking questions, but in the meantime, would anyone like to hear this new letter? No, don't reach for it. So far the only fingerprints on it are mine and, well, whoever's. So let's leave it that way. Everyone take a look first." I waved it. "Letters cut and pasted again."

I cleared my throat.

"Hector Me No More. Back to the begining
koin a phrase after the attic
Lying in wait
we bring lauds
we bring lentes
The strange truth is straying dark
Like unto the antic satyrs
Who will fardles bear
Striving mainly for the stodgy
striving smply for Gehenna
Striving lastly for surcease
striving fit for all
For Billy

"Now that's a mouthful," I commented, then quickly listed any strange spellings I noted. "Let's see, any guesses?"

"Who's Billy?" asked Calliope.

I kept a straight face. "I can't say," I answered. I didn't say 'I don't know.'

Janet's teeth were chattering. It was California cold, that chill that comes from the ocean in the early morning hours. "Add up the third letters."

I knew what she meant. I took a quick look. "Tee, Kay, Ell, hmmm, should be an Oh, but coin is misspelled. We'll count it anyway. Ah, an Ess, an Eee, and—that's it. What does TKLOSE mean?"

"It sounds like 'to close'," said Derrick Gleason, "as if a life were being closed."

"It might be an African word," Janet Austin, "or an African name. Perhaps a secret society of some sort."

"I think you didn't have enough time to put together a decent letter," said Lou.

I said nothing in reply. Thinly at first, then louder and louder we heard the shrill wail of sirens.

Calliope turned to go.

"You may not leave," I said.

"I want to get dressed before they arrive."

"It's too late for that. We'll want to say we were together from this moment on. And it's safer. The murderer might still be somewhere on the grounds."

Derrick looked startled. "He's here, isn't he? I mean, he's you. I thought that was obvious."

"Let's get this straight," I said. "I didn't do it. But someone pulled a clever stunt, and I think I know how it was done. All it would take is a bank of tape recorders and a computer. Piece of cake. I'm going to tell the police about it, *not* you. But we all hang tight until they're here."

The police cars screeched to a halt, and within a second we heard doors slam and muted footsteps along the grass. I saw them emerge from the darkness, a phalanx of boys in blue. They all wore mustaches, except the women. It's part of the dress code. In their midst strode my old friend Police Lieutenant Herman Schmoller of Homicide.

Elbowing aside our guests, Schmoller took a moment to survey the scene, then stepped inside. His eyes darted from corner to corner, focused on us for a moment, then came to rest on the body. His bulky overcoat, which he brought with him from New England, hid the muscles of his compact steely frame.

Pushing back his glasses from the bridge of his nose, he fumbled for a peppermint, then turned to me.

"Be careful," I said. "There's a stain that wants examining on that side of the bed. I think you'll find a poison in it. And here's a letter I stumbled on when I entered in the dark, so it should only have my prints, Nick's prints, and the murderer's prints. We're all here, and I suppose you'll want to—"

He raised a hand. "Can it, Manny," said Schmoller sharply. "You, all of you, into the Manor together. We'll question you there in a few minutes. Ah—" He turned to Calliope. "Except you, Miss. Sutcliffe!" He turned to Kathy Sutcliffe, an officer I'd met once before. "Escort her to her room long enough to get dressed."

Ellie was walking down the steps as we entered. Normally we might have been treated to the first tendrils of dawn smoking through the stained glass windows, but the front room was bathed in artificial light. Miranda was at her elbow, glaring at me. I smiled sweetly. Without a word we assembled in the parlor.

Angie was already there, giving Maggs a hand as the refreshments were laid out. Lou reached for a crescent roll and marmalade, but everyone else stared off into space. It reminded me of the old days at

Pontius Pilate, when John had played Right Tackle, and I'd played Left Out. The atmosphere in the locker room before the big game with Holy Maternity could make you sick. It often did. The nervousness fed on itself, until you could barely move, barely see, sitting in front of the rank lockers. We were boys who thought we were men.

Nick didn't play football. He ran crosscountry.

Most of the people in the parlor hadn't seen death much, I guess, at least before it'd been prettied up by the mortician. There are certain unavoidable consequences of dying no one thinks about. The muscles relax, all of them, and that can have disastrous results. The corpse is wooden and empty and too too normal. You can't take it back. Everything in our upbringing tells us that someone will make it better. You don't really get sent to bed without dinner. Someone sneaks the meat loaf upstairs. You don't really have to know the right answers. Go for the essay questions. You don't really have to pay the bills. Just get some ready-cash from your Masterbounce to pay the VISA.

Lou was still chewing, although his snack was long gone. He might have been muttering, I don't know. Janet played with her hands, wringing them silently, hunched over, staring at the floor. Ellie was talking in a low voice to Derrick Gleason, but I couldn't hear a word. Calliope was closer, and listening.

Angie came over to me and rubbed my shoulders. "What happened?" she asked. "I mean, I heard what happened, but what was it like? Who did it?"

I whispered in her ear, "Someone's trying to tag me with it."

"Who?"

"Don't know. Don't know why, unless—no, that's impossible. People don't remember that long."

"Can I help?"

"Maybe later." It was begining to occur to me that things might get sticky. "I'll let you know."

Miranda was now whispering to Calliope, but I couldn't catch a word. Now that was a poser. I had a funny feeling watching them. Calliope then rose and said something to Lou Mercer. I was about to walk over, join the conversation, when Schmoller entered.

"Good evening—I mean good morning, ladies and gentlemen. My name is Herman Schmoller. I'm with Homicide, and I am in charge of this case. I was not unaware of this gathering. Ms. Kaufman and I discussed the guest list a few days ago at our weekly luncheon. We'll do this as quickly as possible, but I'm afraid we'll need your cooperation. I'd like to take your stories here, so we don't have to make a trip to the station."

There was a chorus of assent.

"I will be asking you how you spent the night, what noises you heard, and, I'm afraid, in what way you knew the deceased—"

A sob escaped Janet's lips. She tried to hold it in, but it burst out, until she was absorbed in a full-blown crying jag, a hoarse wail, head buried in hands. There was rage in Derrick's carriage, his hands were clenched in fists.

Ellie was over in a moment with a glass of water. Seating herself next to Janet, she put her arm around the author, hugging her gently.

"There, there," she said. "This won't last. The sun will rise. There'll be a ray perhaps, on some future date." Janet sobbed the louder.

I still didn't feel a thing. Aren't you sorry he's dead? I asked myself. I wasn't. I tried to make myself feel something, anything. Nothing came. Was I a fish? Angie was still sitting next to me. I put my arm around her waist. She snuggled closer. No, I still had feelings, emotions. Just none to spare for Nick.

"I'm sorry," said Schmoller, pushing his glasses back on his nose. "We must begin." At times like these that little bit of New England creeps out in his accent. He reached for a peppermint and sighed.

"Well," said Lou, rising and striking a dramatic pose, "I want to say this in front of everyone. I hated Nick Patterson. You'll find out why when you do some checking, so I'll tell you now. My agent had the contract arranged—I was going to do a screenplay for one of Nick's books. Yes, I do screenplays—but under a pseudonym. I've got to eat, like everyone else. You can't make a living on poetry, and kudos don't buy groceries. So I write screenplays, sometimes even for," and he winced, "television. I'm not proud of it, but I'm telling you so you know. I hope it doesn't have to go out of this room, but if it does, it does."

He took a deep breath.

"So Nick found out who was writing the screenplay. We'd had a run-in, years ago, in college. He never forgot. I—I suckerpunched him. You would have, too. He took advantage of a girl I knew. Not a close friend, but just someone I knew. It maddened me. He always seemed to land on his feet. The campus police knew about it, but said without a complaint they couldn't do anything, and besides, it'd be his word against hers. So I saw he got what was coming to him.

"You can see where this is going. When he found out I was writing the screenplay he not only got me removed, but he did his best to make it hard for me to get work anywhere. I don't know what lies he was spreading about me, but doors were starting to close all over. I got hints that a story was making the rounds, something about me and the Viet Cong. I don't know. So I've got every reason to hate him.

"And he hung my screen name over my head. He threatened to reveal it. 'Where will the pure poet be then?' he asked me once, on the phone, laughing at me. So I've got the motive. But I didn't do it. I left the Manor tonight, went to bed, and went to sleep. I didn't stir until the phone rang."

He was leaving a little something out. I was about to bring up his little visit with Calliope, when she spoke up.

"I'd like to say something too. I didn't go right to bed when our meeting broke up last night. In fact, I'd been in bed only an hour or so when the phone rang."

"One at a time, please," said Schmoller. "You're Calliope Metropoulos, I believe. Please allow me to ask Mr. Mercer a few questions before you—"

"I just wanted you to know," she burst in, "that I spent most of the night with Miranda Devlin, upstairs in her room, catching up on our old college days. I didn't hear any funny noises. I just wasn't around."

"That's right," said Murrie. "She was with me the whole night."

10.

That's when I knew I was in trouble. I got to feeling in my back pocket. My wallet was there. Good. I might need it.

Schmoller was talking. I had to listen now, catch every word. "Let's do this by the numbers—this is important. A man is dead, and it is my job to determine when, how, and—who."

"Do your duty, officer," said Derrick. "Personally, I never met the guy before today, but I haven't a good thing to say about him. After what I've learned about him tonight—"

He stopped in mid-sentence and Janet stopped in mid-sob.

"What did you learn about him?" asked Schmoller, taking off his jacket and laying it on a chair. His short sleeves revealed the muscles that won him a bronze in the Graeco-Roman.

"Just what I learned from observation tonight," said Derrick hastily. "He was a callous man, an insensitive man. It's not surprising to me that he made enemies."

Schmoller sighed. He could see it was going to be a five-peppermint night. Carefully he unwrapped one of the little candies and said, "I'd like you to come with me one at a time. Ms. Kaufman, may we use the kitchen?"

"Check with Ms. Magdalene," she replied. Maggs nodded.

No one asked her, but Ellie assumed she'd be listening in, and, considering her past association with Schmoller and his parents, I was not surprised when he raised no objection as she followed him out of the door. An officer came back a few moments later and asked Janet to follow him. I gave it a ten count, then stretched and told the cop left behind with us that I had to visit the head. He nodded.

Maggs has her rooms next to the kitchen. She likes it that way. I slipped inside her rooms, then groped my way to the thin wall.

There's no light, of course. She doesn't need any, and refuses to have the room wired. I knew her record collection was shelved on the wall closest to the kitchen. Stubbing my toes only twice, I flattened my ear against the wall and listened.

The acoustics weren't perfect, but I caught enough. Janet was talking about events in the past. At first she came through pretty clear. She said, "Yes, I knew Nick Patterson before today."

Then she got softer and it got more difficult. I caught the words 'date rape', and I heard Nick's name, and the phrase 'ten or twelve years ago'. It must have been rough going. There were long pauses. That's all

I ever learned about it. No one told me anything else then or later. She moved again and I could hear her clearly say she'd been with Derrick part of the evening, that they could vouch for each other.

Janet left and was replaced by Miranda. She must have been leaning against the wall as she spoke because I caught almost every word she said. I fumed at one thing she said in particular.

"Calliope and I were giggling, you know, girl talk, when I heard a loud noise. I went downstairs, thinking it might be an intruder. Manny was just coming in. He wouldn't say where he'd been. He just stomped off."

I couldn't hear what Schmoller was saying, but Murrie started up again.

"No, he didn't want Nick Patterson here. When he heard about it last week he tried to wriggle out of it. He wanted out in the worst way. He lied about a fictitious vacation he'd been planning. He tried to leave. Ms. Kaufman insisted he work, though.... No, I don't know why."

Schmoller was speaking again. Then Murrie answered.

"No. I didn't get one of those calls everyone one else got. I can tell you why, though. I'd recognize his voice, Manny's that is, if he tried to fake Nick's voice. No, that's all right, Ms. Kaufman. Let me finish. They're saying they all got a call at virtually the same time. Don't kid yourself. You know Manny and computers. He could jimmy something real easy. No, I don't know why he'd want to get Nick. I'm not saying he did. I just don't think you should close that avenue yet."

Then she moved, and I couldn't hear a thing. They were shuffling chairs and I figured they were getting ready for the next guest.

"Who's there?" said a voice ten feet away, causing me to jump. After I swallowed my heart I said through gritted teeth, "Don't do that, Maggs! You scared me to death." She moves silent as a hobbit when she chooses.

"I had a feeling you were here," she smiled. "You're up next, Manny. Get out there—and take the other door."

Maggs' back door opens next to the elevator. It was a good thing. An officer found me in the hallway a moment or two after I exited. He indicated with a shake of his head I was to follow him. I did.

"So," I said, taking a seat at the round table. A pot of coffee sat untouched at the center. "What have we come up with so far?"

"Padilla," said Schmoller, "where were you," he consulted his notes, "around two A.M.?"

"I don't know anything about two A.M. I don't check my clock much during the night."

"Aside from the time you found the body, was there a time when you left your room?"

"Yes, but I don't know the time." Something told me not to kid around. "I heard a noise, and went out to investigate. I was gone maybe five, six minutes. Then I went back to my room."

"What did you see?"

"I think I saw one of our guests, maybe two. I think they came into the house, maybe as a prank, then left. I thought I heard them talking, but I probably scared them off."

"Who were they?"

"I'm not sure. They could have been a male and a female."

"What were they doing together?"

"Please, Schmoller. I'm not a dorm mom. We had five adults as guests, three men, two women. Under such circumstances, well, *sub rose ad nauseum.*"

Schmoller took a deep breath, then chose his words carefully. "Can anyone vouch for your whereabouts during the night?"

I frowned. "Is this a joke? You saw Angie in the parlor. She was with me. Do I have to spell it out?"

"So she heard the noise too?" he said. Ellie sighed with relief.

"No," I said, the frustration evident in my voice. It was no use lying about this. "She was in the little girl's room at the time. She never heard the noise."

There was silence for a moment.

"Tell me how you found the body."

So I told him the story, from begining to end.

"It's a pretty strange story," said Schmoller, when I was done.

"If that's your attitude I'm not going to talk to you," I said heatedly. "I know what you're thinking, dammit, and I had nothing to do with it. Listen, Ms. Kaufman. I have some suggestions for you, since Bonehead seems to have made up his mind." I wanted to tell her that Miranda, for reasons I did not know, was lying, but not yet, not in front of Schmoller. "First of all, check with the phone company. They'll be able to confirm that the calls came into the four guest rooms at the same moment. Then you'll have to try to backtrack. *If* they can trace the calls. They may find they all came from the same source. And then I suggest you take the sheets from the guests rooms and have them analyzed for body hair, secretions, what not. There may be some correspondences."

Schmoller reached for a peppermint.

"Thanks, Padilla, but I can do my own job. You don't seem very broke up about all this."

"I'm not. Is that a crime?"

"But you two went to high school together. I've checked."

"So?"

"I've got another question—what do you have against Nick Patterson? You were seen giving him the cold shoulder last night—you and the guy from the *Herald,* John Ronald. He went to the same school too, didn't he?"

I gave it a thought. Did I need to tell the story? I didn't want to. It was none of his damn business. But I realized they'd find out with a little checking, and it would look a lot worse if they found out before I told. So I took a deep breath and told him. No emotion. Just the facts.

"We were friends in school. Me, Nick, John, and a guy named William Benton. Billy. Billy Benton. Yeah, there was a Billy in two of those letters. We buddied around from about the second grade on. They called us the Four Musketeers.

"But Nick was different. Like the three of us would share the work on any project, but not Nick. He always had an excuse. He cut his thumb by accident, or his back was bothering him, or he was wearing his best clothes.

"And he'd take the credit when we had a good idea. Why'd we hang around him? I don't know. Nick was always that kind of guy, getting his way, landing on his feet. In junior high he was the darling of the teachers. And in high school, he got the girl we all hung around with. Her name? I'm not even sure I can remember. Sally, I think." *Susan,* I thought to myself. *Susan, I remember you.*

"But that isn't what split us up. That's just the background.

"One day we were all hanging out at Nick's house. That was rare, because we never went there. He was always at our houses, eating our food, messing with our stuff, and bragging about how his stuff was better. But we never got to go to his place, so how were we to know if he was lying?

"So here we were, finally at his folks' house, and they were gone. It was our junior year in high school. I guess he wanted to impress us, because he mixed us drinks at his father's bar. Mine tasted awful. I didn't touch it. Nick had three or four.

"Then he unlocked his father's gun closet.

"I told him to stop horsing around, but he kept pointing the guns at us, and letting them go off. They were all unloaded, but the click alone would just about cause us all to mess our pants. I told him it wasn't funny, we all did, but he kept on."

I stopped to check the rage in my voice.

"Then he fired a blank at Billy. Man, we thought Billy was dead, because he just dropped. But when the smoke cleared Billy started moving, and he was crying, saying he'd had enough. Nick thought it was funny, laughed at him, asked if he wanted to be a wimp all his life. I said, 'Let's go.' We just about got to the door when Nick fired at us one more time."

"I thought it was another blank. That's what Nick said later, too. Billy dropped to his knees with the funniest look, then fell forward on his face. I thought Billy was just scared, but when the blood came up through his shirt I knew it was over. Nick just kind of stood there glassy-eyed until the police came. John went into hysterics. He didn't come back to school for months. He ended up graduating a whole year after the rest of us, because he couldn't get over it. Me? I was sick for a week. I mean, throwing up and everything.

"But what got me was that Nick came to school the next day. Didn't miss a beat. He said he wasn't sorry.

He said he couldn't be, because it was an accident. He acted like nothing happened. And as far as he was concerned, nothing had. It was just one of those things. He kept on joking and carrying on just like before.

"The Bentons, they just packed up and moved out of town. I couldn't make heads or tails of life for quite awhile. Meanwhile Nick used crocodile tears when he wanted to hit up on some chick. How'd we know? Because Nick would brag about his conquests in the locker room, crowing the line he used about being haunted by the dying look on Billy's face.

"So I can't be very sad he's dead. To my mind he hasn't been alive for a long time. No, I don't forget. Is that enough of a story for you, Schmoller?"

But Schmoller said, "Angela can't verify your story of a noise, then."

"No, she can't. But if I *had* been faking, don't you think I'd arrange things so she could provide an alibi?"

"Did she answer the last phone call or did you?"

"I answered."

"So she didn't hear Nick talking? She only has your word for it?"

"This is ridiculous."

"Answer the question, Padilla."

"No. She didn't listen in."

"Ms. Kaufman, I may have to ask Padilla to come with me to the station, for a little more questioning. Perhaps you'd like to call your lawyer to warn him—"

"What?!" I exploded.

"Mr. Padilla," Ellie was saying. "I am sure this is merely a precaution on Detective Schmoller's part. It is his duty to leave no stone unturned."

"Are you kidding? He thinks I did it."

Schmoller said nothing. That spoke louder than words.

"All right. I'm going up to my room now, though, to change."

"No, you're not," said Schmoller.

"Uh uh," I disagreed. "Last time I spent a night in the lockup I had to throw away my clothes. Have a heart. Let me change shirts. These clothes were a gift from Angie. I'd rather put on a set due for the rag bag."

Schmoller looked to Ellie, who nodded.

"Okay," he said. "But take one of the officers with you." He turned to a blonde specimen. "You, Clague. Follow him up."

"I'll be back, and I *won't* forget this," I said, shoving a finger within an inch of Schmoller's face. He'd have been within his rights to break it off, but Ellie was there, and he likes her and he owes her, so he did nothing.

It had been my intention to produce the two scraps of paper I'd rescued from the trash can, but no more. They were mine now. I needed time and I needed space, and I wasn't going to get either, it looked like. I was going to have to blow. This wasn't going to be easy, but I'd already given the matter some thought.

With Clague right behind I stomped up the stairs. Angie heard the noise and came out to greet me, and we walked in together shoulder to shoulder. I leaned over to kiss her, and whispered, "Distract him. I'm making my break."

So when I opened the drawer to grab a new shirt, Angie threw off her robe and fell into bed, wearing only her nightie. She fiddled with the top two buttons, and they opened up quite nicely. I turned to the officer.

"I got to use the can. Do you need to follow me?"

"No," he said dryly, making a point of looking at Angie by not looking at her. "Just hurry."

Angie wears a few of her years around the middle, but to my mind that's just a sign of maturity. I'm not attracted to the thin sticks other guys go gaga over. Angie's figure is otherwise intact, and it still has the power to cloud men's minds. I watched the cop pull up a chair so he could sit while he didn't stare at Angie. He was asking a question about the roller derby. This would work out fine.

I locked the door of the bathroom, opened the window, and pulled back the screen. I dropped the new clothes, then picked them up, and threw them down the portal. A change wouldn't hurt me on the road. Then I stood on the sink and pulled back the screen. Lifting myself with a grunt, I squeezed through, then flipped over onto my ledge. It wasn't built to support my weight, but I stood on it less than a second. Grabbing the drain pipe I shimmied to the ground, pulling the clean clothes with me. Then I walked as fast as I could without running to the garage. Betsy would be there waiting. She'd never let me down before and I knew she wouldn't let me down now.

11.

Betsy is an old Volkwagen Bug. I keep her in the garage and save her for special occasions—like when I need a car with no registration and fake plates.

I didn't figure I'd have but maybe two or three minutes to get out of there. Two police officers leaned against their cars out on the street, yawning. I waved. They waved back. I used the side door to the garage.

Betsy was there, waiting for me. I unhooked the battery charger, and started her up. She made a harsh noise, like always, and idled high, but she was ready.

Thirty seconds later I was on the street and down the block. The officers waved again. One was stooping to listen in on the horn. I had my head start.

If you've ever driven around Belle Eyrie, you know it's hard to get around unless you know where you're going. Some of the hills are pretty steep, and the streets are deliberately laid out so you can't travel in a straight line in any direction more than a few hundred yards. Almost none of the homes have visible street numbers and most of the street signs are blocked by branches or are regularly removed. I knew where I was going, though, and I stood to make pretty good time because of it.

There are two entrances to the hillsides of Belle Eyrie. Both are on the south side, arched gates emptying on to Sunset Boulevard, not far from the Westwood district. A couple of cruising patrol cars could block the entrances to Belle Eyrie, and I'd be history. I'd already blown any chance of bail. So the main road was out.

Or any road. It was still pretty dark. I'd taken Betsy out on a test run a couple of times to practice for this eventuality. I was ready now.

I'm not going to tell you exactly where I did this, because I may have to do it again, but I will tell you I went north instead of south. Within a mile of the manor I drove over the curb, between two homes, and beyond into one of the many ravines that dug into that hilly area.

It took me half a minute, but I found the fire break, and I took off through the scrub. It was a bumpy ride, but Betsy was up to it. A couple of the hills I tackled were pretty steep, and I took most of that ride in first gear. We were making a lot of noise, no doubt about it, but I knew where I was going. If anyone was in pursuit, which I doubted, they'd have to go by feel. And I had a couple of surprises planned.

There was one bad moment. The earth on one particularly steep hill had grown damp. Perhaps it was the run-off from someone's automatic sprinkler. Whatever, I slipped back down and stalled. It took some doing to get Betsy started again, but once she did I gunned her. Before I could lose my nerve we plowed up that hill again and made it—barely. Spraying dirt and mud in our wake we plunged down the hill and between some pretty tough scrub. I thought

I caught a glimpse of two eyes staring back in the darkness. Probably only a jackrabbit, but it swerved, so I didn't have to.

I was pretty sure no one else could get over that hill or squeeze through that tight fit. We settled into a game of run and gun as Betsy and I took the firebreaks over the Angeles Hills.

A half hour later I emerged onto a San Fernando highway and began Phase One of my plan.

I had to leave behind a computer spoor. That's pretty easy if you know how. I stopped at five 7-11's in quick order and used my card for a few hundred at each. I'd need the stake once I stopped using my plastics, and it formed the begining of my trail. Then I bought some gas. I needed to leave a record of a purchase before I left L.A.

Then north up the 101, as fast as I dared.

By now I knew they had to be on to me. This first hour would be simply a matter of luck.

I didn't start to breathe easier until Camarillo. The sun was sneaking up, the traffic was a little thicker, and I could see any approaching black and white. My head was swimming. I'd only had a few winks before the mess had started. I needed to make a call to Angie, and fortunately that would serve my purposes quite nicely.

I stopped in Santa Barbara to buy breakfast on one of my cards, then charged a call to my room at the manor. Angie answered.

"It took you long enough," she said.

"How's it going?" I asked. "Hope I didn't get you in too much trouble."

"Nothing I couldn't handle. However, thanks to you I'm not going to be allowed to drive to the restaurant this morning. They say I'm needed for more questioning."

"Sorry, honey," I said.

"No problem. You owe me, though. What did you do, anyway? Rob a bank?"

"Worse. I got on Murrie's bad side. Look, I'm sure this line is bugged, so I can't stay long. I just wanted to tell you I love you and thank you for lending me your car."

She almost missed a beat. It was of course my car, and not hers. "You took my car!" she exploded. She certainly couldn't act as if she'd allowed it. That would make her an accessory. "You get my car back here, buster, or there'll be hell to pay."

"Later today, okay?"

"Yeah, right."

"Later, honey."

"Later." I hung up.

Now they'd be on the lookout for Angie's old Gremlin, at least until someone checked and found it still parked a block away. I got back in the Vee Dub and headed north.

A couple of hours later, in Santa Maria, I made my final feint. Charging another meal and filling my tank with the gas card, I called ahead to a motel in Salinas and reserved a room in my own name, leaving a card number as a security. Then, using a lot of change, I made another phone call to a friend in Pacific Grove.

I didn't want to do this to anybody, but it was going to be necessary to make the picture complete. And the guy owed me a favor, a big favor, anyway. I told him he had a chance to pay back the one he owed. You don't have to know his name but he really exists and he knows who he is.

Giving the name of the motel, I asked him to wait three hours, then check in, using my name. To keep the computer trail alive, someone had to check into that motel. I warned him, however, to wear a broad brim hat so he couldn't be readily identified, and to leave the engine running so he could take off immediately. He could drop off the key in a mail box later.

Then I headed East.

There's a winding road, a real sick-maker, that snakes around the mountains. The sign said forty but the truckers take it at seventy-five. I had to use it another time, when the Cajon Pass froze over and traffic was rerouted. It added an extra five hours to a drive at a time when I was only eighty minutes from home, but I figured it was one more item to file for when it was needed. It was needed.

By the time I was done I was feeling a little green. The road drops you off a few miles south of Bakersfield and a few miles north of that graveyard of trucks, that sheer eight-mile grade they call the Grapevine. The truck stop looked pretty good, and I pulled off the road at the last exit before the Grapevine and explored my options.

I took out the two scraps of paper and stared at them. I had a choice to make. I could look for Susan Delgado B—, or travel to Palm Springs to see William Benton, Sr. After a moment I stuffed the Susan scrap back in my pocket and concentrated on the other one.

Now I needed to plan a route. I could take off through the desert to Barstow, then head for my goal, or I could head south, and travel back through L.A. before going east again.

I decided I was safer in L.A. They wouldn't look for me there. I could take the 210 and stay north of downtown.

Besides, I'm not happy when I'm away from the megalopolis. I like L.A. I can't help it. It's so many different places crammed into sprawling mess. There's so many things wrong with it, and a lot of it can't be fixed, but I don't know anywhere else I'd rather be. So I drove.

Now I paid cash for gas, for everything. I didn't want to exist anymore. Time to hide my tracks.

As I drove I started to get sleepy. I was having trouble keeping my hands on the steering wheel. My head was nodding. Traffic ground to a halt around Pomona. It was dinner time. I couldn't stand it anymore. I pulled off the freeway. I ate.

It's a law that you have to carry ten extra pounds in Pomona, no matter who you are. The waitress smiled at me through chubby cheeks as she woke me up. I'd fallen asleep waiting for my pie. I tipped her ten and told her to share it with the chef. Around eight I figured the traffic had thinned enough and I got back on the freeway. East again.

It wasn't so bad, that last ninety minutes or so. Betsy hadn't driven so far in awhile. She was starting to complain, and she didn't have a radio to keep me distracted. The full moon was rising, and the windmills, scattered across the desert hills like dandlelions, gleamed in the silver light. Bats blocked the stars. Night drew on, and the temperature didn't drop. It was hot.

Finally I drove by the giant dinosaurs. There are two of them, the Tyrannasauros and the Brontosauros. Some fellow built them years ago. They were part of some dream that died with him, but the dinosaurs are still there. I knew I wasn't far from Palm Springs.

Palm Springs used to be the place to go. It still is, for a few thousand college students on spring break. But the rich people have taken to the newer communities nearby, the Rancho Mirages and Indian Wells, where the streets are named after the really big lounge lizards, and the rooms run double my weekly salary per night.

Palm Springs is just as hot as it used to be, but it's a little sleepier. It looks a little dusty, but it's a little cheaper. And that was good, because I was going to have to pay cash.

I found a room, and parked the VW where it couldn't be seen from the street.

By the time I took a shower and changed into the other set of clothes it was getting closer to midnight. I took a walk down the street and found an all-night laundry. I changed several bills into quarters, then slipped into the public phone booth. I called my pal up north.

He had a few choice words for me when he realized who I was, but once he calmed down he could hardly wait to tell me about it. As it turned out, he'd checked in, then driven around the block to watch—against my instructions—and it nearly cost him. The rest of the rooms were evacuated and my room was stormed by thirty officers, including two separate SWAT teams. The film crews had been tipped off somehow, so all the local stations had footage, but they didn't know who was supposed to have been inside. The rumors suggested Libyan terrorists. After he was done laughing I told him there might be a chance his picture had been taken. I told him if he was arrested he was to rat on me. Then I gave him my motel phone number.

He told me he'd worn a hat, and shaved his beard once he got home. I apologized. He'd been working on that beard for years. He told me he'd been thinking about shaving for a long time, but I knew what a sacrifice it was. Now *I* owed *him*.

I had one last task for the day. I walked to a liquor store and bought a couple of papers, a toothbrush, toothpaste, and a few other essentials. Once I got back in the room I took time to read.

I was famous. The murder was page one. NICK STRIKES OUT! said one. NICK GETS HIS THIRD read the other. They ran my file photo. I was wanted, no doubt. John Ronald had written a good story for the *Herald,* covering some of the fuss of last night's meeting, and including a few details of the death. I'd been right. It had been poison. I should have felt honored, but all I could feel was sleepy.

I needed two things tomorrow, I decided. The first would be easy. There was a phone directory in my room. The number I wanted was probably in there. The other would be more difficult. I needed a computer and a modem. Tomorrow, I thought, tomorrow, and fell asleep in the chair.

12.

I woke up with the shakes. It was finally starting to hit me. Nick was dead. I wasn't upset. I wasn't sad. But I'd realized that not so deep down inside I wished I'd done it.

I wanted him dead. I had wanted him dead a long time, and had never thought about why.

I'd never wanted to think about him, but he'd got so famous it was hard not to. I had never wanted to see him again, but that had proved impossible. I had never wanted to speak to him, but he had seen to it I had no choice.

I wanted him to be sorry about Billy, but he wouldn't.

At least not for me. You can't be God, but we all try. Nick never owed me anything. This was something between him and whoever.

Or maybe he *had* owed me something, something for the years of friendship we'd offered, even though he was a stinker and never deserved it.

And he certainly owed something to Billy's family, something he never gave them, which I know for a fact because I asked.

An apology.

What had I wanted? Blood?

Maybe.

It was becoming obvious I had never thought things through. I'd built walls around certain parts of my life. I got to thinking about John and I. We'd kept in touch all these years, but we'd never talked about *it*.

I was glad Nick was dead.

I was going to nail his murderer, because whoever it was had done a pretty good job of messing up my life in the bargain. And I was going to find out Murrie's stake in all this.

The possibility occured to me that I'd been the real target, that someone who really wanted me had used Nick as the focus of a convoluted plot.

I couldn't even begin to untangle that one yet.

You can lie on your back in the morning only so long before you just have to get up. Nature's call is the only way I get started some days. I happen to be one of those people who can't get back in bed, so once I'm up, I'm up.

I opened up my wallet and started counting my cash. I couldn't go overboard, but I'd be okay for a few days. I had one piece of fake ID, an extra driver's license. That might be enough.

I sighed and shaved sans creme with one of those penny-whistle disposable razors. You figure to lose about fifteen cents worth of hamburger with one of those.

Breakfast was at a roadside cafe. The morning papers were full of the murder. I read while I ate.

"The mysterious death of Nick Patterson took a strange twist with the disappearance of Manuel Padilla, an associate of Dr. Ellen Kaufman."

Nice job, John, I thought, shuffling the *Herald* a little.

"Although not officially a suspect, the flight of Padilla is considered suspicious by the authorities." Lieutenant Herman Schmoller noted, "We've got a few questions we want to ask him. He knew Nick Patterson from childhood, and might have a few leads."

"Leads are precisely what the police seem to lack. According to Padilla's deposition before his disappearance, Patterson's door was locked when he tried to enter in response to a call that seemed to come from the deceased. It is expected that the autopsy, the results of which are due this afternoon, will reveal that Patterson died from one or more poisons dissolved in a bottle of mineral water found in his room.

"Although no official confirmation has been forthcoming, it is believed that Nick Patterson, the creator of the famous Furies series of books, received what is described as a Third Letter. He had admitted to media the night before that he had received his First and Second. Both, upon examination, seemed to contain vague threats.

"Police have requested the four other writers present at the time of Patterson's death remain in the Los Angeles area for the present. All have accepted the invitation of Dr. Ellen Kaufman to remain in her newly constructed guest wing."

There was more—an outline of Patterson's career, and a thumbnail sketch of the four other guests, but I learned nothing else from the newspaper. They printed the same photo of me as last night.

I was anxious to keep my driving to a minimum so I walked. About half a mile from the restaurant I realized I'd made a mistake.

We Angelenos think we're used to heat, but no one gets used to the desert, not even the residents. They live and die by their air conditioning. It had been warm when I set out, but now, around ten A.M., it was already topping a hundred. The mall was still a mile away. I thought about turning back. Sweat was pouring down my face and soaking my back. No one else was out walking. I stood out.

Palm Springs is an oven. The people here bake quietly over years. You can see it in their faces—nut brown and lined with tiny wrinkles. They wear their shirts open, and no one out here ever heard of a tie. Palm Springs has a sound track, you bet, and it's Western, old as the hills, the gullies, the badlands. The rocks are thrust through the bones of the earth, covered with barren soil save for an occasional shrub or cactus. It's an older world, a tougher world, than L.A. Something, perhaps a desire for open spaces, or a need for solitude, drove them out here where the summers burn and the winters kill—for winter in Palm Springs dips below freezing, and the dryness burns your lungs.

It's a world of illusion. People pretend they can live here. And they pretend it's green. Both take their toll. The green grass ends where the sprinklers stop. The place is beautiful if you have tunnel vision.

A hot wind slashed the streets, forcing me to stop dead in my tracks. Someone was watering their lawn, and a precious spray spilled over onto six inches of sidewalk. I stood under the mist for a minute or so, then gave up and walked back to my room.

There was no help for it but to change back to my first set of clothes. Then, firing Betsy up, I drove to the mall. Betsy was built before air conditioning, but I had all the windows down and the moving air helped. A little.

The heat was getting to me. I was nauseous now. I tried swallowing some air, but nothing helped.

Then into the bowels of the mall. An immediate drop of thirty degrees made the hairs on my arms stand on end. I stuck my hands in my pocket and walked into a computer store.

I saw what I wanted immediately—one of those Monterey 1000s, a lap model with a modem. I could get some real work done with it. But I looked at a lower-priced model until one of the salesmen swooped down for the kill.

He played me like a fish. What did I need? What kind of work did I do? Did I have much experience? I misspoke enough to give him the impression I was a live one, with a little knowledge and too much ready cash.

Then he explained why the 1000 was the model for me.

But, I countered, I'd only brought enough cash for the Mersey 350. So the salesman explained the magic of credit to me.

I was new in town, I warned him. I had a driver's license, but most of my credit cards—I half smiled and hinted at a divorce and he nodded knowingly.

He must've needed the sale. I left behind three hundred dollars and walked out with a couple of thousands' worth of hardware. Understand, I had every intention of paying off the rest of the debt when the dust settled. But I had the Monterey in my hands now, as a nobody, and that was the important thing.

I'd had to park in the sun, and the car was an oven. Would there be heat damage to the computer? I worried all the way to the motel.

I spent a half hour recovering, first under the shower, then panting on the overstuffed chair. When I could, I got busy.

It took me only a few minutes to hook up the computer to the television set, and the modem to the phone. I booted the thing and was ready to work.

First I wanted to get a look at our phones at the Manor. Through the modem I hooked up with the computer in my rooms. I have a program that keeps track of all phone calls in and out of the various lines at Ellie's mansion. The log told me what I though it would—someone had called the four guestrooms simultaneously, about five minutes after I'd been called. They must have received a taped message. The source of that tape, however, startled me.

According to the phone log, the messages had come from my room.

That they had come through my line I didn't doubt. Someone had the know-how to route their machine through my number.

Then I decided to get a look at Schmoller's files.

I happen to know where he lives and he doesn't know I know. He doesn't know I've learned how to patch into his system, and that his password—it's a name, a feminine name—is not the name of his beloved wife or granddaughter. I called up his hard disk directory, and with a few strokes grabbed File:Patterson on the screen.

There was next to nothing in it. I stared at the screen in frustration. Evidently he hadn't had time to update his files or, since the case was mint new, he didn't need the benefit of a file to jog his memory. He was carrying this case in his head.

On the off chance I called up his current work screen. *Voila!* I was in luck. He'd called up File: Patterson himself. As I watched, however, characters were added to the screen. Schmoller was hard at work.

He didn't add much, but it was something. Bless his heart, he'd had the sheets checked. There were enough traces of pubic hair, semen, and miscellaneous body secretions to establish that 1) two different males spent time with Calliope; 2) one of them had been Nick; 3) Lou Mercer had probably been the other. There was a note to take blood samples from the four remaining guests. Then Schmoller typed: 'Am certain Gleason and Austin spent time together, but no evidence of tryst.' Tryst?

There was a final notation that the five books found in Nick's room had been inscribed to Angelica Del Monica.

It was eerie, waiting for Schmoller to type. I gingerly placed the keyboard on the bed. I was afraid to touch a key. Abruptly the screen went blank. Schmoller had turned his computer off, and it had cut my connection too.

There was no reason to call up the screen again. I'd learned all I could so I turned to another task. I won't tell you how I did it, but I made some calls, routing them through one of my billing numbers in another county. It prevents tracing. I gave my room at the Manor a buzz. There was no answer. So I followed the same procedure and tried the restaurant.

It took a second but they got Angie to the phone. I could hear her yelling in the background, so one of the cooks must have messed up the guacamole. Some good old boy must have dumped a load of quarters in the juke box—as one Truckin' song ended another began. Angie picked up the phone.

It wasn't a long conversation. I let her know I was okay, but not where I was. She told me I was getting to be a celebrity. My picture was in all the papers. She'd cut out the biggest one and tacked it on the wall.

I told her I wasn't sure when I'd be coming home, so could she keep a candle burning? She snorted and cut the connection.

One last call. There were two rings and Miranda answered. I hung up. Again. It rang once and Miranda answered. I hung up. Again. It rang seven times. Ellie answered.

"Hello?"

"It's me, Ms. Kaufman," I said. "Just a quick call. I'm fine. Did Angie get a chance to say hello?"

"She did."

"That's all I want to know."

"There are reasons for everything, Mr. Padilla."

"It depends whose side you're on."

"There are no sides, Mr. Padilla. We miss you. When shall we see you?"

"Later. Soon."

I hung up.

I pulled out the phone book and looked up the important address.

It was there.

First stop was a thrift store. It wasn't air-conditioned, but it was open. My head swimming, I made my choices—black slacks, black tie, short-sleeved white shirt, black shoes. They had a big Bible bound in cracked black fake leather. That was pretty much all I needed.

After a quick change I became a door-to-door evangelist. No one would look at my face.

I spent an hour in a restaurant, enjoying the cool and preparing my story. Summer's the slow season, so no one bothered me. As the afternoon waned I prepared for Phase Two. It was still pretty hot, but I figured I could bear it now. I was barely right.

I drove five miles to the edge of Palm Springs. There was less green, more scrub, and about the only thing that grew was the rusting bodies of trucks and cars set on blocks. A couple of the homes looked abandoned. I parked two blocks away.

Bible in hand, I walked towards the sun and stopped at a tired yellow home. I pushed open the white picket fence. The mailbox read: "The Fredericks." They were the next-door neighbors to the Bentons. Molly and William Benton of Cactus Lane. Parents of Billy.

13.

That was the one thing I remembered after Billy's death—the word that went around the school, that there'd been some kind of settlement from the Patterson family. And we heard they'd gone to the desert to live, to get away. Palm Springs stuck in my head. Perhaps my parents mentioned it once over the dinner table. That had been the big factor in choosing my hiding place.

I opened the gate and stepped past the fence, keeping an ear open for dogs. The taste of dry grass filled my mouth. The air was full of it. The residents evidently kept a tight lock on their water bill.

It's fifty-fifty if they'll let you in the door when you knock. Most folks are familiar with the type—dressed like a square, holy book in hand, face scrubbed a little too well. Some folks let them in out of loneliness. After all, it's someone to talk to. A lot of these guys are good listeners. That's their job. Look out for the left out.

I had an advantage. I don't look squeaky-clean. I'm, well, swarthy. Okay, brown. And I know there's something about my eyes that makes it clear I'm not an eighteen-year-old jerk serving a two-year-sentence. I know my age shows beneath those brows. I look interesting.

I knocked on the door and a darling woman answered. She wore a yellow dress, with a clean apron draped around her middle. Her hands, large-knuckled from arthritis, rested at her side. Her hair was golden grey, and her face a delight. Some people get prettier with age, no lie.

"Hi, Ma'am," I said brightly. "Is your husband at home? I'd like to spend a few minutes with you talking about God's word."

"No, I'm afraid he passed away years ago," she said, in a slightly hoarse voice. "No, don't apologize. You may come in, if you want. What church are you with?"

"Manor Christians," I said. "But that's not important." We sat on a tired couch that faced an old-model television. Weary rabbit ears rested on top of the set, which told me she didn't have cable, which told me she probably couldn't pick up more than one or two stations. There were black and white photographs everywhere, and damn few books.

An hour later I knew something about each one of those photographs. I learned about her husband who had died ten years before. I learned about her children who never visited. There was a plate of cookies and a pot of tea on the table. She'd had her share of joy and sorrow, but she was all right. Since I was planning to use her, I let her use me first.

When it was time for me to go she invited me to stay for dinner but I shook my head gently. I asked if she knew her neighbors very well, and if she thought they were in.

"The Bentons. They don't go anywhere. They don't do nothing."

"So I could drop by any time and they'd be in."

"They wouldn't talk to you. They're moody. They never go out. Never." She set her finger to her chin and thought. "Except this week. They were gone for a couple days."

I tried to restrain myself.

"Really? Do you know where?" I asked conversationally.

"They don't talk to me."

"Well, sorry I got to go. I just wanted to say how nice it is to meet someone who doesn't own a VCR or cable. It leaves more time to study the Word."

"Well, to tell you the truth, I can't afford it. But it's nice of you to say that. Most people think I'm backward. That's about the only thing the Bentons are willing to talk about—their gadgets. William Benton tried to get me to buy a tape player once. I told him no. You'd've thought I was a cavewoman. Say, aren't you going to leave a card?"

"We don't work like that," I said. "Your job is to turn around and be kind to others. I'll be back someday. I promise."

When I left I figured I had an hour of sunshine left. It was a tossup whether I should tackle the Bentons now or wait until tomorrow. I was feeling nervous, though, like I couldn't hide forever, so I swallowed and walked over to their gate.

The truth was, I was losing my nerve. I didn't want to do this. I didn't want to see these people who were wounded more deeply than I. This was the shadow across my school years, the line between childhood and cynicism, and though they had a greater claim to the pain, I didn't want to share it.

I don't think I look like I used to. It's been a lot of years. It never occurred to me to don a disguise. Disguises are a joke. The best disguise is no disguise. Your attitude, your clothes, your station in life, are better disguises. This was no *cholo* in jeans and a white T-shirt. I wasn't propping up no walls no more, lunch balanced on my knee, half-sitting, half-standing at the old schoolyard.

I walked up to the house. There were fenders and old tires scattered around the yard. The paint was peeling. It probably used to be blue. The garage was open and a beat-up Chevy was parked within.

I knocked. There was a sound within.

"Who is it?" shouted a suspicious voice.

"Manor Christians. Can you spare a few minutes?"

"Go away."

"Only take a minute, Sir. Read a little scripture."

"Go away."

"Spread a little sunshine. I'm just another wanderer."

This time I heard the scrape of a chair and the trudge of a tired step.

William Benton, Mr. Benton to me, answered the door. I could see Molly behind him, staring over his shoulder. They weren't used to visitors, that was certain.

"Who'd you say you were?" he asked, peering through furrowed brows.

"Sandy Wilson, Manor Christians." I help up the Bible. "Come to share the word. I can come back tomorrow."

Benton weighed a good seventy pounds more than when I knew him, and he didn't wear it well. His chin was covered with a grey grizzle. He wore a faded pair of green slacks and a tank top T-shirt spread too thin over his hairy belly. A cigarette rested on his lips as he talked.

Molly hovered behind his shoulder, a worried look on her face. Her hair was thin and colorless, her cheeks hollow.

"What church was that?" he asked gruffly.

"Manor Christian."

"Never heard of them."

"We're not well-known."

"We don't go to church."

"That's not why I'm here."

"Why are you here?"

"To see if I can help."

"With what?" he asked, more suspicious than ever.

"With whatever. We're called to wander, to spread love and kindness to—"

"You were always a bull muffin artist, Manny," he said, his expression never changing. "Damn, you haven't changed."

"Pardon me, Sir, my name is Sandy—"

"Cram it, Manny, and come on in. I had half a mind to call you myself before—that—happened."

Okay, so next time I'll wear a disguise. He pushed open the screen door and I followed him in.

They didn't have much use for lights. I guess they didn't need them. The TV was on and that provided all they needed. I rammed my shin against a low table in the darkness. They sat down and so did I.

No one bothered to turn off the TV. There was some movie on the cable, which had reached the obligatory half-nude scene. It lasted about five seconds, like most of them did, just enough to raise the rating to PG-13.

I could see, only barely, an old reel-to-reel in the corner, and a new CD player on the shelf. There was a battered stereo, with new speakers, and the largest machine you ever want to see under a phone that could only be described as baroque.

The smoke was getting to me. It had settled into the furniture, into the curtains, into the corners. As my eyes grew used to the darkness I spotted a couple of empty bottles of beer next to my chair.

"I'm sorry," I said. "This must be your seat. Do you want it back?"

"No," said Benton. Molly sat down on the couch, bent over at the waist, her hands clamping her mouth.

"You look the same," he said.

"So do the two of you," I replied.

"Don't lie to me. Molly!" he turned to his wife. "Get me that beer I asked for." He turned back to me. "We look like hell. I ain't seen you since the funeral. How come you never called?"

"I didn't know where you lived."

"That's another lie. I told Nick's family to tell the rest of you."

"They never did."

"Oh."

We sat in silence. I didn't like it. These were my suspects.

Molly seemed to be taking a long time getting that bottle. I looked over in her direction. Benton must've been thinking the same thing because he called out over his shoulder, "Hey, woman, get over here."

He must've seen me looking around the room. He pointed to the phone machine.

"You like it?" he asked.

"I've never seen one like it."

"Brand new. I can do almost anything with it. Make all kinds of calls, three or four at once."

Molly reapppreared with two chilled bottles on a tray. Benton grabbed both of them.

"Beer?" He asked, thrusting one in my direction.

"No thanks," I said. I wasn't about to let a poisoner catch me so quickly. He gave me a funny look, twisted it open, and took a swig. "See, it's okay."

"No," I said hastily. "I don't drink. Anymore."

"Since when? I remember when I caught you and Billy with those brews you swiped from my fridge. Think I forgot about that? No way. Well, no use wasting a cold one." He took a deep swallow.

"Look, I can't stay long, I just came—"

"Damn right you can't stay. You're a fugitive. I saw you on the news last night. You're famous. I wondered if you'd come around here. Although I expected the police first."

"Why?"

"William," said Molly, pensively, "don't—"

"Ah, the cops know already, if they got any brains. Look, I don't have to apologize. You can see things haven't been going so good since Billy died. You'd think a couple decades would change things, but I can't get him out of my mind. Thinking about the year he shoulda graduated from high school, then college. Thinking about his hitch in the Army, then his first job, and his promotions, and raises, and his wife and his kids. No, it ain't healthy, living the life he never got, but it's all I got, the life I never had. Does that make sense? We lost it all. I thought moving out here might make me forget. But I couldn't. Not never. I thought of suing that damn bastard, or his father. But what good would that a done?"

"I thought you got a settlement from the Pattersons?"

"I didn't get diddly. What did I know? I signed this form, and they gave me some money that sounded like a lot, but you know, it didn't go far after taxes, and they knew it wouldn't. They had big money, that damn kid and his father, the hot-shot lawyer. Me? I was just this stiff. They saw me coming."

He cleared his throat, a long and loud operation. My eyes were smarting from the smells and the smoke.

"When I heard you'd hooked up with that lady Whatsername on the Westside, the one I always see in the news, I told Molly we ought to look you up. I thought to myself, you knew Billy too. Maybe she would help. But I never called. I figured you'd forget anyway."

"I didn't," I said. "I never forgot. Neither did John."

"That's nice. Nice to know you could bring yourself to remember. Hope it wasn't any great sacrifice."

I said nothing.

"All right," he said after awhile. "Let me tell you something. Nick called me a couple weeks ago."

I looked up.

"Yeah, Nick. Least it sounded like him, anyway. I almost hung up, but he begged me not to. He said he had something to say to me, something important, but he couldn't say it over the phone. He said someone was out to get him. He wasn't sure they would, but he didn't want to leave any accounts unsettled. He called three more times. I wanted to believe him but— you know what I'm saying?—Nick was always so slick. Even in high school, it was like he was Mr. Business Card. I felt like a kid when he talked to me in those days, me, an adult with a blue-collar job. You know what I mean?"

"Yeah," I said. "That was Nick."

"So finally he said he wanted to meet with us. His treat. I thought about it along time. He sent me this chit for a hotel in L.A., real fancy. I didn't want to go, but the missus reminds me we ain't been out of here for going on twenty years. I figure she's right. I wrote him a letter, telling him we'd come."

He paused to light another cigarette. "So we went. I got there and they didn't know anything about no reservation. It was a fancy pants hotel, real nice. I felt like a jerk, standing in what I thought what my nice suit, but you can tell these freddies think I'm nothing.

"I thought the missus was going to cry, right then and there. I was ready to kill Nick. I was ready to get back in that car and drive back here and never leave no more till I die.

"Then I realized, this Nick guy has been ruining my life. Now he's trying to play games with my head. No way. I took out my credit card and charged the room. I figured what the hell. I never use it for nothing anyway. It's just so I can cash checks. We have a great time, going to restaurants, go to see a play, driving around L.A. We looked at the footprints in the concrete. We took a tour bus. We saw a show taped. We had a chicken dinner at Knott's. Things we never had time to do before. It was great. Anyway, I charge everything. What the hell, I figure, make these fairies walk up and down the stairs to press my pants and shine my shoes. I deserve it. And I decide if Nick comes by I'm going to grind my fist in his face, and I'm going to enjoy it. Because I got the proof he stiffed me, because I kept that piece of paper.

"Then we got the word he's dead. Then I get to thinking, maybe it wasn't his voice. Maybe someone who wanted to kill that mother set me up, and here I am, Mr. Big Shot, in L.A. for the first time in a long time, and suddenly Nick's dead. And I used my card everywhere. The police are going to know I was there. Sooner or later, when they check, they're going to know.

"Maybe I should've called them, but I decided I'd hightail it out of there. No panic. But we packed up and left. Right, woman?"

Molly nodded. She looked like she was going to cry.

"That's it?" I asked.

"Ain't that what you came for? To find out what we knew?"

"Sort of."

"Sort of is right," he said, pulling out a pistol from underneath his chair. "I figured you'd come here, you son of a bitch. Not but that I don't admire you for offing Nick. I'm glad, I'm damn glad he's dead, but I ain't going to fry for it."

"Fry?"

"You know. The electric chair."

"Oh!" I answered. "I get it. Common mistake. We don't fry people in this state. We gas 'em."

"Nice try, Manny, but I ain't going to take the fall."

"What are you talking about?" I yelled. I started to rise but he waved the gun.

"It's loaded," he said.

I looked at Molly. Now she was crying, shaking, nearly in hysterics.

"You called the police, didn't you?" I said to her. "When you got that beer, you called the damn police!"

She nodded yes.

14.

One of my few complaints about this country is that just about any yahoo can own and operate a gun. It's insane. No, we're not arguing. I've read the document, and it says you can organize a militia, not arm the loony patrol.

Nick's dad had been an idiot. He'd owned guns. Billy was dead. Evidently Benton hadn't learned his lessons. But now you know why I don't carry a gun. I do not forget Billy.

You don't argue with a gun.

He was pointing that thing at me, and Molly was starting to scream. Despite that I could still hear a distinct siren approaching in the distance. Benton was sweating and his finger was twitching.

"Don't move," he rasped. "I'll shoot."

"I believe you," I said calmly. "Relax. I don't have a gun. Look." I slowly stood up and smoothed my pockets. It was painfully obvious there was nothing underneath.

"Okay okay," he said. "But don't move. The cops are almost here. Maybe there's a reward for you. I don't know. You were stupid to come here, stupid. Did you think I was stupid, just because I had to work for a living."

"No," I said honestly. "I always admired you when I was a kid. I still do. And Billy thought the world of you. Now, we didn't admire just anyone. We all thought Nick's dad was a jerk. Everyone did. But you, you were worth looking up to."

"Yeah, right."

Molly was calming down, but I could tell the police were only a half mile away.

"Look at this stuff around here. You've got a college degree's worth of gadgets here. I'll tell you, most highbrow students would electrocute themselves first before they could handle all the stuff you got here. Like this, for instance." I took a chance, walked to the CD player and gently pulled it away from the shelf. With a quick movement I unhooked the connection to the amplifier. "Where'd you get this thing? Is it a Merlin? You can't find this in L.A. What did you pay for it?"

"It was a steal," he said proudly. "I've got a connection, a guy back east. There isn't another one west of the Mississippi. Hey, be careful!"

I'm quick when I have to be. I took three steps forward and laid it against the barrel of the gun.

"Let's go," I said fiercely.

"What?"

"Shoot and the machine's just scrap." He tried to jerk the gun back, and I moved the player with it. I had to get out of there.

"Wha-what—"

"Let's walk to the window. NOW!"

We walked together. Molly watched in silent horror. The window was closed for the sake of the air conditioner, but the wall beneath it was rotting. I leaned back and kicked it. It fell with a crash into the scrub outside.

"It's me and the machine," I said. "I don't want to hurt it. But I will."

He wasn't thinking. He had all the cards, but I made him think I held the trump. The CD player was replacable, but I wasn't. I backed out the window, cutting my right leg slightly. Then I turned and ran off in the darkness.

Before I reached his back fence I paused to lay down his player. The one who dies with the most toys wins, right? Then I dove over the fence as a shot rang out.

Beatrice Frederick heard the shot and she was standing at her doorstep. The black and whites heard it too, and the boys in blue were busting down the door to rescue the Bentons from the mad fugitive.

"Sandy?" said Mrs. Frederick as I ran up to her door.

"I need your help, Beatrice. Do you trust me?"

"What's happening. What did you do?"

"My name is Manny Padilla. Did you see the report last night about Nick Patterson?"

She nodded mutely.

"I'm the guy that's running. I didn't do it. But I'm going to find the guy who did. I can't do it behind bars. If you tell me to go, I'll go. Can you help me?"

She motioned me indoors.

I followed her through the living room, to the kitchen, and to a utility cupboard. She pulled a little latch and door within opened. Stairs led below.

"My husband, God rest his soul, had our home built with a bomb cellar. It keeps the preserves cool. Come here."

"You don't have to do this," I said.

"You're the first person to listen to me in ten years. Maybe you were using me. I don't know. But you really listened." She leaned over and kissed me on the cheek.

With a broom she swept aside some cobwebs, and laid down some old boxes on top of the dusty floor. "Sit here and wait."

I was left alone in the dark. The minutes started to pass. I could hear almost nothing. No phone, no computer, no light, no contact. For good or ill I had put myself in a corner. Now I had to believe it was a secure corner. I had to trust a woman whom I'd used. At least I'd told her the truth the second time around.

So I waited. Once you've made your move you have to live with it. But I couldn't stop thinking. And there was lots to think about.

How much of what Benton told me was the truth? A guy like him could have managed the stunt with the phone calls. He was sharp. There was no question now he'd been stalling, waiting for the police to come. He might have enjoyed spinning that yarn while we waited.

I was furious about Murrie's lie. What was she hiding? Why was she shielding Calliope? To be honest, I wouldn't have tagged Calliope. She'd gotten what she'd wanted from Nick—and from Lou Mercer, and would've from me to, if I'd felt like it. I'm not criticizing. I don't admire that lifestyle, but we make our own choices, and I'm too tired nowadays to live other peoples' lives for them. I didn't see her killing Nick. If she didn't like him I saw her humiliating him, setting him up and throwing him for a loss.

I was beginning to wonder about Derrick. Part of the time he acted like a jerk, but he'd really been attracted to Janet. I can't blame him. And there was a connection between Nick and Janet. I'd heard enough to suspect he'd taken advantage of her. I wanted another look at Schmoller's file. But that would have to wait. Not yet. Not till I got back.

If I got back to the apartment. How long would I need to hide? I hadn't given Beatrice any instructions. And now I had to go to the bathroom.

In the darkness my hearing became more acute than ever. Every noise, no matter how muffled, seemed significant. When the police came there could be no mistaking their tread. Each step caused my heart to jump. I didn't think Beatrice would give me away, but then, how well did I know her?

They seemed to be crossing directly over my head. Was there one, two, three? I couldn't tell. What would I do if that door opened, sending a blinding shaft of light into the pitch-dark cellar? If she turned me in I'd have nowhere to go.

After awhile the footsteps stopped. I waited. Nothing happened. Then there was a scraping noise, and the cellar door opened.

"You can come up now," said Beatrice Frederick.

I rubbed my eyes as they adjusted to the indoor lights. It occured to me that this, too, might be a set-up, but I didn't care anymore. My bladder was about to burst. I only hoped they'd let me use the restroom before we got in the car.

It was just the two of us. All the curtains were closed, and the air conditioner was rattling loudly.

"They're gone," she said. "I hope you were telling the truth."

"I was. I am. Did you see them drive off?"

"I think so. If there were only three cars they've gone."

I took a deep breath.

"Did they ask for me by name?"

"Yes. They said they wanted you for questioning."

"Hoo boy. I can't thank you enough. Would it be asking too much if I waited an hour before I leave. Is that all right with you?"

"Sure," she said. "Do you play scrabble?"

I chuckled. "Yes. But can I use the bathroom first?"

We had time for two games—I lost them both fair and square—before I decided to take a chance and go. I wrote down my phone number and told Beatrice to call it when things settled down. As I walked to the door I stopped and took her hands in mine.

"I don't get the chance to meet good people very often," I said. "It's important to me, more important than this case, more important than—"

But I couldn't finish the sentence, and I guess I didn't have to. She turned off her porch and house lights.

Slowly, very slowly, I opened the door and stepped into the darkness. The lights were burning at the Benton residence, and I thought I saw a silhouette in the window. I walked away with quick but silent steps, gently opening and closing the gate, and walking down the street.

I wanted to bolt, to run the three blocks to my car. The small of my back tingled and I shuddered as I imagined what it would be like to be thrown forward from the impact of a bullet. My breathing was ragged. The heat was still intense. I was immediately coated with sweat. My stomach screamed but I jammed my hands in my pockets and kept going.

Betsy was parked where I'd left her. I looked around to see if I was being watched. Then I shrugged. How would I know? As swiftly as I could, I opened the door, turned on the ignition, and sped away.

The streets seemed deserted until I drew close to Palm Springs. A few of the local lizards had emerged from under their rocks and were driving to town too. The dilapidated cars and trucks looked to be held together with baling wire and electric tape. Betsy fit right in.

I had a funny feeling as I drove up the motel. I kept another car between me and my lodgings and took as good a look as I could manage. The parking lot was pretty empty. Still...

I drove around the block. Bingo. There were four police cars parked behind the building. I kept on going.

I'd done my best to keep Betsy under wraps, so I wasn't sure they had a description of her. I figured my best bet was to stick in the middle of traffic and get out of town. The road to the freeway was long and dark. I was afraid to go too fast and get pulled over for a ticket, and I couldn't stand going slower.

When it finally happened it was almost a relief. In my mirror I saw the flashing lights go on and speed up behind me. The siren shrieked once. I pulled to the side. I had run the good race, I had fought the good fight.

The patrol car sped past me.

They had their eye on someone else. I breathed a silent prayer and sped up until I pulled on the freeway.

I pulled over at a truck stop about fifteen miles down the road. They had a machine that sold stamps at a premium, and I obtained an envelope and a sheet of paper also. I penned a letter to the motel, and thrust it, along with some cash, into the envelope. The address was in the phone book. I'd done my duty, paid my bill. I still had my hopes I'd be able to recover the computer later. To the best of my recollection I hadn't saved any data on the disk. If I had, they'd know all about me.

Back on the road, I realized I was naturally heading west, back to LA. I wasn't ready to give myself up, not yet. I needed a base, somewhere to go.

I could probably get lost as well as anyone in L.A. I decided it was time to chance it, to get up close and personal.

It was time to pay a call on Preacher Joe.

15.

Driving west in the dark, I was nagged by the stone I had left unturned. That second scrap of paper. "Susan Delgado B—" it had read. Nick had written to her, made some attempt to contact her that she'd rebuffed. I had hoped that a visit to the Bentons would settle everything. Would I have to look for Susan as well? And how? That 'B' was probably the first letter of her married name. She could live anywhere in the area, the country, the world, for that matter.

Sometimes the worst way to find the answer is to look for it. I ignored the nagging, and let my mind wander.

Against my will it wandered back to Billy.

As long as I focused my anger on Nick I was able to forget the real wound, the real hurt. Now it almost seemed to me that Billy was demanding my attention.

I was thinking back to The Game. Ask anyone who went to Pontius Pilate High School twenty years ago. That was the day we played San Juan Zarate High School, which we knew as St. Zorro.

Why is that memory in black and white? I can't draw color out of those images. Perhaps it was the distance we experienced during the event, when we began to realize a myth was being created.

Just thinking about The Game made my heart beat faster, made me press the accelerator the harder. Whoa! I had to lift my foot from the gas pedal.

It was the high tide of our school years, the moment when everything came together, the evening when all things were possible.

St. Zorro was the largest private school in the city, located on the west side of town. It openly recruited student athletes, stretching the boundaries of its district with false or borrowed addresses. Its graduates went on to fame and fortune. Once a year they drubbed us.

Ours was a small high school in East Los Angeles, and our team frankly mediocre. We were just costumed kids, but to our minds we were gladiators.

We hadn't won a thing all year, and they were undefeated when we met in our last game. They were headed to the playoffs. We were going nowhere.

They bussed us to St. Zorro, with its modern stadium that shamed our field with its rickety wooden bleachers. Our noses were pressed to the window as we stared in amazement at the beautiful homes and clean streets. The sun was setting, and the golden light made everything look like a commercial. For most of us, the real world of television, with its new paint, comfortable homes, blond families, and immaculate living rooms made our own lives seem unreal, tawdry, an embarrassment. We lived in mansions compared to the old country, but our sights had been set higher. Our back yards all had a rusting swing set and slide, set adrift in a sea of unmown grass. No one had money for a new coat of paint, and dinner was rice and beans most nights. Our nervousness was exacerbated by our self-perceived unworthiness. We had no right to these neighborhoods. We were not as good as them.

Somewhere behind us our mamas and papas were making their biannual trek to the West Side, those who weren't stuck in the night shift. Stuffed in the cars were the brothers and sisters and *tias* and *tios* and cousins to the nth degree, dressed as nicely as they were able, bathed and washed and perfumed and bundled in layers of sweaters and coats. Yet we knew we would look unwashed and ignorant and foolish compared to the relaxed superiority at St. Zorro.

New model cars abounded, passing us, honking, the riders gesticulating. They knew who we were. Our ancient bus wheezed and gasped. Who else could it be?

And then Billy stood up and started talking.

I don't remember anything about what he said, except that it was funny, and we started laughing until our sides hurt. He was pointing at the homes and the cars, and reminding us we might be greasers and white trash, and that we still might not have a chance, but we still had more beans than anyone anytime anywhere.

What is it about high school football? Cheerleaders jumping up and down, the constant pounding of drums and blaring of horns, hysterics in the stands— the whole evening was an assault of sound. Some may say it is not important, but you wouldn't know it those precious few hours the game is played.

Our side of the stands was surrounded by police— an insult always foisted by a belief that we were dangerous. We knew our parents were being searched for weapons, that purses were being opened, jackets turned inside out. It was part of the humiliation.

The game began before we knew it. It was only a few minutes old and we were down 12-0. It didn't seem to matter. Something funny was going on. Instead of daunting us, those first few minutes seemed to fill us with a deadly intensity. The game turned into a war.

We were still unable to gain any yardage, but we stopped them cold after that. There were so few of us most of us had to play the whole game, but reserves of strength we didn't know existed began to surface.

I remember the wild look in John Ronald's eyes, as he made tackle after tackle with a ferocity we hadn't seen before. Billy Benton carried the ball into the middle of the line again and again, always gaining enough yards so that his punts kept St. Zorro deep in their own territory. The first half was coming to a close and the score hadn't changed.

Then Juan Ortega, one of the ends, was injured. He fought it, but they carried him off, and for only the third time that year I ran off the bench and into the game. Mine was the only clean jersey out there. That didn't last. I was plugging a hole, barely holding my own, thrown in the dirt, punched, kicked, and bitten, but I stayed out there.

My memory of the second half is fuzzy. Someone said they kept a film of it at the school, but I never watched it. Early in the half the score became 12-7 when their All-State halfback fumbled near the end zone and John fell on it. After that, the rains came down, locking us in a quagmire.

Even though they looked to be victorious, St. Zorro was being humilated. Those who stood on their sideline hung their heads in shame. They were expected to kill us. Now they would barely win.

With less than a minute to go we called a time-out. We had the ball, but Billy had collaped in a heap, doubled over in pain. There was a stunned silence on both sides of the field.

Billy's ring finger was dislocated, twisted at the joint to an impossible angle. The coach and the principal were running out to the huddle. Billy turned to me and said, "Pull it out, dammit, pull it out."

Just the sight of that finger made me sick, but when you're coated with mud and muck, and your head is ringing, and every bone and muscle hurts, you can accomplish strange things. I reached down and jerked. There was a horrible popping sound and most of the guys looked away.

Billy stood up, ashen grey, and said, "Let's go."

The principal, tears streaming down his face, shouted, "I've never been so proud!" as the referee hustled him off the field.

But we were already walking to the line, towards fresh troops and shouted taunts about our sisters and our mothers and our homes.

I still don't know what happened. I remember something about running down field and knocking over one, and then another defensive back. A third stopped and took a swing at me, striking me in the stomach and the side of the head. I fell head over heels backwards, but out of the corner of my eye I saw a streak. When I rose and looked down field there were zeros on the clock and Billy was standing in the end zone.

Our side of the stands emptied, and so did theirs—ours to the field, they to their cars, afraid of our knives, I imagine. But all that happened was a few thousand timid *mestizos* jumped up and down in the middle of a grassy field, and no one got any sleep before they had to go back to work next morning.

That was the night Susan Delgado abandoned Nick and went out with Billy. Nick was furious. It was like a victory for John and me. Nor did we have much sympathy for Nick the next day when he complained that Billy had stolen 'his' girl. Susan had gone out with all of us, I pointed out. She belonged to herself. Maybe we should have shown more feigned sympathy.

Everything seemed to matter so much in those days. We thought everything we did was important. We played every game like it was our last.

Saturday through Wednesday after the game Susan went out with Billy Benton.

Thursday he was dead.

I shook my head. Reliving the past accomplished nothing. I was still traveling from nowhere to nowhere, with no clear idea of what I wanted or needed to do. I was still suspicious of William Benton, but since I'd botched my little scheme I'd lost both an opportunity to crack this thing and a hiding place.

Little details of the evening kept coming back, insistant, demanding. Where we ate before the game, the color of Mama's dress that night, where Susan and Billy went that night, the coach stamping on his hat, the driver of the bus...

Susan.

I was shaking badly. I couldn't stop it.

Billy was gone.

But Susan—

Then—

Not Susan.

Suddenly I had to know why Nick had written to her.

I was losing control of the car when it hit. I pulled over the side, put on my emergency blinkers, and stopped. One deep breath, and another.

Susan.

How many times had Susan come into my thoughts these past few days? Susan Delgado. Before the death she'd been our ideal, our idol, in the best sense. Both beautiful and friendly—approachable and inviolate. She'd gone out with each of us in our turn and played no favorites.

But after the funeral we hadn't seen much of each other. We'd all drifted apart, and our senior years seemed dry and empty. The death cast a pall over the rest of our high school sojourn. Only on graduation was I able to begin to put it behind me. John and I had kept in touch with each other, and with no one else from those years. Even the grandeur of The Game was spoiled, part of a Golden Age that passed before we knew what it was we had.

Where was Susan now? Had she married? What was her last name? Did she even live in the state?

It was the middle of the night and there was no place to go, nowhere to find out.

I wanted to talk to Ellie. She had contacts and could trace almost anyone. Without doubt her lines were tapped—probably with her permission. Who could I go see to start my own search?

I was now driving through the eastern suburbs, still over an hour away from the coast. I pulled off the freeway and stopped at a convenience store to get a soda. Then to the public phone outside and a call.

Angie answered on the second ring. She'd been sleeping fitfully. She didn't ask where I was.

"Listen. I know your line is probably tapped, but I need a favor."

"Okay." She waited.

"I don't need a favor from you. That would make you an accessory."

"Okay."

"I need a favor from someone else."

I think she got it. "Okay. I'll look into it. Listen, Manny, they know what car you're driving."

"How?" I asked, upset.

"I think the ice queen told them."

Another score to settle with Miranda. "I'll call you later," I said. "I'm okay."

"I'm okay, too, Manny. And I got my books," she added brightly.

"What?"

"Those five books. The police released them. Ellen made sure they were delivered to me at the restaurant. The last ones he autographed. You know he put the date on them too? The last books he ever autographed! John Ronald had them take a picture of me holding the books for the *Herald*. What do you think they're worth?"

"Say goodnight, Grace," I said. She did.

Back on the freeway and west.

16.

Ellie says it is a lot easier to hide out in the open. Or as my cousin Raúl used to say, people don't see you so easy when you holler in their face. (Raúl used to holler in people's face all the time, and they all knew it was him.)

Ellie told me once there was a warrant out for her arrest (she never told me why), so she got a job as a journalist and covered the story of the intensive yet unsuccessful Tri-state womanhunt. When I asked her what finally happened she told me the statute of limitations ran out during the World War. She wouldn't tell me which World War.

Of course that advice only works when it's successful. I decided to give it a shot, however, and spent the rest of the night in Koreatown.

There were a couple of reasons for that. First of all, there was a good chance my picture hadn't made the front pages in the Korean language newspapers. Even if it had, I figured I was pretty safe, because we all look alike to them.

The other reason was Sam Park's All Night Eatorium.

Sam saw me enter and didn't blink an eye. I knew *he* read the *Times,* so he couldn't have missed my mug, but he won't forget that Ellie cleared his daughter of the grade scandal at Cal Tech. I took a seat at the counter and ordered the #2 Dinner.

I sat by myself, for the most part. I was an outsider to the regulars and did not exist, which suited me fine. A little later Sam came by and shot the breeze with me. He kept half an eye on my fork until I ate all my kimchee. He doesn't believe me when I tell him I like it, but if you can't acquire the taste you might as well forget Korean cuisine.

Outside traffic continued at a slow but steady pace, even though my watch read three A.M.

Time moves slowly when you've got nowhere to go. It was unsettling. Life is always like this for the homeless in L.A. All dressed up and no place to go. Each haven temporary, no time to plan, no opportunity to clean and renew, just a struggle to get through an hour.

Of course I *had* a home. I just couldn't go there, yet.

I must have passed out from exhaustion at some point, because I woke to the sound of an English-language newspaper slapped down on the seat next to me. Sam had sent one of his boys to get me something to read. He is the soul of politeness, and it must have cost him an effort to 'accidentally' wake me, even though he probably guessed sleep was the last thing I could afford. I picked up the paper. It was a copy of the *Sentinel,* a black newspaper you mostly find downtown. I was happy to see I hadn't made that paper either. I reread the sports page seven or eight times until I had the high school box scores memorized.

Around six A.M. I figured it was safe to see Preacher Joe, so I settled my bill and left. Sam doesn't let me pay, but I left behind a pretty large tip.

I don't drive to Preacher Joe's Bar-B-Q Ribs and Bibs Emporium unless the sun's up. It used to be I could drive anywhere in L.A. There are places, though, where the bad guys are winning.

It's sad. Most of the people in the neighborhood work hard. They dream. They just can't afford to live anywhere else. There are bars on all the windows, and they keep the doors closed at night and sleep low for fear of stray bullets.

I remember when I used to visit Joe and Babbs. We'd sit on the front porch together with sweaty glasses of lemonade. As often as not there'd be a little something extra in the drink. The kids would play in the street, and the music from a hundred different radios would fill the air. Girls would flirt, boys would wave, dads would holler, grandmothers would nap, all on the front porch.

Now the gangs roam at night, and you just don't know. Maybe they're trying to even a drug debt, but mistake Place for Avenue or Street. The house gets shot up and the murderers rush home to watch the report on the TV news. If you live there you don't go out at night. The graffiti marks the otherwise unseen borders. If it weren't so deadly it would be pathetic, this desperate attempt at identity. I always check to make sure I'm not wearing the wrong color when I go there. It can be fatal.

Preacher Joe and Babbs were already working when I drove up. The place wasn't quite open for breakfast, but when I knocked on the pane Joe opened up immediately.

"I wondered when you'd show up," he said, shaking my hand, then wiping it off on his apron. It was newly washed, but I could see ages of deep-down stains. He was smiling, and the gold tooth gleamed.

"Yeah," I said, "here I am."

"You doing okay?"

"I think I got this thing licked. I've got to track down a couple of people, though, and I need a favor. I want to borrow your car. Mine's starting to get noticed."

"That's pretty easy," he said, winking and pointing to the kitchen. "You know the way. Tell Jazmine I said it was okay."

In about half an hour they'd be slinging pancakes and flipping eggs, but Babbs was in the back right now laying the chicken and ribs over the racks as she prepared to slow cook them. There was a big barrel of patented Soothe Your Soul Out Of The Bowl Bar-B-Q Sauce ready to spread, and she was applying the first of the layers. She smiled when she saw me enter.

I leaned over and kissed her while she splashed the sauce around. "How are you, honey?" she asked.

Babbs is one of those women who might be twenty-five, might be fifty-five. She smiles like tomorrow might be better and today is shaping up all right. I happen to know her daughter Jazmine is pushing thirty. I've told Preacher Joe on more than one occasion that I'm going to run off with Babbs, and I've half a mind to one of these days.

Babbs has told me more than once she might go.

"I'm fine. So's everyone else."

"Guess you ain't got a home nowadays."

"'Fraid not," I said. "Not too much longer, though, and I'll have this doped out."

"Now ain't that Kaufman lady taking care of you?"

"I got a little more at stake than her this time out."

"Anything I can do to help?" she asked.

"Pray for me. And save me some chicken. I'll be passing back through later."

There's a door that opens inwards behind the refrigerator. You have to really squeeze to get back there, and then you walk down a short flight of stairs to the corridor.

Once upon a time a rich eccentric owned the whole block. Joe and I can't figure if there are other undiscovered tunnels, but there's one for sure between the restaurant on one corner of the block and Joe's home at the opposite point of the diamond. The city doesn't know about it, but I do, and every now and then it's handy.

There's a string of bulbs from one end to the other, but it's not well lit and you can't see the walls. I thought I saw a door to the right once, but I don't like to spend too long down there. The air is thick and musty and although I'm not superstitious there's something forbidding about it. I always tell myself I'm going to come back someday with a mask for my mouth and a good strong flashlight, but I never seem to get around to it.

It takes a couple of minutes to walk from one end to the other. I don't know the exact distance, and Joe hasn't bothered to measure. Some trips seem to take longer than others. All I know is I'm always relieved when I make the far door, breathing heavier than I should.

I knocked on the door before I opened, and yelled, "Company," as I entered. There was a swirl of cloth, and Jazmine sat back down, wearing a robe.

"Manny!" she said with a smile. "It's good to see you. Do you need a lawyer?" she asked hopefully.

"Yet I may," I answered. "But first I need a car."

She reached into her purse. "Take mine."

"Your dad said I should use his."

"You don't want to drive that tank. Drive mine. Leave the key on the table when you come back."

It didn't take much urging. Since it was too early for me to get my work done, I sat down and had a little breakfast with her, and we talked business. She'd been a public defender for five years, but was thinking of going into practice for herself.

So I asked her about Josh and she shrugged. No on had heard from him for half a year. He might be in jail, he might be dead. He was probably doing whatever it was he did and they weren't likely to see him until he needed cash.

Joe and his family could have moved out years ago, but he's told me more than once it might kill the neighborhood. Not only can he hire some kids on occasion, but when people come to his place they keep their money in the community. One time he told me that the money in some ethnic communities circulates fifteen to twenty times on the average before leaving the neighborhood, but money is spent only once in the black community.

He doesn't mention it, but the other reason he doesn't leave is that a lot of folks who depend on him for a free meal would be out of luck if he split.

Just before she left I asked Jazmine if I could use the shower. I was getting a little tired of myself. She went one better, and pulled out some of her father's clothes for me to wear. We're not an exact match, and we don't share the same styles, but a half hour later when I was done I thought I looked pretty smart in the porkpie hat. She found me a pair of dark glasses, something I never wear, and I no longer felt like myself.

I drove Jazmine's compact to Santa Monica. The wind was brisk at Cylia Li's house, but the sun was fine and the air smelled salty and sweet.

Cylia and I go way back, and we still get along despite a lot of shared experiences. Her schedule doesn't vary much, and I knew she wasn't going anywhere much that day. She works out of her home most of the time, and almost never sees an office. She does free-lance cataloging for several of the university libraries in the area. I parked down the street and watched the house until her boy friend left. Him I got no use for. He spends too much time with the Nestor weight machines and I can't recall seeing a book in his hands, but it's Cylia's life, not mine. He drove off to the gym on schedule. I started up the car and took his spot.

Clothes unmake the man. She had to look at me twice before she realized who I was. Her mouth formed a soundless 'O', and she waved me in.

Her home is full of that new wave furniture—metal made up to look like plastic, particleboard dressed to look like driftwood. The fax machine was humming in the corner. I sat in an off-center chair and we looked at each other.

"You look good, Cylia," I said.

"You look awful," she replied, giggling a little. "That isn't your car, is it?"

"No," I answered, "but I have the owner's permission. I'm a fugitive, not a thief."

She giggled again. "Well, you didn't come here to visit. What do you want?"

"I need a favor."

"The computer?"

"Yes, that, and something else."

She made a face. "I'd like to let you stay, but Bo will be back at five. You should've heard him talk about you when he read the paper."

"Woah," I said. "Time out. You never told me Neanderthal could read."

"There was a picture." She leaned forward and smiled. "He's a little jealous of you, you know."

"No lie. Don't worry. I don't need a hiding place. I need you to perform an unethical and semilegal act."

"Oh. Is that all? What gives?"

"I need you to go to my old high school, Pontius Pi—I mean St. Peter the Pilot. Tell them you're Mary Matsumoto, an old classmate of mine."

She arched her eyebrows. "Earth calling Manny. I'm Chinese, remember?"

"Honest," I said, "The principal is the same guy they had when I was there, and he won't have a clue. I'm not kidding," I insisted, to her disbelieving look. "Tell them you're an old friend, or you're on the reunion committee or something. You figure it out. See if they have a record of an address or phone number for Susan Delgado. I don't know what her name would be if she married. Can you do that?"

"Is that all?"

"Unless you're worried about driving there."

"Are you kidding? Hey, is this another girlfriend?"

"No kidding," I said, brushing aside the question. "I need to find her."

She shrugged. "Sure. I can do it. And I'll remember this too. Don't get mad next time I call you a Cuban or a Colombian."

"Thanks. Really."

She stood up and smoothed her dress. The smile left her face and she looked long and hard at me.

"How do you feel?" she asked at last.

I thought about it. "I feel good," I said, surprised myself. "I got a lot of friends. I feel real good."

Cylia and I don't kiss good-bye. There are some doors that close behind you and you don't try to open them.

I looked out the window after she'd gone, watching the joggers and bikers drift by. There were a few sailing ships at sea. Things always look good on the West Side.

I know how to boot Cylia's computer system. I'm the one who helped her buy it. It was time for another break-in. Long distance, of course.

Most colleges have a telecode so they can transfer data over the wires fairly easily. Most of this is pretty faceless, and the work of people like me is made simple by a basically stupid attitude on the part of most institutions of higher learning. While you will find it costs you good money to get your own academic records, and there are certain parts of your file which remain confidential to you barring a court order, just about anyone who claims they are checking references can get anything they want by asking. So it was that Goodman College got a call from Lynwood Temporary Services, asking for records of two students, Miranda Devlin and Calliope Metropoulos. I included a phony Tax ID I'd been saving for the right occasion.

Goodman is a Women's College that is part of the East Valley Cluster. I've been there. Ivy on the walls helps hold the buildings together. Chocolate is hidden under pillows because everyone's on a diet. English and History majors are their specialities. What they used to politely call a 'finishing school,' because most of the girls were finished with college when got married. There were plenty of young hormone bombs attending the engineering school across the street to be had, and a lot of them were.

It's supposed to be a secret but I know Miranda's Social Security number, and I can fake her signature when I have to. As for Calliope, Miranda had said they'd attended the same college and she might have been telling the truth. A pair like that would meet in college or not at all. I fabricated Calliope's number and John Hancock on a consent form I jury-rigged on Cylia's word processor. Hoping for the best, I faxed everything to Goodman and waited.

A note was transmitted to my screen advising me that the number submitted for Calliope was incorrect. For some reason they printed Calliope's correct Social Security ID underneath her name. I made the alterations and resubmitted the form. Soon both files were in my hands.

It was an interesting mix. Miranda's record was spotless, though not brilliant. Calliope had been her assigned roommate from day one, and the two remained paired all four years.

Calliope's file was more revealing.

She'd been in trouble, academic and otherwise, from the start. There was one scholastic and two disciplinary suspensions, along with a number of disparaging remarks from counselors and professors. I gathered from various euphemisms that she'd done everything but put a revolving door in her room.

Her grades, when she did not withdraw or garner an incomplete, were average. Except for—

Three A's, one each her last three semesters. All English courses. All taught by an adjunct named Patterson.

17.

I did some mental arithmetic. I knew Miranda's age. Figuring Nick's age from my year of graduation, adding six years for college and graduate school, there was no reason a young Nick Patterson might not have been making his first forays into academia while Murrie and Calliope sang alma mater mine. I was not surprised to discover he'd taught once upon a time. I really knew nothing about him from the time he left high school to the period when I was made aware of his literary activities. He could have been a vivisectionist for all I knew.

What classes had he taught? I took a closer look. Creative Writing Intensives, One, Two, and Three. Intensive. Yeah, I'll bet. Whatever happened to an apple for the teacher?

I'm not a judgemental person, although I admit to having my own ideas about good and bad taste. I was more interested in a connection that seemed to go back a long ways. Teacher and student seemed to have done quite well by themselves since then.

I leafed through the pages. No written comments from Professor Patterson. How about his records? Should I chance it? I did. I requested his records.

They were not forthcoming. I typed in a second request.

I was informed that the LAPD had confiscated the relevant files.

It occured to me that other, wiser heads might be undertaking the investigation with far more resources and energy, but no one would have as much stake in it as I.

Except the murderer, of course.

It was nearly noon as I stacked up all my papers and turned off the machines. I checked Cylia's icebox, but she was on a health kick again so her Twinkies were missing. I made myself a salad and waited.

She came back around one, looking quite pleased with herself. She makes a great co-conspirator.

As it turned out one of the administration officials had remembered Mary Matsumoto quite well—and had convinced himself that Cylia Li looked Japanese, which she decidedly does not. They had coffee together, and then, though he admitted it meant bending the rules, he wrote out Susan Delgado Baker's address. That was her last name now, Baker. Cylia promised to say hello for him when she saw Susan, and had left when she could.

"How did your morning go?" she asked when she was through recounting her adventure.

"Not too bad," I said. "Could've been better. Look, I'd better run. I hope you don't mind."

"Well," she said, "sometimes Bo comes home early. It really would be better, at least until this dies down."

I shook her hand. "Thanks Cylia. You're a real friend."

"So are you. Listen, friend, don't open any mail. You might get your Third."

I winked at her and walked to Jazmine's car.

Susan lived in Pasadena now. I'm not as good a navigator there as I'd like but I figured I'd aim the car north and east, and figure it out when I got there.

The sky was blue in Santa Monica, but that beautiful ocean breeze does more than cool the air on the coast. It blows the smog inland, and as I drifted east the sky got greyer and greyer. The skyscrapers of the financial district were wavering shafts only partially visible through the clouds of auto emissions.

I wanted to stay on the freeways as long as possible, so I took the San Berdoo to the Pasadena to the Glendale to the Foothill Freeway. As I drove by Eagle Rock I waved. I like that rock, and it really looks like an Eagle.

When I finally got off, not too far from the Huntington Library, I made a conscious effort to go slow. Pasadena catches speeders photographically, and they mail you a picture of yourself with your speed on the bottom, along with address to mail your check. I didn't want Jazmine's insurance rates to rise, so I was as careful as possible.

No matter where you live in Pasadena, the smog is as bad as it gets in Southern California. The wind blows it against the mountains, where it rests snugly until the sun sets. People there like to taste their air. It's hotter in the summer and colder in the winter than Belle Eyrie. Once a year, on New Year's Day, the place looks gorgeous. It never rains that day, the sun comes out, and all across the country, in living rooms from Wisconsin to Indiana to MainePaw turns to Maw and says, 'Maw! We ought to load up the car and move there!'

Parts of Pasadena are gorgeous. Old-style homes are perched on Indiana streets or Colorado hills. Manicured lawns and sculptured shrubberies are guarded by lawn jockeys, pelicans, and Virgin Marys. Drive a half a mile and you find the barrios and ghettos. Susan lived in a neighborhood in between.

I spotted her address and parked. It was a modest home, bright blue and white, with an open garage and no car within. The name Baker had been carved deep into a slab of stained wood, then hung to swing from the porch. A kid's plastic big wheel was parked in front of the door.

She drove up while I watched. It was all I could do not to stare. She climbed out of the front seat of a Volvo.

She hadn't changed at all. Her barely brown, slightly round face was still crowned by the stark black hair that rested comfortably on her shoulders with the gentlest of waves. She wore a mid-calf skirt and a short-sleeved embroidered blouse. She was smiling. I wanted to cross the street to see if she'd remember me.

But as she bent over to lift her little girl I saw she *had* changed. She was a little thicker around the middle. The muscles in her calves were more pronounced. Her arms were a little flabbier. From the side I could see a few wrinkles around her eyes and neck. Her little girl reached up to hug her, then dropped to the ground and ran to the door.

I loved her more than ever.

I wondered for a moment why I'd cut her from my life when Billy died. I'd been a ruthless surgeon, I realized, hacking and slicing good tissue as well as bad.

My eyes misted as I watched her follow her daughter to the door, then fish in her purse for keys. I was going to get out, I was going to introduce myself. I would ask her a few questions and—

I would ask nothing. If she had been involved in Nick's death, I didn't want to know. There was no reason to interrupt her life. I doubted now that she could have done anything to Nick. It looked to me that she had gone on with her life while I let old wounds fester. She'd gone on living.

I turned the key and drove away as fast as I could.

It was time to stop running, time to admit I was not one of the Furies. If there was justice to be administered, it would be dealt by the law, not by an angry and tired fool. My judgement was getting clouded.

I'd drive home, turn myself in, then hand over everything I'd discovered to Herman Schmoller. Let him wrestle with it. Ellie was probably chewing over the business right now, and would be giving Hermy-baby a call as soon as she was done dictating another chapter for her new book.

Traffic was starting to clog the freeways, so long before I got to the interchange I escaped to the city streets. I made pretty good time. There are certain streets that snake through the city and no one seems to use them. No, I'm not going to tell you which ones.

The afternoon was nearly gone when I pulled into Preacher Joe's garage. His older daughter, Janizetta (Dr. Jackson to you) was home, and she let me in. Jazmine had washed and pressed the clothes I'd purchased from the Thrift Store in Palm Springs, and I changed into those, then sat down and talked with Janizetta for a few minutes. Once I'd caught up on who'd been doing what and who wasn't talking to who I excused myself and called Angie at the restaurant.

"Is that you, honey?" she asked excitedly.

"Slow down," I answered. "What's up?"

"Ellen says to tell you she wants you back. Now. She says everything is okay."

"When did you talk to her?" I asked.

"Right after you called this morning. I drove over and we had a little conversation, like you suggested."

"Is it safe?" I asked.

"I didn't ask," she admitted, "but I don't think she'd have said what she did unless things were all right. Are you sure you're okay?"

I thought about Susan, and the way life turns out, and how you can't go back, and that any chain of events that had brought Angie and I together was its own justification.

"I'm okay. Really. I've learned a few things. Don't know if it'll help or not, but I can't run anymore. Oh, who's staying at the Manor?"

"They all are, all four of them, including that Jezebel Janet, who's a sweet girl, and you keep your eyes off her!"

"Cheaper than a hotel, eh?"

"I guess as long as they have to stay in town, it's as good as anything, and the food can't be beat. Are you going to the Manor?"

"I'm going to the Manor."

"I'll meet you there," she said.

"What about the restaurant?"

She made a rude sound, and we hung up.

Again I tackled the corridor, and emerged in the kitchen of the Ribs 'n Bibs Emporium. I could hear the hum of conversation. Another good day for business. Babbs burst into the back room, saw me, and gave me a hug. She thrust a chicken wing in my hand.

I ate in the kitchen 'with the help' as she put it, which in this case meant Joe and Babbs, taking a break

while the new kid served up beans, slaw, and barbe-
cue. I told them a little about where I'd been, but
nothing of what I'd done or whom I'd seen. At last I
stood up from the table.

"Time to face the music," I said as we walked to the
street. "Thanks for the meal."

"Give a call if you can't make bail," said Joe,
shaking me, then hugging. We laughed.

He walked out with me, while I fumbled for the
keys to Betsy. Turning for a last word with him, I
glimpsed a flash of blue out of the corner of my eye.
I whirled.

Two of L.A.'s finest were staring me in the eye.
They looked vaguely familiar to me. I must have seen
them during one of Ellie's investigations. No matter.
They knew exactly who I was. Without a word one
reached for his handcuffs.

I pretended to faint. As I collapsed to the ground
Preacher Joe knelt to my side. I dropped my keys
gently behind his foot. With his heel he clamped them
to the sidewalk and nodded. The last thing I wanted
was to leave Betsy parked in the open in this neighborhood. I could count on Joe. He'd take care of
things. He'd repark her.

"I'm serious," he said, looking for all the world as
if he was ready to take my head off. "No one eats free.
You come across with three dollars and ninety-five
cents or these gentlemen here will take you away."

"Out of the way, sir," said one of them gruffly,
pushing him aside. "Manuel Padilla, you have the
right to remain silent. If you give up the right to
remain—"

"Manuel Padilla!" shouted Preacher Joe in horror.
"Ain't that the guy on the news?" He leapt behind the
other officer. "Save me, Officer, save me. Don't let

him get me. He stiffed me for a dinner, and I came out here—"

"—silent anything you say can and will—" continued the officer. Typical L.A. cop—he was blonde with a mustache, and his partner was black with a mustache. I decided to help him out. "—be used against me in a court of law," I continued. "I have the right for an attorney to be present during all questioning. If I cannot afford an attorney one will be appointed for me by the court. I understand these rights. What's going on here and who's this Padilla guy we're talking about?"

They weren't having any of it. Within a moment I was stuffed into the back seat of the police car. They called in their catch on the horn, and were quite pleased about it. This might mean an interview for the eleven o'clock news. We didn't get halfway to the lockup, however, when a call came for them to turn around and head for the Manor. I was wanted by Police Lieutenant Herman Schmoller and he was holed up with Ellie.

"Sorry guys," I shrugged. "Boy, will they be mad when we get there and they find out I'm not that Padilla guy. Well, it's your neck."

Sirens blaring, we made the Manor in record time. I had to help them with directions once we got to Belle Eyrie. It can be real confusing if you don't know where you're going, and these boys worked one of the downtowns.

They dragged me up the tree-lined Manor walk. I was a little nervous about showing my face as I walked up the step, officers in tow, and stepped through the front door. Schmoller was waiting for us, and ordered them to take off the cuffs.

I'm not sure Angie had been invited, but she was there with the rest of them—Calliope Metropoulos,

Derrick Gleason, holding hands with Janet Austin, Lou Mercer, Ellie, of course, and Miranda. John Ronald was seated in the corner with his tape recorder. He represented a single concession to the fourth estate. That was nice of Ellie.

I wasn't quite sure of my status, but Ellie herself poured me a drink of water, and pointed Schmoller and myself to chairs on opposite sides of the room. John and I nodded to each other. Maggs came in and stayed long enough to give me a peck on the cheek. Miranda—

I refused to look at Miranda. Not that she was eager to make friends either. Schmoller shifted uneasily, and the two officers stood behind him, unsure of what was to transpire. They weren't alone.

"Very dramatic," said Lou. "I hope this little show will be the beginning of the end of our sojourn here. Not that you haven't been the perfect host, but my publishers, er, employers, are expecting copy. This is not my working environment."

"I will not take long," said Ellie. "I apologize to all and sundry," she continued, nodding in my direction, "for any inconvenience caused by my inability to penetrate the mystery of the Third Letter."

"Then you understand it?" asked Schmoller.

"I am afraid so. That is why I have called you all together. It is now possible to state with certainty who is responsible for the death of Mr. Nick Patterson, author, entrepreneur, and erstwhile college professor."

Miranda tried not to look surprised, but Calliope jumped.

"It should have been obvious from the start, but in retrospect I understand why I did not want to accept the truth." She looked very tired and stopped speaking.

I couldn't stand it any longer.

"All right, Ms. Kaufman," I said. "I've done a little research on my own, and I'll be glad to share it to see if it corroborates your findings, but how about first you end the suspense and tell us? Who killed Nick Patterson?"

She favored me with a puzzled look. "Mr. Padilla, I had my hopes that you, more than anyone else, with your enterprise and initiative, would have already realized the truth."

"Please, Ms. Kaufman, just tell us. Who killed him?"

She didn't blink. She said:

"You did."

18.

"I knew it!" shouted Miranda. "I knew it!" Her eyes were daggers. She had never looked so happy.

Schmoller rose, and with his officers approached. In his defense I will say he looked saddened, even disappointed. He had expected better of me. That was as close a vote of confidence I was ever likely to get from him.

I never saw her rise, but Ellie was standing in front of me.

"That will not be necessary. Mr. Padilla asked the question in such a way that the particular answer was necessary. But that was not a complete answer. For he was not alone is his guilt." She paused to let us chew on that.

"Be seated all of you again. And excuse if you will my little game."

I sat down. As Ellie glided back to her seat I noticed Angie had slipped behind Schmoller. Heavens knows what she'd planned to do, but she was known for her swinging elbows during her Roller Derby days.

Schmoller didn't want to sit down. He stood and glared, and his fingers were itching. Was I going to slip through his fingers? Angie stepped and stood behind me. For the rest, they sat stunned, except for Derrick, who produced a stub of a pencil, licked it, and began to make a few notes in his memorandum book.

Ellie wasn't going to start until Schmoller took his seat again and she got her way. It took thirty or forty seconds, but at the end of that time she nodded and said, "Thank you," in her sweetest tone.

"Honestly, Mr. Padilla. What were you thinking when you boasted—no, do not protest, that *is* the proper word—boasted to Ms. Austin regarding what you have learned about blunt instruments and arsenical buns while in my service? That remark alone has put your life in jeopardy. Not from myself, mind you, but from that thin blue line that protects our society from anarchy. They were searching for you, guns at the ready."

I smiled and shrugged. Angie boxed one of my ears. "Always bragging to the ladies. I know you," she scolded.

But Ellie ignored her and continued, "It was more than a question of method and opportunity. It was a question of hatred, deep and abiding hatred festering over a number of years.

"Ms. Metropoulos," she said, and Miranda tensed. "Your association with Mr. Patterson seems to have been a tangled one, going back much farther than is generally known. On the whole, however, it seems to have been an amiable relationship, or, at the least, a mutually gratifying one. I can uncover no evidence to the contrary. It occurs to me that some," and she glanced at Murrie, "might have overreacted and out of

unwarranted assumptions acted to protect your reputation—perhaps out of habit—"

"The weevil tree where no flan ordureth," I said.

"What the hell is he talking about *now?*" snarled
Schmoller.

"It is of no import," smiled Ellie. "Suffice it to say
that any misguided obstruction of justice will prove at
the last to have been both venal *and* unnecessary. Shall
we leave it at that unless events demand otherwise?"

Schmoller glowered, slumped a bit, but said nothing.

"Mr. Gleason, it occured to me that you might have
acted out of a misplaced sense of chivalry. Your
sudden friendship with another member of our company might have clouded your judgement, and in
outrage you could have taken justice in your own
hands."

Janet, bless her heart, gazed at him all the more
sweetly.

"On further consideration I realized that course of
action was beyond your talents."

Derrick looked mildly surprised. "Thank you, I
think."

"You have found your niche," she smiled. "It is well
for all concerned.

"Of Ms. Austin's motivation or lack of it we will not
speak. It will be not necessary. Her motive was
sufficient unto the task, but I now know she is
innocent.

"Mr. Mercer, your confession might have been
timed to blunt suspicion. So I considered, but
concluded that bluff and bluster do not always translate into action. Do not frown. I am aware of your
nocturnal activities that evening, and postulated Ms.
Metropoulos as a possible ally. Your actions in
concert with those of Mr. Patterson would have

allowed you more than anyone else that night the requisite time to poison that fatal vial."

That was good, I thought to myself. Fatal Vial. Very good.

She now turned to Schmoller. "Lieutenant Schmoller, I am given to understand William Benton has been detained for questioning by the Palm Springs Police Department upon your request."

He raised his right eyebrow. "How did you know? That's true, of course. He was in Los Angeles during the period in question. We have the receipts. He's been telling a ridiculous story about having been invited to L.A. by Patterson himself."

"Perhaps ridiculously true," said Ellie. "You will be releasing him shortly. For the benefit of those who do not know, Mr. Patterson was involved in the accidental death of William Benton's son, named also William Benton. That, I assume, was the 'Billy' referred to in the postscript to the Third Letter. I am indebted to both Mr. Padilla and Mr. Ronald for information regarding this matter."

John nodded but said nothing. What was he thinking? I hadn't called him during my flight. Why?

"As I eliminated—to my satisfaction solely, I am sure—one possibility after another, I was left to consider that the pain that led to this death might have its roots even deeper, that there might be another victim of the younger Benton's tragedy.

"There *were* other candidates," she said, look directly at me. "It might have been necessary to inform Lieutenant Schmoller of their identities had I not discovered who hated Nick Patterson most of all."

She paused.

"I am reluctant to admit my own recalcitrance to focus upon the Third Letter. I cannot explain this rationally. It offended my vanity, I suppose, to depend upon a such a crutch.

"But it proved quite easy once I turned my full attention to it.

"You will recall—" and there was silence in the room "—that the key to the first two letters lay in a rather infantile trick involving literally the third letter of the alphabet, the letter 'c'. That datum seemed to fail with the Third Letter. Allow me to reread it."

She fumbled for a photocopy and read aloud:

"Hector Me No More. Back to the begining
koin a phrase after the attic
Lying in wait
we bring lauds
we bring lentes
The strange truth is straying dark
Like unto the antic satyrs
Who will fardles bear
Striving mainly for the stodgy
striving smply for Gehenna
Striving lastly for surcease
striving fit for all
For Billy"

She cleared her throat. "Regarding the bulk of the work, I'll leave psychological decipherment to those who've a taste for it. There is, however, more than one alphabet. Indeed, there is one alphabet which provided the exemplars from which we derive the word. The choice of Gehenna, satyr, and Hector should have made it obvious, but it was the phrase 'koin a', or *koine*. *Koine* superceded the literary *attic* and became *lingua franca* of the ancient world, if I may mix metaphors. It was at once clear that—"

"Oh my goodness," said Lou. "Pardon me. I have another dark secret—I went to seminary for a year. Alpha, Beta, Gamma, Delta. So the third letter is 'g'."

It was all Schmoller could do not to rip the paper from her hands. Holding himself in check, he stepped behind her and looked over her shoulder, running his eyes across the page, once, twice, until he nodded. A look of disgust covered his face.

One by one each took a look at the paper. For each the moment of discovery was different. I saw fear, pity, sorrow, despair, and anger—and on the face of Miranda utter indifference. Lou Mercer swore. But I now knew I was at fault, as was everyone else in the room in greater or lesser degree.

No words. No music. Lights out. Home Olga.

19.

John Ronald's knuckles were white as his pencil sped across the notepad. He'd be calling in the story within seconds, but his face said he'd be living it for years.

Regardless of personal pain, John's a professional. His story made the afternoon edition. The headline in bold letters spelled out the message hidden behind the third letter "G": "I KILLED MYSELF".

I went numb. I had to. Ellie had been right. It was my fault. I hadn't pulled any trigger, swung any blunt instrument, but it was my fault. And John's fault. And the fault of anyone who had ever come into contact with Nick.

But mostly it was Nick's fault, and I didn't know what to feel—anger? grief? rage? guilt?

I wanted to shake him, to ask, what did you do that for? If I'd known it was that bad I could have helped. We could've talked.

But he had tried to talk to John and me that night. We'd given him the cold shoulder. I'd done my best to avoid him for years. If he'd have bared his soul I might have laughed in his face.

Nobody made him do it, I said to myself. And Echo said, do it.

I don't recall anyone officially calling an end to our little gathering. There was the sound of an ignition in the parking lot, and I glanced out the window. Janet and Derrick were standing together hand in hand, looking into each other's eyes. They were singing, singing a little song that Derrick had made famous:

Hi old friend,
It's not the end,
If you must go
Then let's pretend
It's next time already,
It's next time again.

Schmoller got busier than ever. There were a lot of loose ends he'd want to confirm, but you could tell he was convinced. Nick Patterson killed himself.

Lou Mercer just sat for the longest time, staring into space, chewing on the ends of his beard. One time he grinned at me weakly. "Hell of a note," he whispered. "Hell of a note."

I shrugged. "You never know," I answered. It was a time for cliches, for emotional Band-Aids, for any device that might put a little space between us and reality.

Then he pursed his lips. "You know, I've wanted him dead for so long, imagined him dead, pictured myself doing it, but I'm such a coward I hated myself for fantasizing something I'd never do." His voice trailed off. "Now I'd do anything to bring him back. Why?"

Miranda had her arms around Calliope, and she was saying, "I'm sorry. I'm really sorry."

"Yeah," said Calliope. "Who'd've thought he'd kill himself?"

Miranda's face darkened. "I'm talking about you. I'm sorry I thought I had to protect you."

"Is that why you lied?" she asked.

"Well," said Murrie weakly, "I guess it felt like the old days to me, when I had to cover for you again and again."

Calliope smiled. "Thank you," She turned to me. "So, what are *you* doing tonight?"

"Having dinner at my place," said Angie.

"Just asking. Just asking." She paused. She looked to me and whispered: "Where are you going for dessert?"

20.

There are no tidy endings to this one. Nick made sure of that. It took Schmoller awhile, but he eventually pieced it all together. As you might expect, Nick had planned his end in a small and mean way. First, he set up the Bentons with that visit to L.A. They were cleared, of course, but the old wounds had been reopened, and would take time to heal. I heard later that William, Sr. spent a little while in the hospital with a mild heart attack when it was all over.

Give Schmoller credit. Eventually he found the phone machine I knew had to exist. Nick had plastered an automatic dialer in his wall—after setting the timer to ring all three guest rooms simultaneously, five minutes after a different taped message woke me. He had poisoned himself according to a strict schedule, and set me up to be found with the body. Split-second timing and he'd pulled it off.

We hadn't seen each other for years, but he'd wanted to get in a last dig.

Thinking it over, it made sense that he'd wanted to get in a fight with Lou Mercer, to cast suspicion his way.

Those burning embers in the waste can—had he planned that too, hoping someone would fish out enough evidence to point to either the Bentons or Susan?

If so, Susan hadn't risen to the bait. I should call her, I really should. But I can't make myself do it.

De mortuis nihil nisi bonum. Speak no evil of the dead.

Maybe.

They said this was his way of saying sorry for Billy's death. They said he'd been haunted by guilt all these years and that he couldn't forgive himself. Some suggested if his friends hadn't deserted him he'd never have come to this pass.

I don't know. Nick could've said he was sorry to Billy's parents. He could've gone to the funeral. He could've showed just a little emotion.

Or maybe not. We're all made different. If some of the bozos are right, we're really nothing but the product of our individual double-helix. We really can't help what we do. The whole world's on automatic pilot. Karma, *neh?*

Neh. I'll accept the fact we've got certain ingrown characteristics, but as Ellie says, there are chances and choices, and even if the results are bad you can make the right call. You may be born with a temper, but no one forces you to own a gun. You may be born an alcoholic, but no one makes you keep a full liquor cabinent, 'just for company.' Or, as Sister Mary Regina used to say at Pontius Pilate, 'Avoid the near-occasions of sin.'

Nick had to plan, really plan, to hurt us with his death. This wasn't just the impulsive act of a guy at the end of his rope. It was the parting shot of a stinker who thought he could take a few people with him when he pulled down the curtain on his life.

One night I pounded the walls, I was so angry. Another night I was so blue I could barely move.

And yet—and yet—if I could rewind the Rolex I'd have taken Nick aside, at the doorway when I said goodbye to John Ronald, and stood him a drink. I should've let him talk. I've listened to bores for hours; I could've stood a boor for twenty minutes.

Of course it might have been only a holding action. If Nick was really intent on self destruction, nothing would have swayed his course.

I suppose they had a funeral, but I don't know anything about it. My mouth was dry all the time, and my head hurt. I kept turning off the radio, never knowing how it got on in the first place. All I knew was that nothing sounded good—not rock n' roll, not soul, not salsa. It got on my nerves, all of it. But I needed something. I couldn't get Nick out of my mind.

Sunday afternoon it hit me, and I knew what I had to do. I left a note on the table telling Ellie I'd be back later, and I drove to the Inspired Evangelical African Lutheran Baptist Church of Imperial Heights, Rev. Luther T. Jefferson, pastor. It was getting dark, but the singing was wafting out into the street, and the light was shining out of the stained glass windows. I parked on the street and walked in.

Luther looked up as I entered, but he never missed a beat. He was pounding on that battered piano, and with a wave of his head in my direction, continued to bang out a honky tonk rhythm. His robes flew wildly about as he danced, feet flying left and right while his fingers were a blur above the keyboard.

They don't hand out hymnals at Luther's church. After he and the choir belt out a stanza or two you start singing along with them, and it isn't long before you're standing and waving your arms, singing the same words first fast, then slow, now high, now low.

A glance would tell you there was one major difference between me and the congregation, but no one is out of place at the Evangelical Inspired. Soon I was swaying arm in arm with a couple of gentlemen in the front row, as we sang one of Luther's compositions. "There's no sin that's unforgiven," we sang, "nothing busted He can't fix."

Again and again and again.

Sweat was pouring from everyone in that little bandbox of a building. Behind the tired beams of the loft the choir stood, housewives and bank tellers and single working mothers, transformed, transfigured, by the brutal spotlights that pinned them to the altar, and the ecstatic smiles and tightly-closed eyes that masked the pain of everyday living.

In the middle of one number, with no cue apparent to me, all grew silent as the soloist trilled the same words we'd been singing, dancing over the notes we'd been struggling to reach. Her hair was close-cropped to her head, her teeth were masked by braces. I figured her for forty, perhaps forty-five.

Then Luther changed keys, and the battered Steinway became a harp. "Amazing Grace," he sang, "how sweet the sound..."

I started to cry. I shook and wept. Strong arms supported me as I started to collapse. "...that saved a wretch like me..."

This was the one place, perhaps in all of Los Angeles, where no one would judge or point or stare. "I once was lost, but now am found..."

Everyone was singing, everyone was crying, with me, for me, swaying together young and old, lame and blind.

"...was blind, but now I see."

The service went on for hours. It took me awhile, but I got control of myself. When the end came I stayed for the cookies and the talk. I didn't need a radio in the truck when I left, because I was singing. Good thing, too, because it was stolen while I was inside. It didn't matter. I sang all the way home.

Two more things. I never got that computer back. The one I bought in Palm Springs. Someone had swiped it from the room I abandoned. The manager and I went around in circles about that, but I finally gave up.

And about a month later Ellie made plans for another televised literary debate. I passed. I told her I was heading for San Diego. Angie and I took off for Palm Springs.

Beatrice Frederick was there, that sweet lady, almost as if she knew I was coming. She didn't seem to be in the least surprised when I knocked on her door.

"Mr. Padilla. How good of you to drop in."

I introduced Angie, and although Beatrice offered to cook, we ended up at a local restaurant—*not* Mexican. Angie can't bring herself to enjoy the competition, anywhere.

"Why did you come up to visit me?" Beatrice asked me during dessert. There was a ballad playing on the radio, something about love and divorce and loving again.

"I promised, didn't I?"

"Well, yes," she said. "But you didn't have to."

"No, I didn't have to," I agreed. "But I wanted to."

"Why?"

I leaned back in my chair and thought for a moment. My stomach was full, Angie was watching the sunset through a smudged window, and the temperature was down to a reasonable 95.

"Why?" I answered. "Because I'm damn lucky to know so many good people in this world. I'm damn lucky that I not only got a lot of friends, but there's islands of goodness you only discover by accident. I guess I've learned you'd better live with the goodness you got while you can."

"Oh," she said.

"Besides, they know how to bake here. Who's for another piece of pie?"